SHIP PASSENGER LISTS

PENNSYLVANIA AND DELAWARE (1641-1825)

EDITED AND INDEXED BY

CARL BOYER, 3rd

Published by

FAMILY LINE PUBLICATIONS
Rear 63 East Main Street
Westminster, Maryland 21157

GENEALOGY * LOCAL HISTORY * EARLY MAPS
MARYLAND * PENNSYLVANIA * DELAWARE * VIRGINIA
and WASHINGTON, D.C.

Send for Free Catalog for hundreds of titles pertaining to these areas

Originally published by the compiler 1980
COPYRIGHT 1980 BY CARL BOYER, 3RD
LIBRARY OF CONGRESS CATALOG CARD NUMBER: 79-57204

Published by FAMILY LINE PUBLICATIONS 1992
ISBN: 0-940907-24-0

CONTENTS

PREFACE

The task of collecting and publishing four volumes of the ship passenger lists mentioned in Harold Lancour's bibliography was conceived while this genealogist was compiling two volumes on the ancestry of his children, *Slade-Babcock Genealogy* and *Ancestral Lines*. It became apparent that one of the most time consuming and frustrating efforts a genealogist makes is the search for and through the many journals and books listed by Lancour. Thus it become the goal to publish those articles which were not in publication in readily accessible volumes, at the same time repeating enough of Lancour, with updated information, to guide the reader to the other necessary sources in print.

This has finally been completed, with the exception of the eleven volume index to Pennsylvania naturalizations and the works of the Pennsylvania German Folklore Society, which will be reprinted, in the latter case, by the Genealogical Publishing Company.

The past few years have seen great progress in this field. With this volume, which contains thirty-two of the eighty-two sources cited by Lancour, and Tepper's *Emigrants to Pennsylvania*, which contains twelve more, and with the fact that seven of the Lancour-listed sources are essentially duplicates, the task of searching for one's immigrant ancestor has been made much simpler.

Perhaps even more exciting is the recent news of the impending (at the time of this writing) publication of P. William Filby's immense *Passenger and Immigration Lists Index* by Gale Research. It will still be necessary to look at the original lists after one has consulted Filby's work, but this will be a magnificent resource from which one can begin.

Of course this editor's contribution to the literature has been little, but the index is important, and the retyping of the foreign language sources, often from difficult type faces, will prove to be helpful. Reception by the genealogical public has been excellent, and this has made an essentially boring task worth the while.

I would like to thank Carol at the Bunny Hutch in Santa Monica for making it easy to continue my work while I waited for my daughter to finish her ballet lessons, and Benn Howard of Academy West for his occasional friendly rejoinders.

This volume is dedicated to the memory of my mother, Elizabeth Timm Boyer, who passed away December 1, 1979, but who always gave me support and encouragement as long as she lived.

Carl Boyer, 3rd

P. O. Box 333 (24200 Cheryl Kelton Place)
Newhall, California 91322

January 5, 1980

Note concerning the second printing:

With this printing changes have been made to this page for purposes of bringing it up to date, and minor corrections have been made to pages 125, 239, 240 and 258. In addition, the imprint on the title page has been changed.

The initial press run of this title was about 950 copies, or some 200 more than that ordered for the other titles in the series of *Ship Passenger Lists*. In spite of the increased size of the printing, and stiffer competition from the Genealogical Publishing Company, this larger printing sold more quickly than earlier smaller printings of the other titles. For that, I am thankful.

Carl Boyer, 3rd

Newhall
August 6, 1981

Those interested in obtaining titles from the publisher may obtain a brochure by sending their name and address to the publisher at the address given at the bottom of the copyright page.

SHIP PASSENGER LISTS

"Einwanderer in Pennsylvania vor 1700," *Jahrbuch für Ausland-deutsche Sippenkunde*, 1 (1936), 53-54 [Lancour No. 116].

Arets, Leonhard, von Krefeld, 1683.

Bebber van, Jakob Isaaks, Bäcker aus Krefeld, 1687.

Bebber van, Jakob Isaaks und Matthias, Söhne des vorigen, 1684 und 1687.

Berends, Klaus von Hamburg, 1700.

Biedermann, Ludwig, aus Anhalt, 1694.

Bleickers, Johannes, von Krefeld, 1683.

Bonn, Hermann und Peter, vor 1689.

Buchholtz, Heinrich und Frau, 1685.

Dilbeck, Isaak.

Doeden oder Duten, Jan, vor 1689.

Engel, Paul.

Fabritius, Jakob, aus Glogau, lutherischer Pfarrer, 1669 in New York, seit 1671 in Pennsylvanien.

Falkner, Daniel, aus Langenreinsdorf i. Sa., 1694. Später lutherischer Pfarrer in New Jersey.

Falkner, Justus, Bruder des vorigen, 1700; später lutherischer Pfarrer in New York.

Frey, Heinrich, aus Altheim im Elsass, 1685.

Geissler, Daniel, um 1694.

Gottschalk, Georg, von Lindau a. Bodensee, um 1694.

Harberdink, Levin, um 1696.

Hartsfelder, Georg, vor 1676.

Heinrichs, oder Hendricks, Gerhard, von Kriegsheim, 1685 mit Frau und Tochter.

Zabriskie, Zaborowsky, Albrecht, * um 1638 in Insterburg, eingew. 1662. Indianerdolmetscher und Farmer in New Jersey. In den Urkunden: Cawbrisco, Tabberscue, Saboroscus, Sobriscoe, Saberesco u. dgl. mehr. Das Zabriskie-Haus in New Bridge, New Jersey, wurde in der Revolution beschlagnahmt und von der Regierung später dem General von Steuben geschenkt.

Zips, Adrian Henrichsen, vergl: Diederichs.

Hoffen, in den, Evert, von Mühlheim, 1699 mit 4 Kindern.

Houfer, Franz.

Jacobs, Isaak.

Jansen, Dirck.

Jansen, Dirck, ,der Knecht'.

Jansen, Klaus, 1685.

Jawert, Johannes, 1700.

Karsdorf, Hermann, von Hamburg, 1700 mit Familie.

Kassel, Johannes, von Kriegsheim, 1686 mit 5 Kindern.

Kastner, Paul, vor 1691.

Kelpius, Johanes, aus Siebenbürgen, 1694.

Klassen, Kornelius, von Hamburg 1700.

Klever, Peter, vor 1691.
Klostermanns, Annecke, von Mühlheim, vor 1689.
Klümtes, Jakob Jansen, vor 1689.
Kolk, Dietrich, op den oder von, vor 1689.
Köster, Heinrich Bernhard, aus Blumenberg in Lippe 1694; 1700 wieder nach Deutschland zurück.
Kramer, Andries, vor 1691.
Kriskum, Andries.
Künders, Thones, von Krefeld, 1683.
Kürlis, oder Keurlis, Peter, von Krefeld 1683.
Kuster, Paul, Maurer, von Krefeld, um 1693 mit Frau und 3 Söhnen, † 1707.
Lensen, Jan, von Krefeld, 1683.
Levering, Gerhart und Wigart, von Mühlheim 1685.
Lindermann, Johannes, von Mühlheim 1689.
Loof, Anton.
Lütkens, Daniel, 1694.
Luycken, Jan, von Krefeld 1683.
Matthäi, Konrad, 1694.
Millan, Hans, vor 1689.
Müller, Georg, 1700.
Neuss, Jan, Silberschmied von Krefeld.
Op den Graeff, Abraham, Dietrich und Hermann, von Krefeld 1683.
Pannebecker, Heinrich, von Flomborn in der Pfalz.
Papen, Heifert, von Mühlheim, 1685.
Pastorius, Franz Daniel, Gründer von Germantown 1683.
Pettinger, Johannes, um 1693.
Roosen, Paul, von Hamburg 1700.
Rüttinghausen, Gerhart, aus Broich bei Mühlheim, erst in New York, seit 1688 in Germantown.
Schäfer, Isaak, vor 1689.
Schäffer, Peter, aus Finnland, eingedeutschtes Mitglied der Kelpiusgruppe, 1694.
Scherges, oder Scherkes, David.
Schumacher, Jakob, 1683.
Schumacher, Peter, von Kriegsheim, 1685 mit 4 Kindern und einer Verwandten.
Schumacher, Sarah, von Kriegsheim, mit 7 Kindern.
Seelig, Johannes, aus Lemgo, 1694.
Sell, Martin, um 1694.
Sellen, Heinrich und Dietrich, aus Krefeld, vor 1689.
Silans, Johannes, vor 1689.
Simens, oder Seimens, Jan, von Krefeld, 1683; Walter von Krefeld 1684.
Sintern, Isaak und Familie, von Hamburg, 1700.
Siverts, Kornelius, von Friesland, vor 1689.
Strepers, Wilhelm, von Krefeld 1683.
Tamsen, Klaus.
Tellner, Jakob, aus Krefeld, Hauptgestalt der frühen pennsylvanischen Mennoniteneinwanderung; in Nordamerika 1679-81, 1684-98, †

London um 1712.
Theissen, Reinert, von Krefeld, 1683.
Tünies, Abraham, von Krefeld, 1683.
Umstatt, Hans Peter, von Krefeld, 1685.
Warmer, Christian, um 1694.
Wertmüller, Georg, aus der Schweiz, 1683.
Wulff, Paul, aus Fendern in Holstein, vor 1688.
Zimmermann, Heinrich, Arzt aus der Schweiz, 1698. Sein Sohn Eman-
    uel, angesehener Berater des pennsylvanischen Sektentums, hinter-
    liess 7 Söhne, von denen 6 vielköpfige Familien hatten. Die
    Nachkommen haben ihren Namen in Carpenter umgewandelt.
Zimmermann, Maria Margareta, Witwe des schwäbischen Magisters
    Johann Jakob, Anregers der Chiliastenauswanderung nach Pennsyl-
    vanien, mit ihren 4 Kindern 1694 eingewandert.

"A Partial List of the Families Who Resided in Bucks County, Penn-
    sylvania, Prior to 1687, with the Date of Their Arrival," *The
    Pennsylvania Magazine of History and Biography*, 9 (1885), 223-233
    [Lancour No. 117A].

This article, which contains "A Registry of All the People in the
County of Bucks within the Province of Pennsylvania That Have Come
to Settle the Said County," from J. H. Battle's *History of Bucks
County, Pennsylvania* (Philadelphia: A. Warner & Co., 1887, pages
672-680), has been reprinted in *Emigrants to Pennsylvania* (Baltimore: Genealogical Publishing Company, Inc., 1977), edited by
Michael Tepper, pages 19 to 29.

"The Sailing of the Ship 'Submission' in the Year 1682, with a True
    Copy of the Vessel's Log," *Publications of the Genealogical
    Society of Pennsylvania*, 1 (1895-1898), 7-13 [Lancour No. 118].

Following are excerpts from the article by L. Taylor Dickson.

The log of the ship "Submission," of which the following is a
copy, commences the fourth day of the week, sixth day of the
seventh month (September) and ends on the seventh day of the week
[Saturday], the twenty-first day of the eighth month, 1682. The
vessel at this day being near the mouth of the Chesapeake Bay,
which appears by the entry made on the nineteenth day of October,
at which time the odor from the pines was noticed, "supposing ourselves not to be within 80 leagues." Phineas Pemberton in his
record states that they arrived in the Choptank, Maryland, on the
second day of ninth month, 1682, thus making the voyage in fifty-
eight days from port to port, the last days of the passage not
being recorded in the log.

As Captain Settle was bound for another port, and the weather
being overcast, it is highly probable that upon the twenty-first
day of the seventh month he did not know where he was, and therefore did not complete the log.

Many of the passengers remained in Maryland for a considerable
time (some of them married there), and then walked to Appoquini-
mink, the lowest section of New Castle County, about forty miles
from the place of landing, and twenty miles south of the established town of New Castle....

The Log of the "Submission."

Voyage of the
Submission
from Liverpool to
Pennsylvania
1682.

An acct of our passage towards Pens[ylvania——the passengers
Subscribers, went Abord the vessel Submission from the port of
Liverpoole $5\frac{\text{th}}{}\ \frac{7}{\text{mo}}$ 1682. The master's name James Settle, the mate
Samuel Rigg——Brian ffleetwood the Carpenter, Anthony Busshell the
cooper, Ellijah Cobham, Thomas Bullock, Peter Travis, John Royle,
Thomas Hateley, servants. Henry Blivin, Michael Colon, appren-
tices. Heads ii.

The Passengers names & ages & number as——near as cold be well
taken.

	ffree Passengers.			Passengers		
Of Lancashire.	[James Harrison	54 years	Anna Harrison	58 years	2	-0
	[Agnes Harrison	80 --	Richard Radclif	21 --	2	-0
	[Robert Bond	14 --	Joseph Steward	14½ --	2	-0
	[Phineas Pemberton	33½ -	Phebe Pemberton	22½ --	2	-0
	[Abigail Pemberton	2½ --	Ralph Pemberton	70 --	1	-0
	[Joseph Mather	18 --	Joseph Pemberton	(16 weeks age)		-0
	[Lydia Wharmsby		Elizabeth Bradbury	16 --	2	-0
	[Allis Dickinson		Jane Lyon	16½ --	2	-0
Of Cheshire.	[James Clayton	50	Jane Clayton	48 --	2	-0
	[James Clayton	16	Sarah Clayton	14 --	2	-0
	[John Clayton	11	Mary Clayton	8 --	1	-0
	[Joseph Clayton	5	Lydia Cleaton	5 --	1	-0
	[Randulph Blackshaw	60	Allis Blackshaw	43 --	2	-0
	[Phebe Blackshaw	16	Sarah Blackshaw	14 --	2	-0
	[Abraham Blackshaw	10	Jacob Blackshaw	8 --	1	-0
	[Mary Blackshaw	6	Nehemiah Blackshaw	3 --	1	-0
	[Martha Blackshaw	1	freight free			
	[	His servants.				
	[Roger Bradbury	49	Ellenor Bradbury	46 --	2	-0
	[Jacob Bradbury	18	Martha Bradbury	14 --	2	-0
	[Joseph Bradbury	10	Sarah Bradbury	8 --	1	-0
	[Roger Bradbury	2				

From Wales.	[Ellis Jones	45	Jane Jones	40 --	1 -0
	[Barbary Jones	13	Dorothy Jones	10 --	1 -0
	[Mary Jones	12½	Isaac Jones	(4 months)	0 -i
	[Rebeckah Winn	20	Jane Mede	15 --	2 -i
	[Marjory Mede	11½			

whole passengers 37

heads 49
hed the owners servants for sale
Janeclif Hodges & Ellen Holland.
    1682 about 4 afternoon set sails & came to an anker black
Rock about 6 from whence & sent 3 letters by boat one Roger
Longworth one for Henry Haydock one for Thomas Jonjois....
2—— 2. the sea very rough the wind high about 4 in the [————?]
[2 Oct.] dyed Abraham the son of Randulph Blackshaw about 6 in the
morning A great head sea broke over the ship & staved the
boat & took the most part of it away, broke up the main
hatches that were both nailed & corked & took them away
that they were not seen where they went, broke the boat's
mast & hyst that were lashed in the midship, broke of the
gunnell head in the midship & broke the forre shet & took
severall things of the decks & severall things that were in
the boat it cast betwix decks. At 9 in the morning the boy
was put overboard, about 4 in the afternoon A great sea
fell on our Rudder & broke it about 1 yard or Something
more from the head, was again pieced as well as it cold
that night——not being discovered until about 10 at night &
was made pretty firm the next day....

————

"List of the Pilgrims of the 'Welcome'," *Memoirs of the Historical
Society of Pennsylvania*, 1 (1864), 467-471 [Lancour No. 119].

    Bibliographical entries in Lancour, numbered 117 through 122 and
124 are superseded by two volumes published in Baltimore by the
Welcome Society in 1970, the first being *Passengers and Ships Prior
to 1684*, edited by Walter L. Sheppard, and the second being George
E. McCracken's *The Welcome Claimants Proved, Disproved and Doubt-
ful, with an Account of Some of Their Descendants*, the first with
245 pages, maps, charts and indexed, and the second with 660 pages,
frontispiece and index. Sheppard's volume includes reprints of
articles by Balderston, Roach, Sheppard, Dallett, Bunting and Dickson with corrections, additions and new material. McCracken's book
is described as an "exhaustive study of 304 claimants, along with
the genealogies of the descendants to the third generation," with a
forty-six page index. Dr. McCracken wrote to this compiler on 15
September 1977: "Only one change need be made and that is that
Caleb Pusey and his family should be removed from the probable
column to the proved."

———

Marion Balderston. "The Real *Welcome* Passengers," *The Huntington Library Quarterly*, 26 (1962), 31-56 [Lancour No. 120].

See the note following the entry for Lancour No. 119 on the page preceding.

———

George E. McCracken. "Welcome Notes," *The American Genealogist*, 38 (1962), 152ff. [Lancour No. 121].

See the note following the entry for Lancour No. 119 on the page preceding.

———

J. H. Battle. *History of Bucks County, Pennsylvania*. Philadelphia: A. Warner & Co., 1887 [Lancour No. 122].

Pages 440-441 contain the names of several passengers arriving on the *Friends' Adventure*, July 1682, and on the *Endeavor* in July 1683. This item has been superseded by Walter L. Sheppard's work described in the note following the entry for Lancour No. 119 on page 11, above. An additional article, "Early Shipping to the Jersey Shore of the Delaware," contains sixteen ship passenger lists of various sizes for 1675-1681, thus making Sheppard's volume even more valuable.

———

Charles H. Browning. *Welsh Settlement of Pennsylvania*. Philadelphia: William J. Campbell, 1912 [Lancour No. 123].

This 631 page volume has been out of print for some years. Containing material which is "highly suspect," it purports to be a history of the settlement of "Welsh tract" lands granted by William Penn in 1681, containing the names of a great many emigrants and the ships on which some of them arrived. This book should be used with great caution, with all statements verified by original sources.

———

"A Partial List of the Families Who Arrived at Philadelphia between 1682 and 1687. With the Dates of Their Arrival," *The Pennsylvania Magazine of History and Biography*, 8 (1884), 328-340 [Lancour No. 124].

This article has been reprinted in *Emigrants to Pennsylvania*
(Baltimore: Genealogical Publishing Company, Inc., 1977) on pages
6 to 18.   It has been superseded by Sheppard's work, cited in the
note to Lancour No. 119, page 11 above.

––––––––

Albert Cook Myers.   *Quaker Arrivals at Philadelphia, 1682-1750;
Being a List of Certificates of Removal Received at Philadelphia
Monthly Meeting of Friends*.   Philadelphia: Ferris & Leach, 1902
[Lancour No. 125].

This work has been reprinted by the Genealogical Publishing
Company in 1959, 1967 and 1978.   It contains dates of removal, but
not the names of ships.

––––––––

Albert Cook Myers.   *Immigration of the Irish Quakers into Pennsylvania, 1682-1750*.   Swarthmore: Albert Cook Myers, 1902 [Lancour
No. 126].

Pages 277 to 390 of this illustrated volume totaled 499 pages
contains "List of Certificates of Removal from Ireland Received at
the Monthly Meetings of Friends in Pennsylvania, 1682-1750; with
Genealogical Notes from Friends' Records of Ireland and Pennsylvania, Genealogies, County Histories, and Other Books and Manu-
scripts."   No ship is mentioned.   The 1969 reprint is available
from the Genealogical Publishing Company, Baltimore.

–––––– –

William I. Hull.   *William Penn and the Dutch Quaker Migration to
Pennsylvania*.   Swarthmore: Swarthmore College, 1935 [Lancour No.
127].

This 445 page volume is the second number of the Swarthmore College monographs on Quaker History, and has been reprinted (1970) by
the Genealogical Publishing Company, Baltimore.   While no ship is
mentioned, Hull's work does give a list of the early Dutch and German settlers of Germantown.

––––––––

Ammon Stapleton.   *Memorials of the Huguenots in America, with
Special Reference to Their Emigration to Pennsylvania*.   Carlisle,
Pa.:   Huguenot Publishing Co., 1901 [Lancour No. 128].

This 164 page work was reprinted by the Genealogical Publishing
Company, Baltimore, in 1969, but was out of print by 1977.   It con-

tains an alphabetical list of immigrants believed to be Huguenots who came to Pennsylvania before 1776, largely extracted from Lancour Numbers 144 and 145. No ship is mentioned.

"Naturalizations, Germantown, Pa., 3/7/1691/92; Copia Naturalisationis of Francis Daniel Pastorius and of 61 Persons More of German Town from William Penn, Esq.," *National Genealogical Society Quarterly*, 28 (1940), 7-8 [Lancour No. 129].

*William Penn, Proprietor of the Province of Pennsilvania, etc. By the King and Queen's authority, to all to whom these Presents shall come Sends Greeting, etc. Whereas

*Francis Daniel Pastorius
Jacob Telner
Dirick Isaacs op de Graef
*Herman Isaacs op de Graef
Tennis Conderts
Abraham Isaacs op de Graef
Jacob Isaacs
Johannes Cassels
Hewart Papen
Herman Bon
*Albertus Brandt
Jacob Schumacher
Walter Simens
Dirick Keyser
Arnold Cassel
Dirick Keyser, Junr.
*Jan Lensen
Clas Tamsen
Hans Milan
Dirick Sellen
Hendrick Sellen
Paul Wolff
Lenart Arens
Arent Klinken
Paul Kastner
Willem Streipers
Koendradt Backer
Viet Scherkes
Hans Peter Umstad
Anthony Duplouvys
Heinrich Kesselberg
Reinert Tisson
Jan Lucken

*Peter Clever
Jan Duplouvys
Peter Schumacher
Peter Schumacher, Junr.
Isaac Dilbeeck
John Doeden
Abraham Tennis
Willm Rittinghuysen
*Claes Rittinghuysen
Johannes Kusters
Henrich Buchholts
*Isaac Jacobs
Matthis Jacobs
Wiggert Levering
*Isaac Schoeffer
Heinrich Frey
*Hanns Andress Kramer
*Jurgen Schumacher
Isack Schumacher
Peter Kurlis
Gerhard Levering
Johannes Bleickers
Herman op de Trap
Dirick op de Kolck
Cornelis Siverts
Reinier Hermans
Anthony Loof
Andrees Souplis
Jan Williams
(Added below:
"Peter Keyser
Dirrck Keyser")
high and low Germans, Inhabitants

---

*...land-owners, Citizens...1683, 1692, 1698....

and Owners of land in German-Town and in the County of Philadelphia, being foreigners, and so not freemen, according to the accep-
tion of the Law of England, Have requested to be made freemen of
the said Province, pursuant to the Powers granted by the King's
Letters patent, and Act of Union and Naturalization, etc. made in
this Government, Now Know ye, that for the further Incouragement of
the Industry and Sobriety of the said Inhabitants, And for the better and further Security of their Estates reall and personal, to
them and their heirs, They the said Inhabitants having Solemnly
promised (upon Record in the County Court of Philadelphia aforesaid) faith and Allegiance to William and Mary, King and Queen of
England, etc. and fidelity and lawful Obedience to me, according to
the King's Letters, patents aforesaid, I doe declare and by these
Presents Confirm them the said Inhabitants before named to be Freemen of this Government, And that they shall be accordingly held and
reputed in as full and ample manner as any person or persons residing therein, And that they the said Freemen have liberty and freedom hereby to trade and traffick in this Colony or in any of the
King's Dominions and Plantations, as other good Subjects do without
any manner of Lett, Hinderance or Molestation whatsoever.

Witness Thomas Lloyd, Deputy Governr. of the Province of Pennsilvania, etc. Given at Philadelphia aforesaid, with the assent of
the Provincial Council, the Seventh day of the third month Anno
Domi 1691, and in the third year of the reign of King William and
Queen Mary over England, etc....

W. F. Corbit. "Welsh Emigration to Pennsylvania. An Old Charter
Party," *The Pennsylvania Magazine of History and Biography*, 1
(1877), 330-332 [Lancour No. 130].

This article has been reprinted in *Emigrants to Pennsylvania*
(Baltimore, 1977), pages 30-32.

Albert Bernhardt Faust and Gaius Marcus Brumbaugh. *Lists of Swiss
Emigrants in the Eighteenth Century to the American Colonies*,
2 vols. in 1. Baltimore: Genealogical Publishing Company, 1976
[Lancour No. 131].

This reprint includes "Notes on Swiss Immigrants" by Leo Schelbert. The lists include people from Zurich, 1734-1744, and from
Bern and Basil [*sic*], 1709-1795.

Friedrich Krebs. *Emigrants from the Palatinate to the American Colonies in the 18th Century*, ed. Milton Rubincam. Norristown: Pennsylvania German Society, 1953 [Lancour No. 132].

This thirty-two page pamphlet is available in a 1964 reprint by Commercial Printing House, Lancaster, Pennsylvania.

———

Adolf Gerber. *Beiträge zur Auswanderung nach Amerika im 18. Jahrhundert aus Altwürttembergischen Kirchenbüchern.* Stuttgart: J. F. Steinkopf, 1928 [Lancour No. 133].

This work, together with Lancour No. 134, have been supplemented with material from Nos. 145 and 146 in the production of an English edition, No. 135, below.

———

Adolf Gerber. *Neue Beiträge zur Auswanderung nach Amerika im 18. Jahrhundert aus Altwürttembergischen Kirchenbuchern unter Hinzuziehung anderer Quellen.* Stuttgart: J. F. Steinkopf [1929?] [Lancour No. 134].

This work, together with Lancour No. 133, have been supplemented with material from Nos. 145 and 146 in the production of an English edition, No. 135, below.

———

Adolf Gerber. "Emigrants from Wuerttemberg; the Adolf Gerber Lists. Edited by Donald Herbert Yoder, Union Theological Seminary," *The Pennsylvania German Folklore Society Yearbook*, 10 (1945), 103-227 [Lancour No. 135].

This work will be included, with corrections, in a edition of the genealogical publications of the Pennsylvania German Folklore Society to be published by the Genealogical Publishing Company, Inc., 111 Water Street, Baltimore, MD 21202.

———

Otto Langguth. "Pennsylvania German Pioneers from the County of Wertheim. Translated and Edited by Don Yoder, Ph.D., Muhlenberg College," *The Pennsylvania German Folklore Society Yearbook*, 12 (1947), 147-289 [Lancour No. 136].

This work will be included, with corrections, in the volume noted under Lancour No. 135, above.

———

Adolf Gerber. *Die Nassau-Dillenburger Auswanderung nach Amerika im 18. Jahrhundert; das Verhalten der Regierungen dazu und die späteren Schicksale der Auswanderer.* Flensburg: Flensburger Nachrichten, Deutscher Verlag G.m.b.H., 1930 [Lancour No. 137].

The compiler wishes to acknowledge the very helpful assistance of Waldo Arthur Tulk, Assistant Librarian of The Historical Society of Pennsylvania, in securing a copy of this work, which was very difficult to locate.

Vorwort

Die vorliegende Schrift beruht im wesentlichen auf den sehr umfangreichen handschriftlichen Quellen, welche jetzt im Staatsarchiv zu Wiesbaden aufbewahrt werden, und auf welche zuerst von meinem verstorbenen Freunde Marion D. Learned in seinem ,Guide to the Manuscript Materials relating to American History in the German State Archives', Washington, D. C., 1912 hingewiesen worden ist. Während die grosse Mehrzahl dieser Akten noch keine Bearbeitung gefunden hat, sind die Hauptdokumente des Jahres 1709 von Julius Goebel in ,Deutsch-Amerikan. Geschichtsblätter' Band XII, 1912 herausgegeben worden. Die Irrtümer seiner Einleitung sind grossenteils von Geheimrat Wagner, dem damaligen Direktor des Staatsarchivs, in ,Nassauische Heimatblätter', Band XVIII, April 1914 berichtigt, und einige neue Quellennachweise hinzugefügt.

Von andern Drucken kamen noch folgende in Betracht: Der anonym erschienene Sammelband, ,Das verlangte / nicht erlangte Canaan usw.', Leipzig u. Franckfurt 1711 = Canaan; Theodore Frelinghuysen Chambers, ,The Early Germans of New Jersey usw.', 1895 = Chambers; J. Daniel Rupp, ,Chronologisch geordnete Sammlung von mehr als 30 000 Namen von....Einwanderern in Pennsylvanien von 1727-1776', 2. Aufl., Philadelphia, 1876 = Rupp oder R, und A. J. Weidenbach, ,Nassauische Territorien vom Besitzstande unmittelbar vor der französischen Revolution bis 1866' in ,Annalen des Vereins f. Nass. Altertumskunde und Geschichtsforschung', Band X, 1870.

Bei der Wiedergabe von Auszügen aus handschriftlichen Quellen habe ich, obwohl es sich vielfach um wenig sorgfältig geschriebene Konzepte oder Abschriften handelte, dennoch die Orthographie derselben nach Möglichkeit bewahrt und nur den Gebrauch von kleinen und grossen Buchstaben und die Interpunktion den heutigen Regeln angeglichen, bei Zitaten aus Drucken dagegen nichts geändert.

Von verschiedenen Schreibungen von Vor- oder Familiennamen habe ich meistens nur eine gegeben, auch auf die so häufig wechselnde Vorsetzung oder Auslassung von Johann kein Gewicht gelegt.

Bei amerikanischen Staaten und deren Einteilungen habe ich mich mitunter der gebräuchlichen Abkürzungen bedient: Pa. = Pennsylvanien, N. J. = New Jersey, N. Y. = New York, Co = County, Twp = Township.

Im übrigen gereicht es mir zu besonderer Freude, den Herren Staatsarchivdirektor Dr. Domarus, Archivrat Dr. O. Heinemann,

Staatsarchivar, und Dr. Bier, Staatsarchivar, zu Wiesbaden sowie
Herrn Prof. Dr. R. W. Kelsey zu Haverford, Pa. auch an dieser
Stelle für die Förderung meiner Arbeit verbindlichen Dank auszu-
sprechen. Ausserdem verdanke ich mehreren Herren Pfarrern die Erlaubnis zur Einsicht in ihre Taufbücher und den Herren Pfarrern W.
Metzler, W. v. Oven, G. Weber, K. Werner und K. H. Zunn Mitteilungen aus denselben, der Buchdruckerei E. Weidenbach die Ueberlassung
der Gesamtansicht von Dillenburg im 17. Jahrhundert und den „Flensburger Nachrichten" die sorgfältige Vorbereitung des Druckes.
Schönau im Schwarzwald im November 1930.

Dr. Adolf Gerber.

I. Die Auswanderung von 1709

Die Auswanderung von 1709 beschränkte sich nicht auf das freund-
lich zwischen seinen Hügeln und Wäldern eingebettete Fürstentum
Nassau-Dillenburg, wo damals Fürst Wilhelm als der vorletzte seiner
Linie regierte. Sie dehnte sich von der Pfalz über ganz Südwest-
deutschland aus.

Der schon lang andauernde Spanische Erbfolgekrieg hatte auch
deutsches Gebiet nicht unberührt gelassen und Teile der Pfalz
schwer verwüstet. Obgleich er sich jetzt, am Vorabend von Prinz
Eugens und Marlboroughs grossem Siege bei Malplaquet, einem erfol-
greichen Ausgang zuneigte, so machten sich doch seine Begleitum-
stände auch in den nicht unmittelbar betroffenen Gegenden mehr und
mehr fühlbar: Teuerung, zurückgehender Arbeitsverdienst, Vermehr-
ung der ohnehin hohen Abgaben und infolgedessen fortschreitende
Verschuldung und Verarmung der weniger Bemittelten.

Dazu war der letzte Winter ein überaus strenger gewesen. In der
Pfalz waren sehr grosse Schäden in den Weinbergen angerichtet. Im
Nassau-Dillenburgischen und im Weilburgischen waren die Winter-
saaten verdorben und die Missernte vorauszusehen, welche sich tat-
sächlich einstellte. So berichtete der Keller (Amtmann) von Drei-
dorf unterm 15. Sept., dass die Untertanen seiner Stadt und Amts,
‚Gott erbarme ess, diessmahl keine Früchte, es möge sein Korn,
Gersten oder anders, verkauffen könte, weilen dass Korn mehrentheils verdorben', nur allein aus Not etwas Hafer, um ‚Krigss- und
Schatzungssgelder' (vgl. Anm. 2) zu geben. Aehnlich hatte es im
Bericht des Oberschultheissen von Herborn vom 8. desselben Monats
gelautet: ‚Wenige Früchte werten diessesmahl in hiesigen Ampt, es
geschehe dann auss Noth, die Schatzungs- und Kriegsgelder darvon zu
bezahlen, konnen verkaufft werten, maasen die Kornernte so gering
gewessen, das, wann auch ein Gemeind der ander mit der Saath fort-
helffe wolte, so konten dennoch sämptliche Kornfelder nicht besaam-
et werten' und gegen die Fasten würden ‚die mehrerste ihre eigene
Brothfrüchte nicht mehr haben'.

Unter solchen Umständen ist es wohl begreiflich, dass gedruckte
und mündliche Berichte von der mit einem Nimbus umwobenen „Insul",
worunter damals öfter Carolina als Pennsylvanien verstanden wurde,
verbunden mit dem Glauben, dass die Königen von England die Ueber-

fahrt dahin veranstalten würde, nicht nur das allgemeine Tagesge-
spräch wurden, sondern eine Volksbewegung auslösten, in welche
einer den anderen nachzog.

Fürst Wilhelm von Nassau-Dillenburg sah diese Bewegung von Anfang
an als töricht und unheilschwanger an, liess aber zunächst die,
welche um Erlaubnis zum Wegzug nachsuchten, auf ihre eigene Verant-
wortung hin ziehen, vorausgesetzt, dass sie zuvor ihren Verpflichtungen gegen ihre Gläubiger und ihn nachgekommen waren. So heisst
es in der Anweisung zur Dimission (Entbindung von Untertanen-
pflicht) dreier Flammersbacher vom 6. Juni: ,Wan Supplicanten sich
von der thörichten weiten Reiss vnd ihrem vnd der Ihren augen-
scheinlichem Verderben nicht abhalten lassen wollen, so lassen wir
die Verkauffung ihrer Güter nach völlig bezahlten Schulden vnd ent-
richteten 10. Pfennig (zehnprozentige Vermögensabgabe) zwar ge-
scheen, wollen aber an allem Vnheil vnschuldig vnd an keine Wieder-
aufnahm ins Land gehalten sein.' Auch in der Verordnung, welche er
bei den sich täglich mehrenden Gesuchen am 25. d. Monats an seine
Amtleute erliess, ging er noch nicht von diesem Standpunkt ab, wenn
er darin sagt: ,[Es] fänden sich zwar Vrsachen vnd Mittel, selbige
ab- vnd hinzuhalten, wir wollen vnss jedoch noch zur Zeit damit
contentiren, dass wir an all ihrem künfftigen Ergehen vnd Vnheil
keine Schuld tragen, befehlen aber alles Ernstes, dass du dahin
selbst vnd durch Heimberger (Bürgermeister) vnd Vorsteher auff den
Dorffschafften allen Fleises sehest, damit keiner, er habe dann
zuvor seine Schuld vberall richtig gemacht...auch den Zehenden
Pfennig abgestattet, dimittiret vnd weggelasen werde'.

So nachgiebig der Fürst sich hier den Auswanderen, welche vorste-
hende Verpflichtungen erfüllten, gegenüber erweist, so wenig war er
geneigt, das heimliche Fortziehen zu dulden, welches meistens durch
das Streben, sich einer oder der anderen Verpflichtung zu entzie-
hen, hervorgerufen wurde und obendrein eine Verletzung des Unter-
taneneides mit sich brachte. So besagt ein Regierungsschreiben
nach Freusburg vom 20. Juli, er habe kürzlich ,dem ärgerlichen,
unbesonnenen, theils auch bosshafft und meineydigen, mithin höchst
straffbaaren heimlichen Flüchten dero Unterthanen nach der Insul
Carolina zu Steuer ein scharff verpoentes Edict unter anderen dahin
publiciren lassen, dass alle ihre Güter...eingezogen und confis-
ciret werden solte'. Ein etwa intendierter Verkauf sei null und
nichtig, Käufer und Verkäufer den Umständen nach dazu noch, ,mit
wohlverdienter Straffe anzusehen'.

Dementsprechend liess er denn auch z. B. die Güter des heimlich
ausgetretenen Schwung von Dillbrecht einziehen, während sein Verhalten den ordnungsmässigen Auswanderern gegenüber noch längere
Zeit dasselbe blieb, wenn er sich auch nicht ganz in ihre Not
hineinzudenken vermochte und von seinem Standpunkt aus in ihrem
Fortziehen Undankbarkeit für alles, was er in den Kriegstroublen
zu ihrer Erledigung von nicht weniger als dreiviertel aller erhaltenen Dimissionsgesuche fällt nämlich in die Zeit zwischen dem 20.
Juli und dem 19. August, also nach obigem Edikt gegen das heimliche

Flüchten. Als aber trotz der vielen aus Holland und England anlan-
genden Nachrichten über die Not der Fortgezogenen noch täglich neue
Gesuche einliefen, fühlte er sich schliesslich genötigt, am 30.
August gegen die ganze Auswanderung vorzugehen und eine scharfe
Verordnung folgenden Inhalts zu erlassen:

Er betrachte es als Gewissenspflicht, fortan keinem, wer der auch
sei, durch seine Einwilligung bei der Auswanderung beförderlich zu
sein. Diejenigen, welche gleichwohl sich nicht abhalten lassen
wollten, sollten sich gegenwärtig halten, dass sie niemals ins Land
zurückkehren dürften, und höchstens drei Wochen zur Verkaufung
ihrer beweglichen Güter hätten. Ihre unbeweglichen sollten nach
Befriedigung ihrer Creditores aber dem Fiscus anheim fallen, damit
sie nicht ,bey diessen theuerund beschwerlichen Zeiten' noch den
ganzen Winter über im Lande blieben und den geringen Vorrat an
Lebensmitteln mit aufzehrten, und damit ihre Güter mit den darauf
ruhenden *onera*[1] an andere verliehen werden könnten und dadurch
diese *onera* von denen, ,die im Landte bleiben und sich ehrlich neh-
ren und der göttlichen Vorsehung gerne vertrauen und stille halten', abgebracht würden. Sollten indessen Kinder von solchen an
dieser ,Abzugsseuchen' kra... seienden zurückbleiben und von Freund-
en oder Verwandten in Obhut genommen werden, so solle die Konfiskation zum Besten dieser armen unschuldigen Kinder unterbleiben.

Als diese Verordnung wenige Tage später den versammelten Heim-
bergern des Dillenburger Amts vorgelesen wurde, gaben sie zu erkennen, dass sie nicht glaubten, ,das dieserthalben künfftighin etwass
mehr vorfallen würde, inmassen die abgezogene Leuthe häuffig widrum
revertirten'. Auch das Fehlen weiterer Akten spricht dafür, dass
die Auswanderung damals aufhörte oder doch ganz gering wurde.

Was die einzelnen Auswanderer betrifft, so finden sich die Namen
der bis gegen Ende Juni dimittierten fast alle in einer Original-
liste in chronologischer Folge und in einer Abschrift derselben in
lokaler Anordnung, während die Namen der später dimittierten und
einiger ohne Dimission fortgezogenen teils aus ihren Gesuchen,
teils aus der Driedorfer ,Specification' oder der Ebersbacher
,Lista' der wirklich fortgezogenen zu entnehmen sind. Diese
Gesuche mit den dazu eingeforderten und abgestatteten Gutachten der
Amtleute oder Heimberger und die ,Specification' und ,Lista' geben
meistens zugleich näheren Aufschluss über die Verhältnisse der Auswanderer. Danach waren es arme oder ganz wenig bemittelte Leute,
wie denn zwei Mandelner in ihrem Gesuch geradezu sagen, sie bäten
um ihren Abschied ,gleich anttern armen vndt verdorbenn auch' und
wie ein Gondersdorfer ,gleich anderen mittel- und geldarmen Leuten'
nach der Insul Carolina will. Daher heisst es auch in den Gutachten gewöhnlich entweder in Worten oder doch dem Sinne nach, sie
könnten ,ohne Schaden', d. h. ohne nennenswerten finanziellen Nach-
teil für die herrschaftliche Kasse dimittiert werden. Dagegen ist
es wohl schwerlich ein Zufall, wenn bei einem Oberndorfer, welcher
noch einen nützlichen Untertan abgeben könnte, ein Dimissionsver-
merk fehlt. Die meisten besassen zwar noch ein eigen Heim, wenn es

manchmal auch nur ein ‚klein Bäugen' gewesen sein mag, waren aber
mehr oder weniger tief verschuldet, sodass nach dem Verkauf des
Ihrigen wenig, mitunter garnichts zum Mitnehmen übrig blieb. Ihre
immer wiederkehrende Sorge war, woher das Brod für sich und Frau
und Kinder nehmen, wie die Beschwerung, insonderheit die Kriegs-
und Schatzungsgelder, aufbringen. Diese Lasten waren so schwer und
so mannigfaltig, dass der Fürst selber in einem eigenhändigen
Schreiben an seine Regierung von den ‚harte undt mit allerhandt
Nahmen vndt Farbe angestrichene Kriegs- vnd Oneragelder'[2] spricht,
welche er womöglich gern zum wenigsten zeitweise gelindert gesehen
hätte. Unter solchen Umständen darf es nicht wundernehmen, dass
nur zwei Fortziehende 50 bezw. 60 Reichsthaler mitnehmen konnten
und zwei andere hundert oder etwas mehr oder weniger. Keiner hätte
die Reise für sich und Familie aus eigenen Mitteln bestreiten können. Alle waren auf die erhoffte englische Beihilfe angewiesen.
Nicht wenige freilich hatten sich vor der Reise anders besonnen
und es doch vorgezogen, ihr schweres Los in der Heimat weiter zu
tragen. Einige davon waren schon zurückgetreten, ehe noch über ihr
Gesuch entschieden war, manche bald, nachdem sie ihre Dimission in
Händen hatten. Einzelne kehrten noch unterwegs wieder um. Bei den
Aemtern Driedorf und Ebersbach zeigen die oben erwähnten Listen,
wer schliesslich wirklich fortgezogen war, bei dem Amt Haiger beweist es eine ähnliche ‚Specification' mit anschliessender Korres-
pondenz, bei den übrigen Aemtern sind die Taufbücher von einigem
Nutzen, lassen aber doch Zweifel übrig. Das folgende Namenver-
zeichnis kann daher nur auf annähernde Zuverlässigkeit Anspruch er-
heben. Jedenfalls sind einige nirgends aufgeführte ‚heimlich
Geflüchtete' hinzuzufügen. Die Kinderzahl kann nicht überall bestimmt angegeben werden, weil die Akten sie in einigen Fällen nur
für mehrere Familien gemeinsam, in anderen verschieden oder garnicht verzeichnen. Hauptabkürzungen sind: A. = Anna vor andern
Taufnamen; Dim. = Dimission; F = Frau; Fam = Familie; Hs = Hans;
Joh. = Johann; Johs = Johannes; K = Kind oder Kinder; TB =
Taufbuch.

Amt Burbach
Holzhausen: Johs Hoffmann, Müller, F u. 4 K. - Lützeln: Jacob
Benner, Auswärtiger, Fam. - Oberdresselndorf: Jost Henr. Ströh-
mann, Schwager von Hoffmann, F u. 4 K. Hessicher Schäfer an seine
Stelle. - Würgendorf (Wirg..): Theis Kühn, 3 K. — Die übrigen
Supplicanten blieben. Einer davon wegen noch nicht verbüssten
Forstfrevels nicht dimittiert.

Amt Dillenburg
Oberschelt: Joh. Jörg Hartman und Johs Jacob, Auswärtige, jeder
F u. zus. 5 K. — Vielleicht zogen zwei in den Dillenburger Kor-
respondenzen als heiml. Auswanderer verzeichnete Niederschelter
auch fort.

Amt Driedorf
Driedorf: Simon Deubig, F u. 2 K.; Johs Stahl, F u. 4 K. -

Heiligenborn: Johs Henrich's ledige Tochter.; Joh. Friedr. Maul, F
u. 1 K. - Hohenroth: Johs Maul, Fam. - Rabenscheid: Henr.
Thomas, F u. 6 oder 7 K. - Seilhofen: Joh. Henr. Crantz, F, ohne
Dim. fort, zurückgekehrt, fortgewiesen. — Alle übrigen, darunter
sämtl. sechs Mademühlener, blieben und finden sich dementsprechend
z. T. auch später in TB.

Amt Ebersbach

Mandeln: Joh. Peter Didrich, F u. 5 K.; Johs Fincke, Brandenbur-
ger, F u. 3 K. - Rittershausen: Joh. Dan. Busch aus Ebersbach
nebst F, 3 K und Frauen Schwester, Hs Jacob Kesseler's Tochter,
ohne Dim.; Johs Kesseler, obiges Schwager, ledig, ohne Dim.; Hs
Hermann Hartmann, F u. 2 K.; Joh. Conrad Müller, F u. 3 K.; Johs
Müller, Joh. Müller's Wittib zweiter Sohn, ledig, ohne Dim. —
Gemeinde Rittershausen schier gegen alle, den Abtrieb gesucht, alle
Männer mit Ausnahme Kesseler's aber in der Provinz New York wieder
nachweisbar. - Weidelbach: Hs Dan. Reupel (TB Rüpel), F u. 3 K.
- Joh. Henr. Rohrbach, F u. 4 K. ohne Dim.

Amt Haiger

Dillbrecht: Hannes (Joh.) Kring, F u. 5 K.; Henr. Schwung, ? K,
ohne Dim. - Flammersbach: Henr. Bender (Benner); Joh. Georg
Reiffenberg; (Joh. Koch vielleicht vergessen.) — Dagegen hatten
sieben, näml. die vier Steinhacher und die drei Haigerer Bürger
sofort ihren Entschluss bereut und nichts von dem Ihrigen veräussert. Drei andere: Tilman Noë (Noh) von Allendorf, Johs Müll von
Haigerseelbach und Joh. Henr. Schäfer von Langenaubach blieben
wahrscheinlich. Joh. Jost Döner von Sechshelden und Jost Hormel
von Langenaubach waren abgezogen, aber zurückgekehrt, und ersterer
bereits ,ohne Consequenz' als Untertan wieder angenommen.

Amt Herborn

Amroff (Amdorf): Henr. Hoffmann, Tagelöhner u. Lumpensammler, F
u. 3 K, vielleicht vor Wegzug gestorben. - Bicken: Joh. Niclass
Class, F u. ? K.; Joh. Conrad Kreuder (-ter), F u. 3 K.; Joh. Conrad Weber, F u. 5 K. - Breitscheid: Frantz Donsbach; Joh. Jost
Görg und Joh. Görg Koppenstein, jeder F u. zus. 7 K., andere tüch-
tige Untertanen an ihre Stelle.; Johs Möller, handelte mit Flachs
und Papier.; Johs Pettri's Wwe. - Burg: Hs Peter Gring, Vieh-
hirte, Fam. - Fleisbach: Henr. Peter, Bender, war 5 Jahr Soldat,
F u. 2 K. - Gondersdorf: Johs Maager (Maag?), F u. 1 K.; Joh.
Deiss Müller, F u. ? K. Drei Gebrüder, Joh. Henr., Joh. Jost u.
Joh. Stoffel Müller, Beisitzer, hinterlassen Mutter und 5 Geschw.
- Herborn: Joh. Henr. Geissler, Steindecker, F u. 2 K.; Hs Henr.
Hinder, F u. 4 K.; Joh. Marcus Koenig, laut TB 1708 aus Halber-
stadt, ,anjetzo allhier wohnhaft als ein Buchdrucker', F u. 3 K.;
Jost Müller; Eberwein Richter, F u. 5 K.; Matthias Theiss, F u. 5
K.; Joh. Conrad Wabel, F u. 5 K.; Nickel Wabel, F u. 3 K.; Joh.
Henr. Weiss, F u. 4 K.; Martin Weiss, Handwerker, Fam.; Joh. Jost
Wilhelmi, F u. 3 K. - Horbach: Jost Henr. Bast, F u. 5 K, in
chronolog. Liste ohne Ort zwischen zwei Schönbachern, findet sich
in TB. - Medenbach: Peter Funck, F u. 4 K.; Chr. Petri, 1 K.;

Joh. Jacob Wendel, F u. 1 K.   - Merkenbach: Theiss Becker, F u. ?
K.; Joh. Conrad Petter, Dim. wahrscheinlich.   - Offenbach: Hs
Georg Arnhold (?), Arnold ?, F u. 6 K.; Joh. Henr. Conradt, F u. ?
K.; Jost Roth, F u. ? K.; Enners Schäfer, F u. ? K.; Joh. Henr.
Schäfer, F, abgezogen, vielleicht zurück.; Joh. Enters (Andreas)
Schmitt, F u. 4 K.   - Roth: Peter Görg, F u. 3 K, anderer an
seine Stelle.   - Schönbach: Joh. Georg Best, F u. 1 K.; Joh. Jost
Schmitt, F u. 4 K.   - Sinn: Joh. Philipbuss Peter, Fam.; Conrad
Assbach, Auswärtiger, Tuchmacher in Herborn, Fam, Dim. ?   — Mehr-
ere andere blieben gewiss.

Amt Tringenstein (Eisemroth)

Eisemroth: Joh. Jost Blecher, F u. 2 K.; Joh. Jost Leisegang's
Tochter A. Cath.; Joh. Conrad Merte (=Martin), Johs Merten, Hs und
Hs Georg Schäfer, jeder F u. zus. 8 K.; Joh. Jörg Schmitt, F u. 1
K.   - Oberndorf: Joh. Jost Becker, Darmstädter, F.   - Ueberntal:
Joh. Adam Hauss, F u. 2 K.   — Joh. Conr. Petter in Oberndorf
schwerlich dimittiert.

Diejenigen unter den Vorstehenden, welche nach mehr oder weniger
langem Liegen in Holland England erreichten, erlebten dort mit
allen andern armen deutschen Auswanderern zunächst die grosse Ent-
täuschung, dass nichts zu einer baldigen Fortsetzung ihrer Reise
vorgekehrt war.   Dann kann es nicht ausgeblieben sein, dass auch
von ihnen unter den Tausenden waren, welche dort zu Grunde gingen.
Im Weiteren darf wohl angenommen werden, dass die Ueberlebenden
sich möglichst an ihren Nassau-Siegenschen Landsmann, den Pfarrer
Joh. Friedrich Häger, mit dem wir manche von ihnen am Hudson wieder
finden, anschlossen und dass es ihnen zum Teil durch seinen Einfluss gelang, den reichlich 3000 zugeteilt zu werden, welche in der
Provinz New York für die englische Regierung Pech gewinnen und
schliesslich Land erhalten sollten.   Auch das bedeutete jedoch noch
keineswegs das Ende ihrer Leiden, denn sie mussten 18 Wochen von
Weihnachten bis gegen Ostern in den Schiffen liegen, ehe diese mit
der Flotte in See stechen konnten.   Laut Bericht des Londoner Pfarrers Anton Wilhelm Böhme vom 26. Mai 1710 (Canaan S. 9 f.) blieben
von einigen Auswandererfamilien während dieser Zeit weder Eltern
noch Kinder übrig.   ‚Die letzteren Brieffe von Portsmouth / so im
April geschrieben / melden / dass in einem Schiffe bey die 80 See-
len gestorben seyn / und dass noch bey die hundert kranck liegen /
deren viele den vorigen / allem Ansehen nach / folgen dörfften.'
Die Ursach wird theils den engen und compacten Lager-Stätten /
theils der Unbarmhertzigkeit des Schiff-Herrn / der sie nicht mit
guter und gesunder Speise versiehet / wohl aber aus der Leute Todt
und Untergang seinen Gewinn machet / beygemessen'.   Nach einem andern Bericht wären im Ganzen 470 in den Schiffen und noch 250
gleich nach ihrer im Juni erfolgenden Landung gestorben.

Nach Rupp und zwei andern oben im Vorwort aufgeführten Quellen,
und dem unten abgedruckten Briefe von 1749 verteilen sich die überlebenden Nassau-Dillenburger, von denen wir wissen, wie folgt: In
der Stadt New York 1710 A. Elisab. Maul, Wwe des unterwegs verstor-

benen Johs, Friedr. Maul und wahrscheinlich auch Joh. Paul Deubig,
hinterlassene Waise von Simon und Frau, dazu früher oder später
Conrad Müller und Frau; in Livingston Manor am Hudson mit Pfarrer
Joh. Friedr. Häger: Dan. Busch, Joh. Henr. Conradt, Herm. Hartman, Henr. Hoffmann ?, Joh. Henr. Krantz, Conrad Martin, Joh. Georg
Reiffenberg, Georg u. Johs Schäfer, Joh. Georg Schmidt, die letzten
drei wegen der Häufigkeit der Namen nicht völlig sicher, dazu aber
unter den Arnold, Becker, Bender, Dietrich, Finck, Geissler, Georg,
Lauer, Stahl, Theis, Weiss u. a. jedenfalls noch Familienglieder
bekannter oder unbekannter Dillenburger, da Conrad Scholl (s. u. S.
45) 1767 noch viele Dillenburger unter den deutschen Einwanderern
von 1710 in der Gegend des Mohawk fand; in Burnetsfield[3] 1749 Johs
Müller u. seine Frau A. Maria geb. Jacob, welche auch jedenfalls
Nassauerin war; in Amwell, Hunterdon Co, New Jersey 1719 oder 1720
Henr. Bast, Joh. Phil. Peter u. dessen laut TB 1697 geb. Sohn Godt-
fried, welche damals jeder 50 Morgen Land, 12 Kühe und 8 Pferde besassen (s. Goebel S. 188), und von denen der erste und dritte
später als Hendrick Bast und Godfrey Peters vorkommen, und letzterer nochmals 1749 als Testamentzeuge, endlich gleichfalls in
N. J. vor 1720 Marcus Koenig (s. Chambers S. 633, 534 u. 35). —
Nach Carolina dürfte 1710 kein Nassau-Dillenburger hingelangt sein.
    Zum Schlusse geben wir zwei Teilnehmern an der grossen Auswan-
derung in einem 40 Jahre später in die Heimat gerichteten,
abschriftlich erhaltenen Briefe das Wort:
    „Unsern Gruss zuvor! Hertzgeliebter Bruder nebst allen Gefreund-
ten mit ihren Familien!
    Seythdeme dass ich Anna Maria von euch auss Täutschland in
America bin, ich niemahlen die Gelegenheit habe finden können, von
meinem Leben und Beschaffenheit euch ein wenig zu berichten. Nach-
deme aber nun ein guther Freund von der Pfaltz Nahmens Stephan
Franck, ein Nachbahr von uns in die Pfaltz verreisset und in eurer
Gegend zu thun hat, so habe nicht unterlassen können, um euch
Gefreunde aufzusuchen und zu erfahren, wie es mit euch stehet.
Berichte euch, das wir im Jahr 710 zu Neujorg sind ankommen von
unsserer langen und beschwerlichen Reiss und daselbst in der Ernde
mein Mann Henrich Heger an einer schnellen Kranckheit, da er mittag
gesund und abens [todt], gestorben. Das Söhnlein, wo uns in
Teutschland gebohren, Nahmens Henr. Heger, ist hier getraut [= ver-
heiratet] und hat 11 lebendige Kinder. Im Jahr 711 habe ich wieder
getraut. Mein jetz noch unter Gottes Gnaden lebender Mann Nahmens
Johannes Müller [ist] von Rütershaussen aus dem Ambt Ebersbach, mit
welchem in friedlich gesegneter Ehe erzeuget 5 Söhn und drey Döch-
ter, welche der Herr bishero bey Leben erhalten, darvon 4 Söhn und
2 Töchter getraudt.
    Uebrigens melde, dass, obschon der Zug und Anfang im Lande sehr
schwer gefallen, so hat uns doch Gott gesegnet, eigen Land, Brod,
Vieh und Nahrung beschehret, dass wir können leben und dem Herren
nicht genung darfür dancken können, wünschen also nicht mehr, in
euer verlassenes Egypten zu wohnen, sondern, wann wir wünschen kön-

ten, wolten lieber euch zu uns wünschen. Allein es ist Niemand zu
rathen, dann die Reisse ist sehr beschwärlich und viel Ungemach
unterworffen, dass Leben und Todt nicht weit von einander stehen.
Ich habe erfahren, dass die Fürstl. Nassauische Herrschafften
wären aussgestorben bis Nassau-Ditz, möcht also von euch, liebsten
Schwäger, Berichte haben, wer das Land hat und, ob es noch so sehr
beschwerdt ist als damahlen. Uns belangendt, so haben wir von
allen teutschen Auflagen ein frey Land. [Man] gibt des Jahrs einmahl Tax, der so gering, dass mancher mehr im Zaphauss verdrinckt
auf einmahl, dass des Jahres Tax ist. Was der Bauer erwirbt, ist
gut vor ihn. Mann giebt kein Zehenden, kein Zoll. Jagen und
Fischen ist auch frey, und unsser Land ist sehr fruchtbar mit allem
Gewächs. Ich habe 100 Acker Land von der Cron und habe 100 Acker
Land darzu gekaufft.
　　Liebe Brüder Johannes Jacob, Hellmes (?) Jacob und Stiffbruder
Ebert Jung und mein lieber Bruder Hanss Henr. Müller, ich mögte
gern wissen, wie lang meine Mutter todt ist, und ihr Schwäger alle,
berichtet uns doch mit Brief, wer noch lebet, wie eure Familien
sind und, wie es um euer Wohlsein stehet, welches wir von Hertzen
gern wissen möchten. Dieser Franck, wann er nicht selbst zu euch
kommen solte, wird euch den Weg zeigen, wo ihr ihn Brieff einlief-
fern solt.
　　Lieber Vetter Hanss Jörg Müller, Thomas Müllers Sohn, ich möchte
wissen, ob ihr lebet, ob es euch wohl gehet, und mit wem ihr ge-
trauet seyd. Dass lasst mich wissen. Wir haben nun einander in 40
Jahren nicht mehr gesehen. Mögte wünschen, 2 oder 3 Wochen bey
euch zu seyn, um euch zu behertzigen und Gute Nacht geben. Ein und
ander Sach mehr zu schreiben, were zu viel und kan nicht wohl auf-
gesetz werden. Möchte wünschen, dass ihr und der Franck könten zu-
sammenkommen, mehres zu sprechen. Uebrigens schliesse ich und
wünsche euch alle 1000 Gute Nacht, ich, meine Frau und Kinder. Und
alle guthe Freunde, die unsserer bekandt sind, sind zu 1000 mahlen
gegrüsset und der Gnade Gottes anbefohlen.
　　Euer ergebenster Schwager und Freundt Johannes Müller Barnets-
fieldt in der Provinz Neujorg, Co[u]nti von Albani, 1749 Julj 10.
　　P. S. Ich bitte euch nochmahlen, um Gottes willen, last euch
angelegen seyn und schickt mir gewiss Brieff, sonst ist mein
Schreiben umsonst gethan, und weiss doch nichts um euch.
　　P. S. Conrad Müller ist zu [Neu?]jorg mit seiner Frau gestorben.
Lebet noch ein Sohn...Hartmann und Dan. Busch ist auch todt. Liebe
Schwäger, lasst meinen Bruder in Rüttershaussen dass Schreiben wis-
sen, damit er mir schreiben kann."

II.　Die Auswanderung von 1750-1753

Zur Zeit der zweiten grossen Auswanderung, welche wiederum nicht
auf Nassau beschränkt war, standen die infolge Aussterbens von vier
Linien vereinigten Nassauischen Lande, zuerst unter der Herrschaft
von Wilhelm Carl Heinrich Friso, Prinzen von Oranien und Erbstatt-
halter der Vereinigten Niederlande, und darauf unter der Vormund-

schaftlichen Regierung seiner Wittwe Anne, geb. Kronprinzessin von
England, und des Herzogs Carl von Braunschweig und Lüneburg. Da
diese im Ausland residierten, war es notwendig gewesen, eine beson-
dere aus einem Präsidenten und einer Reihe von Räten bestehende
Landesregierung zu verordnen, welche von Dillenburg aus das frühere
Fürstentum Dillenburg, das Amt Beilstein und die Unterdirectorien
Diez, Hadamar und Siegen verwaltete und wegen des zeitraubenden
Verkehrs mit Holland und Braunschweig manchmal ohne zuvor eingeholte Genehmigung handeln musste.
Das Hauptdokument des Jahres 1750 ist die Relatio 34 vom 2. Mai,
worin die Landesregierung dem Fürsten Auskunft über die bis dahin
erfolgte Auswanderung gibt, ihr Verhalten derselben gegenüber dar-
legt und alleruntertänigst um seine Genehmigung nachsucht. „Es
hatt eine Zeit hero in hiesigen Fürstenthümern, und zwar in Dillen-
burgischen, besonders aber in dem ehemahligen sogenannten Reformirt
[en] Siegnischen Landesantheil und in dem Amte Beilsten eine nicht
geringe Anzahl Unterthanen um Erlassung ihrer Unterthanenpflicht
und Erlaubnis, nach Verkauffung ihres Vermögens nach einer oder der
anderen americanischen Colonie verziehen zu mögen, bey uns in der
Hoffnung nachgesuchet, daselbst ihr Glück besser zu machen und ein
reicheres Auskommen darinnen als in hiesigen Landen zu finden."
Die Unterdirektorien und Beamten seien angewiesen worden, insonderheit den Supplicanten, welche nach Tilgung ihrer Schulden genug
übrig behielten, um sowohl ihre Verpflichtungen gegen die Herrschaft zu erfüllen, als sich und die Ihrigen zu ernähren, die
schädlichen Folgen ihrer verhabenden Reise nachdrücklich zu Gemüthe
zu führen und sie zu ,mehrer Coercir- und Hemmung' ihrer Auswan-
derungslust darauf aufmerksam zu machen, dass ausser dem 10. Pfennig jetzt annoch 2% Abzugsgelder zu zahlen seien. Denen, welche
noch ein Vermögen ,theils von 600 und 900, auch theils von 1000
fl.' übrig behielten, hätten sie ihr Suchen um die Dimissoriales[4]
abgeschlagen, ,andern hingegen, welche nebst denen Ihrigen kaum den
Lebensunterhalt zu finden vermogten, mithin anderen Unterthanen zur
Last lebten, den verlangten Losschein unbedencklich ertheilet'.
„Also haben an Eu. Hoheit wir diesen Vorfall in tiefster Ernie-
drigung unterthänigst einberichten sollen in der unterthänigst
devotesten Zurversicht, Höchstdieselben sothane von uns in Absicht
auf dero Unterthanen bestes gemachte Verfügungen in Gnaden zu
genehmigen geruhen werden, als worüber wir uns die gnädigste Ent-
schliessung in ehrerbietigster Obliegenheit zu unser weiter unter-
thänigsten Verhaltung hiermit erbitten."
Die Antwort beginnt im Stile der Zeit: ,Von Gottes Gnaden Wilhelm Carl Henrich Friso, Printz von Orange, Fürst zu Nassau pp' und
ist mit der eigenhändigen Unterschrift ,Prince d'Orange & Nassau'
versehen. Sie macht die Landesregierung darauf aufmerksam, dass
Supplicanten, welche nicht leibeigen sind, nach Entrichtung der
schuldigen Verpflichtungen die Verziehung auf dem Lande nicht ver-
weigert werden kann, billigt aber im übrigen ihre Bestrebungen,
,durch diensame Vorstellungen besonders die tauchlichen und wohlbe-
mittelten Unterthanen so viel möglich im Lande zu behalten'.

Aus den Jahren 1751 und 1752 liegen keine wichtigeren, die Auswanderung im Ganzen betreffende Akten vor, desto mehr aber aus dem
folgenden Jahre, wo die Rentkammer in einem Promemoria sagt, dass
,bekandtlich sehr viele Unterthanen...nach Penselvanien oder der
Orthen zu ziehen gesonnen' und ,dieselbe ihre Abreisse sehr pres-
siren und mehrentheils zusammen fort wollen'. Sie ist jedoch an
anderer Stelle nicht der Ansicht, dass gnädigster Herrschaft daran
ein Schaden zuwachse, ,insolang nicht guthbemittelte Unterthanen
auch in mehrer Anzahl als biss dahin noch geschehen, forthziehen',
,zumahl ohnehin die Nassausehrbevölckert und fast mehrere Menschen
hat, als der District wohl ernehren kan'. Uebrigens könne ja von
landesherrlicher Macht wegen verordnet werden, dass die Emigranten-
güter nicht höher als ihr ermässigter Taxwert verkauft werden dürften. Dieses Mittel würde besonders Starkbemittelte vom Abziehen
abschrecken.
Dieser Vorschlag wurde jedoch von der Regierung in ihrem Rund-
schreiben vom 22. März nur unvollkommen befolgt. Sie befahl darin
zwar, dass jeder Verkauf ,vor Amt' geschehen müsse, gab aber
gleichzeitig den Beamten auf ,inallewege ohne Zwang' zu verfahren
und es durch Abmahnung der Käufer oder sonst auf schickliche Art zu
erreichen zu suchen, dass die Güter ,über ihr *justum pretium* [wah-
ren Wert] nicht getrieben' würden. Verkauf unter der Hand ward dagegen mit Konfiskation und daneben noch mit namhafter Geldbusse
oder Leibesstrafe bedroht.
Im Postscriptum ad Relatio 42 vom 26. Mai legt sie darauf der
Vormundschaft, welche nach dem inzwischen erfolgten Tode des Fürsten für dessen minderjährigen Sohn eingesetzt war, Rechenschaft ab:
,Ohngeachtet der...in Weeg gelegten Difficultäten [seye] dannoch
die Auswanderung dermaln sehr starck...und, obgleich an der einen
Seite viele unnütze, arme und ohne Schaden zu entbehrende Einwohner
damit [fortgingen, schienen] dennoch an der andern Seite auch ange-
sessene Unterthanen sich die Lust dazu immer mehr ankommen zu lassen.' Um die Emigranten vor den Emissarien, welche sie in ,Sclav-
erey und Elend' brächten, zu schützen, hätte sie sie bei Behändi-
gung der Dimissorialien an den *Commissionarium* des Capitains von
Waldo gewiesen. Sie halte es aber noch für nötig, nach dem Exempel
anderer Reichsstände zur Warnung der Unterthanen eine gedruckte
Verordnung gegen besagte *Emissarii* zu erlassen und öffentlich anzu-
schlagen und lege den Entwurf einer solchen mit Bitte um baldige
Genehmigung bei.
Die von Anne unterzeichnete Antwort ward, da sie sich mit Herzog
Carl verständigen musste, erst am 3. August ausgefertigt. Es wird
darin der Erlass der eingesandten Verordnung gebilligt, zugleich
aber ,bey allzu starck einreisendem Missbrauch der sonstigen *liber-
tates emigrandi* [Auswanderungsfreiheit]' seitens bemittelter Untertanen der Gebrauch der ,Zwangsmittele' für unentbehrlich gehalten,
welche in die unten S. 31 inhaltlich wiedergegebene Verordnung vom
28. Febr. 1764, Absatz 4-6 später aufgenommen wurden. Durch solche
werde den Emigrationen bemittelter Untertanen wenigstens eine ziem-

liche Behinderung in den Weg gelegt, und während der Untersuchung
des Ertrags seiner Grundstücke werde manchem die Lust zur Auswanderung wieder vergehen oder die Zeit der Abreise verstreichen, auch
der unordentlichen Kauflust der Bleibenden ein Ziel gesetzt. Im
übrigen käme noch eine Erhöhung des Abzugsgeldes als ein Nebenmit-
tel in Betracht.

Nach der Relatio 60 vom 1. September wurde nun die Verordnung
gegen die *Emissarii* mit dem Datum des 3. August sofort gedruckt,
dagegen zur Zeit von der Publikation einer weiteren Verordnung mit
den von der Vormundschaft vorgeschlagenen Zwangsmitteln abgesehen,
,da auf die in hiesigen Landen kund gewordene Nachricht, dass die
americanische Colonien mit der darzu bestimmten Anzahl Europäeren
nunmehro angefüllet seyen und keine weitere Colonisten auf dieses
Jahr angenommen würden, seit einigen Monaten hier kein Unterthan
mehr *pro dimissorialibus* nachgesuchet hat'. Erst 1764 wurde darauf
zurückgegriffen.

Gehen wir nun den Ursachen der starken Auswanderung des Jahres
1753 nach, so zeigt der Bericht des Ebersbacher Amtmanns Bausch vom
12. Februar, dass in seinem Amt ein Brief aus Amerika die Hauptver-
anlassung war. Als er vor einigen Wochen gehört habe, dass wieder
so viele Leute nach der Insul ziehen wollten, habe er es anfangs
nicht glauben wollen. Da er nun aber vernehme, dass ,rechte wohl-
habende Leuthe, so über 6, 8 und mehr hundert Gulden und Thaler
Werth besitzen', ihre Habseligkeiten feil böten, habe er sich nach
der Ursache erkundigt und erfahren, ,dass solche guthe Brieffe auss
der Insul kommen'. Er habe sich rechte Mühe geben müssen, etwas
devon zu Gesicht zu bekommen, und habe zu dem Zwecke den Schulmeister angestellt, einen davon abzuschreiben. Derselbe sei von Johs
Hayn (Haün, TB u. R Hein), welcher als Kuhhirt anno 1751 von Rittershausen hinweggezogen. Weil nun dieser Hayn jederzeit ein
,still und erbahr Leben geführet' und darin der meisten Mitgezoge-
nen, so noch viele Verwandte hier hätten, auch des verabredeten
Wahrzeichens seines Briefes gedächte, so mässen die Leute diesem
mehr Glauben als andern noch herumlaufenden ,Federwischen' bei und
machten ,nicht wenig Lermen wegen des Fortziehens'. Die Bauschsche
Abschrift ist, wenn auch sehr vergilbt, erhalten. Was Hayn darin
über Amerika sagt, sei im wesentlichen hier mitgeteilt. Das
Schluss-s, welches ein Mittelding zwischen einem s und sz bildet,
ist dabei als s transcribiert.

„Von diesem Landt zu berichten, so ist unser rechtmässiger Herr,
dem wir geschworen haben, Wilhelm (!) der 2te, König in Engellandt.
Sonsten ist unser gegenwärtiger Gouverner vom König eingesetzt,
Recht und Gerechtigkeit zu befördern und das Böse zu straffen. Es
ist aber nicht wie bey euch, das die Herrschafft den Unterthanen
plaget bis auff das Höchste mit Geldgeben und Frohndiensten, dann
wir sitzen...ruhig unter unsrer Herrschafft. Sie regieren auch
nicht länger als ein Jahr. Dann werden sie oder andere wider
erwählet von den Unterthanen...

Es ist alles frey, alle Handthierung und Profession. Es ist

auch, Gott sey danck! ein fruchtbares Land mit allerley Gewächs,
Frucht genug, auch allerley Frucht, als (=nur) keinen Hirschen (=
Hirse) hab' ich noch gelesen. Wir haben die Zeit, die wir hier im
Landt sein, lauter Wäytzenbrod gebacken. Es ist auch nicht so gar
theuer. Mann kaufft das Buschel um 4 Schilling, das ist bey euch
2 Kornmeste, und ein Schilling ist so viel an eurem Geld als 9 alb,
und 20 Schilling ist ein Pfund. Ich habe aber schon manchen Tag 3,
auch 4, auch bis 5 Schilling verdient...
    Dabey braucht mann kein Holtz zu kauffen. Ich bin hier selber
Förster. Ich und mein Bruder haben eine Stunde lang Waldung, das
schönste Holtz. Es gibt hier allerley Holtz, viererley Eichen,
Tannen, . . Wallnis, Cedern, Casdanien, Hühnerpapeln (?), allerley,
das ich mein Lebtag in Teutschlandt nicht gesehen habe, auch gesund
Wasser, auch gesunde Lufft, auch Vieh genug.
    Es gibt hier Leute, die 10 bis 15 Pferde haben und haben nichts
mit ins Land bracht. Wer fleisig arbeittet, der kan sich hier wohl
ernehren. Mann gibt ja der Herschafft gar wenig. Ein Mann, der
zwey, drey oder 400 Acker Land hat, der gibt des Jahrs 2 auch 3
Schilling, und ein Schilling seind 9 alb, wie ich vorher gemeldet,
auch manchmalen garnichts. Es gibt auch solche Pletz pfeil, wer (=
für den, der) Geld mit ins Land bringet. Die Leute verkauffen und
gehen weiter fort. Es weis noch kein Mensch, wie gros das Land
ist. Euroba ist dagegen als Dillenburg gegen Franckfurt in der
Landkarte. Das beste Landt liegt noch wüste. Sie reissen noch bis
sieben hundert Meilen und finden [kein] Ende.
    Wann ein wohlstehender Mann bey euch seine Sache zu Geld hätte
und Lust, hierher zu ziehen, der kan hier in Ruhe sitzen besser wie
bey euch ein Edelmann. Die Armen auch, aber sie müssen klein
anfangen, dann das Land bringt Frucht genug, wann das Holtz darvon
gereiniget, ohne Besserung. Aber das ist das beste, wann sie ihre
Pfracht bezahlen können, so können sie sich darnach wohl ernehren.
Ein gemeiner Taglöhner hat 2 Schilling und 6 Bens—12 Bens ist ein
Schilling—das ist bey euch ein halber Reichsthaler. So weit ist
mein wahrhafftiger Bericht von diessem Land, von Frucht, Holtz und
Wasser, das schöne Obst nicht zu vergessen. Mehr Obst und Persing
hat hier ein Mann als bey euch ein gantzes Dorff.
    Gottes Wort und Prediger haben wir auch zur Genüge, wer das gerne
höret. Es wird euch wohl bewust sein, das Prediger aus dem Dillen-
burgischen zu uns gekomen sein. Der Wiessler ist bey uns Prediger, der Otterbein ist in der Statt Längester" usw. Datiert: ,In
Penselphanien in Alten Mängel bey Luthwig Haus', (an andrer Stelle
all Mengil),[5] d. 15. Oct. 1752.
    Ein anderer Brief, welcher von Bausch sechs Wochen später von un-
gefähr einem kleinen Mädchen auf der Gasse abgenommen wurde und im
Original erhalten ist, machte wieder ,viel Auffruhr'. Der Schreiber, Daniel Becker, ein Reisegenosse von Johs Hayn, erklärt darin
die Reise für beschwerlich, aber ungefährlich und sagt dann u. a.:
,Ich wünsche doch..., das ihr aus der Egibttische Blage komt, dan
dan ich betaure euch alle in dem Dillenburger Lande'. Eine Reihe

von ihm aufgeführter Handwerker könne in Amerika ,fihl Gölt verdinen'. Ein Mann ässe dort mehr Fleisch als sechs in Deutschland, usw. Datiert: ,auff Rache wey im Daumschieb Liebanon',[6] 12. Nov. 1752, von Philad. über ,Trendaun' zu erreichen.

Im Amte Beilstein war der Ende Januar erfolgende Besuch des gleichfalls erst vor zwei Jahren ausgewanderten Joh. Chr. Schmitt nicht ohne Einfluss auf die Auswanderung. Er war von seiner ziemlich gut bemittelten Familie, welche sich in Heidelberg Twp,[7] Pa. niedergelassen hatte, zur Hauptsache wieder hinausgeschickt, um eine zurückgelassene Schwester nebst Mann und Kindern nachzuholen, hatte sich aber in Rotterdam vom Kaufmann und Schiffsagenten Daniel Havart bereden lassen, gegen freie Rückfahrt Auswanderer zu werben. Als die Regierung gegen Ende März davon erfuhr, wurde er verhaftet, unter starker Bedeckung zuerst nach Beilstein und darauf nach Dillenburg gebracht und dort gefangen gesetzt. Da ihm jedoch keine vorsätzliche Verführung Dillenburger Untertanen nachgewiesen werden konnte und der Heimberger Steup, bei welchem er zwei Jahre als Knecht gedient hatte, nichts als Treue und Aufrichtigkeit bei ihm verspürt zu haben erklärte, wurde der Arrest als genügende Strafe erachtet und er unter Ableistung folgenden Eides aus der Haft entlassen:

„Ich, Johann Christian Schmitt, gelobe und schwöre zu Gott dem Allmächtigen einen leiblichen Eid, dass ich mit keinem der Nassauischen Landesunterthanen hinkünftig mich mit einigem Gespräch von dem Zustand von Pensilvanien und der Gegenden einlassen, noch weniger dieselbe, um mit mir in dieses Land zu ziehen, überreden und ansprechen oder gar einen Contract desfals mit ihnen schliesen, sondern mich dessen gäntzlich enthalten, auch innerhalb 3 Tagen mich aus den hiesigen Landen wegbegeben und mich darin nicht wiederfinden lassen will, so wahr mir Gott helfe durch seinen lieben Sohn.'

Hauptquelle für die einzelnen Auswanderer sind diesmal die Tabellen ,von den seit einigen Jahren her nach America weggezogenen Unterthanen', für welche die Landesregierung Formulare an die Aemter und Unterdirektorien aussandte. Diese Formulare enthielten 12 oder 13 Columnen, worin neben dem Namen des Emigranten folgendes einzutragen war: Das ,Vatterland', d. h. der Heimatsort desselben, seine Conduite, die Stärke seiner Familie, der Wert seiner Mobilia und Barschaft, seine Immobilia nebst deren Wert oder Taxa, Kaufpretium und Käufer, seine Passiva, die Beträge des 10. Pfennigs und des Abzugsgeldes und das Geld, welches er bar mitgenommen. Es fehlen leider die Tabellen von Burbach, Ebersbach, Haiger, Herborn, Siegen und Tringenstein. Bei Ebersbach wird dieser Mangel durch den Brief von Johs Hayn und die Amtsrechnungen einigermassen ersetzt. Bei Haiger und Tringenstein bieten die entsprechenden Rechnungen aber nur drei bezw. einen Namen, und bei Herborn zwar 1753 die Angabe, dass von den Einahmen des Jahres aus dem 10. Pfennig 556. 29. 4 auf die Emigranten entfallen, aber wieder nur einen Namen.

Nach den Tabellen waren die Wegziehenden überwiegend brave, aber
wenig bemittelte Leute. Unter 58 werden 28 fleissig genannt, einer
träg, 14 gut, 13 schlecht oder doch schlechte Haushalter, einer
ehrbar, einer liederlich. Fast alle hatten zwar wiederum ein eigen
Heim und mehr oder weniger Grundstücke, waren aber z. T. stark verschuldet, die Beilsteiner z. B. durchschnittlich mit über 50%.
Nach den Tabellen und den Ebersbacher Amtsrechnungen konnten unter
80 nur 28 Beträge von über 300 Gulden mitnehmen, darunter nur 20
über 500 und 5 von 848 bis 1305. Von den 52, welche weniger als
300 mitnahmen, hatten fünf garnichts übrig behalten, vierzehn 6-75,
dreizehn 75-150 Gulden.
    Vergleicht man jedoch Johs Hayn's und Dan. Becker's Briefe mit
der Ebersbacher Amtsrechnung des Jahres, so zeigt sich eine grosse
Diskrepanz. Denn, während schon die Ueberfahrt für Dan. Becker und
Frau, Johs Hayn und Bruder nebst Frauen und die Gebrüder Henrich
480 Gulden beanspruchte, und dazu noch das Geld für die Land- und
Viehkäufe der drei Familienväter in Amerika hinzukommt, stehen alle
dem in der Amtsrechnung nur 85 von Johs Hayn mitgenommene Gulden
gegenüber. Selbst angenommen, dass Amtmann Bausch die beiden Henrich, welche Vormünder hatten, den Verarmten zurechnete, welche er
laut Regierungsschreiben vom 23. Febr. des Jahres *connivendo* (mit
Zudrückung eines Auges) entlassen durfte, so fehlt es doch bei den
übrigen an einer Erklärung.
    In der nun folgenden Namenliste ist den wenigen uns bekannten
Auswanderern der Jahre 1750-52 die Jahreszahl (ohne die 17) beige-
setzt, den vielen, welche entweder sicher oder doch vielleicht 1753
fortzogen, dagegen keine Zahl beigegeben. Bei denen, welche nach
Rupp in Philadelphia landeten, ist ein R mit der Nummer der
Schiffsliste hinzugefügt, wobei geringe Abweichungen in Ruppschen
Schreibungen oder die Vorsetzung besw. Auslassung eines Johann
nicht vermerkt ist. A vor andern Taufnamen ist wieder als Anna zu
lesen, F, Fam und K als Frau, Familie und Kind oder Kinder.

Amt Beilstein

Arborn: Henr. Hild, Fam v. 6; Chr. Klein, Fam v. 6. - Bach:
Joh. Henr. Wiederslein, Fam v. 2. - Bretthausen: Joh. Chr. Rehi,
Fam v. 5. - Emmerichenhain: Peter Flick, Fam v. 6, entweder
1751, R 168 oder 53 R 200; Joh. Jost Krum's Wwe, Fam v. 8; Gerlach
Stalp, Schuhmacher, Fam v. 4; Joh. Wilh. Stalp, Schmied, Fam v. 7;
Jost Stalp, Fam v. 4. - Erbach: Chr. Henr. Greb, Fam v. 6. R 206
Chr. Henr. u. Joh. Deis Gr. - Haiern: Joh. Peter Stahl, Fam v.
3. - Langenbach: Joh. Chr. Lindorff und Joh. Dan. Pfeiffer mit
Zurücklassung ihrer Familien heiml. fort zur Erkundung Amerikas 51.
R 168 Leidtorff u. J. D. Phil. Pfeiffer; Conrad Graa, Fam v. 6. R
206; Joh. Chr. Rübsamen, Fam v. 4. R 206 ausser Chr. noch Joh.
Theis Rübs. - Liebenscheid: Peter Höchst, Schuhmacher, Fam v. 9;
Chr. Kupfer, Fam v. 8. - Marienberg: Joh. Christmann, Fam v. 3,
51. R 167; Johs Peter Leys, Fam ? R 206. - Nenderoth: Wilh.
Becker, Fam v. 5. R 206 W. Becker Grün (!); Chr. Hild, Fam v. 9;

Peter Hild, Fam v. 7; Johs Köhler, Fam v. 6; Jost Ludwig, Fam v. 6;
Friedr. Michel, Fam v. 5. - Niedershausen: Joh. Peter Russ,
Schuhmacherbursche, cca 50-52; Conrad Michel, Schäfer, Fam v. 7. -
Obershausen: Conrad Becker, Schmied, Fam v. 6. R 206. - Ober-
rossbach: Phil. Kring, Fam v. 5, zog 51, falls R 167 Joh. Henr. u.
Joh. Jost Gring seine Angehörigen. - Pfuhl: (Joh.) Chr. Schmit,
Fam v. 7, 51. R 168 ausser Chr. noch Joh. Chr. u. Joh. Henr.
Schmidt; Paulus Krum, Fam v. 5, ausser Paulus auch Johs Crum; Chr.
Mann, Fam v. 7. R 206 Chr. mit Jonas, ausserdem noch ein Chr.
krank; Johs Zehrung, Fam v. 6. Sohn Ludwig in Heimat 1764, arre-
tiert. - Rehe: Johs Diehl, led., 53 ?; Joh. Chr. Jung, Kuhhirt,
Fam v. 5. - Salzburg: Maria Elisab. Goebel, led.; Joh. Enger
Weller, Leineweber, Fam v. 5. Vgl. R 208 Joh. G. Wäller u. Joh.
Wilh. Weller. - Stockhausen: Joh. Jacob Haas, Fam v. 4. R 206
Hass; Peter Weyel, Fam v. 4. R 206; Joh. Henr. Widderslein, Fam v.
6; Mathäus Zimmermann, Fam v. 6. R 206 Matheus u. Hermanus Z. -
Unnau: Martin Buchener, Fam v. 7. R 206 Joh. M. Buckner krank mit
Joh. Henr. Buchner und an anderer Stelle Johs B.; Theis Lauer, Fam
v. 6. R 206 Theiss mit Henr. L. - Waigandshain: Joh. Jacob
Fischbach, Fam v. 9. Vgl. R 204 Jost F.; Joh. Chr. Stahl, Fam v. 6.
R 206 Joh. Chr. mit Joh. Gerlach St. - Willingen: Joh. Chr.
Reyss, Fam v. 3; Johs Peter Reyss, Fam v. 4. Vgl. einen Reys u.
Reiss R 146. 50. - Zinnhain: Jacob Schütz, Fam v. 5. R 206.

Grafschaft Diez

Altendiez: Peter Löwenzöller, Fam v. 8; Joh. Georg Minck, Fam v.
6.

Amt Dillenburg

Dillenburg: Joh. Henr. Becker, Wollenweber, Wwer 52. R 192;
Pfarrer Phil. Wilh. Otterbein 52. - Donsbach: Joh. Conrad
Schelt, Landmann und Kuhhirt, F u. 3 K. - Oberschelt: Joh. Jacob
Nickel, Landmann, F u. 2 K. Vgl. Joh. Peter N. R 209.

Amt Driedorf

Driedorf: Joh. Henr. Hardt, F u. 1 K. - Heisterberg: Chris-
toph Betz, allein; Joh. Chr. Theis, F u. 8 K. R 203 Chr. Deiss. -
Hohenroth: Joh. Peter Rumpff, F u. 2 K. Vgl. R 200 J. P. Stumpf;
Joh. Georg Theis, F u. 3 K. - Mademühlen: Joh. Jost Claas, F u.
2 K.; Joh. Georg Goebell, F.; Joh. Adam Stahl, F u. 2 K.; Joh.
Henr. Stahl, F u. 3 K.; Joh. Peter Stahl, F u. 3 K.

Amt Ebersbach

Im Interesse besserer Uebersichtlichkeit seien hier die Auswan-
derer von 1751 und 1753 voneinander getrennt.
1751: Ebersbach: Joh. Dan. Becker, Fam; Wwe Giersbach (u.
Sohn?); Johs Heintz, Fam; Dan. Hoffmann. - Eibelshausen: Johs
Orth. - Mandeln: Johs Franck. - Rittershausen: Gebrüder Joh.
Henr. u. Johs Hayn (TB Hein), beide Fam; Gebrüder Joh. Georg u.
Johs Henrich, beide ledig. Mit Ausnahme Francks und der Wwe Giers-
bach, an deren Stelle Joh. Jost Giersbach erscheint, finden sich
alle diese R 167, und zwar in zwei Gruppen beisammen. Nach Johs
Hayn's oben z. T. abgedrucktem Briefe waren sie, wenigstens Hayns,

4 Monat unterwegs, gelangten aber in 7 Wochen 2 Tagen ohne Sturm
von Cowes bis in den Delaware. Es starben 2 Alte und 11 Kinder,
wogegen 7 geboren wurden.
    1753: Bergebersbach: Gebrüder Joh. Dan. u. Joh. Jost Schlappig.
- Ebersbach: Johs Aurand; A. Christina Giersbach; Johs Gräff;
Henr. Müller; Johs Müller jr.; Georg Schäffer. - Eibelshausen:
Phil. Wagener.
                      Fürstentum Hadamar
    Amt Hadamar, Oberzeuzheim: Jacob Schmiedt, F. R 210.   - Amt
Stuhlgebiet, Bellingen: Peter Baldus, F u. 5 K. R 208.   - Dreis-
bach: Merten Hilsenhäuser, F u. 4 K. Vgl. R 206 Martin Helfeysen;
Peter Müller, F u. 2 K. R 206 Peter M. mit Johs Miller.   - Hahn:
Joh. Best Weber, F u. 2 K. R 206 Sebastian W.   - Todtenberg: Joh.
Henr. Baldus, F u. 3 K. - Waldmühlen: Christ Schütz, F u. 2 K. R
204 Christoph Sch.
                        Amt Haiger
    Allendorf: Jost Henr. Weyel, Fam 52?   - Langenaubach: Hs Jacob
Herwig und Joh. Wilh. Schmit (Amerika?).
                        Amt Herborn
    Herborn: Joh. Zeppenfeldt (Amerika?).
              Aemter Hilchenbach und Siegen
    Eiserfeld: Johs Güding, Bergarbeiter u. Tagelöhner, nach Pa. -
Müsen: Joh. Brumbach's Wwe A. Juliana, Kinder, zu Brüdern in Pa.
- Niederndorf: Thielman Weissgerber, F u. K. Alle diese 50. R
153 Johs Gitting, Joh. Jac. Br., Dilmanus W.
                      Amt Tringenstein
    Eyershausen: Jost Henr. Becker (Amerika?).
Ausserdem aus dem Fürstentum Pfarrer Wilh. Stoy u. Wissler, beide
52. R S. 271.
    Die vielen Vorstehenden, welche sich in R 206 finden, d. h. in
der *Rowand* ihre Ueberfahrt machten, waren Reisegenossen einer
beträchtlichen Anzahl[8] von denjenigen, welche Joh. Chr. Schmitt für
Daniel Havart angeworben hatte, und teilten mithin auch deren
Ueberfahrtsbedingungen. Nach denselben erhielt jede erwachsene
Person oder sogenannte ganze Fracht einen festen Schlafplatz von
sechs Fuss Länge und anderhalb Fuss Breite. Sonntags 1 ℔ Fleisch
mit Erbsen, Reis oder Bohnen; Montags 1 ℔ Mehl, Dienstags 1/2 ℔
Speck mit Erbsen, Reis oder Bohnen; Mittwochs wie Montags; Donners-
tags wie Sonntags; Freitags 1 ℔ Butter und 1/2 ℔ Stockfisch mit
Erbsen, Reis oder Bohnen; Samstags 6 ℔ Brod, 1 ℔ Käse und Erbsen-
suppe. Ferner: 1 Maas Bier des Tags, solangte es gut bleiben kan,
nebst 1 Maas Wasser, nach dem aber 2 Maas Wasser täglich. Von Mor-
gens 6 Uhr bis Abends 6 Uhr Feuer, um darauf zu kochen und die
Kranken und kleinen Kinder zu erwärmen, ,insoweit es Wind und Wet-
ter zulassen'. Für durstige Kranke 2 Fass Essig und 1 Fass Brande-
wein, wie auch Gewürz, ,damit sie nicht durch deren Ermangelung auf
der See ihrer Gesundheit und Lebens beraubt werden', wie auch die
erforderlichen Medizinen.
    Viel geringer als die Zahl derer, welche wir bis Philadelphia

begleiten konnten, ist naturgemäss die Zahl derer, welche wir über
Philadelphia oder einen andern Landungshafen hinaus verfolgen kön-
nen. Die Familie Schmitt und die Gebrüder Hayn blieben, wie wir
bereits oben sahen, in Pennsylvanien, während Dan. Becker sich in
New Jersey niederliess. Die Gebrüder Henrich gingen dorthin oder
nach New York. Johs Diehl, Maria Elisab. Goebel, Joh. Peter Russ
und Joh. Adam Stahl werden ebenso wie Jost Henr. Weyel gleich in
New York gelandet sein. Johs Diehl und die Goebel, welche Wilh.
Seebers Frau geworden war, lebten 1767 in Canajoharie am Mohawk,
Russ 1789 in Claveratz (vielleicht Claverack, Columbia Co) und
Stahl um dieselbe Zeit in Rhinebeck, Duchess Co, N. Y. Eine von
letzterem nach Dillenburg gesandte Vollmacht ist sowohl auf einem
deutsch- als auf einem englischgedruckten Formular ausgefertigt.
Die deutsche ist datiert ,im vierzehnten jahr unserer Independence
und im jahr unsers Herrn' usw. (1789, 10. Sept.). Einer der beiden
Zeugen trägt den in unsern Tagen weltbekannt gewordenen Namen
Rockefeller. Der Vollmacht liegt in dem Akten an anderer Stelle
die Abschrift der Dimissorialien bei, welche als Beispiel aus der
Mitte das Jahrhunderts hier abgedruckt seien:
   „Demnach Joh. Adam Stahl von Mademühlen im Fürstenthum Dillenburg
aus hiesigen Landen ab- und nacher *Americam* zu ziehen gedenket und
dahero um die erforderl. *Dimissoriales* geziemend angestanden, man
auch demselben hierunter zu deferiren kein Bedenken hat, Als werden
ihme solche kraft dieses hierdurch ertheilet und [er] somit der
Unterthanen Pflicht, womit er zeithero hiesig gnädigster Landes-
herrschaft zugethen gewesen, erlassen.
   In Urkund der Landes-Regierung gewöhnl. Unterschrift und vorge-
druckten Insiegel. *Signatum* (gez.) Dillenburg, d. 17ten May 1753.
L. S. Fürstl. Oranien-Nassauische zur Vormundschaftl. Landes-
       Regierung verordnete Präsident, Geh. Räthe, auch Geh.
       Justitz- und Reg. Räthe.
                                        I. E. Spanknabe"
Taxa 4 f. Driedorf
   Jost Henr. Weyel wohnte 1767 in Caritschazery,[9] N. Y. Nach einem
Briefe von ihm an seinen Schwestersohn vom 30. Sept., von dem ein
Teil in der unten S. 37 erwähnten Kinenschen Abschrift erhalten
ist, war er bis dahin von seiner Auswanderung nicht besonders
befriedigt. Er berichtet darin u. a. von dem Untergang eines Aus-
wandererschiffes mit 300 Menschen in der Nordsee, von 300 Gulden,
welche ihn und den Seinigen die Reise nach New York gekostet, von
den teuren Preisen in Amerika und von dem englisch-französischen
Krieg daselbst. Von letzterem sagt er: ,Wir haben 8 Jahr lang
Krieg in America gehabt, nicht einen Krieg, wie in der Welt
bräuchlich ist, sondern einen mordthätigen Krieg durch die blut-
gierige Wilden... Die haben in den 8 Jahr viel 1000 todt geschlagen
und gefangen genommen und haben sie 100 Meil wegs hinweggeführet
bis in eine Stadt, die heist Canida (!). Es ist ein französischer
Ort.'
   Peter Hild und Familie sowie die Familien Ludwig und Stahl, denen

zwei seiner Schwiegersöhne entstammen, werden auf einem Waldoschen
Schiffe direkt nach Boston gefahren sein, denn seine drei verheira-
teten Töchter und deren Männer und eine verwittwete Schwiegertoch-
ter, welche 1786 Erbansprüche in Dillenburg erhoben, wohnten damals
in Waldoborough, Mass. Die von ihnen eingesandte Vollmacht ist be-
glaubigt von Gouverneur James Bowdoin d. 16. Sept. 1786 ,*in the
Eleventh year of the Independence*' *of the U. S. of America* und
trägt das grosse *Sigillum Reipublicae Massachusettensis.*

III. Die Auswanderungen zwischen 1764 und 1798
     Mit dem Aufhören des siebenjährigen Krieges kam neben der Auswan-
derung nach andern Ländern auch die nach Amerika wieder in Aufnah-
me. Während man sie aber in vorhergegangenen Jahrzehnt nur durch
die eine gedruckte Verordnung vom 3. Aug. 1753 einzuschränken
gesucht hatte, ging man jetzt binnen zwei Jahren mit dreien gegen
sie vor.
     Die erste ward von der Landesregierung am 28. Febr. 1764 ohne zu-
vor eingeholte Genehmigung des überlebenden Mitglieds der vormundschaftlichen Regierung, Herzog Carls, erlassen und ihm gegenüber in
der Relatio 35 vom gleichen Datum, wie folgt, begründet. Es seien
unter den Supplicanten gegenwärtig verschiedene ,wohl angesesene',
besonders aber der bekannte bereits in Amerika gewesene Joh. Christ
Lindorff von Langenbach Amts Beilstein und seine ganze in ,wohl-
thuenden' Unterthanen bestehende Familie. Da sie nicht leibeigen
seien — im Amt Beilstein kennt nur Niedershausen Leibeigenschaft —
habe man ihnen die Auswanderung nicht schlechterdings versagen,
sondern nur erschweren können. Zu dem Zwecke sei in der neuen Verordnung neben älteren z. T. verschärften Bestimmungen von den
Zwangsmitteln Gebrauch gemacht, welche in dem vormundschaftlichen
Schreiben vom 3. Aug. 1753 bereits vorgeschlagen, aber damals
zurückgestellt worden seien.
     Der Inhalt der neun Absätze der Verordnung ist kurz folgender:
     1. Wiederholung der Verordnung von 1753.
     2. Wer ohne *Dimissoriales* auswandert, verliert zur Strafe sein
Vermögen.
     3. Wer die *Dimissoriales* erlangt hat, ,soll sich garkeine Hoff-
nung machen / er mag würcklich wegziehen, oder hernach sein Vor-
haben änderen / und wieder bleiben wollen / als Unterthan wiederum
angenommen / oder in denen hiesigen Landen gedultet zu werden /
sondern er hat nebst seiner völligen *Familie* jene auf ewig zu räumen', besonders keine unerzogenen Kinder zur Beschwerde des Landes
zurückzulassen.
     4-6 (neu!) Verkauf und Dimission haben in folgender Weise vor
sich zu gehen: Zunächst reicht der Emigrant seinem Beamten ein
Verzeichnis seiner zu verkaufenden Güter mit den darauf haftenden
Schulden und den Namen des präsumptiven Käufers ein. Darauf unter-
sucht der Beamte den wahren Ertrag eines jeden Stückes und setzt
mit dem Emigranten und dem Käufer zusammen einen leidlichen Preis
fest, von dem der letztere eidlich versichern muss, dass er ihn aus

seinen baren Mitteln, ohne vieles dazu zu borgen, zahlen könne. Erst dann erteilt die Regierung unter Umständen die *Dimissoriales*, falls es nach ihrem Ermessen ohne Schädigung des im Lande Bleibenden geschehen kann. Werden diese Bestimmungen jedoch umgangen, so verfallen die Güter dem Fiscus, und wird der ungehorsame Käufer unnachsichtlich ebenfalls zum Emigriren angehalten.

7. Damit die Herrschaft nicht zu kurz komme, hat der Beamte bei Ansetzung des Vermögens eines jeden Emigranten den Rechnungsbeamten des Ortes zuzuziehen. Andere Gläubiger haben zwei Monate ihre Ansprüche geltend zu machen. Der Käufer darf vor Ablauf solcher Frist und ohne schriftliche Ordre vom Beamten bei Strafe zweifacher Restitution dem Emigranten nichts auszahlen.

8 und 9 handeln von der Aufbewahrung der Akten in der Repositur und von der Kostenlosigkeit der notwendigen Untersuchungen.

Herzog Carl genehmigte unterm 26. März nicht nur nachträglich diese Verordnung, sondern stellte obendrein zur Erwägung, ob nicht, falls das Emigrieren trotzdem fortwähren sollte, die schon 1753 von der Vormundschaft angedeutete willkürliche Erhöhung der Abzugsgelder vorbehalten werden sollte. Da nun in der Tat noch verschiedene ziemlich vermögende und nicht leibeigene Supplicanten, besonders aus dem Amte Beilstein und aus dem Hickengrunde, inständig auf ihrer Dimission beharrten, ward eine solche Massnahme von der Regierung in ihrer Relatio 62 vom 12. April ,ohnumgänglich nothwendig' erachtet und unter demselben Datum eine Zusatzverordnung mit folgender Hauptbestimmung erlassen:

„[Die Regierung] behält...sich 1) in jedem vorkommenden Fall eine willkührliche Bestimm- und Erhöhung des Abzugs-Geldes ausdrücklich bevor / und kan sodann denen zu *emigri*ren [*sic*] gesonnenen überlassen / ob sie gleichwohl mit wenigeren Mitteln ihrer eitelen Hofnung nachfolgen wollen / durch die alleinige *Industrie* ein besonderes Glück in gantz ohnbekannten Landen zu suchen."

Auf diese beiden in erster Linie gegen verheiratete Personen grichtete Verordnungen des Jahres 1764 folgte am 3. Juni 1766 eine Notverordnung gegen das Auswandern Unverheirateter, welche am 17. Juli durch eine gedruckte Verordnung im Namen des nun mündig gewordenen Wilhelm V ersetzt wurde. Anlass zur Notverordnung gab die unvermutete Anzeige, dass junge unverheiratete Leute unter dem Vorgeben, dass sie in Amerika als Dienstboten jährlich 50-60 Reichsthaler bares Geldes sich machen könnten, zur Auswanderung verleitet würden und sich mit den ,anitzo allenthalben im Zug' befindlichen Emigranten heimlich aus dem Land zu machen suchten. Der erste Teil der gedruckten Verordnung dehnt eigentlich nur die längst auf heimliche Auswanderung gesetzte Strafe der Vermögenskonfiskation auf junge, noch unverheiratete Leute aus und verbietet allen und jeden bei Verlust des ihnen Bezahlten ihnen ,so wenig von dem ihrigen etwas abzukaufen / als einigen Vorschuss darauf zu thun'. Der zweite wichtigere Teil schliesst sämtliche Auswanderer, ob jung oder schon älter, von künftigen Erbschaften in der Heimat aus. Unter dem Vorwand, dass verschiedentlich frühere Untertanen sich

ihnen im Nassauischen zugefallene Erbschaften selbst oder durch
Bevollmächtigte nachgeholt hätten, dass aber gleichwohl keine Erbschaft vom Ausland ins Nassauische hereingekommen sei, sowie aus
andern Ursachen wird verfügt,

„dass nach *America*, Russland / oder sonst *emigri*rende Unterthanen
in Zukunft zu keinerley Erbschafft mehr zugelassen / sondern davon
gänzlich ausgeschlossen / fort sogleich / nach erlangten *Dimissori-*
alien und geschehenem Abzug / *pro mortuis* (für tot) gehalten / und
die nächst folgende Anverwandten darzu berechtiget seyn sollen".

Mit all diesen Waffen, wie Bestimmung des Verkaufspreises der
Güter, Beschränkung der Käufer auf die kapitalkräftigen, willkürliche Erhöhung der Abzugsgelder, Ausschluss von allen Erbschaften,
ausgerüstet, war die Regierung in den Stand gesetzt, die Auswanderung von Vermögenden grösstenteils zu verhindern. Die der Unvermög-
enden schwoll jedoch 1773 noch einmal so an wie nie zuvor und wurde
von ihr zum Teil dem Einfluss der alle Jahr sich einfindenden Amerikaner zugeschrieben, denen gegenüber sie sich machtlos fühlte. So
heisst es in Relatio 190 vom 26. Juni 1773:

„Eu. Hoheit müssen wir Pflichten halber unterthänigst berichten,
dass in diesem Jahr mehr Unterthanen, als jemahlen ein Jahr geschehen ist, aus hiesigen Landen nach America emigriret sind. Ob nun
zwaren bisnach solche Emigration den hiesigen Landen unschädlich
gewesen und die Emigranten mehrentheils auss armen und in übler
Aufführung gestandten, überhaupt aber in keinen besonders vermogen-
den Leuthen bestanden, so ist gleichwohl nichts gewisser, als dass
die Unterthanen durch die alle Jahr in den hiesigen Landen sich
einfindende Americaner angeworben und zum Auswanderen verführet
werden. Wir haben zwarn auf diese Leute genaue Aufsicht gehalten,
allein sie wissen, ihre Sache so einzuleiten, dass nicht hinter sie
zu kommen ist." Es sei aber nicht abzusehen, warum ihnen auch nur
ein kurzer Aufenthalt zu gestatten sei.

In seiner eigenhändig mit W. Pr. v. Orange unterzeichneten Antwort, Haag d. 18. Juli, pflichtete der Fürst ihnen mit Bezug auf
diese Amerikaner bei und genehmigte, dass ,diejenige, welche von
Zeit zu Zeit in Unsere Lande zurükkommmen, arretiret und, wann sie
nichts darinnen zu thun haben, sofort daraus verwiesen, diejenige
aber, welche wirkliche Geschäffte daselbst haben, erst nach Verlauf
des zu deren Ausrichtung ihnen bestimmten *Termini* ausgebothen
werden'.

Neue Verfügungen waren nicht nötig. So konnte z. B. die Regierung im Jahre 1784 der Weilburger gegenüber die gute Wirkung ihrer
Emigrations-Verordnungen rühmen und im nächsten Jahr der Hanauer
mitteilen, dass sie dank der angedrohten Vermögenskonfiskation zur
Zeit nicht über heimliche Auswanderung zu klagen habe. Im Gegen-
teil ging sie dazu über, nicht nur mehr und mehr den Wegzug solcher, welche wegen ihrer Armut zur Last fielen oder zu fallen droh-
ten, durch Gewährung einer kleinen Beisteuer zur Reise bis an den
Hafen zu begünstigen, sondern sogar die Auswanderung solcher,
welche Vergehen oder Verbrechen begangen hatten, zu fördern.

Während z. B., wie wir oben S. 10 sahen, 1709 einer wegen eines
noch nicht abgebüssten Forstfrevels zurückgehalten wurde, ward
jetzt einer im gleichen Fall, damit er nur nicht etwa bleibe, von
seinem Amtmann ohne Zahlung der Busse fortgelassen. Einer von
ihrer ganzen Umgegend gefürchteten Diebsfamilie wurden die Abzugsgelder ganz oder zum Teil erlassen. In mehreren Fällen wurde der
Rest einer noch nicht abgesessenen Gefängnisstrafe geschenkt, wobei
ein Häftling in seinem Gnadengesuche darauf hinweist, wie jetzt die
Reise nach Amerika von so vielen angetreten werde, die sich in
,verzweifelten Umständen' befänden. Ja, der Oberschultheiss Reich-
mann von Herborn möchte alles Ernstes sämtliche Insassen des dorti-
gen Zucht- und Arbeitshauses nach Amerika schicken, wenn er den 7.
Mai 1789 der Regierung schreibt: ,Die im Arbeitshaus befindliche
gantze Gesellschaft von hier könnte man zum Vortheil des Publikums
noch mit einer Reissesteuer dem Käsmann [nach Amerika] mitgeben,
wenn sich dieselbe dazu willfährig erklären würde. Ich stelle
unterthänigst anheim, ob nicht der Zuchthaus-Kommission aufzugeben
seyn möchte, diese Züchtlinge darüber zu vernehmen und die Erklärung ehebaldigst einzusenden'.
    Mütter mit unehelichen Kindern und enehelich Geborene, welche
nicht selten auswanderten, wichen dabei, abgesehen von andern Grün-
den, einem starken moralischen Druck, da sie beide andauernd in den
Bastardregistern der Amtsrechnungen geführt wurden. Eine nicht
unbemittelte Frau, welche ein bewegtes Leben hinter sich hatte,
verheiratet gewesen und wieder geschieden war, wollte fort, weil
sie die Verachtung nicht ertragen konnte.
    Arbeitslosigkeit daheim und günstige Nachrichten über den Nah-
rungsstand im Bergbau in Amerika seitens vorangegangener Arbeitsge-
nossen waren der Grund für die Auswanderung mancher Bergleute im
Siegenschen in den Jahren 1796 und 1797. Auch die Hämmer waren
damals dort seit längerer Zeit stillgelegt, und fast modern mutet
die Empörung zweier Tagelöhner darüber an, dass die Hammerschmiede-
meister und -schultheissen sie trotzdem unter Berufung auf ihren
Zunfteid nicht auswandern lassen wollten. So sagt der eine in
seinem Gesuch:
    „Sie verlangen vom Taglöhner, dass er bei ihnen bleiben soll, sie
geben ihm aber nichts zu verdienen, sobald ihr Interesse dadurch
einigen Nachtheil leiden sollte. Die Eigenthümer der Hammerzeit
fanden es für gut, ihr Gewerbe stehen zu lassen und sofort liessen
sie ohne auf den Taglöhner — der unterdessen schmachten mochte —
einige Rücksicht zu nehmen, alle Hämmer das ganze vorige Jahr hin-
durch und bisher noch immer still stehen. Da soll also der Täglöh-
ner mittlerweile von seinem eigenen Schmalz zehren, und wenn es dem
Eigenthümer gefällig ist, will er jenen erst wieder wie sein Last-
thier gebrauchen. Wir hätten doch wohl gerechte Ursache zu ver-
langen, dass, wenn wir bleiben sollten, uns die Hammerschmidtszunft
zuerst das vergüten müste, was wir seit 3-4 Jahren zugesetzt
haben." Und weiter unten nach Zurückweisung der Behauptung, dass
die Siegner Zunft eine besondere geheime Schmiedekunst besässe:

„Ein schwacher Mann taugt garnicht zu ihrer jezigen Schmiederey und, wer nicht einen besonders starken Körperbau besitzt, schmiedet kaum 10-15 Jahre, so ist er schon invalide... Jeder Schlag erschüttert das Innere de Gebeine. Meiner festen Natur habe ich, Spiess, es zu verdanken, dass ich nun schon 26 Jahre geschmiedet habe, aber ich fühle auch, dass ich gearbeitet habe. Vielleicht noch einige Jahre, so bin ich schon zur Arbeit untauglich, allein nichts desto weniger werde ich alsdann doch noch gern essen. Gott helfe mir aber, wenn ich auf die Dankbarkeit der Zunft, in deren Dienst ich meine Kräfte aufgeopfert habe, rechnen sollte." Uebrigens wollten sie in Amerika die Erde bauen und nur im Notfall schmieden.

Der andere erklärt u. a.: „Die bürgerliche Gesellschaft, worinnen ich lebe, muss mich entweder ziehen lassen, oder sie muss mir annehmliche Mittel angeben, wie ich mich und meine Familie ernähren soll, denn ich bin nicht ein Glied von ihr, dass ich vor Mangel umkommen müsse."

Ein Kuriosum ist die Auswanderung von drei Rittershausenern, welche 1000-2000 Gulden im Vermögen hatten. Sie ward herbeigeführt durch einen später als Fälschung nachgewiesenen und auch heute noch deutlich als solche erkennbaren fingierten Brief aus Amerika, welchen der eine sich von einem Schulmeister in Eibelshausen hatte anfertigen lassen, um seiner nicht zur Auswanderung geneigten Frau Lust zu machen, mit ihm zu ziehen. Er enthielt eine dringende und endgiltige Aufforderung herüberzukommen seitens seines Vetters Joh. Jost Hofheinz, welcher es zum Major und zu grossem Besitz gebracht habe, während ein anderer Rittershausener drüben gar General geworden sei. Da dem Lande durch diese Auswanderung ein so beträchtlicher Geldverlust drohte, gab die Landesregierung sich alle erdenkliche Mühe, sie durch den Amtmann davon zurückzuhalten. Sie wies ihn an, die Männer mit ihren Eheweibern und erwachsenen Kindern vor sich kommen zu lassen und ihnen, wenn der Brief auch zuverlassig sein sollte, die Gefährlichkeit ihres Vorhabens und die grosse Ungewissheit ihres künftigen Schicksals vorzustellen, ,da sie zusammen mit ihren Familien und Gütern entweder Schiffbruch leiden und verkommen, [oder] ihre Verwandte, worauf sie jetzt rechnen, mittler Zeit verstorben seyn oder in Kurtzem versterben oder doch in ungünstige Umstände gerathen könnten'. Im Falle sie aber trotzdem auf ihrer Absicht beständen, ihnen zu eröffnen, dass sie 20% ihres Vermögens *pro Fisco* zurücklassen müssten und ,sich nicht die mindeste Hoffnung zu machen hätten, dass sie oder ihre Abkömmlinge...jemahlen als Unterthanen wieder aufgenommen' würden. Abmahnung und Drohung waren in diesem Fall natürlich gleich vergeblich.

Die Akten sind angefüllt mit in der Mehrzahl vergeblichen aber trotzdem mitunter mehr als einmal wiederholten Versuchen der Auswanderer oder ihrer Angehörigen, zurückgelassenes Vermögen oder angefallene Erbschaften vor dem Zugriff des Fiscus zu retten. Bei solchen, welche jung auf die Wanderschaft gegangen waren und später die Auslieferung ihres Vermögens beantragten, kam es eventuell darauf an, ob sie *cum animo revertendi*[10] ausgezogen waren oder von Anfang an Auswanderung beabsichtigt hatten. Bei denen, welche Erbansprüche machten, hing es davon ab, wie es mit der Anwendbarkeit der Verordnung vom 17. Juli 1766 stand, welche die Justizkanzlei bereits in ihrem Promemoria vom 12. Jan. 1786 am liebsten aufgehoben gesehen hätte. Meinte doch Amtmann Gail von Mengerskirchen am 2. Dez. 1793 sogar, dass bei der in den Nassauischen Landen bestehenden Uebervölkerung die Emigrationsstrafen überhaupt wohl ,cessiren' sollten.

Ein Beispiel erfolgreicher Durchsetzung von Ansprüchen beim Fiscus bietet Joh. Jacob Diehl im Frühjahr 1768, obwohl er während der Zeit durch den argwöhnischen und übereifrigen Amtmann Kinen von Haiger mehrfach bei der Regierung verdächtigt und schliesslich gar verhaftet wurde. Zunächst brachte Kinen nämlich in Erfahrung, dass er der Ueberbringer zahlreicher Briefe aus Amerika sei, und veranlasste die Regierung, die sechzehn, welche noch nicht an die Adressaten abgeliefert waren, zu beschlagnahmen. Während diese als unverfänglich festgestellt und freigegeben wurden, spürte er aber noch drei bereits abgelieferte auf, schrieb sie teilweise ab oder liess sie abschreiben und versuchte nun mittels des einen für Amerika ungünstigen nachzuweisen, dass die andern beiden, welche für Amerika günstig waren, geschrieben seien, um Diehl bei der Werbung von Auswanderern behülflich zu sein. Derselbe solle sich nämlich haben verlauten lassen, dass er ,ein oder zween Prediger und dann etwa 40 paar junge ohnverheyrathete Leute' mit zurückzunehmen wünsche. Er, Kinen, gestatte sich deshalb gleichzeitig unterthänigst vorzuschlagen, dass die Verordnung vom 17. Juli 1766 zur Warnung junger Leute nochmals im Lande publiziert werde. Da zur Zeit auch mehrere Dimissionsgesuche eingelaufen waren und auf Diehls Anstiften zurückgeführt wurden, machte die Regierung sich Kinens Verdächtigungen und Befürchtungen zu eigen und liess Diehl gefänglich einziehen und die Verordnung aufs neue ergehen. Diehl rechtfertigte sich jedoch durch Uebersendung der ihm von zwei evangelischen Gemeinden mitgegebenen Berufungen von Predigern und erklärte das übrige für ein aus ersterem hervorgegangenes Missverständnis, so dass er unter Androhung ,unnachlässiger, schwehrer Strafe', im Falle er doch Leute zur Auswanderung veranlasse, aus der Haft entlassen und ihm die Annahme der Prediger freigestellt wurde. Auch liess er sich durch die anfängliche Abweisung seiner eignen Ansprüche und derjenigen seines Bruders Johannes und der Maria Elisabeth Seeber, geb. Goebel, seitens des Fiscus nicht einschüchtern und ruhte nicht, bis er alles ektenmässig erhärtet und binnen Monatsfrist durchgesetzt hatte. Für ihn selber war dabei sein noch jetzt erhaltener Pass aus dem Jahre 1765 von Wichtigkeit, welcher seiner originellen Fassung wegen hier wiedergegeben sei:

„Nachdem Vorzeiger dieses Johann Jacob Diehl zu Rehe nach *America* zu reissen willens ist, und dann hiessiger Orten gesunde und frische Lufft und nicht das Mindeste von einer ansteckenden Seuche

zu verspüren ist, Alss wird jedes Orts Obrigkeit nach Standes Ge-
bühr hiemit ersuchet, vor eingangs gedachten Johann Jacob Diehl aller Orten pass- und repassiren zu lassen, welches in dergleichen
Fällen wiederum beobachtet werden soll, in Urckund des hierunter
getruckten Amtinsiegels.
        Beilstein d. 17ten Junij 1765
    L. S. Fürstl. Oranien-Nassauisches Vorm. Amt hierselbst
                        A. Jeckeln, Rath und Amtmann
    Hauptquelle für die Namen wären diesmal die spezifizierten Son-
derberichte über die Einnahmen aus den 10. Pfennigs- und Abzugsgel-
dern gewesen. Da jedoch kein einziger von diesen erhalten zu sein
scheint, ist man im wesentlichen auf die Gesuche um Dimissorialien
oder Vermögens- bzw. Erbschaftsauslieferungen angewiesen. In den
daneben in Betracht kommenden Amtsrechnungen fehlt bei den verhältnismässig wenigen Namen überdies noch oft das Auswanderungsziel.
Auf die Fälle ist daher im Folgenden in solchen Fällen ein Frage-
zeichen davor gesetzt, wenn auch z. B. 1773 kaum ein anderes Land
ausser Amerika in Frage kommen dürfte. Das Auswanderungsjahr,
diesmal vielfach fraglich, wird wieder mit Auslassung des Jahrhunderts gegeben. Die Hauptabkürzungen sind dieselben wie oben S. 9
u. 24.
                    Amt Beilstein[11]
    Arborn: Elisab. Theis 89; A. Marg. Theis 91; Vaterschwester
einer Theis früher; 2 led. Brüder von Jost Klein cca 66. - Beilstein: Henr. Sartor 73?; Dessen 2 K 84. - Bölsberg: A. Maria
oder Barbara Menck 64? - Emmerichenhain: Phil. Henr. Flick,
starke Fam, und Sebastian Rübsamen, F u. 5 K, 85, wollten in Gegend
von Philadelphia. - Hof bei Marienburg: Wilh. Maier Jahr?; A.
Cath. Schell 69?; Joh. Chr. Steup, F u. 6 K, 85; Franz u. Johs
Steup 88; Joh. Jost Brand, deren Schwager, 88. - Langenbach:
Joh. Christ Lindorff, wirkl. Auswanderung mit Fam, 64. R 244;
Tönges (=Anton) Müller, 18jährig, 88; Dessen Vaterbruder cca 68;
Joh. Tönges Uhr, Schneider, 88. - Marienberg: wahrscheinl.
(Joh.) Sebastian Weber 64. R 244. Besucht 66 u. 84; Joh. Jost
Weber, led., 85. - Rehe: Joh. Jacob Diehl 65. R 250 Thiel; Jost
Henr. Diehl m. Brüdern 69. R 272 er allein. - Salzburg: Martin
Simon, 16jährig, 85; Dessen Vaterbruder Jahr ?. Stockhausen: Joh.
Peter Danecker, Schulmstr., F, 85; Joh. Henr. Rickas (Rickes),
Schneider, 71. R 285 Rickos; Dessen Geschw. A. Gertrud 84 ?, A.
Marg., 20jährig, u. Johs Rickes, F, 87; Deren Schwager Joh. Best
Dencker 87; Vermutl. aus diesem Amt Sebastian Müller Jahr ?
                    Amt Burbach
    Niederdresselndorf: Simon Juncker 87; Joh. Adam Helm, F A. Ger-
traut, 88; Joh. Peter Danecker, F A. Maria, 34 Jahr Kuhhirt, 2 K u.
1 Enkelkind, 88, Sohn Schulmstr. in Amerika. - Oberdresseldorf:
Anna Nicolai Jahr ? - Oberwilden: Joh. Jacob Ginsberg, led., 97.
- Salchendorf: Joh. Wilh. Otterbach, Knecht, 85. - Würgendorf:
Joh. Ebert Michel, Schneider, 2 K, 66. R 256 Michael.

Grafschaft Diez
Hahnstätten: Joh. Wilh. Ullius, für hessisches Jägerkorps angeworben 75. - Obernhof: Joh. Henr. Philippar, 15jährig, Schneidergesell, cca 73.

Amt Dillenburg
Dillenburg: Dan. Niederhauss(en) 71. R 284; Elisab. Reinhold,
Kammerschreiberstochter, folgt Herrschaft 79 ? - Wissenbach:
Conrad Franz' Wwe 98; N. Hain, led., 98.

Amt Dreidorf
Driedorf: Andreas Germann 66; Dessen Schwester 88; Chr. Groth
73; A. Ursula Lauer 73; Wilh. Anton Röder, 15jährig, Mullerknecht,
89; Dessen Mutterbruder gleichen Familiennamens fruher. - Honen-
roth: Cath. Sahm 85, Verwandte früher. - Mademühlen: Joh. Chr.
Betz 65. R 250; Joh. Jost Betz 72. R 294; Joh. Henr. Stahl 65 ? -
Munchhausen: Joh. Peter Weyel, schwerl. dimittiert, 89.

Amt Ebersbach
Ebersbach: Joh. Jacob Aurandt 73 R 304; ? Wilhelmina Speck 73;
Soldat Thönges, Beisass, F u. 4 K, 89. - Eibelshausen: ? A.
Elisab. Hofheintz 73; A. Christina u. Maria Christina Müller 73; ?
Bernhard u. Gotfried Roth (Rath??) 73; Jacob Hast (Hass), F u.
deren 4 K, 89; Justina Pfeiffer 89. - Mandeln: Conrad Dietrich,
F u. 8 K, 89. - Oberrossbach: ? Joh. Henr. Tielmann 73. - Off-
dilln: ? Johs Heppener 73; ? Leonhard Hinckel 73; ? Joh. Georg u.
Johs Knaebel (Knebel) 73; ? Leonh. Kretzer 73. - Rittershausen:
A. Elisab. Cuntzin, will dienen, 66; Joh. Jost Hofheintz u. ? Joh.
Jost Schmidt, Soldaten in holländ. Diensten, cca 66; ? Johs Helm
72; ? Johs Georg 73; Joh. Georg Ebert sen. u. Joh. Georg Ebert jr.,
F A. Magdalena u. 7 K, 89; Joh. Jost Fenster's geschiedene Ehefrau
89; Joh. Georg Hofheintz, F A. Maria u. 4 K, 89; Johs Müller jr.,
F A. Maria u. 1 K, 89; Joh. Jacob Weiss, Schmied, led., 89; Dazu
drei, bei denen Behörden Ausw. annahmen: Joh. Dan. Cuntz, Schrei-
nergesell, Joh. Georg Cuntz, Schneidergesell u. N. Weiss, Schneidergesell, alle 89. - Steinbrükken: Jost Busch's Wwe 73. R 305
Joh. Henr. u. Joh. Jost Busch. - Weidelbach: ? Jacob Hoffman 73;
Jacob Sandmann 73 ?; Dessen Geschw. A. Magdalena u. Wilh. Sandmann,
2 K, 84; Johs Orttmann, Wwer, 1 Tochter u. 4 Söhne, Ausw. fragl.,
89.

Amt Haiger
Allendorf: Johs Weber 84. - Dillbrecht: ? Leonh. Kretzer 66;
Joh. Jost Arnold, Schäfer aus dem Darmstädtischen, verlobt m. A.
Magdal. Sandmann oben, 84; Joh. Jost Knoebel, F A. Cath. u. 3 K,
84; Henr. Rupp, Tag- u. Nachtwächter, 50jähr., led., 84; Dessen
Geschw. früher. Fellerdilln: ? Dan. Debus' Wwe 66; Johs Hees vor
67; Conrad Scholl, Erkundungsreise 64-65, wirkl. Auswanderung 66;
Henr. Hees, Frau u. ungeborenes K heiml. verlassend, 73; Leonh.
Büdenbender, lahm, Schneider, F A. Elisab. u. 2 K, 84; Dessen
Schwiegereltern cca 10 Jahr zuvor. - Haiger: ? Chr. Bluhm 66.
Langenaubach: Henr. u. Phil. Schmidt 66 oder früher; ? Conrad

Gross' Wwe 66; Jacob Michael 72. R 294. - Manderbach: ? Joh.
Dan. Heymann 66; Joh. Jacob Kinckel, Schneider, 1 K erster Ehe, 84.
- Niederrossbach: Henr. Kempfer, Ausw. fragl., 73. - Sechshel-
den: Johs Richter, Leineweber, F 84. - Steinbach: Joh. Jost
Frantz, bei Austritt von Kinen vergebl. verfolgt, 64; Joh. Georg
Frantz, Jahr ?

Amt Herborn

Erdbach: ? Joh. Thönges Leng 73; ? Chr. Triesch 73. - Herborn:
Joh. Jost Metzler, F A. Elisab., Tochter Susanna Elisab. u. ? K,
70; Jacob Theis 72. R 294; Joh. Georg Weil, Rotgerber, 15jähr.
Sohn gleichen Namens, 73. R 302; Eine Jüngst besucht Heimat 83-84;
Marg. Elisab. Metzler 86; Deren Mutter 73 ?; Post, desertierender
Husarenkorporal, 79; Dessen Sohn u. Tochter 89; Jost Henr. Hainz
89; Joh. Jacob Hornevius, Schneidermstr., Schwestersohn v. Pfarrer
Stoy 89; Chr. Leuckel's Eltern 89; Joh. Phil. Manger, Chirurg, F u.
3 K, 89; Joh. Peter Schütz sen., Schneidermstr., beleidigt, 89;
Joh. P. Schütz jr., Theologe, Auswanderung angeraten, 89; Joh. Jost
Weber, Baumwollspinner, F u. 9 K, 89. - Herbornseelbach: Anton
Deusing, 1 K, 89. - Merkenbach: Schuldiener Weber 86; Friedr.
Wilh. Käsmann vor 88; Dessen Schw. A. Elisab. Cath. u. Maria
Elisab. 89. - Uckersdorf: Joh. Jacob Schupp 71. R 284; Conrad u.
Joh. Jacob Drewitz 73. R 307 Tre- u. Triewitz; N. Häuser, Jahr ?

Amt Hilchenbach

Allenbach: Jost Henr. Kohl, bejahrter Hammerschmied, F, 2 Söhne
u. 3 Töchter, 96. - Helberhausen: A. Marg. Kunze, verheir. mit
Joh. Henr. Klein, Schiermstr., 73. R 305 (oder 74. R 317). - Hil-
chenbach: Karl Wilh. Fuchs, nicht examin. Chirurg, Bäcker u. Gast-
wirt, F u. 3 K, 95; Andreas Freudenberg, F u. 5 unmündige K, 4
ältere K bleiben, 96. - Müsen: Joh. Jacob Braun's Wwe, Sohn Joh.
Jacob, Bergmann, led., Tochter u. Eidam, 96; Johs Braun, Bergmann,
F u. 2 K, 96; Jost Henr. Höfer, Schreiner, F u. 3 K, 96; A. Magdal.
Jung, elternlos, 1 K, 96; Joh. Henr. Schreiber, Schneider, F u. 1
K, 96. - Ruckersfeld: Joh. Henr. Slötzel, Tischlergeselle 73, 78
züruck. - Schreiberg: Joh. Ebert Schneider, Schreiner, 23jähr.,
96. - Stöcken: Justus Henr. Holdinghausen, Schreiner, elternlos,
23jähr., 96. - Aus diesem Amt noch Joh. Henr. (od. Johs) Hertz,
Strumpfweber 72.

Amt Siegen

Eiserfeld: Joh. Henr. Cron, Joh. Henr. Wertebach u. Joh. Henr.
Zimmer, F u. 1 K, alle drei Bergleute, 96. - Eisern: Hermannus
Schütte, Schlosser, 97. - Fickenhütten: Phil. Fick's Wwe, Söhne
Joh. Engel u. Johs, beide Leineweber, 96; Joh. Peter Flender's Wwe,
Kinder nebst Eidam Franz Spiess und dessen Kinder, 8 Personen, 96.
- Klafeld: Johs Fischbach's Wwe, 3 erwachsene Töchter, 97. -
Niederschelden: Joh. Jacob Becker, Schreiner, 73. R 301; Hermann
Bender, Bergmann, F u. 3 K, 97; Georg Ludw. Schneider, Bergmann,
elternlos, led., 97; Andreas Weber, Bergmann, Fam, 97. - Rins-
dorf: Hermannus Stötzel, Bergmann, F, 97. - Schneppenkauten:
Gottlieb u. Marg. Berg, 96. - Siegen: Joh. Henr. Troepler, Metz-

germstr., F u. ? K, zuletzt obdachlos unter freiem Himmel, 84; Dessen Bruder früher; Louise Engels, Tochter des Bürgermstr., verlobt
m. Carl Friedr. Loss, Sangerhausen, nach New York, 95; Ebert Mer-
tens, Bergmann aus Dielsen, Fam, 96. - Weidenau: Joh. Thomas
Flender, Hammerschmied, Fam, 96. - Willesdorf: Johs Stoltz, F u.
2 K, 84; Maria Mag. Entenener, 1 K, 97; Deren Schw. früher.

Amt Tringenstein

Eisemroth: ? Joh. Jost Sommer 72. - Eyershausen: Johs Wickel
73. - Hirzenhain: A. Marg. Wirth 89; Deren Schw. seit 71 Philadelphia.

Aus verschiedenen anderen Gegenden

Gadelheimer Mühle (Ellar): Phil. Stähler, 12jähr. Waise, 71. -
Löhnberg: Ludw. Henr. Deisman, minderjährig, 72. R 296. - Men-
gerskirchen: Wilh. Beuler, F, 72. - Merzhausen (Hessen Cassel):
A. Elisab. Sonnenschein 89. - Netphen: Aktuarius Bude's Wwe 95.
- Niederquambach: Henr. Wilh. Zimmermann, verlobt m. El. Theis,
Arborn oben, 89. - Probbach: Franz Schäfer, Fam, 87; Dessen
Schwieger früher. - Waldernbach: Gewesener Kaplan Schloos 89.

Ueber die Reise der Auswanderer lässt sich diesmal wenig mehr
mitteilen, als dass sie ausser über Rotterdam oder Amsterdam zu-
letzt auch mitunter über Hamburg erfolgte. Unbemittelte junge
Leute konnten sich nach der Aussage des alten Drewitz in seinem
Verhör am 5. Aug. 1773 bis an den Hafen durchbetteln, während die
Seereise nach wie vor in Amerika abverdient werden konnte.

Was ihre Schicksale dort betrifft, so nahmen drei an dem Frei-
heitskriege teil, und zwar Hertz und Joh. Henr. Rickas auf
nationaler und Ullius auf englischer Seite. Hertz starb in Fort
Washington, Ullius soll in Amerika desertiert sein, und Rickas
besuchte später die Heimat noch wieder. Von den übrigen wissen
wir, dass 2 sich in Maryland ansiedelten, 11 in Pennsylvanien, 1 in
New Jersey und 9 in New York. Lediglich beabsichtigte Niederlas-
sungen sind hier nicht mit aufgezählt.

In der Grafschaft Baltimore wohnten 1791 A. Maria (oder Barbara)
Erdmann, geb. Menck, und Phil. Stähler.

In Philadelphia lebte 1788 Friedr. Wilh. Käsmann, 1789 eine Wirth
und 1791 Susanna Elisab. geb. Metzler als Frau des Fabrikanten Carl
Bartholomaeus; in Tulpehoken zur gleichen Zeit deren Mutter A.
Elisab. als Frau von Moritz Dobel, in Reading 1784 Sebastian Weber;
in Elsass Township nahe Reading 1789 Joh. Henr. Klein mit seiner
Frau A. Marg. geb. Kunze; in Maiden Creek, Berks Co 1771 Sebastian
Müller (Miller); in Chambersburgh, Franklin Co 1788 Dan. Nieder-
hauss(en) mit seiner Frau Elisab. geb. Reinhold; in ‚Saltz Krick'
Twp,[12] Vollmacht von Lancaster, 1802 Joh. Jost Hofheinz, welcher in
dem fingierten Brief (s. o. S. 36) als Major und begüterter Landmann dargestellt war und nun als ‚armer Greis' um die Auslieferung
seines Vermögens bittet.

In Memsfeld oder Mämsf. N. J., 8 Meilen von Burlington und 28 von
Philad., 1791 Joh. Henr. Philippar mit Frau u. 5 K: Samuel,
Elisab., Rebecca, Maria, Lucrecia.

In der Stadt New York waren 1789 Henr. Hees und der ehemalige Husarenkorporal Post, welcher dort eine Handlung betrieb; in Canajoharie oder Nachbarschaft 1767 der oben ausführl. besprochene Joh. Jacob Diehl; in einem Orte, welcher in den Akten fast ganz durchstrichen ist, 1789 Jost Henr. Franz; in Wallckill, 25 Stunden von New York, 1767 Johs Hees; in Grossen Flooth[13] zur selben Zeit Adam Bengel, Conrad Scholl, Henr. und Phil. Schmidt. Scholl schrieb am 20. Sept. an seinen Eidam und Hees am 2. Nov. an seinen Vater. Von beiden Briefen sind Teile in der oben S. 37 erwähnten Kinenschen Abschrift vorhanden.

Hees ist Lehrer. Er schätzt sich überglücklich, jährlich 132 Reichsthaler Schullohn nebst mindestens 40 Rthl. Nebenverdiensten zu haben, d. h. ,an baarem Gelde 172 Rthl., dabei einen freyen Tisch', was nur zu begreiflich ist, wenn man bedenkt, dass der Beilsteiner Schulmeister, allerdings laut Amtsrechnung von 1722, nur 9 Gulden ,Dienerbesoldung' erhielt. Er ist überhaupt ganz begeistert von Amerika. Selbst wenn jemand seine Ueberfahrt dort abverdienen müsse, tue er besser, in Amerika 3 oder 4 Jahre zu dienen als in Deutschland ,vor immer in Armuth und Noth'. Für einen, der nur ,Bauernwerck' tun könne, sei 100 Rthl. ein geringer Jahreslohn.

Scholl ist Landmann. Der Eingang seines Briefes ist von Wichtigkeit für die Dillenburger Auswanderung nach der damaligen Provinz New York im allgemeinen, wenn auch seine Bemerkung, dass die 1710, also vor 57 Jahren, Eingewanderten noch meistens am Leben seien, natürlich der Einschränkung bedarf. Er beginnt:
,,Wir sind nicht auf Hasenklebers Land gangen, sondern wir sind vor uns selber und wohnen bey den hintersten Einwohnern hinter denen Wilden, allwo nichts als Deutsche wohnen, welche anno 1710 sind hereingekommen und noch mehrentheils bei Leben sind und viel Dillenburger sind. Wir ziehen aber noch den Herbst etwas näher nach dem Meer zu, allwo unser 20 Familien haben Land gekauft, alle miteinander Dillenburger, worunter meine näheste Nachbarn seind, die beyde Brüder Philip und Henrich Schmidt von Langenaubach und Joh. Adam Bengel, welche auch alle mit einander noch frisch und gesund sind. Wier vier haben so viel Land fast wie die ganze Fellerdillner Gemeind erb- und eigenthümlich''. Weiter unten sagt er dann Tochter und Schwiegersohn: ,,Ihr müsset nicht dencken, dass wir euch in der Egyptischen Dienstbarkeit auch lassen, dann ihr müsset auch hierher, dann hier ist Land genug und frey und sehr gutes Land, dann unser Brod ist nichts als Waitzen, vom Korn wissen wir nichts.''

Ausserhalb der Jahre 1709, 1750-53 und 1764-98 sind im 18. Jahrh. nur ganz wenige Auswanderer[14] in den Dillenburger Akten verzeichnet. In den ersten Jahren des folgenden Jahrhunderts schwillt aber ihre Zahl noch einmal bedeutend an.

Anmerkungen

[1] *Onera*, gewöhnl. Beschwerung, schliesst hier ausser Abgaben auch Frohndienste ein.

[2] Abgesehen von mancherlei geringen Abgaben gab es 1709 die Mai- und Herbstbede oder -beedt, ursprünglich eine Heeressteuer, die zu Oculi und Laurentii fällige Herrenschatzung, die grosse ordinäre Schatzung, die Kriegsgelder und die Fourage Zulagsgelder für die am Mittelrhein auf Postierung gestandene Kavallerie, letztere drei im Amt Herborn im Betrage von rund 3335, 4112 und irrtüml. rund 194, korrigiert 139 Reichsthalern.

Das bei Veranlagung der grossen Schatzung beobachtete Verfahren war, dass zunächst der Schatzungsfuss des Jahres und damit der Betrag eines Herrenziels festgesetzt wurde. Darauf ward in verschiedenen Jahren zu verschiedenen Zeiten, 1709 im Januar, April, Juli und Oktober, die Zahl der Herrenziele ausgeschrieben, welche in dem Jahre in den ersten sechs Monaten je 2, in den folgenden drei je 1-1/2 und in den letzten drei zusammen 4 betrug, so dass im Ganzen der Betrag von 20-1/2 Zielen zu zahlen war. Dieser wurde mit Ausnahme der ganz armen Leuten gewährten Ermässigungen ratenweise dem Fürsten übersandt. Die Ermässigungen beliefen sich im Amt Herborn, wo sie als Nachlasszettel anstatt ,Aussgiefft' bzw. ,Aussgab' gebucht sind, 1707 auf rund 30, 1708 auf 46, 1709 auf 94 Rthl., wurden mithin in unserm Jahre verdoppelt.

Wie schwer diese Kriegs- und Schatzungsgelder auf dem Einzelnen lasteten, hing davon ab, in welchem Verhältnis sie zu dem Ertrag seiner Güter oder seiner meist durch Schuldzinsen verminderten Einnahme standen. Bei einem Fleisbacher Auswanderer überstieg die Beschwerung den Ertrag, so dass er bereit war, seine mit 110 Rthl. eingeschätzten Güter für 30 hinzugeben.

[3] Burnetsfield, nicht Barnetsf., wie in der folgenden Briefabschrift, ist das jetzige Herkimer, N. Y.

[4] *Dimissoriales*, Dimissions- oder Entlassungsschein. Vgl. den Schein S. 34.

[5] All Mengil (Alten Mängel) am Fuss der Blue Mountains war ein wenig fruchtbarer District in den jetzigen Twps Albany u. Greenwich, Berks Co, Pa., wo ,alles mangelte'.

[6] Rachewey wahrscheinlich Rockaway, Morris Co, N. J.

[7] Offenbar Heidelberg Twp in Berks Co, Pa.

[8] Es waren: Joh. Chr. Bentz, Joh. Peter Braun von Derschen, Joh. Martin Buchner, Joh. Martin Diehl, Joh. Best Heun, Johs Wilh. Jung, Johs Stefan Klöckner (verschrieben — cken), Joh. Peter Meyer, Johs Schäfer, Joh. Best Schneider, Philippus Schumann, Johs Sehlbach und wahrscheinlich Joh. Chr. Weinbrenner als Sohn der Wwe W.

[9] Caritschazery nicht identifiziert. Ein Great Chazy Fluss in Clinton Co, N. Y.

[10] *Cum animo revertendi*, mit der Absicht zurückzukehren. Die Rückkehr erfolgte bisweilen erst nach 10, 20, 30 und mehr Jahren, war mithin ganz unbestimmbar, ebenso das Ziel der Wanderung.

[11] Vom volkswirtschaftl. Standpunkt ist es beachtenswert, dass

Beilsteiner Ausw. 1773 gestattet wurde, für etwa 1000 Gulden Zeuge aus der Dresslerischen Fabrik in Siegen abgabenfrei mitzunehmen. Der Amtmann hofft in seiner Befürwortung, dass die Fabrik dadurch vielleicht künftig Absatz nach Amerika bekommen möchte, und rühmt das Bestreben der Landesregierung, derlei Fabriken auf alle mögliche Art ,in mehreren Flor zu bringen'.

[12]Ein Salt Creek Twp scheint nicht nachweisbar. Es gibt jedoch ein Salt Lick Twp in Fayette Co fast 200 Meilen von Lancaster und darin ein creek, das mitunter Salt Creek genannt wird.

[13]Memsfeld statt Mansfield, Burlington Co, N. J. Wallekill ist Wallkill, Ulster Co, N. Y. Grossen Flooth höchstwahrscheinlich Great Flat, wie die Herkimer Village Section genannt wurde.

[14]Z. B. Martin Kupfer, Emmerichenhain etwa 1738, Johs Jonas, Niedermeisen 1749, Joh. Georg Blum, Eyershausen 1763.

Als Frucht anderer Studien schliesse ich hier zwei Ausw. an, von denen der eine um die Mitte des Jahrhunderts bereits in Pennsylvanien sesshaft war und der andere 1796 nach Amerika ging. Es sind dies Kaspar Kinterleitner, dessen Erbschaftsakten der Freiherr Friedrich von und zu Gemmingen mir gütigst vorgelegt hat, und Franz Bernhard Stritt, dessen letztwillige Verfügung vor der Reise nach Amerika im Gemeindearchiv zu Pfaffenburg im Wiesental aufbewahrt wird.

[Dr. Gerber's work has been presented in its entirety, above. However, in some circumstances the punctuation has been altered slightly in order to avoid confusing the American reader. Most notably, the use of the dash in between the names of those emigrating from a particular village has been altered to the use of a semi-colon, the dash being preserved in between the villages. Also, in the original each footnote was set off by a following), and this was deleted here.—Editor.]

Provincial Council, Pennsylvania (Colony). *Minutes of the Provin-*
cial Council of Pennsylvania, from the Organization to the Termi-
nation of the Proprietary Government, Published by the State,
vols. 3-4. Harrisburg: T. Fenn & Co., 1840, 1851 [Lancour No.
138].

The following excerpts dealing with immigration have been copied
from Volume 3, pages 299-301, 303-305, 307, 346-348, 350-351, 390-
392, 409-411, 414, 436-437, 440-442, 444, 457, 460-461, 483-490,
498-501, 554-559, 564, 614-616, 642-643, and 647, and from Volume
4, pages 58-60, 72-73, 99-100, and 331-332, of the *original* edition.

At a Council held at the Courtho. of Philadia., Septemr. 21st,
1727. Present:
The Honble PATRICK GORDON, Esqr., Lieut. Governour.
   James Logan,   William Fishbourn,)
   Richard Hill,   ) Esq'rs.
A Paper being drawn up to be signed by those Palatines, who
should come into this Province with an Intention to settle therein,
pursuant to the order of this Board, was this day presented, read &
approved, & is in these Words:
We Subscribers, Natives and late Inhabitants of the Palatinate
upon the Rhine & Places adjacent, having transported ourselves and
Families into this Province of Pensilvania, a Colony subject to the
Crown of Great Britain, in hopes and Expectation of finding a
Retreat & peaceable Settlement therein, Do Solemnly promise &
Engage, that We will be faithfull & bear true Allegiance to his
present MAJESTY KING GEORGE THE SECOND, and His Successors Kings of
Great Britain, and will be faithfull to the Proprietor of this Pro-
vince; And that We will demean ourselves peaceably to all His said
Majesties Subjects, and strictly observe & conform to the Laws of
England and of this Province, to the utmost of our Power and best
of our understanding.
A Signed List was then laid before the Board, of the Names of one
hundred & nine Palatines, who with their Families, making in all
about Four hundred Persons, were imported into this Province in the
Ship William and Sarah, William Hill, Master, from Rotterdam, but
last from Dover, as by Clearance from the Officers of his Majesties
Customs there; And the said Master being asked, if he had any
License from the Court of Great Britain for transporting those
People, & what their Intentions were in coming hither, said that he
had no other License or Allowance for their Transportation than the
above Clearance, and that he believed they designed to settle in
this Province. They were then called in, and the several Persons
whose Names are subjoyned did repeat & subscribe the foregoing
Declaration, yizt:

G. M. Wey, V. D. M.,   Hendrick Meyer,
Hans Jerig Siegler,   Hans Jerig Anspag,
Jacob Gons,   Philip Sroygar,
Hans Jorig Swab,   Elias Meyer,
Michael Peatley,   Johannes Leyb,
Unicus Meyer,   Hans Jerig Milder,
Hans Martin Lerystein,   Pastor Springler,
Hans Michael Fiell,   Hans Martin Wilder,
Hans Jerig Hereylf,   Martin Prill,
Abraham Beni,   Peter Seytz,
Jacob Josi,   Johannes Ekman,
Hans Bernard Wolf,   Johannes Berret,
Frederick Heiligas,   Andrew Holtspan,
Andrew Simmierman,   Tobias Frye,
Philip Feruser,   Joseph Welbrogt,
Hans Michael Pagman,   Jacob Meyer,
Hans Serick Wigler,   Abraham Thurn,
Hans Filkisynger,   Hans Jerig Wiegle,
Sebastian Creef,   Hans Jerig Craemen,
Hans Adam Milder,   Hans Jerig Reter,
Hans Jerig Wolf,   Diodorick Roida,
Johan Habaraker,   Philip Jacob Reylender,
Anspel Anspag,   Ernest Roade,
Hans Jerig Bowman,   Philip Siegler,
Alexr. Diebenderf,   Rudolph Wilke.

Sundry of these forreigners lying sick on board never came to be qualified.

At a Council held in the Courtho. of Philadia., Septemr. 27th, 1727. Present:

The Honble PATRICK GORDON, Esqr., Lieut. Govr.
    James Logan,   Isaac Norris,   )
    Richard Hill,   Saml. Preston,) Esq'rs.

A List was presented to the Board of the Names of Fifty three Palatines, who with their Families making in all about two hundred Persons, were imported into this Province in the Ship James Good-will, David Crockat, Mr., from Rotterdam, but last from Falmouth, as by the Masters Affidavit signed by the Officers of the Customs there, It appeared upon Enquiry that the Master had no particular License for their Transportation. They were then called in, and the several Persons whose Names are subjoyned, did repeat & sign the Declaration inserted in the preceeding Minute, vizt:

Michael Sigrist,   Jurg Steiniger,
Michael Tanner,   Joseph Clap,
Joseph Schurgh,   John Adam Philple,
Hans Haggy,   Jurgh Clap,
Jorgan Miller,   Lodowick Clap,
Hans Leaman,   Christian Miller,
Hans Langneker,   Jurgh Coch,

Hendrick Aberlee,
Raynard Jung,
Jacob Wygart,
William Wygart,
Tewalt Leatherman,
Hans Michael Kuntz,
Jurg Michael Kuntz,
Ulrick Stoupher,
Ulrick Zugg,
Peter Zugg,
Barthol Sigrist,
Abraham Abaersoll,
Jacob Fritz,
Adam Kiener,
William Kiener,
Hans Kiener,
Christian Webber,
Hans Michl. Fredler,
Philip Schaberger,
Hendrick Wolfe.

Jacob Walter, Senr.,
Jacob Walter, Junr.,
Christopher Kirkhof,
Hendrick Schultz,
Jacob Siegle,
Jacob Gass, Senr.,
Jacob Gass, Junr.,
Frederick Gass,
John Miller,
Joseph Miller,
Hans Miller,
Hans Foster,
Jacob Arnett,
Paul Hein,
Hans Hein,
Bastian Meree,
Michael Lybert,
Jurgh Zengh,
Jacob Ganwyer,

Mr. Logan acquainted the Board, that last night he received a
Letter from John Wright, Esqr., one of the Justices of Peace of
Chester County, giving Account that one Thomas Wright was killed by
some Indians at Snaketown, forty miles above Conestogoe, which Letter, together with the Depositions of John Wilkins, Esther Burt and
Mary Wright, and an Inquisition taken upon the dead Body were all
laid before the Board....

At a Council held at the Courtho. of Philadia., Septr. 30th,
1727. Present:
  The Honble PATRICK GORDON, Esqr. Lieut. Govr.
    James Logan,   William Fishbourn,)
    Richard Hill,   Clement Plumsted.   ) Esq'rs.
A List was presented to the Board of the Names of Seventy Palatines, who with their Families, making in all about Three hundred
Persons, were imported in the Ship Malley, Jno. Hodgeson, Master,
from Rotterdam, but last from Deal, as by a Clearance from the
Officers of the Customs there, It appeared upon Enquiry that they
were come hither with an Intention to settle in this Province, and
that the Master had no Special License for their Transportation.
They were called in, and the Persons whose names are subjoyned, did
repeat and Subscribe the Declaration inserted in the Minute of the
21st Instant, viz:

Hans Erick Ower,
Francis Stouper,
Hans Stouper,
Hans Jacob Bender,
Michael Spooner,
Hans Erick Keel,

Jost Moyser,
Christian Moyser,
Ulrick Sheillinbergen,
Michel Schenk,
Christian Waltone,
Hans Moyser,

Hans Erick Heyriger,
Lutterick Vellerey,
Hans Ower Parent,
Letterick Pieter,
Hans Adam Soulder,
Hans Michael Smith,
Johannes Sneyder,
Andreas Elicks,
Porcas Hoffman,
Felix Goadts,
Johannes Crowse,
Weyan Teale,
Michel Sebastian,
Augustin Weder,
Mans Lenord Hoffman,
Hans Teyger,
Martin Hosuer,
Hendrick Penhort,
Hendrick Fultz,
Hans Erick Teluer,
Merick Foux,
Stephanus Raper,
Erick Lutwich Zell,
Samuel Baire,
Hans Rinck,
Hans Erick Sheillinberg,
David Marten,
Jacob Marten,
Henrick Hoffman,

Hans You,
Jacob Shir,
Hans Erick Crable,
Henrick Meyer,
Michel Crable,
Samuel Overhoulster,
Felton Younge,
Jacob Roust,
Hans Cooble,
Jacob Baer,
Hans Funck,
Michel Frances,
Peter Goadts,
Christian Solderman,
.Samuel Good,
Jacob Hower,
Rodulph Landish,
Rodulph Baine,
Martin Kindegy,
Jacob Wanner,
Orick Leepe,
Christian Willand
James Miller,
Martin Kearstucker,
John Mather Euger,
Johannes Pealer,
Hans Miller,
Hans Mickle,
Hans Erick Felter.

At a Council held at Philadelphia, October 2d, 1727. Present:
The Honble PATRICK GORDON, Esqr., Lieut. Governour.

Richard Hill,   Clemt. Plumstead,   )
Willm. Fishbourn,   ) Esq'rs.

A List was presented to the Board of Fifty three Palatines, who
with their Families, making in all about one hundred and forty Persons, were imported in the Ship Adventure, Jno. Davies, Master,
from Rotterdam, but last from Plymouth, as by Clearance from the
Officers of the Customs there, It appeared upon Enquiry that the
Master had no particular License for their Transportation. They
were then called in, & having declared that they intended to settle
& live peaceably in this Province, the several Persons whose names
are Subjoyned, did repeat & subscribe the Declaration inserted in
the Minute of the 21st of September last, vizt:

Michael Miller,
Joannes Radler,
Joannes Layman,
Casper Veye,
Jacob Lydie,

Frans Baltzar Frans,
Joannes Cortes,
Nicolas Crou,
Palzer Lyme,
Jacob Wihelmus,

Jacques Simonel,	Ulrick Ryser,
Michael Keysar,	Joan Carlo Horlaeker,
Joannes Ulrick,	Nicolas Keysar,
Hans Adam Oser,	Johannes Peter Hoff,
Peter Shilling,	Christopher Ulrick,
Mathias Ryseling,	Christian Bikler,
Jacob Bowman,	Johan Jacob Hoffman,
Peter Roole,	Daniel Bowman,
John Seyham....	

At a Council held at the courtho. of Philadia., Octr. 16th, 1727.
Present:
The Honble PATRICK GORDON, Esqr., Lieut. Governour.

Richard Hill,	William Fishbourn,	)
Samuel Preston,	Clement Plumsted.	) Esquires.

A List was presented to the Board of the Names of Forty six Palatines, who with their Families, making in all about Two hundred
Persons, were imported here in the Ship Friendship of Bristol, John
Davies, Mr., from Rotterdam, but last from Cows, as by Clearance
from the Officers of the Customs there, bearing the date 20th day
of June last, It appeared upon Enquiry that there was no Special
License granted for their Transportation, & that they are come
hither with a Design to settle in this Province. They were then
called in, & the several Persons whose names are subjoyned did
repeat & sign the Declaration inserted in the Minute of the 21st
September last.

Peter Tagman,	Hillis Castle,
Joannes Forrer,	Jerem Miller,
Andreas Swartz,	Albrecht Bowman,
Henry Strickler,	Hans Jerig Miller,
Jacob Histant,	Nicholas Bogart,
Jno. Histant,	Hans Jerig Hoffman,
Abraham Swartz,	Nicholas Crosman,
Christian Meyer,	Mathias Swyzer,
Joannes Feyseg,	Peter Wilde,
Peter Pixseler,	Jacob Sneppelen,
Hans Reser,	Philip Reemer,
Peter Leeman,	Palatine Gratz,
Hans Jerig Lowman,	Henry Sneppeley,
Christian Crorebit,	Vincent Mayer,
Martin Schaffenes,	Henry Schenholl,
Henry Lier,	Joannes Hosle....
Adam Lepert,	

At a Council held at the Courtho. of Philadia., August 24th,
1728. Present:
The Honble PATRICK GORDON, Esqr., Lieut. Governour.

Richard Hill,	Thomas Laurence,	)
Willm. Fishbourn,		) Esq'rs.

A List was presented to the Board of the Names of Eighty Palatines, who with their Families making in all about Two hundred
Persons, were imported in the Ship Mortonhouse, John Coultas,
Master, from Rotterdam, but last from Deal, as by Clearance from
the Officers of the Customs there, bearing the Date the fifteenth
day of June, 1728.

It appeared upon Enquiry that there was no Special License
granted for their Transportation, they were then called in, & having declared that their Intentions were to settle & live peaceably
in this Province; the several Persons, whose names are subjoyned,
did repeat & sign the Declaration inserted in the Minute of the
21st of September last.

Hans Martin Miller,
Hans Jacob Miller,
Hans Lendert Miller,
Conrad Keer,
Dirik Oordt,
Jacob Hoogh,
Jacob Joost,
Clement Tonkleberg,
Pieter Tonkleberg,
Frederick Tonkleberg,
Joan Joost, Smit,
Joan Pieter Melch,
Venunt Stowfer,
Michael Honest,
Godfrey Kenk,
Joannes Coopman,
Bultes Gering,
Hendrick Raan,
Michael Scybel,
Joannes Trankhuy,
Hans Ulrick Dodder,
Hans Dirik Haak,
Hans Dirik Roodt,
Jonas Keeler,
Michael Detemer,
Martin Schoup,
Jacob Stown,
Jacob Brummer,
Joannes Crist,
Joan Elbret Keeler,
Martin Vogelhove,
Joan Mathias Pieter,
Joannes Roare,
Dirik Begtol,
Jacob Bruelasher,
Philip Snolt,
Christopher Benker,

Uldrick Shurk,
Uldrick Shurk, Jun.
·Joannes Shurk,
Dirik Smith,
Philip Engert,
Christopher Sullenger,
Walter Kenler,
Hans Meyer,
Wilhelm Dillinger,
Rodolph Heler,
Bernard Hensell,
Joannes Triktingest,
Stephen Haltsbeilder,
Joannes Kits Miller,
Michael Rank,
Pieter Lorts,
John Lagerom,
Frederick Leder,
Casper Heydering,
Joannes Edesman,
Joannes Stock,
Hans Faks,
Jonnnes [Joannes?] Boot,
Jacob Kegenhover,
Chistian Newswang,
Joannes Kerer,
Velde Grae,
Michael Keiler,
Joannes Weyhelm,
Joannes Bare,
Frans Latshow,
Hans Benlie,
Jacob Witsel,
Jacob Heystoe,
Hans Wolf Dillinger,
Andreas Evie,
Hendrick Ishelman,

Peter Middlecalf,   Joannes Morgestern,
Christopher Meng,   Joannes Naycomal,
Abraham Wolf,

At a Council in the Courtho. of Philadia., Sept. 4th, 1728.
Present:
The Honble PATRICK GORDON, Esqr., Lieut. Governour.
  Richard Hill,   Thomas Laurence.)
  Clement Plumsted,   ) Esq'rs.
with other Magistrates of the City.
A List was presented of the Names of Thirty Palatines, who with
their Families, making in all about One hundred Persons, were
imported here in the Ship Albany, Lazarus Oxman Master, from
Rotterdam, but last from Portsmouth, as by Clearance from the Officers of the Customs there, bearing Date the 22nd of June, 1728. It
appeared the Master had no Special License for their Transportation: they were then called in, & having declared that they were
come hither with Intention to settle & live peaceably in this Province, the Several Persons whose Names are Subjoyned, did repeat &
sign the Declaration inserted in the Minute of the 21st of September last.

Georg Frederick Berbesdorf,   Hans Jerig Beigel,
Frederick Christof von Strysflas,   Michael Keim,
Mathias Kaplin,   Casper Reshil,
Daniel Bengal,   Alexander Zaartman,
Simon Shaller,   Jacob Weis,
Philip Showman,   Joannes Schenefelt,
Philip Glaser,   Jerig Boog,
Hans Adam Mire,   Jerig Moots,
Laurence Belits,   Jerig Gertner,
Henry Stelfelt,   Andrew Ablin,
Casper Oort,   Hans Miller,
Fred. Egelberger,   John Bloeman,
Conrad Feboy,   Hans Jerig Riger,
Jacob Danbach,   Martin Calb,
Jacob Beigel,   Joannes Earle Keil,

  N. B. This Minute ought to have been Enter'd after the following [dated Sept. 1st, which dealt with Indian relations]....

At a Council held in the Courtho. of Philadia., Septemr. 11th,
1728. Present:
The Honble PATRICK GORDON, Esqr., Lieut. Govr.
               Thomas Laurence, Esquire,
with others of the City Magistrates.
A List was presented of the Names of Forty two Palatines, who
with their Families, making in all about Ninety Persons, were imported here in the Ship James Goodwill, David Crockat Master, from
Rotterdam, but last from Deal, as by Clearance from the officers of
the Customs there, bearing Date the fifteenth day of June, 1728.

It appeared there was no special License granted for their Transportation: they were then called in, and having declared that they
were come hither with Intention to settle & live peaceably in this
Province, the several Persons whose Names are subjoyned, did repeat
& sign the Declaration inserted in the Minute of the 21st of September last.

Johan Casper Steffer,
Johan Casper Steffer, Jun'r.
Uldrick Engelar,
Andreas Knaft,
George Graff,
Joh. Leon'd Holsteinder,
Michael Neff,
Jacob Funk,
Mathias Firrumsler,
Johan Egidius Grin,
Joannes Gurk,
Johan Leon'd Keller,
Isaac Crison,
Jacob Herman,
Thomas Koppenhoffer,
Christian Graaf,
Martin Valk,
Hans Michael Ruiter,
Martin Moeser,
Hendrick Philip Seller,
Frederick Sholl,
Jacob Beyer,
Michael Korr,
Adam Engeler,
Loerenc Durr,
Hans Adam Moesser,
George Shoemaker,
Jacob Kin,
Leon'd Hinker,
Jacob Meckeling,
Teobald Meckeling,
Hans George Seyller,
Jacob Sint,
Hans Vierybank,
Andreas Stickler,
Hans Jacob Slaure,
Joannes Ruspag,
Hans George Metler,
Adam Surmer....

At the Courthouse of Philadelphia, August 19th, 1729. Present:
The Honble PATRICK GORDON, Esqr., Lieut. Governour,
with the Mayor, & several of the City & County Magistrates.
A List was Presented of the Names of Seventy five Palatines, who
with their Families, making in all about One hundred & Eighty Persons, were imported here in the Ship Mortonhouse, James Coultas
Mr., from Rotterdam, but last from Deal, as by Clearance thence
dated 21st of June last.
It appeared that the Master had no special License for their
Transportation, they were then called in, & having declared that
their Intentions were to settle & live peaceably in this Province,
the several Persons whose Names are subjoyned, did repeat & sign
the Declaration inserted in the Minute of 21st of September, 1727.

Dirick Truer,
John Philip Rank,
John Miller,
Conrad Werness,
Casper Dorest,
Dilman Coll,
Michael Urelick,
Michael Boarst,
John Haake,
John Daniel Worley,
Valentine Fikus,
John Adam Moor,
John Rice,
John Stephen Regensberger,
Dirick Adam Weidle,
Ulrick Croll,
Adam Shamback,
Conrod Killinor,

Rudolph Moore,
Hans Jacob Ratslue,
Uldery Roat;
Nicholas Peffell,
Hendrick Doabs,
Ultiner Snebler,
Hendrick Plino,
Hans Hendrick Ubera,
Christopher Brown,
John Christ Croll,
Hendrick Warner,
Gerard Miller,
Andrew Mayes,
Hans Michael Heyder,
Jacob Creeple,
Peiter Weegar,
Hendrick Sligloff,
Hendrick Sootera,
Hans Uldrick Fry,
Christopher Fry,
Jacob Bowman,
Joan Casper Inkeler,
John Miller,
Jacob Over,
David Mantandon,
Christian Longinacre,
Dirick Greeseman,
Carol Arant Mooselback,

Joannes Brinkler,
Moret Creetor,
Jacob Reyser,
Jacob Fetter,
Richard Fetter,
Philip Jacob Back,
George Daniel Back,
Michael Weever,
Wendel Wyant,
Andrew Bastian,
Adam Bastian,
Martin Alstadt,
Rudolph Walder,
Hendrick Keelhaver,
Simon Reel,
Nicolas Carver,
Jacob Eshelman,
Welder Keyser,
Abraham Kensinger,
Reynd. Halder,
Baltzar Roer,
Christopher Bumgarner,
Johannes Orde,
Johannes Dirick Greeseman,
Frederick Marsh,
Peter Moll,
Joannes Middle.

At the Courtho. of Philadia., September 15th, 1729. Present:
The Honble PATRICK GORDON, Esqr. Lieut. Govr,
with the Mayor & several of the City & County Magistrates.
A List was presented of the Names of Fifty nine Palatines, who
with their Families, making in all about One hundred & twenty six
Persons, were imported here in the Ship Allen, James Craigie, Master, from Rotterdam, but last from Cows, as by Clearance thence
dated 7th of July last.
It appeared that the Master had no special License for their
Transportation: they were then called in, & having declared that
their Intentions were to settle & live peaceably in this Province,
the several Persons whose Names are subjoyned, did repeat & sign
the Declaration inserted in the Minute of the 21st of September,
1727.

Alexander Mack,
Joannes Mack,
Felte Mack,
Alexander Mack, Jun'r,
Jo. Hendrick Kalklieser,
Andreas Ponne,

John Martin Crist,
Hisbert Benter,
Hans Contee,
Jacob Possart,
Jacob Wise,
Christian Snyder,

William Knipper,
Jacob Lisley,
Christopher Matten,
Paul Libekip,
Christopher Kalklieser,
Christian Cropp,
Andreas Cropp,
Jacob Cropp,
Christian Cropp, Jun'r,
Hans Slachter,
Joannes Pellickhover,
Joannes Kipping,
Hans Erick Cogh,
John Michael Amwig,
Hans Ulrick Kisle,
Elrick Eley,
Rinard Hammer,
Samuel Galler,
Conrad Iller,
Hans Casper Kulp,
John Jacob Knight,
Alexander Till,
Hendrick Peter Midledorf,

Jacob Snyder,
Joannes Flickinger,
Felte Beecher,
John Jacob Hopback,
Joannes Mackinterfeer,
Christian Kitsintander,
Lenhart Amwigh,
Mathias Snyder,
Joseph Prunder,
Mathias Ultand,
Johannes Prunder,
Jerig Hoffart,
Joannes Perger,
Joannes Weightman,
Philip Mich'l. Fiersler,
Valentine Perhart Hisle,
Hans Jerig Clauser,
Hendrick Holstein,
Feltin Rafer,
Jerig Fetter,
David Lisley,
Jacob Possart,
Daniel Crop....

At the Courtho. of Philadia., Augt. 29th, 1730. Present:
The Honble PATRICK GORDON, Esqr., Lt. Governr.
with the Mayor of Philadelphia, & several of the City Magistrates.
A List was presented of the Names of Seventy Seven Palatines, who
with their Families, making in all about Two hundred & Sixty Persons, were imported here in the Ship Thistle of Glasgow, Colin Dunlap Mr., from Rotterdam, but last from Dover, as by Clearance from
that Port. The Master being examined, said he had no particular
License for their Transportation: they were then called in, &
having declared that their Intentions were to settle & live peaceably in this Province, the several Persons whose Names follow, did
repeat and sign the Declaration inserted in the Minute of the 21st
of Sepr., 1727, & likewise took & subscribed the Declaration of
Fidelity and Abjuration.

Johs. George Lodwick Has,
Bernard Sigmund,
Hans Jacob Doll,
Johannes Dunkell,
Christopher Better,
Johan Peter Osler,
Leonard Graw,
Jeremias Hess,
Velde Grisimer,
Casper Frisman,

Mathias Thais,
Peter Biswanger,
Fredrick Reimer,
Nichel Fizer,
Jacob Nagell,
Johan Casper Smiet,
Johan Siningern,
Ulrick Sherar,
Philip Groscost,
Casper Bittner,

Christian Leman,
Stephen Remer,
Rudolph Draugh,
Johannes Kunn,
Lodwick Dillman,
Johan Hendrick Smitt,
Gerard Zinn,
Christopher Angubrant,
Jean Henrix Fortineux,
Michael Thomas,
Hans Minigh,
Christian Shram,
Jacob Stiffell,
Rudolph Andreas,
Fredrick Peifer,
Leond. Kopplinger,
Johs. Kopplinger,
Wolfer Sperger,
Voldrick Meidleman,
Elias Meidleman,
Jacob Ammon,
Ulrick Steyner,
Dolls. Britelman,
Thomas Hass,
Hendrick Hass,
Johan Ekel Lukembourg,
Henrick Ekenbill,
Hans Simon Murs,

Johan Paulus Dillenhover,
Johannes Sherer,
Johan Justice Sherer,
Hans Georg Hoffman,
Nichol. Kinser,
Johannes Hoffman,
Philip Hauts,
Laurence Koff,
Abraham Transu,
Casper Hartman,
Thomas Hammon,
Hendrick Gutt,
Peter Travinger,
Casper Griger,
Bernard Renn,
Dietrick Kober,
Lutwig Moler,
George Hurtzell,
Lutwig Hurtzell,
Leond. Hoognunk,
Peter Federolph,
Peter Muller,
Fredrick Likenberger,
Valentine Michael,
Christopr. Hendrick,
George Undetenard,
Michael Thomas,
Christian Thomas.

IN THE ABSENCE of the Honble the Lt. Governr.
At the Courtho. of Philadia., Sepr. 5th, 1730. Present:
The Mayor & Recorder of the City, together with several Justices
of the Peace.

A List was Presented of the Names of Forty six Palatines, who
with their Families, making in all about One hundred and Thirty
Persons, were imported here in the Ship Alexr. & Ann, William
Clymer, Master, from Rotterdam, but last from Deal.

The Master being examined said he had no particular License for
their Transportation: they were then called in, & having declared
that their Intentions were to settle & live peaceably in this Province, the several Persons whose Names are subjoined did repeat &
sign the Declaration inserted in the Minute of the 21st of September, 1727, and likewise took & subscribed the Declaration of
Fidelity and Abjuration.

Anthony Muller,
Daniel Cristman,
Adam Fillipott,
Hans Lensenns,
Johan Fredrick Lausseness,

Martin Creiner,
Waldes Langhaer,
Martin Yonger,
Michael Blesser,
Peter Tilman,

Johannes Herler,
Johan Adam Atler,
Martin Muller,
Johan Peter Waller,
Frans. Plumm,
Jacob Muller,
Fredrick Meyer,
Carles Callar,
Hans Ulrick Krinston,
Bernhard Meyer,
Jacob Meyer,
Hans Musulburger,
Martin Burger,
Hans Jacob Oberholts,
Johan Fredrick Waller,
Henrick Marta,
Geo. Michl. Brinsius,
Johan Philip Curnert,

Adam Shuler,
Johannes Vitner,
David Suffoltz,
Michl. Firkman,
Rudolph Mastersundts,
Conrad Yongman,
Leopold Hilligas,
Henrick Cleiner,
Mathias Seltzer,
Johannes Cleiner,
Hans Jerick Ham,
Johan Nicol. Brecher,
Johannes Woldman,
Christian Princeland,
. Johan Sebastian Braft,
Hans Michl. Verdus,
Hans Bartel Hemberger,
Johan Carl Hornberger....

At the Courtho. of Philadia., Novr. 30th, 1730. Present:
The Honble PATRICK GORDON, Esqr., Lt. Govr.
  Henry Brooke,   ) Esq'rs., Members of Council,
  Samuel Hasell.)
  Thomas Griffits, Esqr., Mayor,   ) of Philadia.
  Andrew Hamilton, Esqr., Recorder.)
A List was presented of the Names of Twenty four Palatines, who
with their Families, making in all about Fifty two Persons, were
imported here in the Ship Joyce, William Ford, Master, from Boston.
They were called in, & having declared that their Intentions were
to settle & live peaceably in this Province, the Persons whose
Names are hereunto subjoyned did repeat & sign the Declaration
inserted in the Minute of the 21st of September, 1727, & likewise
took & subscribed the Declaration of Fidelity & Abjuration.

Christian Miller,
Michael Shafer,
Nicolas Swort,
Daniel Swort,
Hans Wichel,
Johan Lutwig Wiche,
Joseph Domm,
John Bear,
Hans Jacob Bear,
Leonart Koll,
Henry Shefer,
Egram Hal,

Johan Cuntz,
Mark Ninger,
Johan Hoff,
Andreas Soffman,
Hans Ulrich Meyer,
Leonard Fodry,
Johan Michael Fisher,
Henrick Kilian,
Johs. Overbaeck,
Zacharias Park,
Godfrey Schultze....

At the Courtho. of Philadia., Augt. 17th, 1731. Present:
The Honble PATRICK GORDON, Esqr., Lt. Govr.
  Samuel Hasell, Esqr., a Member of Council, &

Thomas Griffits, Esqr., Mayor of Philadia.

A List was Presented of the Names of Thirty nine Palatines, who with their Families, making in all One hundred & seven Persons, were imported here in the Ship Samuel, Hugh Peircy, Master, from Rotterdm., but last from Cowes, as by Clearance from that Port. The Master being examined said he had no particular License for their Transportan.; They were then called in, and having declared that their Intentions were to settle & live peaceably in this Province, the several Persons whose Names are subjoyned, did repeat & sign the Declaration inserted in the Minute of 21st of September, 1727, & likewise took & Subscribed the Declaration of Fidelity and Abjuration.

Johan George Crisner,
Johan Fisher,
Johan Michel Glain,
Engelbrod Shrawes,
Johan Henrick Knopp,
Philip Knopp,
Casper Holtzhausen,
Conraat Kert,
Johan Jacob Groust,
Johan Jacob Scheive,
Johan Henrick Hermel,
Frederick Babemeyer,
Lutwig Han,
Johannes Metzger,
Joest Wenst,
Christopher Kink,
Conrad Mellar,
Lutwig Goodbroodt,
Christopher Ritter,
George Sebald Madinger,

Hans George Bender,
Johanes Ditreich,
Hans Georg Loreman,
Philip Fredrick Vogell,
Andreas Erlewyn,
Johannes Millburger,
Hans Ritter,
Lutwig Heck,
Johan Cristofall Bauor,
Lutwig Sourmilg,
Johannes Kauns,
Johannes Pengler,
Hans Adam Wartsman,
Johan Georg Kopp,
Turgen Hendrick,
Barent Tysen,
Georg Carl Wentz,
Hans Jerig Loreman,
Hans Georg Fleger....

At the Courtho. of Philadia., Septr. 11th, 1731. Present:
The Honble Patrick Gordon, Esqr., Lt. Govr.
     Thomas Griffits, Esqr., Mayor of Philadia., &
     William Allen, Esqr., one of His Majesty's Justices of the
          said City, &c.

A List was presented of the Names of Fifty seven Palatines, who with their Families, making in all One hundred & seventy five Persons, were imported here in the Ship Pensylvania Merchant, Jno. Stedman, Master, from Rotterdam, but last from Dover, as by Clearance from that Port. The Master being examined said he had no particular License for their Transportation: They were then called in, & having declared that their Intentions were to settle & live peaceably in this Province, the several Persons whose Names are subjoyned, did repeat & sign the Declaration inserted in the Minute of the 21st Septr., 1727; & likewise took & subscribed the Declaration of Fidelity and Abjuration.

Michael Gabertz,	Johan Jacob Kryhe,
Michael Feider,	Henrick Kreemer,
Johan Michael Moll,	Baltzar Seyler,
Hans Adam Kremmer,	Johan Nicolas Steymutz,
Fredrick Willsheyt,	Johan Adam Egling,
Hartman Hunsucker,	Christopher Beyer,
Johan Bartel Gookar,	Johan Jacob Woltzhoflen,
Jacob Lanius,	Johan Schenkell,
Pieter Smit,	Valentine Snyder,
Abraham Foiber,	Johan Philip Beyer,
Johan Nicolas Re,	Conraat Sybert,
Martin Boger,	Hans Martin Schultz,
Jerig Henrick,	Roolof Kusman,
Christian Smit,	Johannes Reymert,
Hans Georg Keyleir,	-Nocholas Foss,
Jacob Steiner,	Laurence Roodt,
Christain Weysar,	Conrad Koogh,
Johannes Drell,	Jacob Mumma,
Abraham Freeman,	Melchier Willholtz,
Fredrick Gybertz,	Adam Sowyer,
Fredrick Strubel,	Michael Gyger,
Christain Smidt,	Joannes Shaak,
Johan Georg Meyer,	Johan Engelbert Lak,
Johan Georg Bergstroster,	Johan Georg Smidt,
Johan Henrick Smidt,	Hans Michl. Horloger,
Johan Barent Arent,	Burkhort Killmer,
Christofoll Moll,	Johannes Bischoff,
Valentine Schultz,	Andreas Beyer.
Frank Kryhe,	

At the Courtho. of Philadia., Sepr. 21st, 1731. Present:
The Honble PATRICK GORDON, Esqr., Lt. Govr.
    Clement Plumsted,   ) Esq'rs., Members of Council.
    Thomas Laurence.   )
    Derick Jansen, Esqr., one of His Majties Justices of Peace for
    the County of Philadelphia.
A List was presented of the Names of One hundred & six Palatines,
who with their Families, making in all Two hundred & sixty nine
Persons, were imported here in the Ship Britannia, of London, Michael Franklyn, Mr., from Rotterdam, but last from Cowes, as by
Clearance from that Port. The Master being Examined said he had
no particular License for their Transportation. They were then
called in, & having declared that their Intentions were to settle &
live Peaceably in this Province, the several persons whose Names
are subjoyned, did repeat and sign the Declaration inserted in the
Minute of the 21st of Septr., 1727, & likewise took & subscribed
the Declaration of Fidelity & Abjuration.
    Johannes Bartholomay Rieger,   Hans Michael Willhelm,
    Louis Timothee,   Joseph Beyer,

Geles Gelesen,
Gisbertus Boors,
Johannes Boors,
Jacob Swenkoel,
Henric Geber,
Johannes Geber,
Johan Henric Geber,
Jacob Ritsch,
Lucas Vetter,
David Vetter,
Johannes Alberts,
Abraham Allshousen,
Johan Henrick Bahn,
Hans Michael Blatnert,
Veith Bruninger,
Johan Jacob Beyer,
Johan Adam Beyer,
Henric Blicker,
Leonard Bock,
Hans Boshung,
Hans George Ebert,
Hans Michael Ebert,
Johannes Eshleman,
Johannes Agender,
Johannes Frey,
Hans Michael Deibellbissin,
Hans George Deibellbissin,
Christopher Lehman,
Johan Philip Lutz,
Hans Peter Lederman,
Michael Meyer,
Hans Jacob Mentz,
Jacob Meyer,
Christofall Meyer,
Johan Thomas Meyer,
Hans Henrick Martin,
Jacob Mier,
Michel Moths,
Johan Casper Muntz,
Christian Muller,
Herman Muller,
Mathias Nehs,
Johan Nehs,
Dewald Nehs,
Hans Georg Nehs,
Mathias Nehs, junr.,
Georg Passage,
Gabriel Roscher,
Johannes Roth,

Hans Georg Gunt,
Hans Georg Friedle,
Jacob Gunt,
Hans Peter Garner,
Hans Michael Henninger,
Rudolph Holsinger,
Hans Leonard Haltzarfall,
Erasmus Haltzarfall,
Henric Herbertz,
Jacob Hachman,
Johan Heistand,
Michael Horsch,
Daniel Hubert,
Christian Hubert,
Jacob Carl,
Ulrick Keyser,
Henrick Kram,
Nicolas Kennell,
Jacob Kobell,
Abraham Kern,
George Dietric Kohl,
Johannes Kirkner,
Gottfried Krafft,
Valentine Klain,
Wilhelm Kerkes,
Wendel Lautermilch,

Leonart Steininger,
Michel Nehs,
Hans Georg Muller,
Johan Leonard Bihlmeir,
Johan Martin Sakreider,
Johan Michel Schrotner,
Michel Stocker,
Georg Wilhelm Schwartz,
Henric Lutwig Schwartz,
Johan Adam Schroter,
Valentine Siegmund,
Jacob Sumaker,
Johannes Smiedt,
Christofall Trubar,
Hans Vogler,
Leonard Virohn,
Oswald Wald,
Hans Martin Wetzell,
Georg Wanamaker,
Johan Jacob Weynand,
Casper Weis,
Jacob Wirtz,

Jacob Rohr,   Jacob Nehs....
Johan Adam Ruppert,

At the Courtho. of Philadia., Octobr. 14th, 1731. Present:
The Honble PATRICK GORDON, Esqr., Lt. Govr.
   Clement Plumsted,) Esq'rs., Members of Council.
   Ralph Asheton.   )
   Thomas Griffits, Esqr., one of His Majesty's Justices of the
     Peace for the City of Philadelphia.
A List was presented of the Names of Thirty three Palatines, who
with their Families, making in all Seventy eight Persons, were
imported in the Snow Louther, Joseph Fisher, Master, from Rotterdam, but last from Dover, as by Clearance from that Port. The Master being Examined, said he had no particular License for their
Transportation. They were then called in, & having declared that
their Intentions were to settle & live Peaceably in this Province,
the several Persons whose Names are subjoyned, did repeat & sign
the Declaration inserted in the Minute of the 21st of Septemr.,
1727, and likewise took & subscribed the Declaration of Fidelity
& Abjuration:

Gottfried Lehman,	Philip Kintz,
Johan Christian Lehman,	Dorst Hooste,
Jacob Michol,	Hans Reeche,
Jacob Keesey,	Anthony Bankauf,
John Vendal Keesey,	Johan Nicolas Smiet,
Hans Jacob Brunner,	Johannes Ulrick,
Hans Bonun,	Johannes Conrad Frank,
Johann Matthias Cramer,	Jacob Snively,
Hans Georg Haunrig,	Christopher Newbert,
Philip Pieter Viṣenant,	Joseph Christop. Bauman,
Johan Pieter Visenant,	Christian Ernest Hagenmuller,
Henrick Hovervass,	Dorts Bowman,
Philip Eckford,	Hans Philip Ulrick,
Ulrick Michal,	Caspar Bectar,
Jacob Holtzinger,	George Scholltz,
Christopher Omborn,	Daniel Veisiger,...
Melchior Heydon,	

At the Courthouse of Philadelphia, May 15th, 1732, Present:
The Honourable the Governor,
With Severals of the Magistrates.
   Thirteen Palatines, who with their Families, making in all ————
Persons, were imported here in the Ship Norris, Thomas Lloyd, Mar.,
from Boston, did this day take & Subscribe the Effect of the Oaths
of Allegiance, Supremacy & Abjuration; and likewise did repeat and
Sign the Declaration inserted in the Minute of the 21st September,
1727.

Casper Shirch,	Johannes Behn,
Marting Osiner,	Christian Kininger,

Mathias Weber,
Johan Philip Weber,
Johan Herb Minicher,
Johan Michael Sigmund,
Johan Ditrich Yungman,

Johannes Herman,
Valentine Westheber,
Johan George Libenstein,
Michael Anderras....

At the Courthouse of Philadelphia, Aug. 11th, 1732. Present:
The Honourable the Governor,
With the Mayor of the City & Other Magistrates.
A List was Presented of the Names of One Hundred and six Palatines, who with their Families, making in all about Two hundred and
Seventy nine Persons, were imported here in the Ship Samuel, of
London, Hugh Piercy, Master, from Rotterdam, but last from Cowes,
as by the Clearance of the Officers of the Customs there. The Master having been examined and these Forreigners having declared
their Intentions of settling in this Province, & living peaceably
therein, the Persons whose Names are Subjoined took & subscribed
the Effect of the Oaths of Allegiance, Supremacy, &c., and likewise
did repeat & Sign the Declaration directed by Order of Council of
the 21st of Septr., 1727.

Martin Gerhard,
John Bendler,
Johan George Nungeser,
Nicolas Corber,
George Philip Windermuth,
Lorentz Knochel,
Hans Jacob Breckly,
Christopher Breckly,
Mathias Breckly,
Ulrick Breckly,
Samuel Brand,
John Heneberger,
Michael Dierstein,
Henrick Ebby,
Johan Jacob Belerth,
Gottfrid Staal,
Hans George Klingman,
Michael George,
Jacob Oberholzer,
Hans Mosiman,
Peter Wetzstain,
Christian Bendler,
Henrick Ramsaur,
Hans Adam Naig,
Julius Dehr,
Johan George Glasbreumer,
Johan Sebalt Schremer,
Wendal Brechbeil,
Johan George Kleinhans,

Johan Adam Anderas,
Christain Frants,
Christain Frants, Jun.,
Frederick Keiffer,
Jacob Crist,
Samuel Scheer,
Jacob Fleiser,
Leonhard Deebler,
George Deebler,
Oswald Hosteller,
George Bender,
John Lentz,
John Brechbil,
Jacob Stauffer,
Johan Nicolas Strass,
Hans George Goedke,
Johan Leond. Keffer,
Mardin Weigall,
Fredrick Mulchslager,
Michael Kreider,
Johannes Miller,
Hans Carl Balsner,
Christain Balsner,
Fridrick Aldorffer,
Anastasius Uller,
Johannes Ziger,
Hans Jerig Steyer,
Jerig Heyl,
Peter Stey,

Hans Wendell Hoill,
Wilhelm Bergemer,
Christian Bury,
Andreas Muller,
Andreas Stantzenberger,
Johannes Ulrick,
Johan Peter Hailman,
Christian Geeman,
Benedict Geeman,
Johan Leonhard Zeigler,
Johan Fredrick Shitz,
Johan Philip Shitz,
Peter Baltsbach,
Jacob Kneehler,
Martin Biller,
Johan Jacob Erdman,
George Lodwig Hornisch,
Jacob Keiffer,
Casper Wartman,
Jorich Klingman,
Jacob Gutt,
Ulrich Burckholter,
Paulus Boger,
Johan Philip Boger,
   E.

Wendel Berndheisel,
Johan Berndheisel,
Hans Michl. Bumgartner,
John Bumgartner,
Jacob Albrich,
Fredrick Hartman,
Wendel Gerlach,
John Helfurt,
Jacob Weyes,
Ulrich Fisheir,
Henrich Berret,
Peter Shellenburger,
Jacob Gochnauer,
Christian Gochnauer,
Peter Frith,
Andreas Shetler,
Hans Jerig Quickle,
Carl Seyl,
Wendel Werbel,
Philip Werbel,
Augustmus Wendel,
Peter Schneider,
Elias Meyer,
Adam Hillegas....

At the Courthouse of Philadia., Septr. 11th, 1732.   Present:
The Honourable the Governor.
The Mayor & Recorder of the City, &c.
A List was presented of the Names of Seventy Palatines, who with
their families, making in all One hundred & Sixty eight Persons,
were imported here in the Ship Pennsylva. Merchant, John Stedman,
Mr., from Rotterdam, but last from Plymouth, as by Clearance
thence.
The Master having been examined, & these forreigners declaring
their Intentions to settle and live peaceably in this Province, the
Persons whose Names are subjoyned, took & subscribed the Effect of
the Oaths to the Governmt., & the Declaration prescribed by Order
of Council Sepr. 21st, 1727.

Jasper Casparing,
Matthias Zollicoffer,
Jacob Gis,
Conraad Frick,
Michael Reyn,
Hendrick Christian,
Johan Jacob Buss,
Michael Noall,
Johan Seleberger,
Philip Frank,

Jacob Hans,
Hans Michl. Moog,
Vandal Fifar,
Joan Nicolas Miller,
Johan Peter Strack,
Benedict Eiselman,
Michael Witmar,
Geo Mich. Sweynhart,
Hans Mich. Crumurin,
Philip Cavel,

Michael Jerle,
Leonhard Jerle,
Hans Geo. Graaf,
Geo. Michl. Holsteiner,
Hans Jerig Smit,
Jacob Rod,
Hans Jorg Cuntz,
Christopher Stedler,
Johan Georg. Couger,
Simon Carlz,
Matthias Hayser,
Adam Lower,
Hartman Lower,
Simon Peter Holsteiner,
Paulus Reyter,
Hendrick Reyter,
Johan George Bootz,
Wilhelm Chriesmerg,
Georg Mentz,
Hichael Slinager,
Dietrich Ganff,
Bernhart Wolffinger,
Bastian Wagener,
Johannes Fause,
Jerich Palk Graaf,
    E.

Cornelius Kereim,
Hans Rootclie,
Wolf Copenhaver,
Michael Copenhaver,
Johannes Weaver,
Matthias Menigen,
Conraad Honig,
Johan George Ein,
Daniel Millar,
Johannes Hoorle,
Christian Steinback,
Ulrick Cranklook,
Paulus Linsenbegler,
Hans Jacob Meyer,
Jacob Shaad,
Michael Caup,
George Fredrick Capp,
Gabriel Konigh,
Hans Leond. Conraad,
Carl Olignar,
Wendel Weinheimer,
Adam Zeyler,
Hans Jorig Mindhard,
Matthias Shaup,
Fredrick Erm.

At the Courthouse aforesaid, Sepr. 19th, 1732. Present:
The Honourable the Governor.
The Mayor & other Magistrates.
One hundred & twelve Palatines, who with their Families, making
in all Three hundred & thirty Persons, were imported in the Ship
Johnson, of London, David Crockat, Mr., from Rotterdam, but last
from Deal, as by Clearance thence, were in like manner qualified,
whose Names are subjoyned.

Hans Stimman,
Johan George Stimman,
Laurens Hartman,
Johannes Erwig,
Paulus Wegerlin,
Hans Jacob Muller,
Johan Georg Muller,
Valentine Beyer,
Henrick Sain,
Conradt Behen,
Jacob Muller,
Johs. Michl. Lochtner,
Hans Francis Yegener,
Thomas Mattern,

Johannes Messinger,
Bernhard Pifer,
Mathias Brounwart,
Johan Jacob Rohr,
Christo. Ernhardt,
Conrad Bollon,
Andreas Lohr,
Lorentz Webern,
Tobias Hogle,
Johan Jacob Kuntz,
Christopher Rise,
Fredrick Rise,
Joh. Wilhelm Kollin,
Adam Hiber,

Andreas Overbeck,
Hans Jacob Kraus,
Jacob Rousch,
Hans Valent. Renner,
Daniel Schuhl,
Johan Martin Shilling,
Isai Cusehuah,
Nicolas Ewick,
Paulus Wynhamer,
Johannes Bastian,
Lorentz Bastian,
Johannes Bastian,
Johannes Bowman,
Lodwig Friedler,
Anthorn Gilbert,
Johan Balzar Bott,
Johan Philip Yerigh,
Valentine Wild,
Nicolaus Wild,
Fredrick Muller,
Thomas Souder,
Hans Adam Werner,
Johan Valtin Umstadt,
Johannes Soffrenz,
Bartholomius Mortz,
Lorentz Kuntz,
Ludwig Lehman,
Johannes Jorig Paltz,
Nicolaus Eveland,
Johan Martin Bower,
Johannes Everman,
Johannes Albrecht,
Hans Erick Young,
Conraad Sadler,
Johan Adam Leberger,
Christopher Englandt,
Johan Christo. Beyer,
Leonhardt Momma,
Henrick Ostwald,
Leonhard Weyer,
Johannes Smitz,
    E.

Andreas Hemler,
Johan Conrad Scheymer,
Hans Martin Bulinger,
Johan Martin Bulinger,
Hans Philip Timmerman,
Johan Michael Dietur,
Johannes Dietur,
Laurenz Bader,
Rudolph Bonner,
Henrick Appell,
Johan Fredr. Bomgartner,
Johan Henrick Mull,
Pieter Darbeer,
Pieter Gabell,
. Pieter Schuyler,
Philip Shmid,
Johannes Pieter Shmitt,
Johan Jacob Neithelzer,
Conrootz Schywer,
Hans George Frey,
Johan Jacob Frey,
Gerhard Michel. Scholmeyer,
Johan Scholmeyer,
Johannes Fray,
Johannes Hanawer,
Johs. Henrich Masser Schmids,
Hans Mertin Keplinger,
Thomas Kreyl,
Hans Wilhelm Brand,
Christian Schneider,
Conrad Schneider,
Johan Leond. Hermer,
Johan Pieter Keinter,
Johan Frantz Rouss,
Johan Paulus Lederer,
Fredrick Meyer,
Johan George Gump,
Johan George Samin,
Johan Adam Kryl,
Johannes Kryl,
Johs. Geo. Obercogler.

At the Courthouse aforesaid, Sepr. 21st, 1732. Present:
The Honble the Govr., with the Mayor & other Magistrates.
Seventy two Palatines, who with their Families, making in all One
hundred eighty eight Persons, were imported in the Pink Plaisance,
John Paret, Mr, from Rotterdam, but last from Cowes, as by Clearance thence, were in like manner qualified, & their Names are as
follows:

Johs. Philip Muller,
Johannes Muller,
George Baast,
Johannes Klein,
Conrad Schartz,
Daniel Stauffer,
Melcher Feeler,
Bastain Rudi,
Christian Huter,
Hans Zimmerman,
Samuel Meyer,
Martin Meyer,
Jacob Scheerer,
Paulus Hertsell,
Hans Georg. Wagener,
Hans Huber,
George Pieter Kunst,
Christian Mertin,
Jacob Besaker,
Felix Fifler,
Rudolph Richart,
Matthias Muller,
Johan Jacob Koog,
Johannes Hunsiner,
Johan Frantz Fuchs,
Tobias Bechtluff,
Johannes Velker,
Carl Wagner,
Baltzar Schonberger,
Jacob Kutz,
Stephen Lang,
Christian Strohm,
Rudolph Christian,
Peter Bricker,
Hans Stamfley,
Ulrick Steily,
    E.

Hans Lichtein,
Hans Jacob Keyser,
Paulus Keyser,
Hans Danler,
Matthias Kramer,
Nicolaus Zimmerman,
Ulrick Zimmerman,
Samuel Harndits,
Jacob Bloom,
Hans Sherner,
Andreas Filinger,
Jacob Schweitzer,
Christo. Albrecht Lang,
Johan Wilhelm Staup,
Jurig Bernhardts Mahn,
Frantz Steedel,
Johan Philip Kisner,
Johan Adam Zimmerman,
Hans Ulrich Boucher,
Henrick Hartzell,
Nicolaus Honi,
Andreas Woolf,
Nicolaus Kern,
Hans Melchior Werfle,
Jacob Stoufar,
Johan Landis,
Hans Gesell,
Hans Ulrich Wagener,
Henrich Stertzell,
Hans Leond. Hartsell,
Elias Wagener,
Philip Ott,
Andreas Kramer,
Johan Wolk Bartlett,
Ulrich Ressar,
Michael Sicherner.

At the Courthouse aforesaid, Sepr. 23d, 1732, Present:
The Honble the Governor, with Sundry Magistrates.

Fifty seven Palatines, who with their Families, making in all One hundred & forty five Persons, were imported here in the Ship Adventure, Robert Curson, Mr., from Rotterdam, but last from Cowes, as by Clearance thence, were in like manner qualified, and their Names are as follows:

Hans Michael Muller,
Michael Brand,
Michael Gross,
Johan George Briner,

Matthias Richall,
Henricus Lipps,
Hans Jacob Bauder,
Daniel Colmere,

Friedrick Dintelsbeck,
Hans George Abel,
Hans Martin Ronger,
Hans Paulus Sontsinger,
David Holsteller,
Johannes Artz,
Jorig Moser,
Baltzar Stuver,
Andreas Killiven,
Hieronimus Glantz,
Andreas Horn,
Matthias Walter,
David Fischer,
Michael Moser,
Simon Meyer,
Lorentz Swiner,
George Onrich,
Conratz Lang,
Michel Putz,
Baltzar Bortener,
Hans Leonhard Kneide,
Johannes Haberling,
Johannes Sholtz,
Johannes Wingleplech,
Henrick Steger,
        E.

Matthias Wagener,
Hans Ulrich Hoi,
Bernhard Scheertel,
Michel Koch,
Simon Gallinger,
Johannes Becker,
Paul Lecene,
Jean Lecene,
Andreas Weys,
Jurg Zigell,
Valentine Schyp,
Nicol. Bogart,
Johannes Grairteus,
Conrad Clever,
.Nicholaus Bartel,
Tobias Moser,
Andreas Kap,
Leonhard Moser,
Paulus Moser,
Hans Jorig Lichtner,
Hans Melchior Steecher,
Hans Michal Haag,
Georg. Michal Meck,
Hans Peter Stegger.

At the Courthouse aforesaid, Sepr. 25th, 1732. Present:
The Honourable the Governor, with some of the Magistracy.
One hundred and fifteen Palatines, who with their Families, making in all ———— Persons, were imported here in the Ship Loyal
Judith, of London, Robert Turpin, Master, from Rotterdam but last
from Cowes, as by Clearance thence, were in like manner qualified,
whose Names are as follows:

Johannes Christian Schultz,
Andreas Sherar,
Johan Adam Sherar,
Johan Michal Ebort,
Jacob Stuli,
Johan Adam Abel,
Johan Jacob Abel,
Matthes Barrestein,
Rudolph Brown,
Matthes Schmidt,
Henrick Pabst,
Johan Georg. Schmidt,
Hans Philip Ranseler,
Jacob Randsailer,
Hans Peter Sihaver,

Hans Michl. Kreiger,
Wilhelm Berne,
Hans Georg. Kuntz,
Hans David Lentz,
Paulus Miller,
Hieronimus Muller,
Hans Neddtli,
Peter Souder,
Johan Philip Souder,
Samuel Griffi,
Johan Georg. Hoffman,
Martin Heylman,
Johannes Hailman,
Martin Weybrecht,
Johan Georg. Obermuller,

Christian Rape,
Pieter Kritter,
Jacob Muller,
Henrick Goball,
Johannes Otterbach,
Jurig Burghart,
Hans George Noll,
Peter Rauch,
Friedrick Kihler,
Hans George Wagener,
Michael Pens,
Jacob Kintsell,
Hans Georg. Bellman,
Hans Michl. Reyer,
Johan Carl Reyer,
Johan Martin Reyer,
Christian Eply,
Hans David Eply,
Jacob Lischer,
Lutwig Happell,
Mathias Scheitz,
Conraad Fry,
Philip Leonti Cufi,
Hans Jurig Reser,
Georg. Adam Reser,
Philip Raub,
Michael Raub,
Leonhart Segell,
Bernhard Walter,
Henrick Acker,
Philip Jacob Acker,
Johan Georg. Rich,
Johannes Pintnagle,
Hans Georg. Roup,
Johannes Shuman,
Johannes Esther,
Hans Martin Bower,
George Muller,
Hans George Trihan,
Johannes Schmeltzar,
Johannes Retman,
Johannes Michl. Albert,
  E.

George Christopher Lay,
Johan Georg. Fredrick,
Johan George Honig,
Johan Heit Jorgar,
Andreas Schenck,
Georg. Michl. Schmidt,
Jacob Buhlmayer,
Michael Emert,
Philip Criber,
Johan Michl. Hedocker,
Georg. Peter Shultas,
Johan Peter Cuchar,
George Michael Ray,
Johan George Ullerman,
Hans Jacob Stambach,
Johan Friedrich Heyster,
Hans Georg. Abel,
Johan Fredrick Burghar,
Johannes Vogall,
Johannes Pens,
Andreas Colehendurfer,
Hans Adam Gasser,
Johan Hendrick Edler,
Jonas Wolf,
Leonhard Lotz,
Marcus Yung,
Matthias Yung,
Hendrich Lebergher,
Johan Nicolaus Remer,
Johan Baker,
Baltzar Cunkell,
Johan Georg. Furkhill,
Christian Riim,
Fredrich Shafer,
Hans Martin Weybright,
Johannes Reep,
Hans George Borstler,
Casper Kramer,
Conrad Walther,
Johan Geo. Fred. Emert,
Jacob Schratz.

At the Courthouse aforesaid, Sepr. 26th, 1732. Present:
The Honourable the Governor, with some of the City Magistrates.
Sixty one Palatines, who with their Families, making in all one
hundred ninety one Persons, were imported here in the Ship Mary,
of London, John Gray, Master, from Rotterdam, but last from Cowes

as by Clearance thence, were in like manner qualified, whose Names are subjoyned.

Nicolaus Stahler,
Hans George Froshorn,
Michael Abermann,
Hans Jacob Abermann,
Arnold Reitterson,
Conrad Miller,
Dewald Kase,
Christian Kling,
Jacob Stempul,
Nicholaus Stempel,
Johann Lautermilch,
Hans Adam Miller,
Jacob Hauk,
Christo Keiser,
Reinhold Esel,
Cornelius Teele,
Georg. Philip Behir,
Daniel Billigar,
Albrecht Strous,
Joh. Jacob Driebler,
Conrad Eberman,
Andreas Moser,
Caspar Meyer,
Christian Minier,
Hans Henrich Teany,
Hans Adam Robertus,
Jean Louis Danuy,
Pierre Fleury,
Hans George Kohl,
Martin Erenst,
        E.

Hans Michl. Walots,
Hans Jacob Wartz,
Jacob Wartz,
Stephen Kennemar,
Johannes Meyser,
Henrich Schusler,
Jerig Schusler,
Hans Jacob Schusler,
Henrich Schusler,
Joh. Fred. Rousenburgen,
Jacob Walter,
Jacob Walter, Junr.,
Hermann Sim,
Simon Mullar,
Wendel Ketterle,
Albrecht Haase,
Rhineholt Yssell,
Erick Marcus Emler,
Carel Eisen,
George Cling,
Johannes Wertz,
Michael Durr,
Hans George Ebener,
Hans Geo. Erckenbrecht,
Hans Peter Verley,
George Felte Pickell,
Nicolaus Kent,
Hans Michl. Mantz,
Johannes Pickle,
Christo. Pickle.

At the Courthouse aforesaid, Sepr. 30th, 1732. Present:
The Honourable the Governor with Several Magistrates.

Fifty five Palatines, who with their families, making in all One hundred & seventy Persons, were imported here in the Ship Dragon, Charles Hargrave, Master, from Rotterdam, but last from Plymouth, as by Clearance thence, were in like manner qualified, & their Names are Subjoyned.

Peter Matern,
Hans Georg. Dirh,
Michael Dirr,
Martin Wytknecht,
Christian Hoffman,
Jacob Lypersberger,
Hans Adam Bender,
Hans Wendel Lahber,
Hans Georg. Road,

Peter Schlosser,
Hans Wilhelm Ziegler,
Johannes Shyroktz,
Johan Nicolaus Muller,
Christian Suber,
Johan Philip Hoffman,
Hans Georg. Hagi,
Simon Beltzner,
Johan Philip Slough,

Johan Adam Romich,
Johan Fredrick Romich,
Leonhard Schlosser,
Leonhard Muller,
Johan Wilhelm Frank,
Peter Rowdenbash,
Hendrick Rowdenbash,
Hans Jacob Shoork,
Henrich Gruber,
Hans Peter Wolf,
Johannes Herburger,
Johannes Wirtman,
Jacob Klein,
Hendrick Klein,
Johannes Gyger,
Johan Georg. Kroner,
Johan Dietrich Kroner,
Frantz Sype,
Felix Bronner,
    E.

Andreas Shlowch,
Hans Michl. Rysner,
Hans Rudolph Illig,
Hans Martin Koppler,
Henrick Basler,
Georg. Ludwig Schitz,
Leonhard Pentz,
Michael Graaf,
Tobias Paal,
George Fauntz,
Johan Jacob Byerle,
Christopher Besser,
Hans Ulrick Bare,
Hans Georg. Hayl,
George Hayl,
George Sype,
Lutwig Sype,
Hans Georg. Soldner,...

At the Courtho. of Philadelphia, Octor. 11th, 1732. Present:
The Honble PAT. GORDON, Esqr., Lt. Govr.
With Severals of the City Magistrates.
Forty two Palatines, who with their families, making in all ——
Persons, were imported here in the Ship Pleasant, James Morris,
Master, from Rotterdam, but last from Deal, as by Clearance thence,
were this day qualified as usual, & their Names are Subjoyned:

Balzar Spingler,
Henrich Spingler,
Johannes Keliar,
Johan Georg. Senck,
Georg. Bear,
Frederick Baasler,
Ulrich Bodman,
Ulrich Peters,
Matthias Jurian,
Henrich Eckert,
Hans Georg. Salk,
Philip Schellig,
Conrats Kolb,
Conrats Glassbrenner,
Jacob Hornberger,
Hans Peter Sigmund,
Hans Bern Kuntzer,
Fulk Mullar,
Hans Philip Kresler,
Matthias Ambrosi,
Johannes Gumbor,
    E.

George Hans Peters,
Georg. Spingler,
Jurg. Kullar,
Jacob Friedriech Klim,
Henricus Retz,
Jacob Podom,
Johan Jacob Timmanous,
Isaac Raudebush,
Friedrich Notz,
Hans Adam Schilling,
Johannes Moak,
Ulrich Baasler,
Joh. Casper Winterott,
Georg. Philip Snatherly,
Hans Michl. Snatherly,
Georg. Mess,
Valtin Mullar,
Hans Michel Hoffman,
Johannes Tablemeyer,
Conraad Roup,
Georg. Michel Favian....

At the Court House of Philadelphia, October 17th, 1732. Present:
The Honourable the Lieutenant Governor.
With the Mayor of the City, & other Magistrates.
Sixty one Palatines, who with their Families, making in all One
hundred Sixty nine Persons, were imported here in the Pink John &
William of Sunderland, Constable Tymperton, Master, from Rotterdam,
but last from Dover, as by Clearance thence, were this day quali-
fied as usual, and their Names follow:

Bernhard Wymer,	Conrad Low,
Moritz Laurence,	Ludwig Hoogel,
C. Wolger,	Jacob Weyber,
Georg. Albrecht,	Johannes Schook,
Jacob Brechbiel,	Hans Jacob Reyl,
Laurenz Kieffer,	Georg. Adam Stiess,
Stephen Matthes,	Abraham Dubo,
Bartol Moll,	Hans Georg. Rohrbach,
Hans Georg. Martin,	Joh. Nicolaus Schmidt,
Hans Erhart Vosselman,	Adam Wilt,
Johannes Emich,	Antoni Albrecht,
Felter Scheadecker,	Hans Philip Kleas,
Johannes Deynen,	Conrad Getz,
Pieter Haywigh,	Nicolaus Kooger,
Michal Weysel,	Jacob Kooger,
Friedrich Wyssell,	Jac. Matthias Wenser,
Lutwig Joh. Melchionar,	Sebastian Trockenmiller,
Johannes Yeigie,	Gideon Hoffer,
Joh. Phillipus Reinhart,	Hans Reyl,
Hans Peter Brechbill,	Joh. Shuffeln,
Bendu Brechbill,	Johan Paul Derst,
Hans Brechbill,	Henrich Getz,
Hans Georg. Sprecher,	Matthias Rubichon,
Johannes Nagel,	Johannes Vogler,
Peter Smidt,	Jacob Henrich,
Johannes Housam,	Philip Melchior Moyer,
Joh. Michal Housman,	Johan Georg. Wahnsidel,
Joh. Nicolaus Pauschon,	Johan Pieter Apsell,
Baltzar Gerloch,	Georg. Wypert,
Christian Low,	Johan Jacob Sheare....
E.	

At the Courthouse of Philadelphia, August 17th, 1733. Present:
The Honourable the Lt. Governor.
With severals of the Magistrates.
Ninety Palatines, who with their Families, making in all Two hun-
dred & ninety one Persons, were imported here in the Ship Samuel of
London, Hugh Percy, Master, from Rotterdam, but last from Deal, as
by Clearance thence, this day took and subscribed the Effect of the
Government Oaths, & also the Declaration prescribed by the Order of
Council of the 21st of September, 1727, & their Names are as fol-
lows:

Hans Peter Frey,
Johan Leuistanwallnor,
Hans Georg. Strohaver,
Elias Tayler,
Abraham Koen,
Fredrich Koen,
Johan Johan Zimmer,
Jacob Rausher,
Christian Krops,
Henrich Bishof,
Hans Jurg Ruck,
Hans Georg. Ruck,
Hans Jacob Ruck,
Peter Koentz,
Hans Jacob Ridt,
Hans Leonard Lechner,
Hans Jurg Peck,
Andreas Frey,
Friedrich Lieby,
Friedrich Aldorfer,
Michael Smiet,
Matthias Ley,
Hans Peter Bristell,
Michael Sturtzebach,
Hans Melchier Fries,
Hans Wervell,
Hans Jurg Wervell,
Martin Shibe,
Hans Leonhart Wolf,
Hans Casper Joost,
Solomon Miller,
Hans Wolf Eiseman,
Hans Jacob Hoff,
Hans Jacob Matthis,
Johan Leonhart Weyss,
Johan Jacob Crisinger,
Johan Philip Hetser,
Henrich Aller,
Peter Haller,
Johan Caspar Schafner,
Jacob Kraler,
Peter Drochsel,
Ulrick Flichrer,
Hans Adam Frickrott,
Henrich Fesseler,
   E.

Gilian Schmied,
Christian Lausel,
Hans Casper Eiseman,
Malcher Wagner,
Justus Simonius Wagner,
Hans Jacob Kummerlin,
Hans Adam Lang,
Michael Probst,
Johs. Michael Probst,
Hans Georg. Zoller,
Johan Casper Korber,
Johan Henrich Fisher,
Andreas Wagener,
Johan Koofman,
Johan Henrich Adam,
Johan Wilhelm Fisher,
Casper Muhlhaus,
Andreas Weltz,
Hans Casper Brenner,
Jacob Fegley,
Johan Lorig,
Johannes Shnap,
Lorentz Shnap,
Martin Wonner,
Henrich Peter,
Peter Hansminger,
Johan Conrad Kempf,
Christian Kempf,
Gilbert Kempf,
Henrich Rohd,
Peter Cornelius,
Jacob Gerkehouser,
Nicolas Kan,
Hans Leonhart Emiger,
Marcus Klein,
Johan Peter Knoble,
Elias Hasele,
Lorentz Syboot,
Hans Bernhard Trossell,
Henry Meder,
Christian Danner,
Caspar Martin,
Hans Peter Mock,
Valentine Snyder.

At the Courthouse aforesaid, August 27th, 1733. Present:
The Honourable the Lt. Governor.

And severals of the Magistrates.

Fifty eight Palatines, who with their Families, making in all One hundred & seventy two Persons, were imported here in the Ship Eliza, of London, Edward Lee, Master, from Rotterdam, but last from Dover, as by Clearance thence, were qualified as before, & their Names are:

Johannes Krichner,	Hans Yerech Perger,
Johan Philip Sover,	Jacques Bonnett,
Johannes Mehn,	Wolfgang Mullar,
Johan Michl. Grovul,	Jacob Mullar,
Johan Georg. Petry,	Simon Schearman,
John Hendrich Shitts,	Jurig Shearman,
Conraad Shoot,	Johannis Knoll,
Johan Philip Foust,	Jacob Koobler,
Michael Ruht,	Frantz Weiss,
Johan Henrich Tenich,	Johan Dobalt Troud,
Corab Hetrich,	Jurich Ore,
Henrich Stens,	Johannes George Oder,
Hans Peter Hoffman,	Jacob Server,
Johannis Young,	Jacob Server, Junr.
Johan Peter Foust,	Rudolph Server,
Johan Philip Foust,	Jacob Housenwart,
Jacob Michael Erbe,	Jacob Henrich,
Ulrich Shoe,	Johan Henrich Tabas,
Jacob Shuh,	Jacob Zittell,
Johannes Loats,	Johan Philippus Smitt,
Matthias Whiedman,	Hans Jurg Nordt,
Henrich Still,	Jacob Dillinger,
Simon Linder,	Andreas Klipsedle,
Simon Linder, Junr.	Georg. Henrich Murtz,
George Friedrich Onsell,	Johan Ulrich Cool,
Michael Faeber,	Johannis Fageley,
Aran Spogener,	Henrich Stricker,
Stephan Lauman,	Michael Ranhard,
Balser Mets,	Hans Jacob Mets.

E.

At the Courthouse aforesaid, August 28th, 1733. Present:
The Honourable the Lt. Governor,
With severals of the Magistrates.

Eighty four Palatines, who with their Families making in all Two hundred & twenty six Persons, were imported here in the Ship Hope, of London, Daniel Ried, Master, from Rotterdam, but last from Cowes, as by Clearance thence, were qualified as before, & their Names are:

Ulrich Wisseler,	Peter Arant,
Ulrich Rheinhart,	Daniel Rott,
Hans Grumbacher,	Hans George Wyneck,
Hans Stayman,	Frantz Ratsell,

Peter Stayman,
Hans Stayman, junr.
Christian Stoudar,
Hans Rat,
Nicholas Timberman,
Hans Timberman,
Joseph Fleure,
Joseph Fleure,
Johannis Fleure,
Christian Kur,
Michael Whitmar,
Ulrich Whitmar,
Peter Whitmar,
Peter Esleman,
Christian Esleman,
Ulrich Loninacre,
Ulrich Loninacre, Junr.
Jacob Loninacre,
Jacob Burcki,
Hans Snabley,
Christian Blank,
Hans Georg. Weidnar,
Hans Georg. Brimmer,
Fredrich Becker,
Jacob Lochbaum,
Rudolph Brock,
Christian Reblet,
Barnard Keller,
Conrad Rouf,
Jourg Richter,
Henrich Shmiet,
Michael Ably,
Jacob Robman,
Wilhelm Krans,
Henrich Fegeley,
Matthias Fegeley,
Barnard Fegeley,
Hans Michl. Stenbard,
      E.

Andreas Louck,
Herman Arand,
Johs. Henrich Noumich,
Johan Adam Retsel,
Hans Georg. Crylberger,
Johan Leond. Stain,
Hans Jurg Kohler,
Johan Michl. Beyss,
Hans Jurg Hofnam,
Peter Schmid,
Johan David Dupshler,
Johan Jacob Meckli,
Johan Eorl Grop,
Bastian Tsyster,
Henrich Humberger,
Hans Leond. Humberger,
Peter Seyler,
Christian Yonilev,
Andreas Besinger,
Georg. Henrich Kneysman.,
Georg. Michael Fraitter,
Hans Jurg Gobal,
Hans Jacob Guber,
Johan Christopher Cunnaway,
Johan Adam Simon,
Abraham Miller,
Jacob Bart,
Henrich Tace,
Benedick Wise,
Martin Spittlemayer,
Hans Adam Spittlemayer,
Stephen Slunaeker,
Abraham Grautter,
Hans Jacob Shumbur,
Daniel Haselman,
Rudolph Shnebley,
Hans Michl. Shreyack,
Jacob Shreyack.

At the Courthouse aforesaid, September 18th, 1733. Present:
The Honourable the Lt. Governor,
And Severals of the Magistrates.
Sixty seven Palatines, who with their Families, making in all One
hundred eighty seven Persons, were imported here in the Briganteen
Pennsylvania Merchant, of London, John Stedman, Mr., from Rotter-
dam, but last from Plymouth, as by Clearance thence, were qualified
as before, & their Names are:
Johan Klem,   Alexander Casser,

Gotleb Klem,
Georg. Sholts,
David Sholts,
Andreas Moseman,
Christian Moseman,
Hans Burkhard,
David Burkhard,
Johan Schonfeldt,
Johannes Naiis,
Peirre Marot,
Adreas Kleym,
Jacob Kleym,
George Shait,
Johannes Riegel,
Johs. Riegel, Junr.
Daniel Riegel,
Andreas Oullenbacher,
Johan Valentine Presel,
Michael Walter,
Carolus Burkhard,
Johan Philip Weynandt,
Jacob Knop,
Jacob Ott,
Johan Michael Ott,
Lutwig Evald,
Michl. Ludwig,
Daniel Ludwig,
Philip Smeyer,
Christian Hook,
Hans Jorg Grondt,
Jerg Adam Koch,
Fredrich Glass,
Johannes Gordner,
     E.

Pieter Roodt,
Hans Lauer,
Matthias Kish,
Johan Michl. Stoudt,
Johan Just Ulveyn,
Philip Angulberger,
Michael Seydbender,
Johan Daniel Endt,
Johan Valentine Endt,
Johan Peter Sayling,
Adam Volimer,
Hans Georg. Winter,
Hans Martin Sauter,
Frederich Gotz,
.Johannes Mihm,
Peter Smit,
Johan Adam Beyer,
Joh Christo. Yslebach,
Michael Kelchner,
Georg. Bartol Sheffer,
Paulus Sheffer,
Andreas Vry,
Bernhard Maus,
John Ludwig Sees,
Andreas Boyer,
Hans Georg. Hauk,
Peter Straub,
Johan Jacob Karse,
Matthias Beichler,
Justus Osterut,
Johan Georg. Groom,
Hendrich Smit.

At the Courthouse aforesaid September 28th, 1733. Present:
The Honourable the Lt. Governor,
& Severals of the Magistrates.
Forty three Palatines, who with their Families, making in all One
hundred thirty seven Persons, were imported here in the Briganteen
Richard & Elizabeth, of Philadelphia, Christopher Clymer, Master,
from Rotterdam, but last from Plymouth, as by Clearance thence were
qualified as before, & their Names are:

Frantz Schuller,
Jacob Grib,
David Mertz,
Hans Michael Mertz,
George Leap,
Johan Conrad Leap,

Hans Peter Somey,
Hans Jacob Somey,
Hans Peter Somey, Junr.
Otto Fredrick Somey,
Joseph Shumaker,
Ulrick Burghalter,

Philip Jacob Edelman,
Matthias Bousser,
Matthias Bousser, Junr.
Philip Mire,
Christian Bousser,
David Edelman,
Adam Spohn,
Jacob Hennel,
Michael Wise,
Johan Georg. Shufard,
Johan Yost Heck,
Jacob Huntsider,
Hans Jacob Lebegood,
Jacob Herman,
Hans Jacob Uts,
Hans Jurk Uts,
   E.

Johan Nicol. Segar,
George Schenemansgruber,
Matthias Beck,
Johannes Wollett,
Henry Winterberger,
Hans Sherer,
Jacob Krist,
Marcus Krist,
George Angsted,
Marcus Bigler,
Philip Duderman,
Johannes Weber,
Johannes Rosensteel,
Abraham Wootring,
Matthias Rehsh.

At the Courthouse aforesaid, September 29th, 1733. Present:
The Honourable the Lt. Governor,
& Severals of the Magistrates.
Thirty four Palatines, who with their families, making in all One
hundred & Seventy Persons, were Imported here in the Pink Mary of
Dublin, James Benn, Master, from Rotterdam, but last from Plymo. as
by Clearance thence, were qualified as before, & their Names are:

David Karker,
Hans Georg. Horlocher,
Gottfried Riech,
Johannes Yorde,
Andreas Dries,
Cornelius Dries,
Peter Dries,
Johan Adam Dries,
Jacob Spingler,
Peter Hite,
Elias Strickler,
Johannes Strickler,
Johan Michael Noll,
Philip Thomas Trump,
Henrich Sower,
Johannes Wingertman,
Christian Blaser,
Johannes Teutscher,
Joh. Peter Teutscher,
Johan Georg. Ribble,
Jacob Frank,
Johan Arnold Billig,
Fredrich Funk,
Michael Friedly,

Andreas Nay,
Philip Jacob Rothrock,
Johannes Rothrock,
Christian Sooter,
Hans Michael Hammer,
Johan Michael Teel,
Georg. Pfaffenberger,
Jurk Pfaffenberger,
Jurk Derey,
Christian Retelsberger,
Jacob Hoffman,
Fredrich Durflinger,
Asimus Rambach,
Hans Michel Keller,
Jacob Berkel,
Hans Jacob Berkel,
Nicolaus Mauritz,
Baltzer Breuninger,
Johan Adam Werner,
Jorg. Fredrich Kehler,
Peter Apple,
Johan Peter Kettall,
Johan Jacob Gehtel,
Johannes Lap,

Johannes Reichenbach,   Johannes Slabach,
Nicolaus Sowter,   Johan Henry Slabach,
Johan Martin Brown,   Jacob Lesher....
   E.

At the Courthouse of Philadelphia, Oct. 12th, 1733. Present:
The Honourable the Lt. Governor,
With some of the Magistrates.
Fifteen Palatines, who with their Families, making in all Sixty
two Persons, where imported here in the Ship Charming Betty, John
Ball, Master, from London, were this day qualified as usual, &
their Names are:

John Katner,   Adam Spag,
Geog. Michael Katner,   Nicholas Burger,
Henrich Meikle,   Peter Stocker,
Hans Peter Gruber,   Hans Paul Vogt,
Samuel Ludi,   Johan Lang,
Christian Andereck,   Johan Lang, junr.
Ulrich Lebeegoot,   Nicholas Heltzel....
Johan Lebeegoot,
   E.

At the Courthouse of Philadelphia, September the 12th, 1734.
Present:
The Honourable the Lieutenant Governor.
  The Mayor of the City and others of the Magistracy.
Eighty nine Palatines who, with their Families, making in all two
hundred sixty one Persons, were imported here in the Ship Saint An-
drew, John Stedman, Master, from Rotterdam, but last from Plymouth,
as by Clearance from thence, this day took and subscribed the
Effect of the Government Oaths, and also the Declaration prescribed
by the Order of Council of the 21st of September, 1727, and their
Names are as follows:

Christopher Weigner,   David Seibt,
Melchior Heibner,   Christopher Seibt,
George Heibner,   George Heydrich,
George Krieble,   Gergorius Sholtze,
Baltzar Jackell,   David Meschter,
George Jackell,   George Dreyher,
Christopher Shoebart,   Christopher Dreyher, junr.
Melchior Krieble, Senr.   Melchior Meschter, junr.,
Caspar Krieble,   Baltzar Anders,
George Ander,   George Sholtze,
Baltzar Hoffman,   Melchior Sholtze,
Melchior Krieble, junr.   Christopher Sholtze,
Abraham Jackell,   Caspar John,
George Hoffman, Senr.   Friedrich Scheps,
Baltzar Hoffman, junr.   H. Lutwigh Urdans,
George Rinnald,   Barnhard Steinbach,

Hans Weigner,
George Weigner,
Melchior Weigner,
Baltzar Jackell,
Caspar Jackell,
Jeremias Jackell,
Christopher Jackell,
Gregorius Meisther,
Christopher Reinwalt,
Hans Henrich Jackell,
George Mentzell,
Melchior Mentzell,
Melchior Newman,
Tobias Herttranft,
George Weys,
Caspar Heydrich,
Baltzar Heydrich,
Christopher Newman,
Matthias Jackell,
George Sholtze,
Christopher Weigner,
Christopher Jackell,
George Anders,
Conrad Frey,
Matthias Marker,
Hendrich Romfield....
  E.

Christopher Paus,
George Bansch,
Hans Hubner,
David Shoebart,
Wilhelm Pott,
Degenhart Pott,
Wilhelmus Witzen,
Johannes Van Dulike,
Peter Shoemaker,
Jacob Hendrich Rieger,
Johan Yorg. Runtz,
Valentine Henrich,
Jacob Roomfult,
Nicholas Dek,
Nicholas Winder,
Johannes Wilfang,
Jacob Wilhelm,
Ulrich Spies,
Peter Jager,
Caspar Storller,
George Meyer,
Peter Freidel,
Johannes Singer,
Valentine Dihl,
Abraham Dihl,

At the Courthouse of Philadelphia, September the 23d, 1734.
Present:
The Honourable the Lieutenant Governor.
The Mayor of the City, and others of the Magistracy.
Forty nine Palatines who, with their Families, making in all One
hundred twenty seven Persons, were imported here in the Ship Hope,
Daniel Ried, Master, from Rotterdam, but last from Cowes, as by
Clearance from thence, were this day qualified as usual, whose
Names are:

Jacob Bowman,
Bernhart Richer,
Jacob Koser,
Hans Henrich Hoffman,
Hans Jacob Fisbach,
Johan Wilhelm Graaf,
Michael Geber,
Christian Houser,
Michael Fikel,
Ulrich Buler,
Johannes Rechter,
Philip Esping,

Johannes Keyser,
Jorg. Heynsman,
Johannes Heynsman,
Johan Adam Schrof,
Johan Peter Gross,
Johan Hendrich Klakner,
Peter Stam,
August Henrich Kuntzman,
Johan Henrich Swissman,
Christopher Rabe,
Johan Philip Dolt,
Henrich Stolze,

Christian F[defective print],
Zacharias Slummerfeld,
Johan Wilhelm Ohlbach,
Johannes Yung,
Jost Shmith,
Johan Peter Shmith,
Johannes Noche,
Johan Henrich Otterbach,
Johan Herbert Weber,
George Lubchen,
Johannes Peter Apgardt,
Simon Kirbach,
Johan Arnolt Reish,
     E.

Zacharias Albach,
Simon Bevell,
Johan Henrich Weshbach,
Johan Henrich Otter,
Johan George Antony Miller,
Johan Andreas Miller,
Antony Nobel,
Antony Nobel, junr.
Johan Albert Langerfeldt,
Gotfried Schierwager,
Christian Otto Schultz,
Cornelis Paraet....

At the Courthouse of Philadia, May 29th, 1735. Present:
The Honble PATRICK GORDON, Esqr., Lieut. Governor.
With several of the Magistrates.
Fifty four Palatines and Switzers, who with their Families,
making in all one hundred Seventy Six Persons, were imported here
in the Ship Mercury, of London, William Wilson, Master, from Rotterdam, but last from Cowes, as by Clearance from thence, were this
day qualified as usual, and their Names are hereunto subjoined:

Conrad Wuertz,
Abraham Weidman,
Rudolph Weidman,
Hans Jacob Ratgal,
Jacob Boshart,
Jacob Schenckel,
Hendrich Huber,
Jacob Naaff,
Henry Oswald,
Jacob Frey,
Jacob Meyer,
Jacob Pertshinger,
Henry Bruner,
Hans Kiebur,
Jacob Weidman,
Hans Conrad Koller,
Conrad Naaff,
Jacob Madter,
Hans Muller,
Hans Ott,
Johannes Heit,
Hendrich Schuber,
Martin Schelberger,
Jacob Maurer,
Hendri Scheuchzer,
Jacob Shelberger,
Henry Moseke,
     E.

Jacob Tenzler,
Johan Ulrich Ahner,
Johannes Weiss,
Baltzar Bassert,
Henry Merck,
Hans Meyer,
Caspar Netzly,
Caspar Schweitzer,
Henry Surber,
Hans Uhlrig Amman,
Rudolph Aberley,
Jacob Wyst,
Rudolph Egg,
Rudolph Walter,
Jacob Conrad Naaff,
Jacob Schmit,
Conrad Meyer,
Jacob Naaff,
Caspar Tutt,
Caspar Pleuler,
Jacob Minger,
Abraham Wekerley,
Conrad Rutzchi,
Christian Erhard Newmeiter,
Johannes Molich,
Philip Klein,
Hendrich Forst....

At the Courthouse of Philadia, June 28th, 1735. Present:
The Honourable PATRICK GORDON, Esqr., Lieutenant Governor,
And some Gentlemen of the Magistracy:
Thirteen Palatines, who, with their Families, making in all
thirty nine Persons, were imported here in the Brig Mary, of Philadelphia, James Marshall Master, from London, were this day qualified as usual, and their Names are hereunto subjoyned:

Melchior Scholtze,	Johannes Werchman,
Peter Schwaub,	Solomon Buckstool,
Henrich Werchman,	Henrich Boshart,
Wilhelm Gesel,	Nicholaus Botikofer,
Andreas Widmar,	Jacob Widmar,
Zacharias Friedrich,	Solomon Buckstool, junr....
Andreas Brinker,	
E.	

[The following have been copied from Volume 4.]

At the Court house of Philadelphia, September 1st, 1736.
Present:
The Honble JAMES LOGAN, Esqr., President.

Clement Plumsted,	Samuel Hasell,	) Esquires.
Thomas Laurence,	Charles Read,	)

William Allen, Esqr., Mayor of Philadelphia, and Derick Janssen,
    Esqr., one of the Justices of Philadelphia County.
One hundred fifty one Foreigners from the Palatinate & other
Places, who, with their Families, making in all three hundred
eighty-eight Persons, were imported here in the Ship Harle, of
London, Ralph Harle, Master, from Rotterdam, but last from Cowes,
as by Clearance thence, were this day Qualified as usual, whose
Names are as follows:

Frans Hackert,	Johannes Schnieder,
Johannes Van Laaschet,	Johannes Zacharias,
Johannes Petrus Van Laaschet,	Nicolas Melchior,
Christian Van Laaschet,	Baltzer Stephanns,
Johannes Kirkt,	Johan Lutwig Wyker,
Johan Philip Wick,	Johan Henrich Brunner,
Johan Philip Wergonner,	Abraham Appler,
Abraham Tegast,	Johan Jorig Basil,
Johannes Hannewald,	Ludwig Camerer,
Johannes Lorentz,	Johannes Michael Weygall,
Abraham Tirgartz,	Laborious Merschottz,
Jacob Kemlie,	Christian Schricak,
Johan Valentine Fokt,	Conrad Frankberger,
Johan Mathias Fokt,	Johannes Brosinger,
Johan Daniel Braunn,	Daniel Meyer,
Johan Michael Crowel,	Johannes Rossman,
George Nicolas Sysloof,	Johannes Hess,
Johan Baltzer Sysloof,	Christof Windematt,

Yorig Sysloof,
Wilhelm Hetterling,
Daniel Nargar,
Johan Peter Nargar,
Nicolas Traber,
Michael Dom,
Johan Christopher Treber,
Carl Kern,
Nicolas Rebell,
Johan Jorig Jaky,
Jacob Amandus,
Andreas Yokam,
Leonhart Cranbach,
Emcent Shadlin,
Jacob Hofstedler,
Jacob Eyser,
Johannes Rubell,
Friedrick Bregell,
Jacob Jeyser,
Aaron Cook,
Friedrick Minhart,
Rudolph Hackmann,
Jacob Fellman,
Jacob Sonday,
Cornelius Weygandt,
Abraham Snider,
Nicolas Lang,
Adam Boher,
Ludwig Lay,
Christian Erb,
Johan Jorig Wintermont,
Peter Heironimous,
Peter Rentsh,
Hans Melchior Byer,
Andreas Nargang,
Johannes Butler,
Clemens Stout Ceeker,
Mathias Speck,
Derrick Mart,
Hans Jacob Woyl,
Johan Wilhelm Speck,
Peter Stoutbecker,
Henrich Garhart,
Andreas Brimm,
Johan Jacob Tonaspeck,
Andreas Haillman,
Johan Mathias Brouch,
Hans Peter Fegelin,
Hans Jorig Mien,

Paulus Brunner,
Johan Jorig Vanbott,
Johannes Jorig Shirtler,
Johannes Conrad Grim,
Christian Landes,
Michael Linder,
Thomas Hummel,
Andreas Gross,
Johan Adam Shans,
Leonhart Yeager,
Zacharias Sekler,
Johan Valentine Schere,
Peter Roop,
Michael Noll,
Isaac Adolph Delb,
Johan Jacob Christler,
Johannes Mayer,
Nicolas Anger,
Casper Meyer,
Lutwig Meyer,
Christian Stukly,
Casper Stelling,
Johan Jacob Nuss,
Dewalt Beyer,
Hans Conrats Bab,
Johannes Brunb,
Matthias Dick,
Henrich Wolgamot,
Abraham Wolgamot,
Joseph Wolgamot,
Jorig Adam Warner,
Christian Suder,
Johannes Gerber,
Jonadan Heger,
Matthias Reser,
Jacob Cuntz,
Jacob Hollinger,
Jacob Ledtreman,
Jacob Kochnour,
Herman Crott,
Johan Philip Mentz,
Henrich Wydebach,
Casper Coppersmidt,
Johannes Frankeberger,
Andreas Frank,
Adam Vampull,
Hans Jorig Hantwerg,
Johannes Fuchs,
Godfriedt Grill,

Johannes Rotroke,
Johan Jacob Paalt,
Johan Jacob Zyderman,
Nicolas Post,
Henrich Dubbs,
Andreas Cratz,
Jacob Libhart,
Valentine Noy,

Johan Adam Honanschell,
Johan Peter Vampull,
Jorig Mich Freidrich,
Johan Albrecht Sigle,
Johan Peter Marstiller,
Johan Jorig Lonarb,
Christopher Rudolph....

At the Courthouse of Philadia., September 16th, 1736. Present:
The Honble JAMES LOGAN, Esqr., President.
   Thomas Laurence,   Thomas Griffits,)
   Ralph Assheton,   ) Esqrs.
William Allen, Esqr., Mayor the City of Philadia.
One hundred and twelve Foreigners from the Palatinate, and other
places, who, with their Families, making in all three hundred &
thirty persons, were imported here in the ship Princess Augusta,
Samuel Merchant, Master, from Rotterdam, but last from Cowes, as by
Clearance thence, were this day Qualified as usual, whose Names are
as follows:

Johan Gabriel Lamle,
Hans Jorig Bumgartner,
Hans Philip Flexer,
Jorig Meyer,
Philip Gullman,
Jorig Meyer,
Hans Michel Essig,
Jorig Abraham Essig,
Rudolph Essig,
Johan Jacob Bush,
Wilhelm Huber,
Jacob Miller,
Simon Carl,
Johannes Jorig Ritter,
Hans Jost Dubs,
Stefan Schust,
Jacob Meyer,
Theelman Hirnshall,
Durs Toma,
Hans Jacob Toma,
Martin Thomas,
Dierich Toma,
Hans Jacob Dups,
Joseph Cratzer,
Jacob Kese,
Rudolph Hang,
Hans David Bielman,
Hans Thomas Kurr,
Hans Michal Carle,

Jacob Heckendorn,
Daniel Hechendorn,
Bastian Stoler,
Hans Jacob Griter,
Friedrich Griter,
Martin Griter,
Hans Spitler,
Hans Spitler,
Hans Georg Gerster,
Nicolas Tenne,
David Lortensteyn,
Jacob Bear,
Hans Jacob,
Stephen Jacob,
Johan Books,
Christian Reckty,
Abraham Jacky,
Sebastien Cagnelin,
Dietrich Cagnelin,
Jean Cagnelin,
Jean Comer,
Daniel Kommer,
Deitrich Werlie,
Hans Tisler,
Hans Imberman,
Hans Jacob Keller,
Nicolas Indie,
Jonas Joner,
Jacob Joner,

Gottfried Lantermilch,
Christian Darfen,
Peter Brinharb,
Walter Baruman,
Hans Siber,
Hans Zwalle,
Hans Stockie,
Hans Rudolf Erb,
Peter Pinkly,
Melchior Datweiller,
Jacob Freh,
Lorentz Freh,
Nicolas Freh,
Henrich Freh,
Leonhardt Stein,
Hans Nicolas Schmidt,
Lorentz Simon,
Christian Simon,
Friedrich Gartner,
Hans Jorig Drantman,
Henrich Meyer,
Sebastian Graaf,
Hans Georg Graf,
Hans Adolf Wensel,
Hans Jacob Bietrab,
Christian Schiblen,
Hans Heckendorn,

Bendict Yorhlig,
Christian Slachten,
Peter Delo,
Rudolf Bumgartner,
Jean Francois Chrestien,
Colas Drasbarb,
N. Gerard,
Peter Pinklie,
Hans Pinklie,
Hans Pinklie,
Johannes Keller,
Johannes Keller,
Francis Orich,
Nicolas Orich,
Enoas Nowell,
Joseph Noel,
Peter Noel,
Jacob Christaman,
Michel Haaling,
Marcus Marky,
Hans David Marky,
Jacob Altland,
Nicolas Mesling,
Johan Conrad Ganger,
Georg Nicolas Ganger,
Peter Weyer....

At the Courthouse of Philadia., October 19th, 1736. Present:
                    Clement Plumsted,)
                    Thomas Laurence,   ) Esquires.
                    Ralph Assheton,   )
Thirty-seven Foreigners from the Palatinate, who, with their
Families, making in all one hundred and ten persons, were imported
here in the Brigantine John, of Perth Amboy, George Frazer, Master,
from Rotterdam, but last from Dover, as by Clearance thence, were
this day Qualified as usual, whose Names were as follows:

Abraham Beer,
Peter Quattel Ban,
Johannes Trans,
Johan Georg. Micklyn,
Johan Lutwig Sil,
Lutwig Tretler Walsteller,
Johan Phillippus Quickell,
Johannes Segel,
Johan Peter Pris,
Johan Michal Qnukle,
Jacob Keller,
Fransisens Josephus Hornig,

Johan Adam Ransch,
Johan Jost Meyer,
Johan Georg. Quickle,
Johannes Sler,
Johan Christfel Shinger,
Peter Kohl,
Daniel Spelter,
Johan Henrich Schmidt,
Jacob Plyger,
Abraham Dumbolb,
Erns Fredrich Dumbolb,
Peter Haas,

Johan Casper Schmidt,	Johannes Herr,
Casper Struvel,	Debolt Feit,
Casper Lombarb,	Derrich Shutten,
Georg. Keg,	Nicolas Stop,
Paulus Andoni,	Peter Vean,
Fredrick Clipton,	Godfried Eberhard....
Johannes Geyer,	

At a Council held at Philadelphia, May 14th, 1739. Present:
The Honourable GEORGE THOMAS, Esqr., Lieutenant Governour.

Samuel Preston,	Ralph Assheton,	)
Clement Plumsted,	Samuel Hasell,	) Esqrs.
Thomas Laurence,	Thomas Griffitts,	)

[Material relating first to "Proprietary Quitrents."]
The Petition of the Germans was considered, and the following
Message sent to the Assembly:
"His Honour the Governour in Council to the Gentlemen of the
                          Assembly.
"Gentlemen:
"Upon Application made to me on behalf of several Germans, Inhabitants of this Province, that they may enjoy the Rights and Privi-
leges of English Subjects, and for that end praying to be naturalized, I have made enquiry, and find that those whose Names are
mentioned in a Petition now laid before your House, have regularly
taken up Lands from the Proprietors; that they have taken the Oaths
or Affirmations enjoyned by Law, and have peaceably demeaned themselves since their coming into this Government. From these Con-
siderations, I am willing to join with your House in passing a Bill
for their Naturalization.
                    "GEORGE THOMAS."

———

Fritz Braun and Friedrich Krebs. "Pennsylvania Dutch Pioneers from
    South Palatine Parishes," *The Pennsylvania Dutchman*, 8 (Spring
    1957), 39-42 [Lancour No. 139].

The following translation of an article published originally in
Germany was made by Don Yoder.

The number of Palatine church-registers with annotations on 18th
century emigrants, is small. The following list is comprised of
emigrants from villages in the southern part of the Palatinate:
Bellheim, Freimersheim, Freisbach, Gommersheim, Minfeld, Niederlustadt, Oberlustadt, Otterheim, Weingarten, Westheim, and Zeiskam.
[Readers should note that a few of the emigrants in this list from
Minfeld were mentioned in Friedrich Krebs and Milton Rubincam, *Emigrants from the Palatinate to the American Colonies in the 18th
Century* (Norristown, Pennsylvania: The Pennsylvania German Soci-

ety, 1953); and several emigrants from Minfeld, Niederlustadt, Oberlustadt, Ottersheim, Weingarten, Westheim, and Zeiskam appear in Dr. Krebs' articles, "Pennsylvania Dutch Pioneers", in *The Pennsylvania Dutchman* for Spring 1956 and Summer 1956. In each case fuller information is given in the present article. Emigrants from Ottersheim are completely omitted in the translation because they have been covered completely in the *Dutchman*.]

The sources of the references to emigration are the Lutheran church-registers of Freimersheim, Freisbach, Gommersheim, Minfeld, Weingarten; the Reformed church-registers of Zeiskam and Oberlustadt, the latter serving for both Oberlustadt and Niederlustadt; the *Ausfautheiakten Germersheim*; the Electoral Palatine Archives (*Akten Kurpfalz*) for Westheim; and the Archives of the Johannite Order in the Palatine State Archives in Speyer; as well as materials in the *Heimatstelle Pfalz* in Kaiserslautern.

As far as possible, the birth or baptismal and marriage dates of the emigrants, and parents' and wives' names, were added to the basic emigration data, from the church-registers. In most cases, also, it was possible to locate the emigrants in the published ship-lists of arrivals at Philadelphia, the three-volume work, *Pennsylvania German Pioneers*, by Ralph Beaver Strassburger, edited by William J. Hinke (Norristown, Pennsylvania: The Pennsylvania German Society, 1934).

A word of thanks is due Pastor Dr. Kaul, who furnished the emigration data from the Lutheran church-register of Gommersheim.

The materials on the Bauersachs family, under Weingarten, are a good example of what can be done through the cooperation of Pennsylvania and Palatine genealogists....

Bellheim

1. WILL, ISAAC—born at Bellheim, April 19, 1724, son of the Reformed schoolmaster [*Schuldiener*] *Wilhelm Will* and wife *Anna Eva Schlindwein*; "at present living on the Island of Pennsylvania at Germantown, two hours from Philadelphia" ["*dermahlen auff der Insel Pinsephania zu Germandon 2 Stund von Pilladelphia wohnhafft*"] (Inventory of Wilhelm Will, April 29, 1748).

[*Isaac Will* arrived at Philadelphia, September 30, 1743, on the Ship *Phoenix*.]

Freimersheim

2. ANDRES, GEORG MICHELL—son of the citizen *Hanss Michell Andres* (died 1711) of Freimersheim and wife *Maria Juditha Wiedtemann*; was, according to a conveyance of the widow Maria Juditha Wiedtemann dated April 18, 1733, "married, manumitted, and gone to the New Land"....

[A *Michael Anderras* arrived at Philadelphia, May 15, 1732, on the Ship *Norris*.]

3. BELERT (BOELERT), PHILIPP JACOB—born at Freimersheim, September 8, 1725, and ANNA MARGARETHA BELERT, born at Freimersheim,

March 6, 1737, children of the citizen and town-councilor [*Gemeindsmann*] *Johann Friderich Belert* of Freimersheim and his wife *Anna* nee *Müller of Freimersheim*, "both children about 10 years ago gone away to the Island of Cajenne and since then nothing more heard of them" (Inventory of Widow Anna Müller, dated February 10, 1776).

The above-mentioned *Philipp Jacob Böhlert* married *Maria Barbara Grehl*, born at Freimersheim, June 12, 1725, daughter of the citizen and master-tailor *Philipp Grehl* (died about or before 1760) at Freimersheim and his wife *Margaretha Zachelmeyer (Zagelmejer)* (died in March 1770); wife and children "journeyed to Pennsylvania after obtaining manumission"....

Children, born at Freimersheim:

1. *Eva Margaretha Belert*, born November 14, 1753.
2. *Johann Christoph Belert*, born February 7, 1755.
3. *Johann Michael Belert*, born September 17, 1757.
4. *Johann Adam Belert*, born January 9, 1760.

Freisbach

4. KERN, JOHANN THOMAS—born at Freisbach September 19, 1700, son of *Peter Kern* of Freisbach; married at Friesbach, February 17, 1733, to *(Anna) Maria Margaretha Jopp*, daughter of Michel Jopp of Ottersheim; "went to Pennsylvania."

Children born at Freisbach:

1. *Anna Elisabeth Kern*, born November 20, 1733; "in Pennsylvania."
2. *Johann Christoph Kern*, born January 25, 1736; "in Pennsylvania."

[*Johann Thomas Kern*, aged 36, arrived at Philadelphia, August 30, 1737, on the Ship *Samuel*. The family settled in Lancaster County, Pennsylvania.]

5. KERN, JOHANN JOST—born at Freisbach, 1746, is buried in the old graveyard of Hassinger's Church, between Middleburg and Paxtonville, Snyder County, Pennsylvania. In this cemetery many emigrants from the Upper Rhine country found their last resting place. On the tombstone of John Jost Kern his birthplace is given as "Freischbach, Germany" (i.e., Freisbach, Kreis Germersheim). Also members of the *Bauersachs* family (spelled *Bowersox*) are buried there. See Aaron Gern Gift, "The Hassinger Church," in *The Pennsylvania-German*, September, 1908.

[*Jost Kern* arrived at Philadelphia, October 13, 1766, on the Ship *Betsy*.]

One *Johann Justus Kern* was born at Freisbach, February 20, 1741, son of *Philipp Jacob Kern* and wife *Sophie Margarethe*. Since in the period concerned the Lutheran Church Register of Freisbach contains only the birth of this Johann Justus Kern, he may be identical with the emigrant.

6. MUENCH, JOHANN PETER—married at Freisbach, September 19, 1724, to *Maria Christina Oster*, daughter of *Leonard Oster*. Cf.

below his brother, *Johann Simon Münch*, under Gommersheim.
Children, born at Freisbach:
1. *Philipp Simon Munch*, born August 25, 1728; "in Pennsylvania."
2. *Johann Peter Münch*, born January 13, 1730; in the Church Register there is no reference to his emigration and no death entry.
3. *Johann Georg Münch*, born September 27, 1731; "in Pennsylvania."
4. *Jacob Peter Münch*, born June 28, 1733; "in Pennsylvania."
[*Peter Minech*, aged 39, arrived at Philadelphia, August 30, 1737, on the Ship *Samuel*.]

Gommersheim
7. BERRY, ISAAK—shoemaker, died at Gommersheim, July 24, 1733; married at Gommersheim, February 4, 1723 to *Anna Elisabeth Schwartz*, born at Speyer in 1703, daughter of the cartwright *Wendel Schwartz* and wife *Maria Francisca*.
Children, born at Gommersheim:
1. *Eva Christina Berry*, born August 5, 1724; "in America."
2. *Anna Eva Berry*, born November 7, 1725; "in Georgia."
3. *Maria Barbara Berry*, born January 8, 1728; died at Gommersheim.
4. *Johann Ludwig Berry*, born December 24, 1729; "in Pennsylvania."
5. *Anna Margaretha Berry*, born March 27, 1732; "in Pennsylvania."
8. WALTHER, NICOLAUS—married at Gommersheim, February 21, 1735, to *Anna Elisabeth Schwartz*, widow of the above-mentioned *Isaak Berry*, born at Speyer 1703.
Children, born at Gommersheim:
1. *Anna Apollonia Walther*, born February 5, 1736; died at Gommersheim.
[*Nicholas Walter (Waller)*, aged 41, arrived at Philadelphia, September 5, 1738, on the Ship *Winter Galley*.]
The stepchildren (cf. *Isaak Berry*, above) would have emigrated with this couple.
9. BEYER (BAYER), JOHANN NIKOLAUS—born June, 1677, son of the Magistrate [*Gerichtsmann*] *Christoph Beyer* and wife *Kunigunde*; married *Maria Elisabeth [——]*; "in Pennsylvania."
Children, born at Gommersheim:
1. *Clara Elisabeth Beyer*, born September 19, 1726; "in America."
2. *Georg Jakob Beyer*, born December 12, 1729; "in Pennsylvania."
3. *Maria Magdalena Beyer*, born February 1, 1732; "in Pennsylvania."
4. *Johann Wendell Beyer*, born May 30, 1734; "in Pennsylvania."
5. *Anna Barbara Beyer*, born January 27 1739; "in Penn[a]."

10. BEYER, JOHANN ANDREAS—born December, 1681, brother of the preceding, married *Anna Apollonia [———]*; "in Pennsylvania."
Children, born at Gommersheim:
1. *Thomas Beyer*, born December 18, 1713.
2. *Johann Philipp Beyer*, born February 29, 1717.
3. *Johann Martin Beyer*, born June 23, 1720; "in Pennsylvania."
4. *Eva Elisabeth Beyer*, born September 27, 1725; "in Pennsylvania."

[*Andres Beyer (Beier, Beir, Bayer)*, aged 57, *Johann Philip Bayer* and *Martin Beyer*, aged 18, arrived at Philadelphia, September 5, 1738, on the Ship *Winter Galley*. In the ship-list there is also listed another *Johann Philipp Bayer*.]

11. GIESLER, JOHANN ADAM—married at Gommersheim, May 6, 1732, to *Maria Magdalena Rothmayer*, daughter of *Johannes Rothmayer*.
Children, born at Gommersheim:
1. *Maria Christina Giesler*, born June 23, 1733; "in Pennsylvania."
2. *Johann Michel Giesler*, born February 27, 1737; "in Pennsylvania."
3. *Anna Catharina Giesler*, born February 23, 1739; "in Pennsylvania."

[*Hans Adam Gissler (Geizler, Gesler)* arrived at Philadelphia, September 11, 1738, on the Ship *Robert and Alice*. Perhaps this was the above-mentioned, who could have emigrated alone, letting wife and children follow later.]

12. HOCHLAENDER, JOHANN MICHAEL—cowherd, married *Juliana [———]*; "in Pennsylvania."
Children, born at Gommersheim:
1. *Johann Adam Hochländer*, born 1735, died at Gommersheim, January 25, 1738; Catholic.
2. *Johannes Hochländer*, born August 14, 1737; "with the father in Pennsylvania."

[*Hans Michael Hochlander (Hoglander, Slotsunder)*, aged 32, arrived at Philadelphia, September 5, 1738, on the Ship *Winter Galley*.]

13. KRIEG, MARGARETHA DOROTHEA—born at Gommersheim, April 12, 1730, confirmed at Gommersheim 1745, daughter of *Johann Philipp Krieg*, cooper, and wife *Anna Barbara*; "in Pennsylvania."

14. MUENCH, JOHANN SIMON—weaver, son of the weaver *Johann Philipp Münch*, married at Gommersheim, August 17, 1728, to *(Anna) Maria Katharina Schenk*, daughter of the weaver *Johann Jacob Schenk*; "with children in Pennsylvania." Cf. above, *Johann Peter Münch*, under Freisbach.
Children, born at Gommersheim:
1. *Maria Barbara Münch*, born November 21, 1729; died at Gommersheim, March 17, 1736.
2. *Maria Catharina Münch*, born March 20, 1731; "in Pennsylvania."
3. *Johann Nikolaus Münch*, born June 22, 1732; "in Penn[a]."

4. *Johann Christoph Münch*, born June 6, 1734; "in Pennsylvania."

5. *Maria Apollonia Münch*, born February 26, 1736; "in Pennsylvania."

[*Simon Minech*, aged 35, arrived at Philadelphia, August 30, 1737, on the Ship *Samuel*.]

John Simon Minich is buried at the Bernville Cemetery in Berks County, Pennsylvania. According to his tombstone he was born July 21, 1700, and died February 17, 1782; his wife Catharina was born in January, 1700, and died December 12, 1773. In the church-register of Gommersheim there are no birth-dates given for either the emigrant or his wife. In America the name is spelled Minnig, Muench, and Minnich. See Tombstone Inscriptions, Bernville, Pa., in *The Penn Germania*, 1913.

15. ROMETSCH, JOHANN CASPAR—born at Gommersheim, July 6, 1728 (after the death of his father), son of *Caspar Rometsch* (died at Gommersheim, May 22, 1728) and wife *Anna Margaretha*; "in Pennsylvania."

[*Johann Caspar Rometsch (Rumetsch)*, aged 24, arrived at Philadelphia, September 24, 1753, on the Ship *Peggy*.]

16. SCHOPPING, ANNA BARBARA—born at Gommersheim, October 1705, daughter of the potter *Johann Adam Schopping* (died at Gommersheim, January 18, 1746, aged 72) and wife *Magdalena*; "went to Pennsylvania."

17. SCHREINER, JOHANN ADAM—born *circa* 1682, married *Anna Margaretha [———]*.

Children, born at Gommersheim:

1. *Johann Michael Schreiner*, born 1708; no reference to emigration in the Church Register.

2. *Martin Schreiner*, born January 3, 1716; no reference to emigration in the Church Register.

3. *Anna Maria Schreiner*, born December 7, 1718; died at Gommersheim, July 5, 1727.

4. *Johann Philipp Schreiner*, born September 9, 1721; "in Pennsylvania."

5. *Johann Georg Heinrich Schreiner*, born July 12, 1724; "in America."

6. *Johann Valentin Schreiner*, born December 16, 1728; "in Pennsylvania."

[*Hans Adam Schreiner (Schreyner)*, aged 52, *Johann Michael Schreiner*, aged 28, and *Martin Schreiner*, aged 20, arrived at Philadelphia, September 5, 1738, on the Ship *Winter Galley*.]

18. WALTER, JOHANN JAKOB—born at Gommersheim, January 15, 1729, son of *Johann Jakob Walther* and wife *Anna Maria Krieg*; "in Pennsylvania."

[*Johann Jacob Walther (Walter, Walder)*, aged 25, arrived at Philadelphia, September 24, 1753, on the Ship *Peggy*. Immediately before Johann Jacob in the same list appears the name of a *Johannes (Hans) Walter*, aged 35.]

19. WINGERTER, JOHANN DANIEL—citizen and butcher, son of *David Wingerter* from Kleinfischlingen; married at Gommersheim, August 18,

1733, to *Anna Maria Schreiner*, daughter of *Johann Friedrich Schreiner*.

Children, born at Gommersheim:
1. *Anna Barbara Wingerter*, born June 29, 1734; "in Pennsylvania."
2. *Johann Jakob Wingerter*, born August 20, 1736; "in Pennsylvania."
3. *Anna Margaretha Wingerter*, born March 8, 1738; "in Pennsylvania."
4. *Maria Christina Wingerter*, born September 24, 1740; "in Pennsylvania."

MINFELD

20. BOUQUET (BOCKE), MATHEUS—baptized at Minfeld, September 21, 1727, son of the citizen *Abraham Bocke* and his wife *Elisabeth*, single, emigrated to American presumably with his sisters and his brother-in-law (Document dated February 26, 1762). Cf. below, his brother-in-law, *Hanss Georg Hoffman*.

21. BOUQUET (BOCKE), RACHELL (RAHEL)—baptized at Minfeld, October 11, 1722, sister of the preceding, emigrated as single woman to America (*"West Indien"*) (Document of February 26, 1762).

22. DAUB, NISKLAUS—went to the New Land in 1752. Presumably he is identical with *Nicklaus Daub*, son of *Ludwig Daub*, married at Minfeld, February 7, 1741, to *Anna Maria König*, baptized at Minfeld, July 31, 1718, daughter of *Frantz König* and wife *Rahel*.

23. FOSSELMANN, HANSS ERHARD—baptized at Minfeld, September 25, 1701, son of *Ludwig Fosselman* in Minfeld and wife *Maria Margaretha Schäffer*; married at Minfeld, August 23, 1729, to *Elisabetha Margaretha Probst*, daughter of *Christoph Probst*; emigrated thirty years ago to the New Land (Document dated 1762). Cf. brother-in-law, *Johannes Kauffmann*.

24. GROSS, GEORG MICHAEL—baptized at Minfeld, December 3, 1719, son of *Frantz Gross* in Minfeld and wife *Susanna* nee *Schäffer*; emigrated as single man about 1751 to the New Land.

25. GROSS, ANNA MARIA—baptized at Minfeld, August 27, 1727, sister of the preceding; emigrated to the New Land about 1751.

26. HAEN (HAEHN), (JOHANN) JACOB—widower, married at Minfeld, July 2, 1749, in the parsonage there "on account of great poverty" [*"Wegen grosser Armuth"*], to *Anna Barbara Egert*, widow of *Peter Egert*, deceased farmer (*Hoffmann*) on the Rinkenbergerhof.

27. HEINTZ, MICHAEL—emigrated from Minfeld to America in 1753. Possibly he is identical with *Johann Michael Heintz*, son of *Johann Michael Heintz*, former citizen at Frechenfeld, and wife; married at Minfeld, February 11, 1749, to *Johanna Ulm*, baptized at Minfeld April 18, 1728, daughter of *Johann Michael Ullm*, citizen at Minfeld, and wife *Anna Barbara* nee *Dudenhöfer*.

28. HEINTZ, WENDELL—son of *Michael Heintz* (died 1752), citizen at Freckenfeld, and wife; married at Minfeld, October 30, 1752, to *Eva Barbara Gross*, daughter of *Frantz Gross* and wife *Susanna* nee

Schäffer; went to the New Land in 1767.
[*Wendel Heintz* arrived at Philadelphia, October 6, 1767, on the
Ship *Hamilton*.]
   29. HOFFMAN, HANSS GEORG—son of *Lorentz Hoffman* (died 1749),
former citizen at Rohrbach, and wife; married at Minfeld, April 8,
1749, to *Rosina (Barbara) Bouquet (Bocke)*, baptized at Minfeld,
January 20, 1726, daughter of the citizen *Abraham Bouquet* and wife
Elisabetha; emigrated to America presumably with his brother-in-law
and sister-in-law to America (Document of February 26, 1762). Cf.
above, his brother-in-law, *Matheus Bouquet*.
   30. KAUFFMANN, JOHANNES—mason, baptized at Minfeld, April 23,
1696, son of *Matheus Kauffmann*, shoemaker at Minfeld, and wife
Juliana; married at Minfeld, August 24, 1723, to *Maria Elisabetha
Fosselmann*, baptized at Minfeld, May 25, 1704, daughter of *(Johann)
Ludwig Fosselmann* in Minfeld and wife *Maria Margaretha Schaeffer*;
went about 1750 to Zweibrücken and about 1765 emigrated from Guten-
brunnen (Kreis St. Ingbert) to America. Cf. brother-in-law, *Hans
Erhard Fosselmann*.
   Children, born at Minfeld:
      1. *Catharina Elisabetha Kauffmann*, baptized July 9, 1724.
      2. *Maria Margaretha Kauffmann*, baptized April 20, 1727.
      3. *Johann Jakob Kauffmann*, baptized December 24, 1730.
      4. *Johannes Kauffmann*, baptized December 7, 1732.
      5. *Johann Georg Kauffmann*, baptized September 5, 1734.
      6. *Maria Apollonia Kauffmann*, baptized April 18, 1737.
      7. *Anna Maria Kauffmann*, baptized November 30, 1738.
      8. *Johanna Kauffmann*, baptized September 24, 1740.
      9. *Anna Apollonia Kauffmann*, baptized September 12, 1742.
   [*Johannes Kauffman* arrived at Philadelphia, October 1, 1754, on
the Ship *Phoenix*. With him on the same ship-list is named *Johannes
Kauffman, Jr.*]
   31. KOENIG, ABRAHAM—baptized at Minfeld, April 2, 1724, son of
Frantz König and wife *Rahel*, married at Minfeld, January 7, 1751,
to *Maria Magdalena Kauffmann*, baptized at Minfeld, March 12, 1730,
daughter of the citizen and linen-weaver *Christoph Kauffmann*.
   32. KOENIG, ANNA MARIA—baptized at Minfeld, July 31, 1718, sister of the preceding; married at Minfeld, February 7, 1741, to
Nicklaus Daub; emigrated to the New Land about 1752. Cf. above,
Nicklaus Daub.
   33. OTH (OTT), NICLAUS—son of *Johann Michael Ott*; married
January 30, 1725, to *Maria Margaretha Fosselmann (Vosselmann)*,
baptized at Minfeld, February 7, 1706, daughter of *Ludwig Vosselmann* and wife *Maria Margaretha*; emigrated about 1754 to New England
or America.
   [A *Johann Nickolaus Ott* arrived at Philadelphia, November 2,
1752, on the Ship *Phoenix*.]

NIEDERLUSTADT
   34. OTT, JOHANN ANDREAS—born at Niederlustadt, September 20,

1728, son of *Johann Georg Ott* and wife *Catharina Groh*; "already
gone to the New Land ten years ago" [*"vor zehen Jahren allschon in
das neue Land gezogen"*] (Document of June 20, 1760). The emigration must have taken place around 1750.
[An *Andreas Ott* arrived at Philadelphia, September 22, 1752, on
the Ship *Brothers*.]
    35. ROCH, JOHANN PETER—born at Niederlustadt, August 24, 1724,
son of *Peter Roch*, citizen and farrier at Niederlustadt, and wife
Maria (Anna) Barbara Stadler; married *Margaretha Lutz*. See *The
Dutchman*, Spring 1956, p. 39.

OBERLUSTADT

    36. FAUTH, JOHANN JACOB—born at Oberlustadt, September 7, 1738,
son of *Bernhard Fauth* (Church Register: *Fäth*), and wife *Katherine
Haf*, "went away to America about 18 years ago" (Document of March
18, 1783); married *Louisa Theiss*, born at Oberlustadt, December 24,
1741, daughter of *Johann Adam Theiss* of Oberlustadt and wife *Magdalena Schmitt*, "who married *Jacob Fauth* from here and likewise went
to Pennsylvania" [*"welche ahn Jacob Fauth von dahier verheurathet
und ebenfalls in Pennsilvanien gezogen"*] (Document of December 3,
1765). Cf. also his brother-in-law, *Georg Jakob Heintz*.
[*Jacob Faut* arrived at Philadelphia, August 24, 1765, on the Ship
Polly.]
    37. HAUSHALTER, GEORG SIMON—arrived in Philadelphia on the Ship
Polly, August 24, 1765, with the brothers *Christian* and *Johann
Jakob Wunder* as well as *Johann Jacob Fauth*. Since he wrote his
name immediately after Fauth in the ship's list and the name Haushalter appears in Ober- and Niederlustadt in the period involved,
we may assume that the emigrant is connected with the Haushalter
family listed in the Church Register of Oberlustadt. The only
point of uncertainty is whether the father *Jörg Simon Haushalter*
emigrated with the family or whether the son *Jörg Simon Haushalter*
emigrated alone.
Jörg Simon Haushalter, resident in Ober- or Niederlustadt, married *Anna Maria [———]*, and had the following children, born at
Ober- or Niederlustadt:
    1. *Jörg Simon Haushalter*, born March 20, 1741.
    2. *Christian Haushalter*, born December 3, 1743.
    3. *Eva Maria Haushalter*, born September 5, 1746; died September
        29, 1746.
    4. *Maria Eva Haushalter*, born October 27, 1749.
    5. *Anna Margaretha Haushalter*, born March 1, 1753.
    6. *Johann Jörg Haushalter*, born September 28, 1757.
[*Georg Simon Haushalter* arrived at Philadelphia, August 24, 1765,
on the Ship *Polly*.]
    38. HEINTZ, GEORG JAKOB—from Rhodt unter Rietburg, married
Maria Catharina Theiss, born at Oberlustadt, February 20, 1736,
daughter of *Johann Adam Theiss* of Oberlustadt and Magdalena
Schmitt, "who married Georg Jakob Heintz from Roth and went with

him to Pennsylvania..." (Document of December 3, 1765). Cf. above,
his brother-in-law, *Johann Jakob Fauth.*

39. HOFFMANN, DANIEL—born at Oberlustadt, February 17, 1727,
son of *Johann Jacob Hoffmann* and wife *Susanna Christina Brückner;*
"who went to the New Land" (Document of August 30, 1758).

40. HORTER, GEORG ADAM—born at Oberlustadt, May 27, 1738, son
of *Jacob Horter* and wife *(Maria) Agnes Sohland,* "already gone to
Pennsylvania 12 years ago" (Document of April 20, 1768). The emigration must therefore have taken place around 1756.

41. HORTER, ANNA BARBARA—married before 1733 to *Georg Horter,*
citizen and town councilor at Oberlustadt; died before 1764.
"Whereas *Barbara Horter,* widow and relict of *Georg Horter,* deceased
citizen and at Oberlustadt, went from here about one year ago to
the so-called New England with her son *Velten Horter,* also a son of
hers named *Georg Jacob Horter* had gone there several years previously, so then both brothers and sisters and in-laws of hers still
residing here, namely *Jacob Wunder* and his wife *Anna Maria,* and
Jacob Sager, sent a manuscript letter asking her therein, since one
of them had the desire to go to the above-mentioned New Land, if he
should sell or convert into money the inheritance still coming to
her here and bring it to her. Now since *Jakob Wunder* and his wife
Anna Maria have likewise resolved to go to their respective mother
and brothers and sisters and therefore have petitioned for permission, to convert into cash the properties of their inlaws still
coming to them and take them to them," hence a complete inventory
of the properties of *Georg Jakob* and *Velten Horter* was drawn up and
the results of the sale given to the brother-in-law, *Jacob Wunder,*
who emigrated in 1765 (Document of April 19, 1765).
Children, born in Oberlustadt:

1. *Anna Maria Horter,* born July 21, 1729, married *Johann Jacob
     Wunder* (q.v.).
2. *Georg Jacob Horter,* born July 9, 1733.
3. *Johann Valentin Horter,* born September 16, 1740.
[*Johann Valtin Horter* arrived at Philadelphia, September 26,
1764, on the Ship *Britannia.*]

42. JAHRAUS, GEORG ADAM—born at Oberlustadt, December 27, 1746,
son of *Andreas Jahraus* and wife *(Anna) Margaretha Schmid;* "who
resides in America" (Document of October 30, 1786).

43. SCHMITT, ANNA ELISABETHA—daughter of *Andres Schmitt* of
Oberlustadt and wife *Catharina Jahraus,* "wife of *Friedrich Doll,*
inhabitant of Pennsylvania" (Document of March 30, 1770).

44. SIGRIST, ANNA APOLLONIA—born at Oberlustadt, February 1,
1723, daughter of *Martin Sigrist (Siegerist)* and wife *Catharina
Böhm;* "already gone to Pennsylvania 21 years ago..." (Document of
October 3, 1765). She must therefore have emigrated around 1744.

45. TEIS, GEORG ADAM—arrived at Philadelphia with *Georg
Simon Haushalter* (q.v.) on the Ship *Polly,* August 24, 1765, and his
name is given in the ship's list immediately after Haushalter's.
Perhaps he is identical with *Jörg Adam Theiss,* born at Ober- or

Niederlustadt, February 9, 1739, son of *Andreas Theiss* and wife
Magdalena.

46. WUNDER, JOHANN JAKOB—born at Oberlustadt, January 13, 1727,
son of *Sebastian Wunder* and wife *Anna Maria*; married *Anna Maria
Horter*, born at Oberlustadt, July 21, 1729, daughter of *Georg Horter* and wife *Anna Barbara*. Cf. *Anna Barbara Horter*, above.
   Children, born at Oberlustadt:
   1. *Jörg Adam Wunder*, born January 7, 1753.
   2. *Anna Maria Wunder*, born August 22, 1755.
   3. *Valentin Wunder*, born April 1, 1758.
   4. *Maria Barbara Wunder*, born October 21, 1760.
   5. *Christoph Wunder*, born January 5, 1764.
[*Jacob Wunder* arrived at Philadelphia, August 24, 1765, on the
Ship *Polly*.]

47. WUNDER, CHRISTIAN—born at Oberlustadt, July 13, 1729, brother of the preceding, married *Catharina* [———].
   Children, born at Nieder- or Oberlustadt:
   1. *Maria Eva Wunder*, born April 16, 1757.
   2. *Andreas Wunder*, born October 18, 1751; died February 4,
       1763 [should birth read 1761?].
   3. *Andreas Wunder*, born December 27, 1763.
[*Christian Wunder* arrived at Philadelphia, August 24, 1765, on
the Ship *Polly*.]

WEINGARTEN

48. BAUERSACHS, PAUL—born at Weingarten, September 29, 1744,
son of *Johann David Bauersachs* and wife *Anna Maria Damian* of Böbingen, settled as citizen at Freisbach and from there went to
America (Document of August 5, 1784).
[*Paulus Bauersachs* arrived at Philadelphia, December 4, 1771, on
the Ship *Betsey*.]

The name *Bauersachs* (also spelled *Bauersax* in the Church Register
of Weingarten) is spelled *Bowersox* in America. *Paul Bowersox* died
March 8, 1806, in Center Township, now Snyder County, Pennsylvania,
and is buried at the Hassinger Church Cemetery near Middleburg in
Snyder County (cf. above, *Johann Jost Kern* of Freisbach). According to family tradition in Pennsylvania he had come to America
before 1771, returned to Germany on a visit, and returned to Pennsylvania in 1771. For the children of Paul Bowersox, born in Pennsylvania, see Dr. Charles A. Fisher, *Early Pennsylvania Births*; see
also Aaron Kern Gift, "The Hassinger Church," *The Pennsylvania German*, September 1908. Further information on the family can be had
from the Reverend George E. Bowersox of McSherrystown, Pennsylvania.

49. BAUERSACHS, HANS NICKEL ("NICHEL")—arrived at Philadelphia,
August 15, 1750, on the Ship *Royal Union*. It is probable that this
emigrant belongs to the same family as the above *Paul Bauersachs*.
However, there is in the Church Register of Weingarten no reference
to the emigration of Hans Nickel Bauersachs, nor is his baptism

recorded. Information from Pastor George E. Bowersox, McSherrystown Pennsylvania, has cleared up the mystery:
  Hans Nichol Bauersachs, son of the butcher *Johann Bauersachs* and
wife *Elisabetha "Itsgrund"* (cf. below), was, according to an entry
by Pastor H. M. Mühlenberg in the Old Goshenhoppen Church Register
in Pennsylvania, born November 14, 1702, in "Memelsdorf" and baptized there November 15, 1702. His trade was given as "tailor".
According to the same entry he went in the year 1727 to "Neider...
stadt, 3 hours from Speyer", i.e., Niederlustadt, married there
Maria Elisabetha Gothe, daughter of *Velten Gothe* and wife *Eva
Elisabeth*, and emigrated in 1750 with wife and children to Pennsylvania.
  Children, born at Oberstadt [*sic*] before the emigration:
     1. *Maria Elisabeth Bauersachs*, born April 9, 1735; died before
         1750.
     2. *Maria Barbara Bauersachs*, born August 3, 1738; died June
         9, 1740.
     3. *Johann Valentin Bauersachs*, born July 7, 1741; confirmed at
         Old Goshenhoppen; married December 27, 1764, to *Barbara
         [——]*.
     4. *Jörg Adam Bauersachs*, born February 26, 1744; confirmed at
         Old Goshenhoppen; married *Magdalena Rauenzaner (Routzan)*.
  Both sons served in the Revolutionary War, and after their
release from service settled in Frederick County, Maryland.
References to both families appear in the records of St. David's
Lutheran Church near Hanover, Pennsylvania, on the Maryland border.
The family of *Georg Adam Bowersox* is later named in the records of
St. Mary's Lutheran Church, Silver Run, Maryland, where members of
the family are buried. His own gravestone and that of his wife and
his son Christian are at Uniontown, Maryland. *Georg Adam Bowersox*
took the oath of citizenship to Maryland on June 19, 1779.
  An inquiry to Memmelsdorf, Oberfranken, revealed that the name
Bauersachs never appeared in the records there. In Memmelsdorf
near Ebern in Unterfranken the relationship was proved through the
researches of Pastor Löblein, from the Lutheran Church Register
there: *Johann (Hans) Bauersachs*, widower, married at Memmelsdorf,
November 22, 1698, to *Anna Elisabetha Köhler* of Memmelsdorf. Their
children, born at Memmelsdorf, included 1. *Johannes Bauersachs*,
baptized August 3, 1699; and 2. *Johann Nikolaus Bauersachs*, baptized November 3, 1700.
  Striking is the difference between the birth and baptismal dates
in the Memmelsdorf and Goshenhoppen entries. But we must realize
that the entry in Goshenhoppen was not made by Pastor Mühlenberg
until after 1750. In Memmelsdorf for the period concerned there is
no other entry to be found.
  "Itsgrund": This word appears in the Goshenhoppen Church Register in connection with the reference to the parents of *Johann Nickel Bauersachs*, after the first name of the mother. Undoubtedly it
is a place name, since the Itz, coming from Coburg, flows through

the Memmelsdorf area and into the Main.

Through the entry in the Old Goshenhoppen Church Register in Pennsylvania we have learned where the Bauersachs Family of the Palatinate originated, and that *Johann Nickel Bauersachs* emigrated in 1750 from Niederlustadt to Pennsylvania.

Johannes Bauersachs, baptized at Memmelsdorf August 3, 1699, must likewise have settled in the Palatinate, for in the Lutheran Church Register of Weingarten, on June 9, 1716, is recorded his marriage to *Anna Maria Hubin*, native of Offenbach, single, and on November 27, 1718, the birth of the son *Hans David Bauersachs*, who married (1st) at Weingarten, February 9, 1740, *Anna Maria Damian* from Böbingen and after her death married (2nd) at Weingarten, January 25, 1757, to *Anna Maria Luber (Luwer)* from Oberlustadt. *Johannes Bauersachs* was therefore the grandfather of the emigrant *Paul(us) Bauersachs* and a brother of the emigrant *Johann Nikolaus Bauersachs*.

50. BRUNNEMER, JOHANN PETER—born at Weingarten, April 28, 1726, son of *Johannes Brunnemer* and wife *Anna Margaretha*, had "already gone away to Pennsylvania 18 years ago, without receiving permission..." (Document of March 7, 1767). According to a Power of Attorney drawn up in Augusta County, Virginia, August 15, 1766, Johann Peter Brunnemer was residing there at the time.

51. KLINGLER, THEOBALD—born about 1714, married at Weingarten, November 26, 1737, to *Maria Catharina Gölbert*, daughter of the citizen and town-councilor *Henrich Gelberth (Gölbert)* (died about 1717) at Freimersheim and his wife *Anna Rosina Geiss*; according to a transfer of property of the widow *Anna Rosina Geiss*, dated April 19, 1746, "went to the New Land seven years ago."

[*Debalt Klingler*, age .24, arrived at Philadelphia September 20, 1738, on the Ship *Friendship*.]

WESTHEIM

52. BATTEIGER, JOHANN VALENTIN—born at Westheim, August 27, 1739, son of *Johann Peter Batteiger* and wife *Anna Eva* (in the acts *Maria Eva*); "Valentin 35 years old and absent in America" (Document of May 3, 1777).

[*Johann Valentin Batteiger* arrived at Philadelphia, October 29, 1767, on the Ship *Minerva*.]

53. SCHWAB, GEORG ADAM—born at Westheim, April 26, 1745, son of *Andreas Schwab* and wife *Rosina Barbara*; "resident in Pennsylvania" (Document of March 27, 1765).

ZEISKAM

54. GEISS, PHILIPP JACOB—farrier, born at Freisbach, April 12, 1712, son of *Henrich Geiss*, citizen and town-councilor of Freisbach, and wife *Anna Catharina*; married at Zeiskam and settled there as farrier and citizen. According to an official document of November 9, 1763, they had already gone 12 years ago to America, in the Province of Pennsylvania.... For additional information, see

Pennsylvania Dutchman, Summer 1956, page 58.

55. SCHMITT, LORENZ—citizen, surgeon and barber at Billigheim, baptized at Billigheim, January 31, 1722, son of *Matthes Schmitt*, citizen and town-councilor at Billigheim, and wife *Anna Maria Heckman*; married at Zeiskam, May, 1748, to *Maria Helena (Magdalena) Guth*, daughter of *Johannes Guth* of Zeiskam. After his marriage he moved his residence to Zeiskam. According to the Germersheim records, Lorentz Schmitt's wife, because she wanted to go to the New Land with her husband and her two small sons, had her inheritance paid back in 1751. In an official document of February 4, 1757, it is said of *Helena Schmitt* nee *Guth*, that she "went away to America about 6 years ago". The wife of Lorentz Schmitt appears as Maria Magdalena and as Maria Helena. In the Baptismal Register of Zeiskam is found only the baptism of a Maria Magdalena. At the marriage entry "Magdalena" is stricken out and "Helena" written above. At the entry of the birth of the first child the mother appears as "Maria Magdalena," at the second child's birth as "Maria Helena." For the children see *Pennsylvania Dutchman*, Summer 1956, page 59.

56. SINN (SIEN), SAMUEL—master-baker at Zeiskam, baptized at Zeiskam, August 28, 1710, son of *Johann Peter Sinn*, master-baker at Zeiskam, and wife *Anna Agatha*. For additional details, see *Pennsylvania Dutchman*, Summer 1956, page 59.

57. ZWICKER, JOHANN PETER—citizen and town-councilor at Zeiskam, baptized at Zeiskam, December 21, 1710, son of *Samuel Zwicker* and wife *Susanna Barbara*. For additional details, see *Pennsylvania Dutchman*, Summer 1956, page 59.

It should be noted that the above is not copied absolutely faithfully in every way according to the high standards of scholarship one should expect, simply because the original contained several typographical errors which needed to be corrected. These included omissions of opening or closing quotation marks, misplaced commas, and, on the pages dealing with Oberlustadt, giving the name of Johann Jakob Wunder as such, instead of last name first, as the names were given in every other case. Nonetheless, some errors, such as the phrase, "to American," were retained, with the thought that this *might* have been translated from the original.

————

Friedrich Krebs. "Zur Frühauswanderung aus dem Kurpfälzischen Oberamt Heidelberg nach Amerika (1726-27)," *Südwestdeutsche Blätter für Familien- und Wappenkunde*, 10 (1958), 512 [Lancour No. 140].

The contents of this article have been published in English by Friedrich Krebs in Lancour No. 141, below.

————

Friedrich Krebs. "Annotations to Strassburger and Hinke's Pennsylvania German Pioneers," *The Pennsylvania Genealogical Magazine*,
21 (1960), 235-248 [Lancour No. 141].

Editor's note—.... The following article is a composite of
seven articles published in German genealogical magazines which the
author has sent us for translation and publication. R. D. O.

I

Early Emigration from the County of Heidelberg, in the Electoral
Palatinate, to America 1726-27.

Records deposited in the State Archives at Karlsruhe contain the
following items:

1726-27

Permits to emigrate granted to

Jacob Kiessinger—A poor resident of Sandhofen—to migrate to "the
Island of Pennsylvania."

———— Brecht, widow of Johann Brecht, and her two sons Stephan and
Johann from the village of Schriesheim.

Michel Wedel, a resident of Dossenheim.

Daniel Le Vent, a resident of Hockenheim.

Michel Diel, a citizen of Mannheim-Seckenheim, upon payment of 36
florins, 55 kreuzers.

Michel Boettle (Bettle), citizen of Mannheim-Seckenheim, upon payment of 27 florins, 48 kreuzers, "to the new country." Diel and
Boettle arrived in Philadelphia on the *William and Sarah* and took
the oath of allegiance 21 Sept. 1727.

Johann Jacob Cunz, resident of Walldorf, to "the island of Pennsylvania;" arrived on the *William and Sarah*, took the oath of allegiance 21 Sept. 1727.

Christian Müller, resident of Walldorf, "to the island of Pennsylvania."—identical with either: Christyan Miller, arriving on
the ship *Molly*, oath of allegiance 30 Sept. 1727, or Christian
Miller, arriving on the ship *James Goodwill*, oath of allegiance
27 Sept. 1727.

Johann Alexander Diebendoerfer, resident of Schriesheim; arrived on
the *William and Sarah*, oath of allegiance 21 Sept. 1727.

Anna Marie Will, resident of Schriesheim.

Jacob Mueller, resident of Mannheim-Neckarau.

Andreas Zimmermann, resident of Meckesheim.

Johann Andreas Hill, resident of Mannheim-Sandhofen.

Christoph Walther, resident of Dossenheim, undoubtedly identical
with the Christopher Walther who arrive on the ship *William and
Sarah* 18 Sept. 1727.

Original article "Zur Frü-auswanderung aus dem kurpfalzischen
Oberamt Heidelberg nach Amerika (1726-27)" in *Sueddeautsche Blaet-
ter für Familien- u. Wappenkunde*, June 1958, editor, Konrad v
Alberti, Stuttgart-Sillenbach, West Germany.

II

Emigration from the County of Heidelberg 1741-1749.

The records of the county of Heidelberg on file in the General State Archives at Karlsruhe contain the following items:

1741

Valentin Zweisig (Zweissig), resident of Mauer, upon paying a fee of 3 florins, 30 kreuzers, was permitted to emigrate with his wife and four children "to the new land." "Valdin (Valentin) Zweisig" arrived in Philadelphia on the ship *Molly* 16 Oct. 1741.

Michael Müller, resident of Mauer, upon paying an emigration fee of 6 florins, was permitted to emigrate with his wife and five children. Michael Miller arrived on the ship *Molly*, 16 Oct. 1741.

Joseph Fabian, resident of Mauer...arrived...on the ship *Molly*....

Jacob Hezel, resident of Schatthausen, made application for a permit, and presumably got it, but there seems to be no record of him arriving in Philadelphia.

Jacob Mueller—a cooper from Wiesloch, with the assistance of the town authorities, received permission to emigrate.

1742

Christoph Geister (Geiser?) of Eschelbronn was released from the status of a serf so that he might emigrate. "Christof Geiser" arrived in Philadelphia 21 Sept. 1742.

Indigent brothers Michael and Dieter Danner of Walldorf were permitted to emigrate. They landed as Michael and Dietrich Danner on the ship *Robert and Alice*; took oath of allegiance 24 Sept. 1742.

1743

Caspar Hauck, resident of Helmstadt, received a permit to migrate "to the island of Pennsylvania."

Dietrich Mueller, a baker, and Jacob Hoffmann, a shoemaker, both of Zuzenhausen, were permitted to leave without paying the usual fee because of their being poor. Jacob Hoffman arrived on the ship *Rosannah*, oath of allegiance 26 Sept. 1743.

Abraham Schwann, from Schriesheim.

Hieronimus Trautmann, Johannes Trautmann, Bernhard Tuebinger (Tiebinger) [and] Georg Hoffstaetter all from Schriesheim, after paying the ten per cent tax on the possessions they were taking out with them, received permits to emigrate. "Hyronimus Trauttmann and Bernhart Duebinger" arrived in Philadelphia on the ship *St. Andrew* 7 Oct. 1743.

1744

In the year 1744 permission to emigrate was given to Johann Esaias Stein from Zuzenhausen with wife, one stepson and three stepdaughters.

Johann Adam Krehebuehl from Bammenthal with his wife and three children.

Georg Welcker from Spechbach with his wife and two children, and Conrad Lang, from Spechbach, with his wife and four children.

A group of persons from Zuzenhausen, namely Anna Maria (Regina)
Heylmann, single; Georg Kirsch and his wife and two small children; Anna Dorothea, widow of Georg Licht(n)er and her 16 yr old
son; two single men Johann Jacob Kirsch and Conrad Kirsch.
During the next few years the number of permits practically
reached the zero point.   [The War of the Austrian Succession of
1740-48 ended with the Treaty of Aix la Chapelle.——Ed.]

In 1747 there was one permit granted, namely to a young man who had
been exempted from military service, Christian Rupp, from Dauden-
zell.   He was obliged to pay his ten Pfennig tax amounting to 11
florins and an additional fee of two florins 40 kreuzers for an
emergency locker,   Christian Rupp arrived in Philadelphia on the
ship *Restauration*, oath of allegiance 9 Oct. 1747.

Veit Meister, born at Bargen, son of Georg Bernhard Meister, married at Ort Hoffenheim, near Sinsheim, in 1744, and at that time
paid 3 florins to receive a certificate of manumission.   In 1787
the government of Dilsberg published a statement that he and his
wife and children had emigrated to America in 1751 arriving in
Philadelphia on the *Shirley* 5 Sept. 1751.

Beginning 1749 the number of permits for migration to America
from the county of Heidelberg increased rapidly.

Original article "Zur Amerika-auswanderung aus dem kurpfaelzischen Oberamt Heidelberg 1741-1748" in *Zeitschrift fuer die Geschichte des Ober-rheins*, Band 106, (Der neuen Folge 67, Band) pp.
485-86.   .

III

Emigration from County of Heidelberg 1737, 1738, 1751, and 1754.

The authorities of the County of Heidelberg, Electoral Palatinate, according to records now filed in the State Archives at Karlsruhe, granted permission to a number of persons to emigrate to
America, upon payment of manumission fees.   Such a fee freed the
subject from feudal obligations to his landlord, the local petty
nobleman.

Notable is the fact that of a considerable number of persons who
received permission in 1751 relatively few can be identified in the
lists of ships' passengers arriving in Philadelphia.   There are two
probable explanations: 1. not all ships from Holland or England
came to Philadelphia;   2. some passengers died on board ship during
the voyage.

Following are some emigrants:

1737

Christian Ewig, resident of Wilhelmsfeld, upon payment of a manumission tax of 50 florins, received permission to migrate with
his wife and three children to "the island of Pennsylvania."
Arrived on the *Townshend*, took oath of allegiance Oct. 1737.

Caspar Wedel, resident of Wieblingen (modern Heidelberg-Wieblin-
gen), upon payment of a manumission tax of 9 florins 54 kreuzers,
received permission to emigrate to "the new land."

1738

Johann Georg Arnold of Zuzenhausen, district of Sinsheim, upon pay-

ment of 10 florins as a manumission fee, was granted permission
to emigrate with his wife and children, arrived Philadelphia on
the *Elisabeth* 30 Oct. 1738.

Johann Leonhard Notz, resident of Zuzenhausen, upon payment of 28
florins as a manumission fee, permitted to emigrate. "Lenhart
Notz" arrived on the ship *Two Sisters*, took oath of allegiance
Sept. 1738.

Johannes Roehrer, a resident of Mauer, district of Heidelberg, upon
payment of 10 florins as a manumission fee, permitted to emigrate
to America with his wife and children. ...(Johann Gottfried Rehrer) arrived on the ship *Robert and Alice* 11 Sept. 1738.

For the year 1751 there is an unusually large number of emigration permits:

Peter Benninger, a resident of Epfenbach, district of Sinsheim,
with wife and four children, apparently without payment of the
usual manumission fee.

Heinrich Beck, a resident of Epfenbach, district of Sinsheim, with
wife Anna Margaretha and son Johann Joerg. The latter was
required to pay 11 florins for manumission and 10 florins for un-
paid taxes.

Adam Buckle (Bickle), a schoolmaster of the Reformed Church at
Spechbach, district of Heidelberg, permitted to emigrate with his
wife and children gratis, because he was poor.

Johann Georg Ernst, a resident of Lobenfeld, district of Heidelberg, permitted to emigrate.

Beckenbach, ———, widow, a resident of Eiterbach, applied for a
permit on behalf of herself and her children. After long negoti-
ations, she paid 130 florins as a manumission fee and 177 florins
and an additional 30 florins to satisfy the ten Pfenning tax on
the value of what she took with her. "Casper Beckenbach, Georg
Adam Beckenbach, Georg Leonhardt Beckenbach," all arrived on the
ship *Janet* 7 Oct. 1751.

Elisabeth Hild, daughter of a citizen of Handschuhsheim (modern
Heidelberg—Handschuhsheim) after paying a fee of five florins
received a permit.

Johannes Schilling, a serf, residing at Richardshausen, district of
Sinsheim, paid five florins as a manumission fee and thirteen
florins for the ten Pfennig tax; arrived on the ship *Phoenix*
Sept. 1751.

Andreas Wetzstein, resident of Gauangeloch, district of Heidelberg,
paid ten florins as manumission fee and nine florins to satisfy
the ten Pfennig tax. Permitted to emigrate with wife and two
children.

Samuel Schweigert (Schweikert), resident of Bargen, district of
Sinsheim, after paying ten florins, received a permit.

Leonhardt Scheid, resident of Schriesheim, district of Mannheim,
received a permit. At the same time Adam Heinrich Hoffmann, a
former resident who had departed without paying his manumission
fee, was declared free. (A relative may have paid it for him.)

Johann Michael Roesch, a day-laborer of Dossenheim, district of Heidelberg, permitted to emigrate with his wife and children without making any payment.

Nicklas Reinhard, Caspar Heckmann, Adam Eisenhauer, three day-laborers from Wilhelmsfeld, upon paying the usual fees, received permits to emigrate.

Peter Leyer, from Heiligenkreuzsreinach.

Jacob Reichert, from Heddesbach, district of Heidelberg.

Niclas Zimmermann, from Altneudorf.

These three and their wives desired to emigrate. It is of interest that one of the three couples did not get the desired permit, because his wife was a Roman Catholic, and "in the land to which they plan to emigrate the exercise of the Catholic religion has not been introduced."

Balthasar Koenig, Joerg Happes, Johannes Wagner, Joerg Luecker—four citizens of Schoenau, district of Heidelberg, permitted to depart without paying the usual fees because of their scant means. "Georg Licker, Balzar Koenig, Johanes Wagner and George Happes" arrived on the ship *Queen of Denmark* 4 Oct. 1751.

In 1753 there are two cases on record:

Johannes Musselmann, an Anabaptist from Zuzenhausen, district of Sinsheim, secured a license to marry the daughter of Samuel Petzer, an Anabaptist, of Meckesheim, and also a permit to emigrate to America. "Hans Musselmann" arrived in Philadelphia on the ship *Patience* 17 Sept. 1753.

Georg Martin, resident of Neunkirchen, district of Mosbach, received a permit for himself, his wife, and three children. "Joerg Marthin" arrived in Philadelphia on the ship *Edinburgh* 14 Sept. 1753.

In 1754 the following were permitted to emigrate to America:

Joseph Bubigkoffer—an inhabitant, not a citizen, of Rohrhof, near Bruehl, district of Mannheim, received a permit gratis because of his poverty. "Josef Bubigkoffer" arrived in Philadelphia on the ship *Brothers* 30 Sept. 1754.

Niclaus Federolff, of Dossenheim, district of Heidelberg, received a permit to emigrate to South Carolina with his wife and three children.

Johannes Krauss, day-laborer of Bruchhauserhof (modern Bruchhausen), Sandhausen, district of Heidelberg, was permitted to depart with wife and children without paying the usual fees.

Philipp Leyer, widower from Aglasterhausen, district of Mosbach, and his six children were permitted to emigrate without paying the usual fees, because of his having no means.

David Mueller, resident of Altneudorf, district of Heidelberg, was permitted to emigrate gratis.

Jacob Schifferdecker, resident of Nuenkirchen, district of Mosbach, paid the usual fees and received a permit; arrived in Philadelphia on the ship *Henrietta* 22 Oct. 1754.

Catharina Zimmermann of Moosbrunn, district of Heidelberg, secured

both a license to be married and one to emigrate.
Johann Stephan Martin, son of a citizen in Neckarkatzenbach, district of Mosbach, received manumission after having emigrated. "Hans Steffan Marthin" arrived in Philadelphia on the ship *Shirley* 5 Sept. 1751.
Original article "Die Amerika-auswanderung aus dem kurpfaelzischen Oberamt Heidelberg in den Jahren 1737, 1738, 1751, und 1754," in *Badischische Heimat*, 338. Jahrg., 1958, Heft 3/4 pp. 303-304. Editor Prof. Dr. H. Schwarzweber, Freiburg i. Br.

IV

Emigrants from Wuerttemberg.
A hasty examination of the records of the government of Wuerttemberg for 1749-50, now on file at State Archives in Ludwigsburg, revealed a number of entries concerning persons who had expressed the desire to emigrate to America, i.e., Pennsylvania. A few of them could be identified in the lists of Strassburger-Hinke:
Andreas Herter, from Oberdigisheim, county of Balingen; arrived in Philadelphia on the ship *Osgood* 29 Sept. 1750.
Gottlieb Mittelberger, from Enzweihingen, county of Vaihingen. He "petitions that his divorce be hastened, so that he may be able to take a certificate of divorce with him to Pennsylvania." He made a round trip and published a book about it, *Gottlieb Mittelberger's Voyage to Pennsylvania in the Year 1750 and his return voyage to Germany in the year 1754.*" (Frankfurt/Main, and Leipzig, 1756, 110 pp).
Hans Jerg Felber, from Baach, county of Schondorf, petitioned that he be permitted to emigrate with his wife to Pennsylvania. Arrived on the ship *Elisabeth* 5 Sept. 1751.
Johannes Ese(n)wein, from Baltmannsweiler, county of Schondorf. Arrived on ship *Patience* 11 Aug. 1750.
Hanss Martin Herre, from Zillhausen, county of Balingen, son of the local magistrate and tax collector Simon Herre. According to a record dated 6 May 1765 Hans Herre had married in 1743 Anna Maria Sassler. In 1749 they and three children "had emigrated to the American island of Pennsylvania." "Hans Martin Herr" arrived in October 1749 on the ship *Fane*; oath of allegiance 17 Oct. 1749. In 1765 Hans Herre re-visited his old home, to get his share in the settlement of an estate. For 100 florins he quit-claimed his share to the other heirs. When he was about to return to Pennsylvania, the Wuerttemberg government demanded an emigration fee of 43 florins, 65 Kreuzer, and $4^1/_2$ Heller. He did not pay it. In the year 1770 he petitioned the government to cancel the charge, but it refused. Finally his relatives had to pay the charges.
Original article "Einige Amerika-Auswanderer des 18. Jahrhunderts aus Wuerttemberg." In *Suedwestdeutsche Blaetter fuer Familien- und Wappenkunde*. (Stuttgart, February 1957, Series 9, no. 1, p. 442.) Editor, Reinhold Scholl, Stuttgart-Sillenbuch.

V

Advertisements for Missing Heirs.

Johann Gerlach Bornhuetter, of Daaderhuette (Daaden, a village in
the district of Altenkirchen), Weserwald. He "left for America
more than twenty years ago." Advertisement of government of
Freidewald, Baden, 18 Feb. 1777, published in OPZ ("Oberpostamts
Zeitung") 4 July 1777. "John Gerlach Bornheker," aged 29. Philadelphia 2 Oct. 1753; ship *Edinburgh*.

Johann Wilhelm Strunck of Weitefeld, district of Altenkirchen, left
there "thirteen years ago." Advertisement of government of Freidewald, Baden, 18 Feb. 1777, published in OPZ 4 July 1777. Cf.
Strassburger-Hinke 249 C, 29 Nov. 1764.

Eva Catharina Fath, legitimate daughter of Georg Fath, deceased, of
Offenbach, district of Landau, Palatinate, "left this village as
a single woman more than twenty years ago, went to Pennsylvania,
and has sent no word back since then. Advertisement of government of Landeck Klingenmuenster, Electoral Palatinate, 5 June
1778, published in OPZ 3 July and 9 Nov. 1778.

Jacob and Elisabeth Huth, of Engelstadt, district of Bingen, left
there about thirty years ago and, according to common report,
went to Pennsylvania. Advertisement of government 13 Mch 1778;
published in OPZ 12 May, 30 May, and .. June 1778. "Jacob Huth,"
aged 29, *Loyal Judith* 2 Aug. 1743.

Johannes Juengst, native of Grosskarben, district of Friedberg,
Hessia "went to Pennsylvania twenty-six years ago." Advertisement of government of...Friedberg 13 July 1778, published in OPZ
24 Nov. 1778. Arrived on the ship *Edinburgh* 2 Oct. 1753.

Henrich Kron, native of Essenheim, district of Mainz, "migrated as
early as [1748] from there to America." Advertisement of County
of Oppenheim, Palatinate, .. Jan. 1776, published in OPZ 30 Aug.
and 14 Dec. 1776. "Hendk Crown" arrived on the ship *Hampshire* 7
Sept. 1748.

Veit Meister, son of the deceased court employe at Bargen (district
of Sinsheim, Baden) Georg Bernhard Meister "migrated as early as
1751 with wife and children from the village of Hoffenheim
belonging to the Baron of Gemmingen, district of Sinsheim, to
America." Advertisement of the government of Dilsberg, Electoral
Palatinate 10 Dec. 1787, published in OPZ 8 Feb. 1788. "Veit
Meister" arrived on ship *Shirley* 5 Sept. 1751.

Georg Thomas and Maria Barbara Osterstock, children of the deceased
Johann Philipp Osterstock, subjects to and under the jurisdiction
of Olnhausen (Wuerttemberg) 44 and 53 years old respectively, in
1751 went to America." Advertisement of the government of the
Baron of Berlichingen at Jagsthausen 7 Dec. 1773, published in
the Imperial *Official Post News* 10 Jan. 1780. "Thomas Osterstock" on ship *St. Andrew* 14 Sept. 1751.

Johann Dietrich Reiner, born at Schwaigern, under the rule of the
Count of Neipperg, Wuerttemberg, emigrated in April 1749 with his
wife Maria Margaretha, nee Schleicher, and six children named

Christian about 30 years old, Maria Magdalena 24 years old, Margaretha 22 years old, Sara 20 years old, Johannes 18 years old,
Eberhardt about 16 years old, from their home to Pennsylvania.
Announcement of the Council and state officials, also the Burgo-
master and the court at Bonnigheim in the "Zabergau," Wuerttemberg, 27 Oct. 1777, published OPZ 16 March 1778. The Lutheran
churchbook at the Evangelical parsonage Meimsheim contains the
following: Johann Dietrich Reiner, son of Friedrich Reiner,
citizen and cooper at Schwaigern, was married 9 Oct. 1715 to
Maria Margaretha Schleicher, daughter of the citizen and cobbler
Schleicher. Their children, listed in the Evangelical churchbook, were: Johann Christian, b. 10 April 1718; Maria Magdalena,
b. 21 Sept. 1720; Maria Margaretha, b. 12 Feb. 1723; Maria Sara,
b. 2 May 1724; Georg Philipp, b. 30 Jan. 1727, d. 3 May 1729;
Anna Maria, b. 9 June 1728, d. 8· June 1729; Johannes b. 13 July
1730; Eberharst Friedrich, b. 23 March 1733. "Johan Dietrich
Reiner" arrived on ship *Fane* 17 Oct. 1749.
Original article "Einige Amerika-Auswanderer des 18. Jahrhun-
derts" in *Senftnegger Monatsblatt fuer Genealogie und Heraldik*,
April 1958, Karl Friedrich v. Frank, editor and publisher, Schloss
Senftenegg, Post Ferschnitz, Niederoesterreich.

VI
Emigrants from Oppenheim 1742-49.
The records of the county of Oppenheim, in the former Electoral
Palatinate, which are now filed in the City Archives at Oppenheim
on Rhine, contain information about a few persons who emigrated
during the first half of the 18th century. They furnish evidence
of permits granted, not of actual emigration.
The former county of Oppenheim included the present city of Oppenheim, the market place Nierstein, and the villages of Dexheim,
Schwabsburg, Oberingelheim, Niederingelheim, Daxweiler, Sauerschwa-
benheim, Gorsswinternheim, Wackernheim, Freinweinheim, Bubenheim,
Elsheim, Stadtecken, and Essenheim. The many emigrants from Essenheim are not included in the following list, because they have been
published. In order to avoid repetitition we will list only the
date of the permit, the name, the residence, the fees paid, the
ship, and the date of arrival in Philadelphia.
1742
Permits and manumission certificates to the following residents of
    Stadtecken, namely, Lorentz Blaess, Peter Westerberger, Johann
    Kiel, Friederich Mengel, and Johannes Daum, "to emigrate to Penn-
    sylvania, where they have friends residing." On 3 Sept. 1742 on
    the ship *Loyal Judith* "Lorentz Place, Johannes Kuehl, Johannes
    Domie, Frietz Mengel, and Peter Wasenberger."
Permits granted 17 April 1742, to Friedrich Pfeil, Johann Lehn,
    residents of Gross-winternheim. They arrived 3 Sept. 1742 on the
    same ship.
In the same year a report to the county officials stated that

certain residents of Oberingelheim, namely, Philip Odernheimer,
Peter Weitzel, Ulrich Strassburger, and the widow of Nicolaus
Doerr, had "recently sent their sons, whose names had been entered
on the latest conscription list for military service, to the new
land, and with the knowledge of the entire town, had given each of
them 100 florins and some food for the voyage." The chief magistrate of the village of Oberingelheim was held responsible by the
higher authorities. Johannes Odernheimer, Johann Paul Weytzel,
Johann Heinrich Doerr, and Johann Andreas Strassburger arrived 3
Sept. 1742 on the *Loyal Judith*. The last named returned to Germany
for a visit and came back to Philadelphia on the ship *Mercury* in
October 1769.

25 February 1743 permit granted to Philip Hardt of Niederingelheim,
    upon payment of 10 Pfenning; permits to Nicolaus Runckel and
    Nicolaus Keller of Wackernheim. They arrived 2 Sept. 1743 on the
    Loyal Judith.

3 February 1748 permits "to migrate to the island of Pennsylvania"
    after paying 15 florins and 10 florins for manumission certifi-
    cates and the usual 10 Pfenning fees, to Friedrich Platz (Plotz)
    and Adam Imhaeusser (Immenhauser) of Stadtecken. They arrived on
    the ship *Hampshire* 7 Sept. 1748.

9 March 1748 permits to Franz Graff (Grove), with wife and two
    children, Bartel Kraemer with wife and five children, Adam Weiss
    with wife, all from Grosswinternheim, also Wilhelm Laymeister
    with wife and children from Schwabenheim, all upon paying the 10
    Pfennig fee; to indigents Wolfgang Wolf and ―― Hostermann from
    Grosswinternheim without such payment. They arrived 7 Sept. 1748
    on the *Hampshire*. Their names are given as Frantz Grove, Johann
    Wilhelm Leymeister, Wolfgang Wulff, Hans Jacob Ostermann, and
    Johann Adam Weiss.

29 March 1748 permit to Johann Bischoff from Grosswinternheim, "who
    was so in debt that he had to sell his property and did not know
    how he would be able to support himself." He arrived on the same
    ship, the *Hampshire* 7 Sept. 1748.

14 May 1748 permits to Johann Jacob Runckel and Friedrich Hammer
    from Wackernheim. The former paid 40 florins, the latter 10
    florins. Both arrived with the preceding on the *Hampshire*.
Christian Ramb from Elsheim paid 43 florins for a permit. But his
    name has not been found on the ship's lists.

21 March 1749 permit to Philipp Haber with wife and three children
    from Stadecken paid 54 florins for manumission and 54 florins for
    the 10 Pfenning tax; arrived 27 Sept. 1749 on the *Isaac*.

16 April 1749 permit to Nicolaus Reisinger from Niederingelheim,
    upon paying the 10 Pfenning tax; arrived 26 Sept. 1749 on the
    Dragon.

29 April 1749 to three men from Oberingelheim, Adam Doerr, upon
    payment of the 10 Pfenning tax, Anton Oster and Wendel Runckel,
    gratis, "all three being indigent and having bad records." Doerr
    arrived 9 Sept. 1749 on the *St. Andrew*. Oster arrived 26 Sept.

on the *Dragon*. Runckel remained in Oberingelheim, altho the
authorities were anxious to get rid of him.
14 May 1749 permit to Friedrich Bohr from Wackernheim, after paying
ten florins, arrived 9 Sept. 1949 on the *St. Andrew*.
Christian Meckel from Elsheim had some difficulties. His oldest
son was not emigrating with him. The authorities insisted that his
share of his father's estate be retained and safely invested for
him. Christian with wife and three younger children arrived 27
Sept. 1749 on the *Isaac*.
29 April 1749 Philipp Merz, locksmith, from Nierstein, upon paying
the 10 Pfenning tax, arrived 15 Sept. 1749 on the *Edinburgh*.
Ulrich Jordan (Jordte), an Anabaptist from Haxthaeuserhof near
Ingelheim, also paid the 10 Pfenning tax. He arrived 9 Sept.
1749 on the *St. Andrew*.
The Roman Catholic widow Catharina.Pfeiffer from Essenheim migrated
"without permission of the authorities, secretly, to Pennsylvania." Therefore whatever possessions she had left behind were
confiscated. Johann Rooss and Abraham Schweickart from Niederingelheim also emigrated "secretly," and their property was confiscated.
Original article: "Amerika auswanderer aus dem Oberant [*sic*]
Oppenheim 1742-49," in *Hessische Familienkunde*, Band 3 (1955), Heft
6.

VII

Emigrants to America from the region now a part of the Palatinate
and that of Nahe and Hunsrueck. The records are now filed in the
Archives at Speyer.
Johann Georg and Christian, sons of Conrad Stribeck, citizen and
woolspinner in Hornbach, district of Zweibruecken, by his first
wife Elisabetha Schaeffer, and their mother's brother together
with their grandmother Elisabetha Schaeffer migrated as early as
1735 into the new land, with the knowledge and approval of His
Highness. Since the grandparents were still living and the
children had not received any inheritance from their mother, they
were reported to have taken with them the portion derived from
their grandmother. Elisabeth Shever, Jerich Strebeck, Christian
Strebeck, arrived on the ship *Pennsylvania Merchant* 18 Sept.
1733.
Samuel Mauss, son of the official Friedrich Mauss of Hornbach and
his wife Susanna Mueller, former citizen of Zweibruecken, migrated to America "about 1754." He arrived 14 Sept. 1753 on the
ship *Edinburgh*.
Philipp Wild, son of the citizen and tanner Nickel Wild of Hornbach
and his wife Anna Maria, "about four years ago migrated to the
new land with the knowledge, recognized and to be recognized, of
the government. Before his departure he sold his...inheritance
to his brother Conrad Wild at Oberhausen." Deposition made 3 May
1760.

Catharina Henge, daughter of the deceased citizen and tanner ("Rotgerber") Samuel Mueller at Hornbach and his wife Maria Margaretha
Mauss, had been married to Georg Henge and had had a son, named
Philipp (now sixteen). She was divorced from her husband "pro
adulterii." Later she went to America, where she after having
made the necessary legal depositions was married to a man named
Fischer. (Emigrated before 31 Jan. 1777.)

Ludwig Leiner of Hornbach, "emigrated as a wool weaver." According
to a deposition of his brother Georg Leiner he died in 1784 in
America.

Philipp Bley, son of the citizen and cooper Hanss Werner Bley of
Hornbach and his wife Elisabeth Huber, "twenty-two years ago went
into Alsace and married at Trachenbronn, from where he removed to
America." Deposition made in 1770; (hence Philipp migrated about
1748).

Daniel and Balthasar Zutter, sons of Benedikt Balthasar Zutter of
Hornbach, woolspinner, "left secretly and migrated to America."
(Deposition 7 June 1763.) Daniel and Balthasar Zutter arrived on
ship *Chance* 1 Nov. 1763.

Theobald Pfaff "eight years ago ran away from Eisenbach, district
of Kusel, and emigrated to America. He left nine children behind, of whom three are in the ducal orphanage at Homburg."
(Deposition 29 Jan. 1777.) Theobald Pfaff arrived 26 Oct. 1768
in ship *Betsy*. Note: Pfaff could not have been born in Eisenbach, because the proof of his migration was filed in Hornbach.

Paul Hochstraser, son of the town official Samuel Hochstraser at
Brenschelbach, district of Homburg, in the Saar, and his wife
Elisabetha. He established himself as a tailor in Philadelphia.
(Deposition 18 April 1761.) According to a power of attorney
which Paul Hochstraser and his sister Catharina signed 23 Jan.
1764 at Albany, Province of New York, they were living there.
"Paul Hochstraser" arrived 14 Sept. 1753 in ship *Edinburg*. In
the year 1763 a Jacob Hochstraser emigrated to America, presumably he was a brother of Paul, for local records show that Paul
had a brother of that name.

Heinrich Haller, son of the citizen and tailor Jacob Haller of
Walshausen, district of Zweibruecken, and his first wife Elisabeth Moser, "deserted from the old Ducal Guard and emigrated to
Pennsylvania." He migrated about 1748 without having secured
manumission. Therefore his property, i.e., an inheritance
amounting to 102 florins was confiscated by the government of
Zweibruecken. Presumably identical with Heinrich Haller, 18 Aug.
1750, in the ship *St. Andrew*.

Anna Appolonia Vogelsang, daughter of the citizen Nickel Gentes at
Breitfurt, (district of Homburg, Saar), was married to Georg
Vogelgesang, the younger, (apparently, also a resident of Breit-
furt) living in America. (Deposition 6 May 1765.) Presumably
"Georg Vogelsang" who arrived 21 Oct. 1761 in the *Snow Squirrel*.

Georg Neu, inhabitant and citizen at Breitfurt (d. 18 July 1756)

and his wife Christina Margareta Gentess had the following
children:
1. Joseph Neu, "who about 18 years ago migrated to America and
   is about 40 years old."
2. Peter Neu, "who also some five years ago removed to America
   and is about 30 years old." (Deposition, 8 Feb. 1758.)
Abraham Schmidt, citizen and court employe ("Gerichtsmann") at
Breitfurt, had:
1. Mattheis, "living in America."
2. Georg, unmarried, 30 years old, in America. (Deposition, 7
   Oct. 1760.)
Jacob Welker, son of Wilhelm Welcker of Breitfurt, "who according
to report has gone to America," emigrated before 4 Dec. 1777.
Either "Jacob Welcker," who arrived 26 Oct. 1768 in the ship
Crawford or [the same] who arrived 17 Sept. 1771 in the ship
Minerva.
Heinrich Kunz of Boeckweiler (district of Homburg, Saar), "Heinrich
Kunz, son of the deceased citizen ("Gemeindeman") of the same
name, at Boeckweiler, left this land anno 1764 and, according to
report, in defiance of the highest existing ordinance migrated to
America." Notice in the *Frankfurter Kayserliche Reichs-Ober-
Amtspost Zeitung* of 17 Sept. 1787.... According to local records
Heinrich Kunz had learned the trade of wagon maker and had gone
out in 1764 as a wandering journeyman. On 23 August 1768 he
wrote a letter to Jonathan Heger from Canageschick, Maryland,
which was the last anyone in his home town received from him.
Johannes Keller, son of Daniel Keller of Boeckweiler, was reported
to be "established in the new land and married." He emigrated
before 19 Oct. 1776.
"Children of Wilhelm Schunk of Walsheim, district of Homburg, Saar,
and his wife Catharina Schwartz, namely: Johannes, Catharina,
Elisabeth, Maria, Simon, have been in America the past nine or
ten years." Record 18 Oct. 1781.
The following names of emigrants to America from the region of
Nahe and Hunsrueck were copied from the Lutheran churchbooks at
Hueffelsheim and Loetzbeuren and from the Reformed church books at
Hundsbach.
Johann Georg Reitzel (Reutzel), a cobbler at Hueffelsheim, district
of Kreuznach, and wife (Anna) Sybilla had children:
1. Anna Maria, b. 2 Aug. 1720. "This parish child migrated to
   the new land."
2. Maria Wilhelmina, b. 2 Sept. 1734, "went with her father
   into the new land. 1741."
3. Johann Peter, b. 28 Oct. 1737, "went with his parents 1741
   into the new land."
"Johann Georg Reutzel" arrived 17 Oct. 1741, aged 45 years.
Johannes Wolffskehl, m. 19 Nov. 1730 at Hueffelsheim to Anna Maria
Viel; children born at Hueffelsheim:
1. Elisabetha, b. 28 Dec. 1733.

2. Anna Margaretha, b. 18 Nov. 1735.

3. Maria Agnes, b. 27 Jan. 1738.

All three "went with their father into the new land 1742." "Johannes Wolffskehl," 3 Sept. 1742, ship *Loyal Judith*.

1. Maria, 28 Feb. 1711 "to the new land 1742" (wife of J. Wolffskehl, cf. above).

2. Johan Jacob, b. 22 Nov. 1718 "went 17 May 1767 into the new land."

Johann Michael Rech, b. 1 March 1751 at Hueffelsheim, son of Johann Conrad Rech, and his wife Anna Margreta. "Children and parents went to the new land."

Catharina Elisabetha Schnee, b. 27 Aug. 1730 at Loetzbeuren, district of Zell, Mosel region, daughter of Johannes Schnee and his wife Maria Margretha. "Emigrated to Pennsylvania 1751."

Maria Catharina Hoff, b. 26 May 1732 at Loetzbeuren, daughter of Johann Dieterich and his wife Susanna Elisabetha: "This person and her husband have gone to Pennsylvania."

Johann Wilhelm Lutz, b. 12 Sept. 1732 at Loetzbeuren, son of Matthes Luetz and his wife Elisabetha Catharina, "left for Pennsylvania 1751."

Anna Elisabetha Frantz, b. 25 March 1735 at Loetzbeuren, daughter of Johann Nicol Frantz and his wife Maria Elisabetha: "said to have migrated to Pennsylvania 1751."

Elisabetha Catharina Heyl, b. 4 Jan. 1733 at Hundsbach, district of Kreuznach, "The father of this child has gone to Pennsylvania."

The following names of emigrants were found in "Akt Zweibruecken III No. 3358, Act concerning dismissal...of subjects as well as the exporting of property acquired at marriage (Heirats gut), and the payment of the ten penny tax (1484-1792)," in the Archives at Speyer.

Johann Nickel Beyer, b. at Kleinach, district of Bernkastel, son of Matthias Beyer, also Johann Georg Bartges, son of Matthias Bartges of the same place, both permitted by the government of Sponheim to migrate from Trarbach to Pennsylvania "in order to perfect themselves in the trade they have learned. But if they do not return within three years, they will have to purchase their manumission, and in the mean time their prospective inheritance here is being held as a forfeit."

Michael Bartges, a tanner by trade, was permitted to depart for Pennsylvania on similar conditions. "Michael Bartjes," ship *Two Brothers*, 15 Sept. 1748.

Johann Nickel Neu, son of Christoffel Neu, a weaver by trade, and Johann Peter Velten (Fehlten), son of Conrad Fehlten, a cobbler by trade, received permits to emigrate to America on similar conditions. "Peter Felte," ship *Two Brothers*, 15 Sept. 1748.

Johann Conrad Lahm, a tailor by trade, son of Peter Lahm[,] also John Michel Neu, linen-weaver, son of Philipp Neu, also Matthias Bayer, son of Matthias Bayer, Sr., all of Kleinach, were granted permission by the government of Trarbach 26 April 1741 to go to

Pennsylvania, on condition that they either return within two
years or pay their manumission fees.

That all of them emigrated is proved by the records. However,
Matthias Bayer and Johann Michel Neu are said to have died soon
after their arrival in America.

"Johann Konradt Lahm," aged 22 years, arrived 20 Nov. 1741, in the
ship *Europa*.

Johann Peter Hehn or Henn, son of Nicol Hehn of Horbruch, district
of Bernkastel, according to a report of 11 March 1746 to the
government at Trarbach, ·"emigrated anno 1741 to the so called new
land."

Maria Catharina Lahm and Nickel Lahm, children of Matthias Lahm of
Oberkleinich (district of Bernkastel) according to a report of
the magistrate of Kleinich to the government at Trarbach 8 May
1741, "desire to migrate to the new land."

"Johann Nicklaus Lahm" arrived 29 Sept. 1741, ship *Lydia*.

"This is to inform you that during the past year two young fel-
lows under the pretext of completing their journeyman's stage (in
learning their trade) emigrated to the so called new land. One,
Johann Peter Lorentz, is a native of Hochscheid, the other, Johann
Peter Lahm, is a native of Oberkleinich." Report of a local magistrate to the government of Sponheim 12 May 1741. An entry in the
records of the government at Trarbach confirms that both had emigrated in 1740.

"Peter Lorentz and Peter Laam," 27 Sept. 1740 arrived in Philadelphia on ship *Lydia*.

Original article: "Amerika-Auswanderer des 18. Jahrhunderts aus
der heutigen Pfalz und der Nahe- und Hensrueck-gegend." In *Mitteilungen zur Wanderungsgeschichte der Pfaelzer*, supplement to
Pfaelzische Familien u Wappenkunde, Kaiserslautern, West Germany,
1954. Editor: Dr. Fritz Braun.

[The reader should note that the original article contained more
errors of translation and of a typographical nature than the copy
above, in which some of the more confusing ones were corrected.
The "ten pfenning" tax should have read, as it did once, the "ten
pfennig" tax.]

Frank Reid Differderffer. "The German Immigration into Pennsylvania through the Port of Philadelphia, and 'The Redemptioners',"
The Pennsylvania-German Society Proceedings and Addresses, 10
(1900), 213-216 [Lancour No. 142].

Lancour refers, in entry No. 142, to two lists, the first being
from pages 40-42, a list of the passengers on the *William and
Sarah*, William Hill, Master, which is also reproduced in Egle and
in Strassburger [Lancour Nos. 145 and 146. The second list, copied
below, is also available in the reprint of the 328 page volume of
Proceedings available from the Genealogical Publishing Company of
Baltimore.
This list is from a newspaper advertisement published in Philadelphia eleven days after the *Britannia* arrived in Philadelphia, 18
September 1773, reflecting the possibility, as Differderffer put
it, "that at that particular time the Redemptioner market was not
as brisk as it might have been, and that special efforts were
necessary to work off the human cargo.

Here is a partial list of the passengers on the already named
ship *Britannia*, prepared in the office of Messrs. Joshua Fisher &
Sons, showing the amount of the passage money due by each, as well
as some additional expenses incurred by them on the voyage, most
probably for provisions, which were never over-abundant and
generally insufficient.

Andreas Keym	£26.7	Expenses	2.8
Lena Bekker, his wife	22.2		£59.12
Expense 16 days	1.12		
	£50.1	Jacob Schott	£17.1
		Anna, wife	
Hendrick Soueau	£20.15	Expenses	1.12
Dorothea, his wife	20.11		£18.13
Expenses	1.12		
	£42.18	Christopher Schever	£50.7
		Anna, wife	
John Frederick Camer-			1.12
loo	£23.15		£51.19
Anna, his wife	22.1		
Expenses	1.12	John George Kunkell	
	£47.8	Anna, wife	£41.5
		Catherina, daughter	
Simon Martz		Expenses	3.4
Ann, his wife			£44.9
Anna Margaretta, daughter			
Expenses	£ 2.8	Jacob Steyheler	£19.19
		Catharina, wife	17.18
Augustinus Hess	£19.1	Expenses	1.12
Maria, wife	18.19		£39.9
Anna Margtta daughter	19.4		

Bernard Schmit		Jacob Twytser	£42.7
Margaretta, wife	£61.5	Johanna Barbara, wife	
Turgen, son		Expenses	1.12
Catharina, daughter			£43.19
Expenses	3.4		
	£64.9	Conrad Foltz	
		Susanna, wife	£51.
Andreas Otto	£41.7	Maria, daughter	
Sophi, wife		Expenses	2.8
Expenses	1.12		£53.8
	£42.19		
		William Schwartz	£35.16
John Danl. Roth	£49.8	Anna Maria, wife	
Anna, wife		Expenses	1.12
Expenses	1.12		£37.8
	£51.		
		Christian Nell	£20.
Jacob Wanner	£20.15	Expenses	.16
Maria wife			£20.16
Expensse	1.12		
	£22.7	Johann Jeremiah Snell	£24.19
		Expenses	.16
Daniel Spees	£38.17		£25.15
Anna, wife			
Expenses	1.12	Gerrett Benengé	£23.11
	£40.9	Expenses	.16
			£24.7
Christian Habert	£43.4		
Anna Maria, wife		Anty. Guerin	£21.3.6
Expenses	1.12	Expenses	.16.
	£44.16		£21.19.6
Daniel Spees Jr.	£36.17	Pierie Mullott	£21.
Anna, wife		Expenses	.16
Expenses	1.12		£21.16
	£38.9		
		Gertuna Vogelsand	£17.18
Andreas Kirch			.16
Anna Maria, wife	£44.9		£18.14
Maria Elizabeth			
Expenses	2.8	[The readers should note that	
	£46.17	figures were expenses in British	

Pounds Sterling, which until recently contained twenty shillings
each, with each shilling containing twelve pence; thus decimal
mathematics does not apply.]

The original of the foregoing interesting document is among the
manuscript collections of the Historical Society of Pennsylvania.
Rupp, in his *Thirty Thousand Names*, gives the names of the passen-

gers on the *Britannia*, but not all of them.   This list gives additional ones.

Charles R. Roberts.   "Germanic Immigrants Named in Early Pennsylvania Ship Lists," *The Pennsylvania German Society Proceedings
and Addresses*, 39 (1928), 5-20 [Lancour No. 143].

Between the years 1683 and 1727, how many persons of Germanic
origin settled in Pennsylvania will probably never be known.   Some
writers have estimated the number as high as 50,000.   The Crefeld
colony under Pastorius came in 1683.   In 1694 Johannes Kelpius came
with his band of 40 pietists.   Daniel Falkner and others arrived in
1704.   In 1705 a number of German Reformed residing between Wolfen-
buettel and Halberstadt, fled to Neuwied and then to Holland, and
in 1707 sailed for New York.   Their ship was carried into Delaware
Bay and they eventually settled along the Musconetcong and the Pas-
saic in New Jersey, in what is now known as the German Valley.   In
1708 the Kocherthal colony came to New York, most of whom afterwards came to Pennsylvania.   In 1709 a colony of Swiss, principally
Mennonite, settled in Lancaster county.
     In September, 1717, three ships arrived at Philadelphia with a
total of 363 Palatines.   In 1719 Jonathan Dickinson wrote, "We are
daily expecting ships from London which bring over palatines, in
number about six or seven thousand."   On August 30, 1720, the ship
Laurel arrived with 240 odd Palatines.   Between the years 1708 and
1720, thousands arrived.
     The Provincial Council, by a resolution adopted September 14,
1727, required shipmasters to make lists of all immigrants and that
the immigrants sign an oath of allegiance to the King of England.
The majority of these lists are preserved in the State Library at
Harrisburg.   It was on March 6, 1903, that I saw these original
lists for the first time.   They were in the library proper, as the
Department of Public Records had not yet been established.
     The first ship, record of whose passengers was kept by the Colo-
nial Government, was the William and Sarah, which actually arrived
about September 12, 1727, and not September 18th, and on September
21st not more than 51 of the 317 passengers, 109 of whom were men,
signed the oath of allegiance.   Rev. Dr. Hinke, in Volume 27, has
shown us what errors there are in the published lists.

Immigrants Named in Ship Lists
     The leader of this band was Rev. George Michael Weiss, a Reformed
clergyman, born in 1700 at Eppingen, in the Palatinate.   Michael
Diel, Rudolf Wellecker, George Kremer and Henrich Weller located in
Philadelphia.   Those who settled in Goshenhoppen, now Montgomery
county, where John Frederick Hillegs, born in Alsace, Nov. 24,
1685, died Jan. 6, 1765; John George Welcker, born Feb. 6, 1697,

died March 8, 1782; John Huth, who died suddenly in Philadelphia on
Aug. 14, 1759. His funeral text was: "Mein Leben ist abgerissen
wie ein Weber spull." Michael Zimmerman and Benedict Strohm.
David Schultz in his journal says that Strohm's wife died in April,
1757, and on June 14, 1757, he married again, at the age of 62, a
girl of fifteen. John George Bowman, Sebastian Smith and Ulrich
Stephen settled at Skippack and John George Schwab and Leonard Sel-
tenreich in the Conestoga valley.

John or John Michael Diffenderfer, the ancestor of the founder,
or one of the founders, of this society, Frank Reid Diffenderfer,
was born Jan. 10, 1695, at Neresheim, near Heidelberg, in the Chur
Pfalz, and died in 1778 in Lancaster county. Alexander Diefender-
fer, an ancestor of the writer, died in 1768 in what is now Lehigh
county. They were the sons of John Deubendorffer, born Oct. 8,
1663. The family came from Duebendorf, six miles northeast of
Zurich, Switzerland, formerly Diebeldorf, anciently Tobelindorf.
The family is mentioned as early as 1130 and in 1229 Cuno von Die-
bendorf, Knight, is mentioned in a document of the cloister at
Zinckenburg as a witness.

Joseph Albright settled in Macungie township, now Lehigh county,
where he died in 1744. Some of his descendants removed to Northumberland county. Daniel Levan settled in Maxatawny township,
Berks county, where he died in 1777.

On the ship Adventurer, October 2, 1727, was Ulrich Rieser, born
April 9, 1709, who died Sept. 9, 1784, in Lower Milford township,
now Lehigh county, and John Dieter Bauman, who settled first in
Marlbore township, Philadelphia county, where he operated a grist
mill and about 1755 removed beyond the Blue Mountains, to Towamen-
sing township, now Carbon county, where he died in 1762.

The ship Friendship, October 16, 1727, had among its passengers
Joseph Eberhard, a native of Switzerland, who settled in Lower Milford township, now Lehigh county, was one of the founders of the
Great Swamp church and at his death in 1760 left each of his six
sons a large farm. His brother, Michael Eberhard, settled just
over the county line in Milford township, Bucks county, where he
died in 1772.

On the ship Mortonhouse, August 24, 1728, was Clement Dunkelber-
ger, who died in 1782 in Berks county. His son John removed to
Mahanoy township, Northumberland county. Also, Henrich Wilhelm
Dillinger from Wurtemberg, who settled in Bucks, now Lehigh county.

On the ship James Goodwill, Sept. 11, 1728, came Rev. John Caspar
Stoever, Sr., a native of Frankenberg, in Hesse, a Lutheran clergyman, who located in Virginia, went to Europe in 1737, and died on
board the vessel on his attempted return to America, and Rev. John
Caspar Stoever, Jr., born at Luedorff, in Solinger Amt, Duchy Berg,
in the Palatinate, Dec. 21, 1707, and died at Lebanon May 13, 1779.

Theobald Mechling, born (probably at Lambesheim in Chur Pfalz),
who settled in Lower Milford, now Lehigh county, where a descen-
dant, a member of this society, still owns the land he took up. He

died in April, 1765. Four of his sons removed to Northumberland
county and many descendants reside in Western Pennsylvania and
Ohio. His brother Jacob settled in Germantown.

Egidius Grim, from Wurtemberg, settled in Bucks county, in what
is now Macungie township, Lehigh county, where he died in 1761.

Martin Moser settled in Montgomery county.

Philip Henry Seller settled in Philadelphia county, was an elder
of the Skippack church in 1734 and died July 8, 1769. The town of
Sellersville takes its name from the family.

Frederick Scholl settled first in Philadelphia county and in 1734
in Bucks county, where Hellertown, Northampton county, now is
located. He was an elder of the Lower Saucon church and died in
1754.

On the Mortonhouse, Aug. 19, 1729, was Frederick Ludwig Marsteller, from Darmstadt. He settled on the Skippack creek in New Pro-
vidence township, in Philadelphia, now Montgomery county. He was
one of the founders and deacons of the Lutheran church at Trappe
and his name appears in Latin over the door of this, the oldest
Lutheran church building in America, erected in 1743. He was a
warm friend of Rev. Henry Melchior Muhlenberg, who preached an English sermon at his funeral. He died October 14, 1753. His youngest son, Col. Philip Marsteller, was one of Washington's pall-
bearers.

Michael Weber and his wife Phillis were also passengers on this
ship. He was born in the Palatinate in 1703 and settled in Bucks
county, now Upper Saucon township, Lehigh county, where he died
August 10, 1745, and was buried on his own land. His widow,
Johanna Felicitas, subsequently married Anthony Wilhelm Boehm,
eldest son of Rev. John Philip Boehm.

Wendel Wyandt, or Wieand, born July 14, 1709, at Frensheim in the
Palatinate, settled in Upper Hanover township, Philadelphia county,
and died there in 1787.

Michael Borst died near Lebanon in 1741. George Adam Weidel settled near Lebanon. Jacob Seller lived at Germantown.

On August 29, 1730, came the Thistle, with Peter Miller, born at
Ober Amt Lautern, a graduate of Heidelberg University, and son of a
Reformed minister, who, in 1735, went over to the Brethren at
Ephrata, was called Brother Jabez, and died there Sept. 25, 1796.

Valentine Griesheimer, from Lampedheim, with his wife and four
children, came with a passport given at Worms on April 28, 1730.
He settled in Berks county and died in Hereford township about
1759.

Peter Fetterolf, born at Wachbach, March 20, 1699, settled in
Berks county and died in Hereford township, Aug. 15, 1784. Descendants of his settled in Cameron township, Northumberland county.

Abraham Transue, born in Mutterstadt, in the Palatinate, also was
on board and settled in Bucks county. Rudolph Drach also settled
in Bucks county.

I have here a photostat of the original signatures of the passen-

gers on the ship Brittania, which arrived Sept. 21, 1731. At the
head of the list is the name Johannes Barthalomay Rieger, Hochteut-
scher Prediger. He was born at Oberingelheim, in the Palatinate,
Jan. 25, 1707, and attended the universities of Heidelberg and
Basel, became pastor at Philadelphia and Germantown and in New
Jersey. He died at Lancaster in 1769.

Matthias Smeisser, born at Rugelbach in 1715, died in York
county in 1778.

Leonard Steininger settled in Northampton county and died there
in 1753.

Michael Stocker, John Eigender and John and Hubertus Bartsch
settled in Bucks County.

The ship Snow Lowther arrived October 14, 1731, with Casper
Peter, born in 1698 in Zell, Switzerland, whose three sons are the
ancestors of the large Peters family of Lehigh county.

The ship Samuel came Aug. 11, 1732. On board were John Helfrich,
born in 1699, who settled in Upper Milford township, Bucks county,
now Lehigh, and died Feb. 27, 1764.

Christian and Benedict Gehman, Mennonites, settled in Bucks
county, as did also John George Kleinhantz.

Jacob Gochnaur and Oswald Hostetter settled in Lancaster county.

Anastasius Uhler, born in the Palatinate about 1710, settled in
Lancaster county and died at Lebanon. He was constable of Lebanon
township in 1769.

The ship Pennsylvania arrived Sept. 11, 1732, with 171 passengers. Paul Ritter, born in 1713, settled in Colebrookdale, Berks
county, where he died Feb. 14, 1799. Henry Ritter settled in Lower
Milford township, now Lehigh county, just west of the Great Swamp
Church. A section of the log over the fireplace, with the date
1739, from a house built by him, is in the possession of the Lehigh
County Historical Society. He removed to Salisbury township, where
he died in January, 1797. Casper Ritter settled in Bethlehem township, Northampton county, where he built a mill and died in 1792.

Paul Linsen Bigler settled in Philadelphia county.

The ship Pink Johnson arrived Sept. 19, 1732. The archives gives
110 names, this photostat shows 112. There are many errors. Behn
should be Bohn, Beer, Bey, Rouse, Rausch, Coplinger, Keplinger,
etc. John Moessinger settled in Bucks county. With him was his
son, Michael Messinger, born Nov. 10, 1719, who settled first in
Bucks county and later in Forks township, Northampton county, where
he had a grist mill, became prominent and was a member of the
County Committee of Observation in the Revolution. He died October
24, 1791. He was the ancestor of one of the members of our Executive Committee and has many descendants in Northampton county.

Another passenger was Andreas Oberbeck, from Oberamt Neustadt in
the Palatinate, born about 1690, settled first at Skippack, where
he was elder of the Reformed Church from 1739 to 1744; removed to
Bucks county, where he died in 1765.

The first name on the list is John Steiman. He was born in 1668 at Strassburg, the son of Peter Steinman, who was married June 18, 1645, to Sara Metzgar. She was born Feb. 3, 1623. With him was his son, John George Steinman, born March 18, 1703, who settled in Philadelphia county.

John George Sehm settled in Bucks county and John Dieter settled in what is now Northampton county, where he died in 1758.

The ship Adventurer came Sept. 23, 1732. On it came Mathias Riegel, born in 1709, who settled in Lower Saucon township, the present Northampton county, where he died in 1778. George Riegel, born in 1718, settled in Bucks county, and died May 17, 1798.

Tobias Moser, born 1702, settled in Bucks, now Lehigh county, and died in 1757.

George Breiner settled in Berks county.

Baltzer Bortner, born 1695, settled in Tulpehocken township, Lancaster county, and died in 1747. His son, Jacob, born in 1722, settled in 1761 in Northumberland county and died in 1792.

Mathias Wagner, born 1709, settled in Northampton county.

The ship Loyal Judith arrived Sept. 25, 1732, with Philip Jacob Acker, born 1696, who settled in Macungie township, now Lehigh county, and Henry Acker, born in 1700, who settled in Bucks county.

The ship Dragon arrived Sept. 30, 1732. Among its passengers were Peter Mattern, an ancestor of the writer, who settled in Bucks, now Lehigh county. Some descendants settled in Upper Mahanoy township, Northumberland county.

Felix Brunner settled in Lower Milford township of the present Lehigh county, where he died in 1760.

John Adam Romich, born Feb. 3, 1689, at Ruedenstein, in the Palatinate, a Lutheran and a deacon, in 1762 joined the Moravians in Lynn township, Lehigh county, and died there July 11, 1768.

Leonard Schlosser settled in Bucks, now Lehigh county.

Tobias Bahl settled in Upper Saucon township, Lehigh county, where he died in 1759.

Jacob Dubs, a gunsmith, born Aug. 31, 1710, in Aesch, parish of Birmensdorf, Canton of Zurich, Switzerland, settled in Lower Milford township, the present Lehigh county. He was the ancestor of Rev. Dr. Joseph H. Dubbs.

The ship Pink, John and William [meaning the pink, John and William], arrived Oct. 17, 1732. On it were Sebastian Truckenmiller, born Aug. 1, 1715, died Feb. 1, 1795. He is buried in a field, formerly his own land, in Lehigh county. Some of his descendants settled in Northumberland county. Henry Keck, from Bavaria, is the ancestor of a large Lehigh county family.

On August 17, 1733, the ship Samuel arrived. The archives give 88 males over 16 on board, with one sick, which name Rupp gives, making 89. George Ruch, Senior's age is given as 48. His tombstone states he was born in Zitzendorf, Alsace, in 1664, making him 68. He died in Whitehall township, now Lehigh county, in 1769, aged 104 years and 11 months.

John Lichtenwalner, from Kreuth, in Kolmberg, in Brandenberg was a passenger. His passport, dated April 25, 1733, is still in existence. He settled in Bucks now Lehigh county.

Peter Troxell, from Switzerland, one of the founders of the Egypt Church, Whitehall township, Lehigh county, and who is given as church censor in 1736.

Ulrich Flickinger, born 1702, died 1792, in Whitehall township.

Michael Brobst settled in Albany township, Berks county.

Peter Beisel, whose son Peter, aged 8, became a member of the Northampton County Revolutionary Committee of Observation.

Henry Roth, born in 1688, was one of the two men who gave the land for the Salisbury Church, near Allentown.

The ship Hope arrived August 28, 1733. I have here a photostat of the original list. Rupp says there are 83 over 16; he gives 81. The archives give 79. There are really 84, with some errors in the names.

David Deshler, born in 1711, died in 1792, settled in Germantown, and became a prominent merchant, noted for his honesty and integrity. "As honest as David Deshler" became a proverb. He built the Morris Mansion in 1774, which became the headquarters of Sir William Howe in the Revolution and the residence of President Washington in 1793.

Daniel Roth, a direct ancestor of the writer, born in Switzerland in 1703, died near Allentown in 1737. His son, Hon. Peter Rhoads, reared among Quakers, was a Revolutionary patriot and judge for 30 years.

Jacob Mueckli settled in Whitehall township, and died in 1769.

John Jacob Schreiber, born in Niederbronn, Alsace, in 1699, died in 1750 in Whitehall township.

Michale, Peter and Ulrich Witmer were among the passengers. Peter Witmer, born in 1737, in Hertzheim, Nassau-Dillenberg, Prussia, who in 1766 located near Port Treverton, Snyder county, where he died in 1793, was probably a nephew of these Witmers.

Ulrich, Jacob and Ulrich Lonagcre, Jr., settled in Philadelphia county.

Henrich, Mathias and Bernard Fegley settled in Philadelphia, now Berks county. A member of our Executive Committee descends from one of these men.

Rudolph Schneebele, Christian and Peter Eschelman, John Snabley and Jacob Burki settled in Lancaster county.

On the Brigantine Richard and Elizabeth, Sept. 28, 1733, were John Nicholas Saeger, born 1694, at Reichenbach, Bavaria, who settled in Whitehall township, Bucks county, now Lehigh, and died there in 1762.

Ulrich Burkhalter, from Switzerland, born 1693, died in 1762, in Whitehall township.

On the ship St. Andrew, Sept. 12, 1734, came the important Schwenkfelder colony, which I will not mention in detail at this time. Also Jacob Wildfang, who located in Philadelphia. Descendants are in North Carolina.

On the ship Mercury, May 29, 1735, was a colony of Swiss, headed by Rev. Maurice Goetschy, from Saletz, Switzerland. Rev. Goetschy was sick when the ship arrived and died the following day. His son, John Henry, born March 8, 1718, was a student at the Latin school at Zurich and began to preach to the Reformed settlers at the age of 17, not only at Philadelphia, but at Skippack, Goshenhoppen, Great Swamp, Egypt, Saucon, Maxatawny, Moselem, Oley, Bern and Tulpehocken. He was licensed to preach in 1737 and ordained in 1741 and became a pastor in New Jersey.

John Conrad Wuertz, born Nov. 30, 1706, in the Canton of Zurich, Switzerland, married Anna, daughter of Rev. Maurice Goetschy. He became school teacher, began preaching in 1742, was ordained in 1752 and died at York Sept. 21, 1763.

Ulrich Arner, born in 1699 in Switzerland, settled in Bucks, now Lehigh county.

On the ship Harle, Sept. 1, 1736, was George Zeisloff, born 1709, who, with his wife and several children, was killed by Indians in Lynn township, Northampton county, now Lehigh, March 24, 1756, only two sons surviving. His house is still standing.

John Adam Schaus, born 1704, settled in Bucks county.

The ship Princess Augusta, Sept. 16, 1736, had as a passenger George Nicholas Gauger, born in 1718, who settled in Tulpehocken and whose son John Wilhelm settled in Northumberland county.

The ship Samuel, Aug. 30, 1737, brought John Troxell and his son John Peter Troxell, who was born April 3, 1719, in Switzerland, naturalized in 1748 and in 1756 built a large stone house, with a unique inscription, still standing, in which the Egypt Reformed congregation worshipped. In 1768 he sold his 410 acres and removed to Gwynedd township, Philadelphia county, where he owned a grist and a saw mill. In 1776 he removed to Maryland, where he died Jan. 25, 1799.

Frederick Eberhard, born 1697, died 1751, settled in Bucks county.

Philip Fenstermacher, born in the Palatinate Feb. 27, 1713, died in Longswamp township, Berks county, June 15, 1790.

This is the last ship list given in the Colonial Records.

The ship St. Andrew, Sept. 26, 1737, brought many who settled in Eastern Pennsylvania.

John Erdman, from Pfungstadt, Hesse Darmstadt, settled in Bucks county.

George Frederick Newhard, from Zweibruecken, born 1700, died Nov. 29, 1765, another ancestor of the writer, settled in Whitehall township, Bucks, now Lehigh county. His brother, Michael Newhard, born Feb. 9, 1713, died March 10, 1793, settled in the northern part of the same township, and George Newhard, born 1720, died 1800, settled in Allen township, Northampton county.

Balthazar Beil settled in Upper Saucon township, Bucks, now Lehigh county, as did also John Appel, from Pfungstadt.

George Kern settled in Whitehall township and Philip Seger settled in Lehigh township, Northampton county.

Martin Kocher, born at Holtzenhausen, Nassau Dillenberg, died about 1762, settled in what is now Lehigh county.

On the ship Winter Galley, Sept. 5, 1738, came Christopher Heller, born in 1688 in Petersheim, in the Palatinate. He settled in Northampton county, where he died in 1778. With him was his son Simon Heller, born June 18, 1721, died May 20, 1785, who settled in the same county.

On the ship Glasgow, Sept. 9, 1738, were the following:

Mathias Fenstermacher, born in 1678 in the Palatinate, who settled in Berks county.

Frantz Guildner, who settled in Bucks, now Lehigh county.

John Pontius, born in 1718 in Alsace, settled in Tulpehocken, Berks county. Several of his sons were pioneers in the Buffalo Valley.

September 11, 1738, came the ship Robert and Alice, with John Nicholas Schneider, who was evidently a well educated man, as he wrote a fine hand. He settled in what is now Lehigh county, where he was a Justice of the Peace in Colonial times, when still a part of Bucks county.

The ship Queen Elizabeth arrived Sept. 16, 1738. Here were Reinhard Laubach, aged 70, and his son Christian Laubach, born 1699, died Nov. 19, 1768, who settled in Lower Saucon township, Northampton county.

Anthony Lerch, born Sept. 20, 1720, died Aug. 28, 1793; his brother Pancratius Lerch, who died in 1794, and Peter Lerch, with their father, Andreas Lerch, aged 50, who all settled in Lower Saucon.

The Thistle, Sept. 19, 1738, brought Lorentz Guth, from Zweibruecken, who settled in Whitehall township, was the founder of the Jordan Reformed Church and died in 1770.

The ship Friendship came Sept. 20, 1738, with Jacob Folmer, born in the village of Rosswog, Wurtemberg in 1698, who settled in the Schoharie valley, New York, and later followed Conrad Weiser to Tulpehocken, where he died in 1762. His son Michael located on Limestone Run, in Northumberland county, 1773, was the organizer of Follmer Lutheran Church in Turbot township, and died Sept. 29, 1793. He bequeathed £15 to the Dutch Lutheran Church, £10 towards teaching the poor children. His son, George Jacob Follmer, settled in 1773 in Turbot township, now Montour county. He was a member of the Assembly from Northumberland county in 1776 and 1777, reelected in 1796, 1798, 1799, 1800 and 1801. In 1799 he received 3569 votes and Simon Snyder received 3047. Both were elected, as the two highest. In 1802 he was elected State Senator and died in office Aug. 24, 1804, and is buried at the Follmer Church. During one winter of the Assembly, two or three young lawyers, a little vain of their learning, interlarded their speeches with long quotations from Latin authors. This gave offense to Jacob Follmer, who in reply, remarked that as it was the fashion to make speeches in unknown tongues, he was to be excused if he spoke in the Delaware Indian dialect. This put an end to the Latin quotations.

On the ship Saint Andrew, Oct. 27, 1738, came John Rinehard Bene, who died in Northampton county in 1758. Michael Seider, born March 6, 1709, died Dec. 8, 1783, who settled in Upper Saucon township, then Bucks and now Lehigh county; John Nicholas Stahler, who died in September, 1794 in Northampton county, and George Bibighausen, born Sept. 3, 1708, in Elshof, in Wittgenstein.

The ship Bilander Thistle, Oct. 28, 1738, brought Conrad Merkam, who settled first in Berks county and later in Carbon county.

Peter Steckel, born 1719, settled in Whitehall township, where he died in 1784. His son, Daniel Steckel, died at Bath, Northampton county, aged 101 years and 17 days.

Samuel Eberhard Kopp, born in Lindenfingen, Wurtemberg, Jan. 8, 1700, settled in Bucks county, now Lehigh, where he died March 2, 1757.

On the ship Charming Nancy, Nov. 9, 1738, came Peter Butz, born in 1718, in Hertzogberg, Bavaria. He settled in Berks county and died March 18, 1780.

John Jacob Kuntz, born Feb. 19, 1692, at Niederbronn, Alsace, settled in Berks county. His son, Bernhard Kuntz, born Dec. 3, 1723, died July 14, 1807, settled in Northampton county. They are ancestors of one of our Executive Committee members.

On the ship Samuel, Aug. 27, 1739, came Joseph Biery, from the Canton of Bern, Switzerland, born 1703, who settled in Berks county and died in 1768. Also Casper Doll, born Feb. 2, 1724, died Feb. 4, 1793, in Plainfield township, Northampton county.

The ship Loyal Judith arrived Nov. 25, 1740, with Frederick Wilhelm Nagel, born in 1713, who settled in Moore township, Northampton county, where he died Nov. 29, 1779.

These ship lists, up to the year 1775, if published and edited with notes as the example here given, would make a valuable addition to the history of the Pennsylvania Germans. At the July meeting of the Executive Committee I made the suggestion that this be done and that photostatic copies be made of all the lists. At the request of the Committee, I have therefore given the society this paper.

––––––

Daniel Israel Rupp. *A Collection of Upwards of Thirty Thousand Names of German, Swiss, Dutch, French and Other Immigrants in Pennsylvania from 1727 to 1776, with a Statement of the Names of Ships, Whence They Sailed, and the Date of their Arrival at Philadelphia, Chronologically Arranged, Together with the Necessary Historical and Other Notes, also, an Appendix Containing Lists of More Than One Thousand German and French Names in New York Prior to 1712*, 3rd ed. Leipzig: Degener & Co., 1931 [Lancour No. 144].

This volume, with material from the second edition of 1876, was
reprinted in Baltimore in 1975. However, it contains many errors
and the researcher is advised to consult Strassburger and Hinke
[Lancour No. 146] instead.

William Henry Egle, ed. *Names of Foreigners Who Took the Oath of
Allegiance to the Province and State of Pennsylvania, 1727-1775,
with the Foreign Arrivals, 1786-1808.* Harrisburg: E. K. Meyers,
1892 [Lancour No. 145].

This work, volume 17 of the second series of the *Pennsylvania
Archives*, was reprinted in Baltimore in 1976. It should be used in
conjunction with the work of Strassburger and Hinke [Lancour No.
146], the latter having taken great care in reading the names.

Ralph Beaver Strassburger. *Pennsylvania German Pioneers; a Publication of the Original Lists of Arrivals in the Port of Philadelphia from 1727 to 1808,* edited by John William Hinke. Norristown: Pennsylvania German Society, 1934 [Lancour No. 146].

This three volume work was prepared with great care, volume 2
containing facsimiles of all signatures of those taking the oath of
allegiance and the oaths of abjuration. The first and third
volumes only have been reprinted (Baltimore, 1975).

William John Hinke and John Baer Stoudt, editors. "A List of
German Immigrants to the American Colonies from Zweibruecken in
the Palatinate, 1728-1749," *The Pennsylvania German Folklore
Society Yearbook,* 1 (1936), 101-124 [Lancour No. 147].

This title along with other publications of the Pennsylvania
German Folklore Society is planned for publication by the Genealogical Publishing Company or 111 Water Street, Baltimore, MD
21202. 404 emigrants destined for Pennsylvania and Carolina are
listed.

Fritz Braun. *Auswanderer aus der Umgebung von Ludwigshafen a. Rh.
auf dem Schiff „Thistle of Glasgow" 1730.* Neustadt an der Aisch:
Buchdruckerei Ph. C. W. Schmidt, 1959 [Lancour No. 148].

Mitte June 1730 dürfte das Segelschiff „Thistle of Glasgow" unter

Kapitän Colin Dunlop Rotterdam für die Fahrt nach Amerika verlassen
haben. Es waren 77 Familien oder Einzelpersonen an Bord, insgesamt
260 Personen. Am 19. Juni 1730 hat das Schiff in Dover angelegt
und nach 72tägiger Fahrt ist es am 29. August 1730 in Philadelphia
eingetroffen. In den „Mitteilungen zur Wanderungsgeschichte der
Pfälzer" 1953, Folge 5, wurde ein Namensverzeichnis der Auswanderer
dieses Schiffes abgedruckt. Die Liste ist seinerzeit aus den 508
in dem dreibändigen Werk von Strassburger und Hinke „Pennsylvania
German Pioneers", Norristown, Pa., 1934, veröffentlichten Schiffslisten ausgewählt worden, weil die Passagiere zum grossen Teil aus
Orten um Ludwigshafen ausgewandert sind. Für 13 der auf dem Schiff
genannten Familien oder Einzelpersonen konnten damals Herkunftsorte
genannt werden.

Was kann heute, 6 Jahre nach Abdruck jener Namensliste, über die
Passagiere des Schiffes „Thistle of Glasgow" berichtet werden?

Die für die Wanderungsforschung wertvollsten Angaben, die Herkunftsorte der Auswanderer, fehlen leider in den genannten Schiffslisten. Sie fehlen auch in den Namenslisten der Einwanderer, die
im Court House zu Philadelphia den Untertaneneid für das neue
Vaterland abzulegen hatten. Die allgemeinen Bemerkungen zu den
Listen der einzelnen Schiffe enthalten Angaben über den Namen des
Kapitäns, den Abfahrtshafen, etwaige Zwischenlandungen und über
den Zeitpunkt der Ankunft des Schiffes in Philadelphia. Vielfach
sind auch allgemein gehaltene Herkunftsvermerke gemacht, die aber
bestenfalls territoriale Begrenzungen des Herkunftsgebietes zulassen. Neben Angaben wie „Passagiere" oder „Fremde" ist der Vermerk
„Pfälzer" oft zu lesen; andere Herkunftsvermerke heissen „Zweibrücken", „Württemberg", „Durlach" oder ähnlich. Dass bei dem Wort
„Pfälzer" nicht an die heutige Pfalz, sondern an alle damals zur
Kurpfalz gehörenden Landesteile gedacht werden muss, ist selbstver-
ständlich. Das Wort ist im weitesten Sinne zu verstehen und
schliesst nicht aus, dass auch Auswanderer aus anderen deutschen
Gauen unter ihnen sein können. Für das Schiff „Thistle of Glasgow"
heiss es, dass die Passagiere „Pfälzer" seien.

Wer sich mit Familiennamen beschäftigt, kann das Herkunftsgebiet
der Passagiere eines Schiffes schon aus dem Auftreten von Namen,
die für einen betimmten Teil unseres Vaterlandes charakteristisch
sind, sehr stark einengen. Selbst für die Pfalz lässt sich unterscheiden, ob es sich um die Vorderpfalz oder um den Westrich, um
die Südpfalz oder um die Nordpfalz handelt.

Die Erfahrung zeigt ausserdem, dass sich auf den einzelnen Schiffen Passagiere oder Gruppen von Passagieren in jener Zeit fast immer aus eng begrenzten Gebietsteilen Deutschlands zusammengeschlos-
sen haben. Es gibt vielerlei Ursachen, die neben den allgemeinen
Auswanderungsgründen dazu Anlass gewesen sind: Die Wirkungsbe-
reiche der Werber, die Notwendigkeit des Zusammenschlusses von Verwandten und Freunden, um sich in der Fremde behaupten und durchset-
zen zu können, das Vertrauen zu bestimmten Persönlichkeiten mit
Führungseigenschaften, das Zusammengehen mit Menschen gleicher

Mundart, was im 18. Jahrhundert der besseren Verständigung wegen
ein nicht unwesentlicher Gesichtspunkt war.
  Wenn also die Schiffslisten grösstenteils auch nur die Vor- und
Familiennamen der über 16 Jahre alten männlichen Einzelauswanderer
oder Familienoberhäupter enthalten—nur in einzelnen Listen sind
zusätzlich auch Frauen und Kinder oder das Alter der Auswanderer
angegeben—, so bleiben noch genügend Wege offen, um über die Herkunft der Passagiere ein ständig klarer werdendes Bild gewinnen zu
können.
  Schon 1953 konnte vom Verfasser die Meinung vertreten und belegt
werden, dass die Herkunft der Auswanderer auf dem Schiff „Thistle
of Glasgow" im Raum Ludwigshafen zu suchen ist. Die weitere Nach-
forschung hat dies bestätigt und gezeigt, dass die Auswanderer in
einem verhältnismässig eng begrenzten Gebiet um Ludwigshafen be-
heimatet waren. Nachdem durch derartige Überlegungen und durch die
Zusammenfassung von Lebensdaten aus der Pfalz und aus den USA,
besonders aus Pennsylvanien und Maryland, das Herkunftsgebiet um-
rissen war, konnten einige systematische Nachforschungen in pfälzi-
schen Kirchenbüchern vorgenommen werden. Sie zeitigten ein recht
befriedigendes Ergebnis und der Verfasser hegt die Hoffnung, dass
er aus dem Kreis der Leser im Laufe der Zeit mit weiteren Ergänzungen rechnen darf. Sehr auffallend sind die verwandtschaftlichen
Beziehungen unter den Auswanderern, die durch Einheirat vor und
nach der Auswanderung zustande gekommen waren.
  An diesem Beispiel kann gezeigt werden, was aus dem zunächst
mageren Gerippe einer nur aus Vor- und Zunamen bestehenden Schiffsliste gemacht werden kann. Die Zusammenfassung der Lebensdaten aus
der Pfalz, aus Amerika und selbst aus der Schweiz liefert reich-
haltigen Stoff für die Wiederherstellung in Vergessenheit geratener
Familienzusammenhänge, sie trägt aber auch dazu bei, das Wissen
über die Wanderungsgeschichte der Pfälzer zu erweitern. Die Arbeit
lässt deutlich erkennen, dass die noch nicht ganz sesshaft gewordenen Zuwanderer aus der Schweiz verhältnismässig stark an der Auswanderung beteiligt waren.
  Es werden alle Namen der Passagiere aufgeführt, auch wenn über
einzelne Namen noch keine Ergänzungen vorliegen. In der Schreibweise der Namen hält sich der Verfasser an die Veröffentlichung von
Strassburger und Hinke. Da für die Passagiere des Schiffes
„Thistle of Glasgow" drei Listen vorliegen—eine Schiffsliste und
zwei Eidesleistungen—werden Abweichungen in der Schreibweise der
Namen angegeben. Von beiden Listen der Eidesleistungen in Philadelphia sind Abdrucke der Originalunterschriften vorhanden, sofern
die Auswanderer nur ein Handzeichen angebracht haben, ist dies nach
den Familiennamen durch ein × oder durch den als Handzeichen ver-
wendeten Buchstaben in Klammern angegeben.
JÖRCH Johan(nes): Vgl. HAS Ludwig.
HAS Ludwig (Lutwig, Loudwick): Aus den Aufzeichnungen im Kirchenbuch der lutherischen Gemeinde Hassloch kann eindeutig nachgewiesen werden, dass Johann Georg Ludwig HAAS (HAS) 1730 nach

Amerika ausgewandert ist. Der Auswanderer hat sich in den beiden
Eideslisten selbst als „Johann Jörg Lutwig Hass" eingetragen.
Die Listen sind zweispaltig angelegt. Da der Auswanderer für
seinen Namen beide Spalten in Anspruch genommen hat, waren die
Herausgeber des Buches „Pennsylvania German Pioneers" sich nicht
klar darüber, ob es sich um einen Auswanderer mit drei Vornamen
handelt oder ob es zwei Auswanderer mit den Namen Johan JÖRCH und
Ludwig HAS sein könnten. Die Verfasser hatten keine Möglichkeit
zur Aufklärung des Eintrags und haben deshalb zwei Auswanderer,
JÖRCH und HAS, in den von ihnen veröffentlichten Listen aufgenommen. Nach dieser Klarstellung kann Johan JÖRCH als Auswanderer gestrichen werden.

    Johann Georg Ludwig HAAS (HAASS) wurde am 31. 7. 1701 in Hass-
loch als Sohn des Abraham Hass getauft. Im gleichen Ort fand am
23. 1. 1725 seine Eheschliessung mit Anna Margaretha STAHLER,
Tochter des Ackermanns Johann STAHLER und der Anna Margareta
...statt. Sie wurde am 18. 4. 1703 in Hassloch getauft. Der
Pfarrer hat bei der Eheschliessung im Kirchenbuch den Vermerk
„1730 in die Insul Pensylvania gezogen" nachgetragen.
    Kinder, zu Hassloch geboren:
    Maria Barbara, ᭡ 28. 2. 1726,
    Johann Balthasar, * 1. 9. 1727.

SIGMUND (SIGMUNDT, SIGHMOND) Bernhardt (Bernard): Für die Jahre
    1734 und 1739 ist sein Aufenthalt in Philadelphia, Pa., belegt.
    Er gehörte zu den Organisatoren der ersten reformierten Kirche
    in Philadelphia und war 1739 einer der Kirchenältesten.
DIEHL (THEIL) Hans Jacob: Er dürfte sehr wahrscheinlich aus der
    Umgebung von Hassloch ausgewandert sein.
DUNKEL(L) Johannes (Joannes): 1739 war er einer der Kirchenältes-
    ten der Falckner Schwam Reformierten Kirche (Falkner Swamp, Mont-
    gomery County, Pa.). Vgl. REIMER Friedrich.
BADER (BATTER) Christoph (Christof, Christopher)
OHLER (OHLLER, OLER) Johann Peter (Petter): Er stammt aus Mecken-
    heim und war kurz vor der Auswanderung am 5. 4. 1730 in Hassloch
    bei dem 5. Kind des auf dem gleichen Schiff ausgewanderten Nikel
    FISER (vgl.) Pate.
GRAU Leonard (Löhnhart, Lönhard)
HESS (HES) × Jeremias (Jerrimias): Mit seiner Frau Anna hatte
    Jeremias HESS bereits ein sehr bewegtes Auswanderungsschicksal
    hinter sich, denn genau 21 Jahre zuvor war er schon einmal mit
    seiner Familie zur Auswanderung nach Amerika aufgebrochen.
    Damals erreichte er das Ziel Amerika nicht. Von Holland aus war
    er mit vielen seiner Landsleute auf dem Segelschiff nach England
    gebracht worden und musste sich dort südlich von London im Lager
    Schwarze Heide aufhalten. Da es an Schiffsraum für Amerika
    fehlte, wurde er mit einer Gruppe von Pfälzern nach Irland in die
    Grafschaft Limerick weitergeleitet. Der 1713 durch den Pfarrer
    von Mutterstadt vorgenommene Nachtrag, dass Jeremias HESS mit
    seiner Frau Anna bei der am 29. 12. 1709 in Irland getauften Anna

Maria HEIM, Tochter des aus Mutterstadt stammenden Hans Paul(us)
HEIM und der Anna VOLK, Taufzeuge war, beweist die Anwesenheit
des Jeremias HESS in Irland ebenso wie der Nachtrag bei seinen
eigenen in Mutterstadt geborenen Kindern Hans Conrad und Elisabeth „mortuus in Irrland"—„in Irland gestorben". Als Jeremias
HESS am 2. 6. 1709 in St. Cathrins/England registriert wurde, war
er 34 Jahre alt. Ausser der Frau werden zwei Söhne im Alter von
7 und 5 Jahren und eine Tochter von 2 Jahren genannt. Bei dem
Rücktransport nach Holland im Jahr 1711 heisst es „Jeremias HESS
und 3 Personen".
    Als dem Ehepaar nach der Rückkehr weitere Kinder in Mutterstadt
geboren wurden, erhielt einer der Söhne den Namen des in Irland
verstorbenen Bruders Johann Conrad.
    Auf dem Schiff „Thistle of Glasgow" erreichte die Familie des
Jeremias HESS endlich das erstrebte Ziel.
    Kinder:
    1. Sohn, * um 1703,
    2. Hans Conrad, * 3. 5. 1705 Mutterstadt, „mortuus in Irr-
        land",
    3. Elisabeth, * 21. 10. 1708 Mutterstadt, „mortuus in Irr-
        land",
    4. Christian, * 14. 7. 1713 Mutterstadt, † in Mutterstadt,
    5. Hans Conrad, ∾ 19. 8. 1714 Mutterstadt,
    6. Balthasar, ∾ 8. 12. 1717 Mutterstadt.
LEMAN (K) Christian (Cristian)
GRIESEMER (GRISIMER) (O) Valtein (Velde): Der Auswanderer Johann
    Valentin GRIESHEIMER, Sohn des Hans Velten GRIESSHEIMER und der
    Anna Margaretha..., * 4. 1. 1688 in Lampertheim, † 1759 in Here-
    ford County, Pa., wurde laut Manumissionsschein des Erzbischofs
    zu Mainz, Frantz Ludwig, am 28. 4. 1730 samt Ehefrau und den 4
    Kindern Casper, Johann, Anna Margaretha und Jakob aus der Leib-
    eigenschaft entlassen. Der im Band III des Buches „Pennsylvania
    German Pioneers" abgedruckte Entlassungsschein mit der Bemerkung,
    dass das Untertanenverhältnis nach einer etwaigen Rückkehr wieder
    in Kraft treten werde ist in Pennsylvanien erhalten. Vgl. Bild-
    beilage.
    Die Frau, die Johann Valentin GRIESHEIMER am 17. 7. 1712 in
    Lampertheim geheiratet hat, hiess Anna Margaretha ANDREASS.
    In ihrer neuen Heimat in Pennsylvanien bevorzugten die Grie-
    semer das Leben als Farmer ausserhalb geschlossener Siedlungen.
    Sie schlossen sich in Familiengemeinschaften zusammen und verfüg-
    ten bald über eine eigene Wasserversorgung, über eigene Mühlen
    und Kelteranlagen, sie besassen eigene Webstühle und hatten sich
    Werkstätten wie Schmiede, Schusterei und Sattlerei eingerichtet.
    Zu ihren Wohngebäuden und ausgedehnten Ländereien gehörte ein
    eigener Familienfriedhof. Die Griesemer zählten zu den ange-
    sehensten Familien um Oley, einem Ort und einem Tal zwischen
    Allentown und Reading in Berks County, Pennsylvanien. Hereford
    war der erste Ansiedlungsort, später Goshenhoppen.

Wer heute als Pfälzer durch dieses vor nahezu 250 Jahren überwiegend von Pfälzer Landsleuten besiedelte Gebiet kommt, fühlt
sich von dem Land und seinen Menschen sehr angesprochen. Es sind
viele Dinge, die ein heimisches Gefühl aufkommen lassen: Die
Anordnung und Bauweise der aus dem 18. Jahrhundert erhaltenen
Wohnhäuser und Nebengebäude, von denen einzelne noch mit Schwal-
benschwanzziegeln gedeckt sind, die Blumen- und Gemüsegärten bei
den Wohnhäusern, die mächtigen Rosskastanien oder vereinzelt auch
der alte Birnbaum beim Haus, die Menschen mit uns vertrauten
Gesichtszügen und Lebensgewohnheiten.

In dem Oley benachbarten Spangsville steht noch eine alte Mühle
mit der Aufschrift „D. L. Griesemer and E. Griesemer Mill 1847".
Sie ist gegenwartig im Besitz von Henry Wagner. Etwa 5 Kilometer
westlich von Spangsville erinnert der Ort Griesemersville an die
aus Lampertheim eingewanderte Familie. Griesemersville ist nach
einem Enkel des Auswanderers, Peter GRIESEMER, benannt, der als
erste Häuser des Ortes ein Hotel und ein Geschäftshaus gebaut
hatte. Letzterer, ein Sohn des Caspar, war in I. Ehe mit Esther
HOCH, einer Tochter des Daniel HOCH (Schweizer Herkunft) und der
Mary BERTOLET, verheiratet. Die Bertolet wiederum waren aus Cha-
teau-d'Oex im Kanton Waadt, Schweiz, nach Minfeld/Pfalz eingewan-
dert und von da nach Amerika weitergezogen.

Ein anderer Enkel, Jacob GRIESEMER, war Hauptmann im Unabhäng-
igkeitskrieg.

Kinder, 1-6 zu Lampertheim, 7 in Pennsylvanien geboren:
1. Johann Wilhelm, * 17. 9. 1713; ∞ mit Anna Maria ...; sie
   hatten 6 Kinder: John, * um 1747; Felix, * Juli 1749;
   Anna Maria, * 11. 7. 1752; Catherina, * 12. 4. 1754;
   Gertrude, * 29. 4. 1757; Abraham, * 1759.
2. Casper, * 13. 3. 1715, † in Oley 1794, ⊏ auf dem privaten
   Friedhof, später nach Oley umgebettet; ∞ mit Rebecca
   ESHELMANN.
3. Anna Margaretha, * 12. 9. 1719,
4. Jakob, * 27. 2. 1724,
5. Philipp, * 3. 11. 1725, † 1. 2. 1726,
6. Anna Maria Gerdraut, * Mai 1728; ∞ mit Jacob GERY,
7. Leonard, * 1733, † 1821; er unterhielt in Hereford auf
   seiner Farm eine Töpferei; ∞ mit Elizabeth FABER.

FIEHMAN (FEMAN) (K) Casper (Caspar)
REINER (R) Stefen (Steven)
DRAUG(H) × Rudolph: Es handelt sich zweifellos um Johann Rudolf
DRACH, der mit Maria Elisabetha...verheiratet war. Das Ehepaar
liess am 14. 8. 1728 in Dannstadt eine Tochter Elisabeth taufen.
Patin war Elisabeth OBERBECK geb. DRACH, die Ehefrau des Andreas
OBERBECK, der im Jahre 1732 mit Frau und Kindern nach Amerika
auswandert ist.
KUN × Johannes (Joannes)
HEIM (W) Willem: Wilhelm HEIM stammt aus Mutterstadt und war bei
dem ältesten Sohn des Philip GROSCOST (vgl.), Auswanderer auf dem
gleichen Schiff, Taufzeuge.

Sein Geburtseintrag ist im Kirchenbuch der reformierten Gemeinde
Mutterstadt nicht zu finden. Das Kirchenbuch weist für den in
Frage kommenden Zeitraum nur wenige Namen auf. Es darf angenom-
men werden, dass Wilhelm HEIM ein Bruder zu Anna Margaretha HEIM,
Ehefrau des Hans Philipp GROSSKOST, ist. Ausserdem liegt es
nahe, dass er auch ein Bruder zu Hans Paul HEIM ist, der bei
Jeremias HESS genannt wurde. Letzterer ist mit seinem am 10. 7.
1712 in Mutterstadt geborenen Sohn Johannes oder Hans und wei-
teren Familienangehörigen auf dem Schiff „James Goodwill" am 27.
9. 1727 in Philadelphia angekommen. Hat er den Verwandten die
Anregung zur Auswanderung gegeben?
DITTMAN (DITMAN) × Loudwick
SCHMITT (SMITH) Johan Henrich (Hendrick): (? Dannstadt)
ZINN (ZIN) Gerhart (Gerard)
ANKENBRANTT (ANGUBRANT) Christoph (Cristoph)
FORTINAUX (FORTNE) × Jean Henri (Hanri, Hendrick)
MINNIG (MINIGH) × Hans: (? Dannstadt)
BISWANGER (B) Peter
REIMER (REINER) Friedrich (Friederich, Frik): Friedrich REIMER
    (REYMER) kaufte am 22. 1. 1731 hundert Acker Land von Henry
    PANNEBAKER und dessen Frau Eva...in Frederick Township. Aus
    seinem am 9. 5. 1755 angefertigten Testament geht hervor, dass
    seine Frau den Vornamen Elisabeth trug und dass sein Sohn John
    Peter REIMER als Testamentsvollstrecker eingesetzt war. Fried-
    rich REIMER hatte eine Tochter Elisabeth, die durch ihre Ehe-
    schliessung mit Francis SHUNK von Providence Township Grossmutter
    des späteren Gouverneurs Francis R. SHUNK wurde.
    1740 gehörte Friedrich REIMER wie Johannes DUNKEL (vgl.) zu den
    Kirchenältesten der Falckner Schwam Reformierten Kirche (Falkner
    Swamp, Montgomery County, Pa.).
    In der „Geschichte des Dorfes Mutterstadt" von Heinrich Eyse-
    lein, die als Heft 3 der Beihefte zu den Saarpfälzischen Abhand-
    lungen zur Landes- und Volksforschung im Jahre 1938 veröffent-
    licht wurde, werden verschiedene Namensträger Reimer als Auswan-
    derer nach Amerika in der ersten Hälfte des 18. Jahrhunderts ge-
    nannt. Da die Auswanderer des Schiffes „Thistle of Glasgow" zum
    grössten Teil aus den Gemeinden um Ludwigshafen ausgewandert
    sind, lag es nahe, den Auswanderer Friedrich REIMER im Kirchen-
    buch der reformierten Gemeinde Mutterstadt zu suchen. Tatsäch-
    lich konnte dort Friederich REIMER, verschiedentlich auch Diony-
    sius Friedrich REIMER, verheiratet am 1. 10. 1715 in Mutterstadt
    mit Elisabeth WEYNACHT aus Mutterstadt, gefunden werden. Der
    Vorname der Frau Elisabeth und die Namen der in Amerika im Testa-
    ment genannten Kinder Elisabeth und Johann Peter decken sich mit
    den Eintragungen im Kirchenbuch von Mutterstadt.
    Kinder, zu Mutterstadt geboren:
    1. Elisabetha, ∿ 24. 12. 1716,
    2. Susanna Elisabetha, ∿ 16. 7. 1721,
    3. Anna Barbara, ∿ 2. 1. 1724,

4. Johanna Maria, ∿ 30. 5. 1726,
5. Johann Peter, ∿ 30. 11. 1728.
FISER × Nickel(1), in den USA u. a. FUISSER, FEEZER und FOESER:
Johann Nikolaus FÜSSER, ein Sohn des Christoph FÜSSER, heiratete
am 7. 4. 1722 zu Hassloch Juliane Sophia HAUTZ, Tochter des
Johann Wendel HAUTZ und der Anna Katharina .... Sie ist eine
Schwester zu Philip HAUTS/HAUTZ (vgl.), der auf dem gleichen
Schiff ausgewandert ist. Der Bruder des Johann Nikolaus FÜSSER,
Johann Wendel FÜSSER, ist am 20. 9. 1738 auf dem Schiff „Friend-
ship" in Philadelphia angekommen.
    Das Ehepaar Johann Nikolaus FÜSSER, dem vor der Auswanderung in
Haasloch 5 und später in Pennsylvanien weitere Kinder geboren
wurden, erwarb u. a. am 12. 10. 1737 in Lancaster County, Pa.,
200 Acker Land.
    Kinder, 1-5 zu Hassloch, 6-9 in Amerika geboren:
    1. Maria Catharina, * 26. 12. 1722,
    2. Philipp Jacob, * 3. 3. 1724,
    3. Anna Catharina, * 26. 12. 1725,
    4. Johann Jacob, * 16. 4. 1728,
    5. Philipp Peter, * 5. 4. 1730; Pate war Johann Peter OHLER
        (vgl.) aus Meckenheim, der ebenfalls auf dem Schiff
        „Thistle of Glasgow" ausgewandert ist. Philipp Peter
        FÜSSER hatte in Amerika Catharina ... geheiratet; er
        ist am 12. 12. 1791 gestorben. Unter seinen Kindern
        waren Christina, Margaretha und Maria Elisabeth. Eine
        der Töchter war mit Jacob OBERLE verheiratet.
    6. Maria Margaret, * 10. 5. 1735; ∞ Lancaster County, Pa.,
        am 16. 4. 1754 mit Philipp Lorenz GRÜNEWALD, der am 10.
        6. 1725 in Böhl als Sohn des Joh. Mathes GRÜNEWALD und
        der Maria Catharina ... geboren wurde und als Passa-
        gier des Schiffes „Phoenix" am 15. 9. 1749 in Philadel-
        phia angekommen war.
    7. Susanna; ∞ mit Andreas RHUM (RUHN?),
    8. (? Peter),
    9. (? George).
NAGEL (NAGOLL) Jacob
SCHMIDT (SMITH) Johan Casper (Jan)
ZWINGER Johan
SUMGER Geo.
SCHERER (SHERER) Ulrich (Ulrick)
GROSCOST (O) Philip: Der Auswanderer Hans Philipp GROSSKOST
(GROSSKASTEN) war mit Anna Margaretha HEIM verheiratet. Zwischen
1715 und 1721 wurden dem Ehepaar in Mutterstadt 4 Kinder geboren.
Pate des ältesten Sohnes Wilhelm war Wilhelm HEIM (vgl.), eben-
falls Auswanderer auf diesem Schiff. Charles A. GROSSCOST, ein
Nachkomme in Amerika, ist von der Reformierten Kirche zu den Mor-
monen übergetreten und lebt in Toole im Staat Utah. Auch in
Pennsylvanien und Ohio leben noch Nachfahren.

Kinder, zu Mutterstadt geboren:
1. Wilhelm, ∿ 10. 5. 1715, Paten: Wilhelm HEIM, ledig, und
   Anna Margarethe REISIGER, ledig.
2. Christoph, ∿ 14. 2. 1717; ∞ Mutterstadt 15. 2. 1735 mit
   Johanna STEIGER, T. d. Schultheissen zu Mutterstadt
   Johann Theobald STEIGER. Bei der Eheschliessung ist im
   Kirchenbuch vermerkt, dass der Vater „Bürger in Pennsylvanien" ist.
3. Anna Elisabeth, ∿ 19. 3. 1719.
4. Philipp Daniel, ∿ 8. 11. 1721, Paten: Philipp Daniel
   SAAR und dessen Frau Elisabetha ...
BITTNER (K) Casper: Caspar BÜTTNER stammt aus Maudach; seine Frau
   Maria Elisabetha wurde am 13. 8. 1703 in Dannstadt als Tochter
   des Hans MÜNCH und der Johanna ... getauft. Das Ehepaar Büttner
   lebte in Dannstadt, wo ihm noch vor der Auswanderung am 11. 4.
   1729 ein Sohn Johann Henrich geboren wurde.
DÜTTENHÖFFER (DITTENHÖFFER, TITENHAVER) Johan Paulus: Er wurde am
   3. 10. 1706 als Sohn des Schreiners Hans Georg DÜDENHÖFFER (DIE-
   DENHÖFFER) und der Maria MUNIER zu Hassloch getauft. Die Munier
   stammen aus der Schweiz. Eine Eheschliessung des Auswanderers
   ist im Kirchenbuch Hassloch nicht enthalten; er hat offenbar in
   der Nachbarschaft von Hassloch Anna Maria ... geheiratet.
   Kind, zu Hassloch geboren:
   Johann Christoph, ∿ 3. 8. 1729.
SCHERRER (SHERER) Johannes (Joannes): 1734 gehörte er ·in Philadelphia, Pa., der gleichen Kirchengemeinde an wie Bernhardt SIGMUND
   (vgl.), ebenfalls Passagier auf diesem Schiff.
SCHERER (SCHERRER, SHERER) Johan Augustus (Justice)
CUNTZER (KINSER) Nickel: Johann Nikel KÜNTZER gehörte der refor-
   mierten Kirchengemeinde Wolfersweiler an; unter dem 15. 11. 1715
   ist seine Taufe dort eingetragen. Die Eltern, Hans Bernhard
   KÜNTZER und Anna Catharina SEUBERT (SEIBERT), lebten zu diesem
   Zeitpunkt vermutlich in dem benachbarten Hirstein. Johann Nickel
   KUNTZER lebte als Hufschmied in Tulpehocken, Berks County, Pa.
   Er heiratete am 3. 1. 1742 in I. Ehe Anna Catharina HÖSTER, in
   II. Ehe am 29. 10. 1743 Julianna SCHNEIDER. Am 20. 1. 1794 starb
   er in Tulpehocken und wurde bei der Host Kirche begraben.
   Aus II. Ehe wurden ihm 5 Kinder geboren:
   1. Julianna, * 1747,
   2. Anna Catharine, * 1749,
   3. John Jacob, * 1750,
   4. Anna Elizabeth, * 1752,
   5. Mary Margaret, * 1755.
HOFFMANN (HOFMAN) × Hans George (Geo., Gorg)
HOFFMAN (HOFMAN, HOUF[MAN]) (H) Joannes
HAUTS × Philip: Johann Philipp HAUTZ wurde am 28. 10. 1708 als
   Sohn des Johann Wendel HAUTZ und der Anna Katharina ... in Hassloch getauft. Taufzeuge war Joh.· Philipp DIETZ aus Hassloch.
   Eine Schwester von Johann Philipp HAUTZ, Juliane Sophia, hatte
   1722 Nickel FISER/FÜSSER (vgl.) verheiratet, der mit seiner Familie ebenfalls auf dem Schiff „Thistle of Glasgow" auswanderte.

Johann Philipp HAUTZ heiratete in Amerika Anna Margaret ROYER,
Tochter des aus Bohl stammenden und um 1726/27 nach Amerika ausgewanderten Sebastian ROYER und der Anges FLOCKERTH, die am 1. 6.
1713 in Hassloch geboren war.

Johann Philipp HAUTZ lebte nach seiner Ankunft in Amerika
zunächst in Cocalico Township, Lancaster County, Pa., 1738 war er
in Bethel Township, Berks County (heute Lebanon County), Pa., wo
er 1766 gestorben ist. Von ihm leben zahlreiche Nachkommen in
USA.

Dem Ehepaar wurden in Amerika 10 Kinder geboren:

1. Wendel, * um 1737, † 1797/98; er heiratete am 20. 5. 1760
   Catharina Elisabeth RIEGEL und übersiedelte nach Edinburg, Shenandoah County, Virginia.

2. Magdalena, * um 1738; ∞ am 22. 3. 1757 (in Cocalico Township?) mit Joh. Jacob WERNS, S. d. Conrad WERNS.

3. Elisabeth, * um 1739; ∞ I. am 15. 5. 1759 (in Cocalico
   Township?) mit Johannes WEBER; ∞ II. mit George SIMON.

4. Philipp Lorentz, ∿ 16. 12. 1740 in der Alten Swatara
   Reformierten Kirche in der Nähe des jetzigen Jonestown,
   Pa., Paten: Philipp Lorentz HAUTZ und seine Frau (?
   Eva WALBORN, T. des Christian WALBORN, der um 1709 nach
   New York ausgewandert war). Philipp Lorentz ist im
   Dezember 1796 gestorben. Er heiratete in I. Ehe am 7.
   3. 1764 Anna Maria MUELLER, Tochter des Christopher
   MUELLER; in II. Ehe heiratete er um 1779 Anna Catherina
   DAUB, Tochter des Johann DAUB und der Anna Catherina
   . . .

5. Julianna, * um 1742, † 1784; sie heiratete am 2. 5. 1770
   Johann Jacob LAUBSCHER, der am 3. 4. 1735 als Sohn des
   Conrad LAUBSCHER vom Morschbacherhof und der Anna Margaretha REHBERGER in Obermehlingen geboren wurde.
   Johann Jacob LAUBSCHER war am 3. 11. 1750 mit seinem
   Vater Conrad LAUBSCHER auf dem Schiff „Brotherhood" in
   Philadelphia angekommen und ist 1784 in Lebanon Township, Lancaster County, Pa., gestorben, wo er im Jahr
   1771 eine Farm von 110 Acker Land besass. Die Testa-
   mentseröffnung seines am 15. 10. 1783 verfassten Testa-
   mentes erfolgte am 22. 4. 1784. Die Familie Laubscher
   stammt aus der Schweiz. 1682 hat sich Hanns LAUBSCHER
   aus Meinisberg im Berner Gebiet mit seiner Familie auf
   der Morschbach niedergelassen. Unter dem Datum vom 13.
   11. 1670 konnte der Taufeintrag seines Sohnes Abraham
   in Pieterlen, dem Kirchort von Meinisberg, aufgefunden
   werden. Abraham ist der Vater des genannten Conrad
   LAUBSCHER.

6. Henry, * 1. 10. 1745, † 30. 9. 1796; er heiratete am 12.
   9. 1769 Maria Barbara DUPS. Das Ehepaar lebte in
   Bethel Township, Pa.

7. George, * um 1747, † im Februar oder März 1782; ∞ vor

1772 mit Mary Elizabeth CONRAD.
8. Christopher, * 29. 1. 1753, † 1842.
9. Eva, * um 1754, † vor 1850; sie war mit George GILBERT ver-
    heiratet.
10. Anna Maria, * um 1760; sie heiratete am 5. 6. 1781 Christo-
    pher KNEBLE.

HOFF (POST) Lorentz (Laurence), in den USA HUFF: Der aus der Pfalz
stammende Auswanderer hat sich in Warwick Township, Lancaster
County, Pa., niedergelassen, und lebte dort bis etwa 1760.

TRANSU Abraham: Der Auswanderer Abraham TRANSU (TRANSUE, TRANSOL,
im Kirchenbuch Mutterstadt: TRENTSOLS und TRANTSOLS) heiratete
in I. Ehe am 4. 2. 1721 in Mutterstadt Elisabeth MUSCHLER und
kurze Zeit nach deren Tod in II. Ehe ebenfalls in Mutterstadt am
22. 7. 1727 Anna Margaretha MÜLLER aus (?) Obersietzheim. Er
wanderte mit seiner Frau und 2 Kindern aus und liess sich in
Salisbury Township, Lehigh County, Pa., nieder; er ist um 1770
gestorben. Aus seiner I. Ehe sind 2 von den 3 Kindern mit ihm
nach Amerika gezogen; sein in II. Ehe geborener Sohn Isaak ist
noch vor der Auswanderung gestorben: in Pennsylvanien wurden ihm
3 weitere Kinder geboren.
    Kinder aus I. Ehe, zu Mutterstadt geboren:
1. Anna Katharina, * 15. 3. 1722, † 26. 6. 1799 in Emmaus,
    Pa.; sie heiratete am 1. 1. 1741 Sebastian Henrich
    KNAUSS, * 6. 10. 1714 in Düdelsheim in Oberhessen, der
    mit seinen Eltern nach Amerika ausgewandert war und am
    26. 2. 1777 in Emmaus an Lungenentzündung starb.
    Sebastian Henrich KNAUSS trat 1742 als Reformierter zur
    Moravian Church über und wird als der Gründer des Ortes
    Emmaus in Pennsylvanien genannt (1761).
2. Johann Philipp, * 1. 11. 1724; er ging mit seiner Frau
    nach Bethabara in North Carolina.
3. Anthon, * 22. 12. 1726, † in Mutterstadt.
    Kinder aus II. Ehe:
4. Isaak, * 31. 7. 1729 in Mutterstadt, † vor der Auswande-
    rung.
5. Johann Abraham, * 6. 6. 1731 in Salisbury Township; ∞ um
    1755 mit Anna Magdalena LONG, Tochter des Elias LONG
    (LANG).
6. Johann Jacob, * 28. 7. 1734.
7. Elizabeth, * 20. 6. 1736.

HARTMAN (H) Casper: Karl Kreuter weiss in der Ortsgeschichte
„Maudach im Wandel der Zeiten" zu berichten, dass Kaspar HARTMANN
aus Maudach bereits 1725 mit seiner Frau Anna Regina KLUMB und
deren ledigen Schwester Anna Maria KLUMB „in das neue Land"
ziehen wollte. Damals wurden ein Hausanteil und ein Krautgarten
um den Preis von 180 Gulden abgegeben. Dem Kaufvertrag von 1726
über drei Morgen Ackerland um den Preis von 56 Gulden hat der
Gemeindeschreiber später die Bemerkung angefügt: „Dieses ist
alles bezahlt worden, und der Verkäufer ist mit Weib und Kindern,

Sack und Pack, in das neue Land Anno 1730 gereist". Noch kurz vor der Abreise hatte Kaspar HARTMANN sein eigenes Wohnhaus, $2^3/_4$ Morgan Acker und vier kleine Gärtchen für 240 Gulden veräussert.

HAMMAN (HAMMON) Thomas (Thos.)

SHRAM (K) Christian (Cristian)

STIFFEL (STERFELL) Jacob

ANDREAS (ANDRES) Rudolph (Rudolf)

PEIFER (PF) Frederick (Frédrick)

KÖPPLINGER (CAPLINGER) Leonhart (Leonard)

KEPPLINGER (KEPLINGER, CAPLINGER) Johannes (Johanes, Joannes)

SPERGER (A) Wolfer

BYDLEMAN (MEIDELMANN, MEIDELMAN) Felden (Feld., Velde)

BEITELMAN (BEYDELMANN, BYDLEMAN) Dettrich (Titrick)

BEIDELMAN (BYDLEMAN, MEIDELMANN) Elias (Ellias): Die drei genann-ten Auswanderer BEUTELMANN stammen aus Assenheim. Velten BEUTEL-MANN ist Vater des Elias und Onkel des Johann Dieterich BEUTEL-MANN, letzterer hat sich vermutlich als Neffe der Familie des Velten BEUTELMANN angeschlossen.

Johann Dieterich wurde am 12. 6. 1706 als Sohn des Hans Marti (oder Marx) BEUTELMANN getauft. Bei dem Taufeintrag im Kirchen-buch ist die Mutter nicht angegeben; bei Geschwistern heisst sie Anna Catharina oder auch Maria Catharina (? BAURIN). Es sind keine Anzeichen da, dass Geschwister mit ihm ausgewandert sind, da einige in Dannstadt bzw. Schauernheim geheiratet haben.

Anders ist es mit den Geschwistern des Elias. Sie sind sicher-lich mit den Eltern nach Amerika gezogen, da die jüngsten erst 10 und 13 Jahre alt waren. In den Schiffs- und Eideslisten sind nur die über 16 Jahre alten Söhne eingetragen; so ist nur der 22 Jahre alte Elias in den Listen zu finden.

Velten BEUTELMANN war mit Anna Clara BIERMANN verheiratet. Kinder, zu Assenheim geboren:
1. Maria Elisabeth, ∿ 22. 2. 1706,
2. Elias, ∿ 25. 9. 1707, Paten: Elias BRAND von Wachenheim und Sibila CHRISTMANN.
3. Elisabetha, ∿ 7. 12. 1709,
4. Johann Leonhard, ∿ 3. 10. 1716,
5. Johann Jacob, ∿ 7. 1. 1720.

AMMON (H) Jacob: Es handelt sich vermutlich um eine eingewanderte Schweizer Familie mit dem Namen AMMAN.

STEYNER (STYNER) × Ulrick (Ullwrick)

HESS Thos. (Dommes, Dhommes)

HESS Henrich (Hendrick)

LUKENBILL (LUKENBOURG) × Johan Ekel (Joan)

MEY Hans Simon (In der Schiffsliste: James MORCE). Es kann nicht geklärt werden, ob die verschiedenen Namensträger personengleich sind.

LUKENBILL (LUCKENBILL, LÜCKENBILL) Henrich (Hendrick): Der Name LUCHENBIEHL (LUCHENBÜHL, LUGENBÜHL) kommt in der fraglichen Zeit in der Umgebung von Landau sowie be Zweibrücken und bei Ottweiler

vor. Es handelt sich um eingewanderte Schweizer aus dem Berner
Gebiet.
GUTT × Hendrick
KRIEGER (GRIGER) Caspar (Casper)
TRAWIENER (TRAVINGER) Peter: Er dürfte aus Mutterstadt oder aus
der Umgebung von Mutterstadt stammen.
RENN (REN) Bernhard (Bernard)
KOBER (COVER) Dieterich (Titrick)
MOHLER (MOLER, MAHLER) Lutwig (Loudwick): Der Auswanderer soll
nach Angaben eines Nachkommen, der den Abstammungsort seines Vor-
fahren sucht, am 4. 4. 1696 geboren sein. Nach seinen Angaben
soll der Auswanderer mit Anna (?) ..., geboren am 22. 5. 1698,
verheiratet gewesen und mit Frau und 3 Kindern nach Amerika
gezogen sein, wo er sich in Ephrata, Pa., niederliess und ein
Mitglied der Brethren Church wurde.
    Kinder:
    1. Heinrich, * 20. 1. (od. 4) 1728,
    2. Jacob,
    3. Georg Adam.
HERTZEL (HURTZELL) Ludwig (Loudwick)
HERTZEL (HURTZELL) Geo. (Jerg, Yorg)
FEDEROLF (FEDEROLPH) Peter, in den USA auch FETHERHOLF und FETTER-
OLF: Der Auswanderer stammt aus Wachbach bei Bad Mergentheim.
Mit seiner Familie hat er sich in Macungie, Lehigh County, Pa.,
niedergelassen, wo er 150 Acker Land erworben hat. Von ihm sind
folgende Lebensdaten bekannt:
    Am 20. 3. 1699 wurde er zu Wachbach als Sohn des Johann Jakob
FEDEROLF geboren; noch vor der Auswanderung hat er 1729 Anna
Maria ROTHERMEL aus dem gleichen Ort geheiratet. Sie war das
älteste Kind des nachfolgend genannten Auswanderers Johann
ROTHERMEL und der Sybilla ZIMMERMANN und im Februar 1712 zu Wachbach geboren. Peter FEDEROLF ist am 15. 8. 1784 in Pennsylvanien
gestorben und wurde wie seine Frau auf dem privaten Friedhof auf
der eigenen Farm, die vermutlich zu Hereford Township, Berks
County, gehörte, begraben. Einer seiner Söhne, Jakob FETHEROLF,
wurde am 16. 2. 1742 in Hereford Township, Berks County, geboren.
ROTHERMEL Johann: Er wird in keiner der drei Listen genannt; das
ist verständlich, denn er ist nach den Aufzeichnungen der Familie
Federolf während der Überfahrt gestorben und auf hoher See
bestattet worden.
    Unter den Nachkommen des Auswanderers war lange Zeit die Mein-
ung vertreten, dass der Herkunftsort Wachbach in Holland zu
suchen sei, bis Abraham ROTHERMEL auf zwei Europareisen in den
Jahren 1908 und 1910 aufklären konnte, dass es sich um Wachbach
bei Bad Mergentheim handelt. Er weilte 1910 selbst in Wachbach
und hat im Dezember 1911 vor der Historical Society von Berks
County über den Erfolg seiner Nachforschungen berichtet. Über
Johann ROTHERMEL und seine Nachkommen liegen mehrere Veröffentlichungen vor. Eine alte Familienbibel ist 1880 leider durch
einem Brand in Philadelphia vernichtet worden.

Johann ROTHERMEL aus Wachbach bei Bad Mergentheim war 1688 geboren und hatte 1708 Sybilla ZIMMERMANN geheiratet. Von den sechs zu Wachbach geborenen Kindern sind folgende Daten bekannt:

1. Anna Maria, * Februar 1712; ∞ 1729 mit dem vorgenannten Peter FEDEROLF.
2. Lorenz, ∞ 1746 mit einer Tochter von David KUHNS. Er liess sich in Windsor Township, Berks County, nieder und kaufte dort 1738 150 Acker Land. 2 Kinder: Leonard und Maria.
3. Paul, ∞ 1747 mit Catharine MAURER. Er kaufte 250 Acker Land in Maidencreek Township, Berks County, wo er bis zu seinem Tod lebte. 6 Kinder: Peter, Leonard, Paul, John, Jacob und Barbara.
4. Peter, ∞ mit Magdalena DREIBELBIS, Tochter von Jakob DREIBELBIS. Der Auswanderer Johann Jakob DREIBELBIS wurde am 10. 4. 1709 in Hassloch geboren und ist ledig am 26. 9. 1732 auf dem Schiff „Mary" in Philadelphia angekommen. Peter ROTHERMEL siedelte sich in Richmond Township, Berks County, an, wo er innerhalb von sechs Jahren 450 Acker Land erworben hat. 4 Kinder: Daniel, Peter, Margareth und Abraham.
5. John, * 1722, † 1785; ∞ mit Mary SIEGFRIED, dem ersten weissen Kind, das in Maxatawny Township, Pa., geboren wurde. 4 Kinder: Abraham, Jacob, Daniel und John.
6. Christian, auch er war verheiratet und Vater von 6 Kindern: Margaret, Sybilla, Magdalena, Amanda, Peter und John. 1742 kaufte er 250 Acker in Maidencreek Township und vereinte seine Farm mit der des Bruders Paul.

HOCHGENUG (HOOGINUNK) Leonard (Länhart)

MÜLLER (MOLLER) Peter, in den USA MILLER: Sein Vater war der am 26. 4. 1676 geborene Johannes Müller, Pfarrer in Rothselberg, Alsenborn und Altenkirchen-Miesau. Johann Peter wurde am 25. 12. 1709 in dem Zweikirchlein bei Wolfstein getauft. Am 29. 12. 1725 liess er sich als Theologiestudent in Heidelberg immatrikulieren. Johann Peter MÜLLER gehört zu den auffallendsten Persönlichkeiten unter den aus der Pfalz ausgewanderten Geistlichen. Schon bald nach seiner Ankunft in Philadelphia hat ihn Pastor Jedediah Andrews in einem Bief vom 14. 10. 1730 folgendermassen charakterisiert: „Es ist kürzlich ein theologischer Candidat herübergekommen aus der Pfalz, der auf seiner Anmeldung bei der Synode zur Ordination an Tenant, Andrews und Boyd verwiesen wurde. Er ist eine ausserordentliche Persönlichkeit, was Verstand und Gelehrsamkeit anbetrifft. Wir legten ihm eine Frage bezüglich der Rechtfertigung vor, welche er auf einem ganzen Bogen Papier ausgezeichnet beantwortete. Sein Name ist John Peter Müller und er spricht Latein so fliessend wie wir unsere Muttersprache." Der junge Theologe war 1735 Prediger in Tulpehocken, wurde der geistige Führer der Seventh Day Baptisten (Dunker), gehörte dem Kloster Ephrata an, wurde 1768 Mitglied der American Philosophical

Society und war wegen seiner aussergewöhnlichen geistigen Fähig-
keiten und vielseitigen Verdienste sehr geachtet. Über theolo-
gische Themen führte er einen regen Briefwechsel, im Kloster
Ephrata übersetzte er Tieleman van Braghts „Blutiger Schauplatz
oder Märtyrer-Spiegel" aus dem Holländischen ins Deutsche und
und überwachte den Druck und die Herstellung des Werkes, das 1748
fertig wurde und mit 1514 grossformatigen Seiten als Glanzstück
der Buchdruckerkunst des 18. Jahrhunderts in Amerika gewertet
wird.

Am 25. September 1796 starb Johann Peter MÜLLER, seine Gebeine
ruhen auf dem Klosterfriedhof zu Ephrata, Lancaster County, Pennsylvanien. Der Verfasser hatte Gelegenheit, die Wirkungsstätte
des Johann Peter MULLER in Ephrata aufzusuchen.

Der Grabstein des Johann Peter MÜLLER enthält folgende In-
schrift:

                    Hier Liegt Begraben

                    PETER MILLER

                 Gebuertig im Oberamt
                 Lautern in Chur Pfalz
                 Kam als Reformierter
                 Prediger nach Amerika
                 Im Jahr 1730. Wurde
                 (Un)ter die Gemeine in
                    Ephrata getaufet im
                    Jahr 1735 und genant
               Bruder Jaebez — Auch ward
                 Er nachmals ihr Lehrer
               Bis an sein Ende. Entschlief
                 Den 25ten September 1796
                 Alter 86 Jahr und 9 Monat

LÜNBERGER (LIENENBERGER, LENKENBERGER) Friedrich (Fredrick)
MICHAELS (MICHELL) Carle Vallenthien (Valantine)
HENERICH (HENDRICK) Christofer (Christoph)
THEISS Johann Matheus (Mattheis): Johann Mattheis THEISS stammt
   wie Johann Nickel KÜNTZER aus Hirstein Krs. St. Wendel. Noch vor
   der Auswanderung verehelichte er sich im Jahr 1726. Er siedelte
   sich westlich von Tulpehocken, Berks County, Pa., an und starb
   bereits 1748.
UNDERTENERD Geo.
THOMAS Christian
THOMAS (THOMMAS) Michel (erkrankt): Der an letzter Stelle in der
   Eidesliste genannte Auswanderer Johann Michel THOMAS wurde 1688
   als Sohn des am 24. 2. 1708 in Klein-Schifferstadt begrabenen
   Christian THOMAS und der Anna Margaretha ... geboren. Er hatte
   in Klein-Schifferstadt am 10. 1. 1713 Anna Veronica LANG, Tochter
   des Peter LANG aus Flandern († Klein-Schifferstadt 25. 1. 1719,
   70 Jahre alt), und der Barbara ... († Klein-Schifferstadt 13. 7.
   1719, 65 Jahre alt), geheiratet. Dem Ehepaar wurden vor der Aus-

wanderung 11 Kinder, darunter 9 Söhne, geboren. Mit 7 Söhnen und
einer Tochter haben die Eltern den Weg in die „neue Welt" angetreten.

Kinder, zu Klein-Schifferstadt geboren:
1. Christian, * 1. 1. 1714; ∞ 1745 mit Magdalena ...,
2. Philipp Heinrich, * 12. 9. 1715,
3. Maria Catharina, * 2. 2. 1718, † 7. 5. 1724,
4. Hans Michel, * 3. 10. 1719; ∞ 1744 mit Barbara ...,
5. Gabriel, * 9. 6. 1721, † 18. 1. 1794; ∞ 1744 mit Anna
     Margaret ...,
6. Johannes, * 10. 3. 1723, † 14. 3. 1724,
7. Johann Valentin, * 28. 9. 1724, † 27. 8. 1796; ∞ 1751 mit
     Margaret ...,
8. Anna Catharina, * 29. 5. 1726,
9. Johann Christoph, * 20. 6. 1728, † 6. 9. 1728, Zwilling
     zu
10. Johannes, * 20. 6. 1728; ∞ 1753 mit Catharine ...,
11. Christoph, * 2. 10. 1729; ∞ entsprechend dem Eintrag in
     dem Kirchenbuch der reformierten Gemeinde Frederick,
     Md., am 13. 12. 1757 mit Susan Margaret WEISS.

In einer der Eideslisten hat der Vater selbst unterschrieben,
während sich in der Schiffsliste auch der älteste Sohn Christian
eingetragen hat.

Mit seiner Familie zählt Johann Michel THOMAS zu den ersten
Siedlern in Frederick County, Maryland, wo er 1742 nachgewiesen werden kann. Zuvor muss er auf dem Weg zwischen Philadelphia und Frederick gewohnt haben. In der weiten Ebene
südlich von Adamstown in Richtung zum Potomak-Fluss konnte
der Verfasser eine Reihe prächtiger Farmen besuchen, die auch
heute noch in den Händen von Thomas-Nachkommen aus Klein-
Schifferstadt sind. George Leicester THOMAS, Verfasser und
Herausgeber von drei Bänden „Genealogy of Thomas Family", hat
bei Adamstown eine aus 150 Weihern bestehende Goldfischzucht,
die durch seinen Sohn George Leicester THOMAS Jr. mit einer
bedeutenden Seerosenzucht erweitert worden ist.

Auf dem alten Familienfriedhof nordwestlich von Adamstown erin-
nern die Grabsteine der beiden Söhne Gabriel und Johann Valentin
THOMAS an den Herkunftsort in der Pfalz:

HIER RUHET	HIER RUHET
IM HERN GABRIEL	IM HERN
THOMAS GEBOH	VALLENTINT
REN ZU KLEIN	TAMAS GEBO
SCHIFFERSTAT	REN IN KLEIN
IN DEUTSCHLAND	SCHIFFERSATH
IN DER PALTZS	IN DEUTSCHLAND
DEN 12 JUNE 1721	IN DER PALTZS
GESTORBEN DEN	IM JAHR 1724 DEN
18 JANUARI 1794	30 SEPTEMBER
IST ALT WORTEN 72	UND IST GESTORBEN
JAR 7 MONAD UND	JAHR 1796 DEN
6 TAG	27 AUGUST

Benutzte Quellen:

Bell, The Seibert Family, Washington, Pa., 1959.
Croll, Annals of the Oley Valley in Berks County, Pa., Reading,
    Pa., 1926.
DeChant, Down Oley Valley, Kutztown, Pa., 1953.
Eyselein, Geschichte des Dorfes Mutterstadt, Mutterstadt 1938.
Fisher, Early Pennsylvania Births (1675-1875), Selinsgrove, Pa.,
    1947.
Heimatstelle Pfalz, Kaiserslautern, Auswandererkartel.
Hinke, Life and Letters of the Rev. John Philip Boehm, Founder of
    the Reformed Church in Pennsylvania, 1683-1749, Philadelphia,
    Pa., 1916.
Hinke, Ministers of the German Reformed Congregations in Pennsyl-
    vania and other Colonies in the Eighteenth Century, Lancaster,
    Pa., 1951.
King, Knauss Genealogy. Lukas Knauss (1633-1713) of Düdelsheim,
    Germany, and his American Descendants, Bethlehem, Pa., 1930.
Kirchenbücher Assenheim, Dannstadt, Hassloch, Iggelheim, Mutter-
    stadt und Rheingönheim.
Knittle, Early Eighteenth Century Palatine Emigration, Philadel-
    phia, Pa., 1937.
Kreuter, Maudach im Wandel der Zeiten, Ludwigshafen 1955.
Laubscher Familien-Nachrichten, 1957 Heft 3, 1959 Heft 5.
Martin, The Philip Hautz Family of Pennsylvania in The Detroit
    Society for Genealogical Research, Vol. XX No. 1, Fall 1956.
Meynen, Bibliographie des Deutschtums der kolonialzeitlichen Ein-
    wanderung in Nordamerika (1683-1933), Leipzig 1937.
Prot. Landeskirchenarchiv, Speyer.
Rothermel, The Pioneer Rothermel Family of Berks County, Beitrag in
    Transactions of the Historical Society of Berks County, Vol. III,
    Reading, Pa., 1923.
Staatsarchiv, Speyer.
Strassburger und Hinke, Pennsylvania German Pioneers, 3 Bände, Nor-
    ristown, Pa., 1934.
The Pennsylvania Dutchman, Vol. 8 No. 1 S. 61.
Thomas, Genealogy of Thomas Family, Adamstown, Md., 1951-1954.
Transue, Genealogy of Transue Family, Bethlehem, Pa., 1939 [date
    hard to read in copy].

––––––

"Passengers from the Rhineland to Pennsylvania," *Publications of
the Genealogical Society of Pennsylvania*, 14 (1942), 79 [Lancour
No. 149].

The Pennsylvania Gazette of March 22, 1732-3, thus called the
attention of fifteen derelict passengers to the stern rule of life
and the sea, in German as well as English: "Those Palatines who

came Passengers from Rotterdam, in the Ship John and William, Constable Tymberton, Commander, and have not yet paid their Passages,
nor given Security, are hereby required to make speedy Payment, or
to give good Security to Mr. George McCall, Merchant in Philadelphia; otherwise they may expect to be prosecuted as the Law
directs. Their names are as follows: Hans Emich, Stephen Matts,
Frederich Kooler, Michael Bloemhower, Hans Peter Brechbill, Hans
Brechbill, Philip Melchoir, Nicholas Pashon, George Adam Stees,
Abraham Diebo, Matthais Manser, Hans Riel, Caspar Willaar, Philip
Melchoir Meyer, John George Wahnzodel." In those days, according
to an old opera, No Song, No Supper.—H. E. G.

.   Friedrich Krebs. "Einige Amerika-Auswanderer des 18. Jahrhun-
    derts," *Senftenegger Monatsblatt für Genealogie und Heraldik*, 5
    (1960-1963), 79-82 [Lancour No. 150].

HS = „Pennsylvania German Pioneers" by Ralph Beaver Strassburger,
edited by William John Hinke, Norristown, Pa., 1934. Die nach HS
folgende Zahl zeigt die Liste an, in welcher der betreffende Einwanderer verzeichnet ist, das folgende Datum den Zeitpunkt der Landung in Philadelphia.
   Aus der Stadt Wachenheim an der Weinstrasse, Pfalz.
   Quelle: Familienakten des Stadtarchives Wachenheim.
   Bergt(h)old, Isac, S. d. Mennoniten Jacob B., aus 1. Ehe mit
Susanna Hirsch (Hirschi?) († 1. IV. 1771), war laut einem Inventar
nach Jacob B. († 11. II. 1785) vom 9. III. 1785, damals bereits in
Amerika verstorben. Laut Inventar nach Susanna B vom 4. XII. 1771
war Isac damals 39 Jahre alt. Laut „Hausbuch" hatte er 1772 als
Vorauszahlung auf sein Erbteil und Reisegeld nach Amerika 83 fl 14
kr empfangen (HS 296, Isaac Bergdoll, 16. X. 1772).
   Hirsche (Hirschi), Isaac, S. d. Mennoniten u. Beisassen Hans H.
aus 1. Ehe, in dessen Inventar v. 11. VIII. 1732 er als in Pennsylvanien befindlich genannt wird. (Anm. d. Red.: Vgl. „Pennsylvania
German Society", Vol. XXXV, 1924, S. 161 f. „Hershey".)
   Nagel, Witwe des Johann Jacob N., durfte mit ihren jüngeren Kin-
dern: Anna Maria, Philipp Daniel u. Maria Barbara, nach Pennsyl-
vanien abziehen, gegen Errichtung des 10. Pfennigs, lt. kurpfälz.
Verordnung dd. Mannheim 3. XI. 1750. Inventar zwischen ihr und den
daheim bleibenden Kindern, vom 5. XII. u. 11. XII. 1750 (Anm. d.
Red.: Vielleicht HS 176, 16. X. 1751).
   Steinmetz, Philipp Jacob, S. d. Jacob St. († 15. I. 1784) u. d.
Maria Barbara († 17. I. 1784), „welcher vor ohngefähr 11 Jahren in
Americam gewandert und vor seiner gewesenen Ehefrau Barbara, ge-
bohrnen Habigin eine Tochter namens Maria Cleophe hinterlassen".
Inventar des Jacob S. v. 13. II. 1784.
   Stempel, Nicklaus der Alte, Bürger u. Schreiner, zog mit seinem
Sohne aus 1. Ehe Johann Jacob St., Bürger u. Schreiner, und dessen

Ehefrau Anna Elisabeth, in „Engelland" (Amerika), laut Vermögensteilung zwischen den Abziehenden und seinem zurückbleibenden Sohne aus 2. Ehe Johann Niclaus St., reform. Schuldiener zu Mussbach, vom 17. III. 1732. (HS 25, 26. IX. 1732).

Zimmermann, Friedrich Wilhelm, S. d. Johann Peter Z. u. d. Luise, war lt. Inventar v. 7. IV. 1777(?) u. Testament v. 5. VII. 1777 damals in „Neuengland, Carolinam" wohnhaft.

Aus der Pflege Hassloch, Pfalz[:]
Quelle: Gemeindearchiv Hassloch, Bestand 4 (Pflege), R 1, A 46; Bestand 2, R 2.

Die Pflege Hassloch bestand aus den Orten Hassloch, Böhl und Iggelheim, und zwar zwischen Kurpfalz und Leiningen gemeinschaftlich, doch besass Kurpfalz auch über den Leininger Anteil gewisse Oberhoheit.

In den Rechnungen der Pflege Hassloch sind 1749 für nachstehende Personen Abzugsgelder eingetragen. Soweit sie identifizierbar sind finden wir sie bei HS 133 als Passagiere des Schiffes „Phoenix" verzeichnet, das am 15. IX. 1749 in Philadelphia landete.

Reyer, (Georg) Christoph, * Böhl, S. d. Samuel R., zog von Hassloch mit seiner Schwester Maria Catharina in das „neue Land". Er hatte von 450 fl., sie von 50 fl. den 10. Pfennig zu entrichten. Mit ihnen zogen Conrad Wohlfahrt und Michael Schäffer, beide von Hassloch, Hermann Latur (Latar), Franz Sohl, u. Johann Marx Brendel, alle aus Böhl. Sie hatten von 451 fl., bzw. von 68 fl. 31 kr. und 749 fl. 33 kr. Vermögen das Abzugsgeld zu entrichten. Brendel ist nach den Akten bestimmt mit Weib und Kind nach Pennsylvanien ausgewandert, denn 1759 kam er von dort auf kurzen Besuch zurück, um sein elterliches Erbteil zu beheben, und gleichzeitig auch das Erbe der Kinder des Samuel Reyer in Böhl, wozu er beider Vollmachten aufwies. (Anm. d. Red.: Möglicherweise identisch mit „Marx x Springel" der Liste 133, der nur sein Handzeichen machte, wogegen der Name dazugeschrieben wurde). Aus dem Akte (Gemeindearchiv Hassloch, Bestand 4, A 46) geht hervor, dass Maria Catharina Reyer an den Schmied Georg Meyer in Pennsylvanien verheiratet war.

Bentz, Georg, aus Iggelheim zahlte Abzugsgeld von einem Kapital von 131 fl. 16 kr. und Christ, Christian, aus Iggelheim von einem Kapital von 61 fl. 16 kr.

Aus Külz, Kries Simmern[:]
Quelle: Landschreibereirechnung Simmern 1750, Staatsarchiv Koblenz, Aktenabt. 4 (Kurpfalz) Nr. 3316, 3310.

Cuntz, Henrich, zog mit Weib und 5 Kindern in „das Neue Land" und zahlte 130 fl für den 10. Pfennig und 150 fl für die Manumission. (HS 151, 21. VIII. 1750).

Friedrich Krebs. "Pennsylvania Dutch Pioneers," *The Pennsylvania Dutchman*, 6 (June 1954), 40; (September 1954), 37; (Winter 1954-1955) 39; (Spring 1955), 37-38; 7 (Winter 1956), 38-39; (Spring

1956), 38-39; 8 (Summer 1956), 57-59 [translated by Don Yoder] [Lancour No. 151].

The names of the following emigrants were culled from the collections of the State Archives of Coblenz. The names have been checked against Hinke's *Pennsylvania German Pioneers*.

From Niederbrombach (Kreis Birkenfeld)

1. Pontius, Johann David, born March 3, 1738, and Johann Philipp, sons of Andreas Pontius of Niederbrombach and his wife Anna Marie. Both brothers "emigrated to America around 1767-68." [David Pontzius, Pennsylvania Packet, Oct. 3, 1768.]

2. Apel, Jonas of Niederbrombach went to America in 1768 after he had purchased freedom from serfdom. His wife and three children at first remained in Germany but followed in 1771. [Jonas Apel, Pennsylvania Packet, Oct. 3, 1768.]

From Birkenfeld

3. Wart, Bernhard, born Feb. 21, 1718 in Birkenfeld, tailor. "Is said to have gone to America in or about 1738." [Bern Warth, Loyal Judith, Sept. 3, 1739.]

From Ellenberg (Kreis Birkenfeld)

4. Brener, Peter from Ellenberg emigrated in the year 1768 as a widower with his children to America and nothing was ever heard from him. [Frantz Peter Brenner, Pennsylvania Packet, Oct. 3, 1768.]

5. Maus, Georg Jacob and Franz Carl from Ellenberg set out for America around 1767. [Jacob Maus, Pennsylvania Packet, Oct. 10, 1768.]

From Sohren (Landkreis Zell, Mosel)

6. Albertthal, Franz Niclaus and Johann Niclaus, sons of Balthasar Alberthal and his wife Elisabeth Catharina, emigrated to New England, the former around 1765 and the latter around 1768. Since they left without manumission their property was seized and later also their inheritance, which after taxes was used for the Catholic church, for the poor, and the rest divided among relatives. [Nickellas Alberthal, Tryal, Dec. 12, 1764 and Johann Nickel Alberthal, Sally, Oct. 5, 1767. Franz Nikolaus Alberthal, farmer, and Johann Nicklaus Alberthal, tailor, according to documentation, lived in Hanover Township, Lancaster County.]

From Bockenau (Kreis Kreuznach)

7. Geib, Conrad from Bockenau left with his wife and three children for the new land. [Johann Conrad Geib, Two Brothers, Oct. 13, 1747.]—Kreuznach Official Records 1751.

From Weinsheim (Kreis Kreuznach)

8. Rupperter, Johann Leonhard from Weinsheim in 1752 applied for manumission from Pennsylvania where he married; granted after payment of fees in 1754. [Leonhard Rupperter, Sandwich, Nov. 30, 1750.]

From Ruedesheim (Kreis Kreuznach)

9. Suess, Cyriacus from Ruedesheim, according to Kreuznach official records of 1751, left for the New World.

From Buechenbeuren (Landkreis Zell, Mosel)

10. Maeurer, Philipp (Jacob) from Buechenbeuren around 1750 left
as a "Schuhknecht" for the New World. [Phielib Jacob Maurer,
Patience, Aug. 11, 1750.]

From Engelstadt (Kreis Bingen)

11. Graffert, Christoph, Philipp Peter and Johann Gerhard, sons
of Philipp Peter Graffert and his wife Anna Eva Finkenauer from
Engelstadt left for the New World around 1749. [Christoffel Graffert, Loyal Judith, Sept. 2, 1743, and Philipp Peter Graffert,
Phoenix, Oct. 20, 1744.]

The names of the following immigrants are from two sources: 1)
Oberamtsprotokolle (bailiff minutes) of the city of Heidelberg, for
1741 and 1742, and 2) Lutheran Church Records of Woerrstadt. The
names have been checked against Hinke's *Pennsylvania German
Pioneers*.

From the Heidelberg Area

1. Zweisig, Valentine, from Mauer (Kreis Heidelberg) who has requested freedom from serfdom and permission to emigrate is set
free, with wife and four children, upon payment of 3 Fl. and 30 Kr.
Source: Oberamtsprotokolle of Heidelberg, 1741. [Valdin Zweisig,
Ship Molly, Oct. 17, 1741.]

2. Geiser, Christoph, from Eschelbronn (Kreis Sinsheim, Baden)
who wishes to emigrate is freed from serfdom. Source: Oberamtsprotokolle of Heidelberg, 1742. [Christof Geiser, Ship Francis and
Elizabeth, Sept. 9, 1742.]

3. Danner, Michel and Dieter, from Walldorf who wish to emigrate
are relieved of emigration fees because the sum realized from the
sale of their properties was insufficient to cover their debts.
Source: Oberamtsprotokolle of Heidelberg, 1742. [Michel Danner,
Dietrich Danner, Ship Robert and Alice, Sept. 24, 1742.]

From Woerrstadt (Kreis Alzey)

4. Christian, Philip Jacob. "In 1743 Philip Jacob Christian,
carpenter, and Elizabeth Margaretha, daughter of Joerg Emich Messerschmid, cooper, were engaged on Easter Sunday; and their proclamation was read the following two Sundays. Several days later,
however, the young man secretly left and finally went to England,
from where he expects to sail to Pennsylvania. Whether he arrived
there is not known as of this moment." [Fillip Christian, Ship
Loyal Judith, Sept. 2, 1743.]

5. Baussman, Michel; Weisskopff, Esaias; and Becker, Jacob. "In
1748 Michel Baussmann and Esaias Weisskopff, both of them shoema-
kers and Protestants, and Jacob Becker, a Catholic, left with their
families for Pennsylvania. They arrived safely according to
reports from there." [Johann Michel Bausman, Johan Esaias Weiskob,
Jacob Becker, Ship Judith, Sept. 15, 1748.]

6. Senderling, Johann Niclaus; Stump, Johann Michel; Kraemer,
Johann Peter; Steinbrecker, Johann Valentin; Klein, Johann Heinrich; Cramer, Johann Friedrich; Schedla, Johann Christian. "On May

22, 1749, Johann Niclaus Senderling, Johann Michel Stump, Johann
Peter Kraemer, Johann Valentin Steinbrecher, Johann Heinrich Klein,
Johann Friedrich Cramer, local residents and Johann Christian
Schedla, single son of tailor Johann Heinrich Schedla, left for
Pennsylvania, the former accompanied by their wives and children."
[Johann Friedrich Cremer, Johann Vallentin Steinbrech, Johann Hen-
nerich Klein, Johann Nickel Stump, Johann Nicolas Senderling, Ship
Isaac, Sept. 9, 1749. Johann Peter Kraemer, Ship Saint Andrew,
Sept. 9, 1749.]

7.　Schedla, Johann Heinrich; Gerhardt, Johann Dietrich; Reuter,
Johann Lorentz; Koch, Johann Christian.　"In 1754 the following re-
moved to Pennsylvania or rather into misfortune:　Johann Heinrich
Schedla with family, Johann Dietrich Gerhardt with wife and child-
ren, Johann Lorentz Reuter with wife and child, Johann Christian
Koch with wife and children, along with others, in part single
young men and women, approximately 40 in number.　They had the mis-
fortune of having to spend time in Cologne because the King of
Prussia at first refused to grant them permission to pass through.
This took a considerable period of time.　The group consumed much
of their little wealth and finally they had to travel by land to
Rotterdam at great cost.　I trust that the rest of the local citi-
zenry remaining behind have lost the taste of the New World."
[Dieter Gerhard, Lorentz Rouyter, Henrich Schedler, Christian Koch,
Ship Phoenix, Oct. 1, 1754.]

The following listings of Palatine emigrants to America in the
eighteenth century are derived from several manuscript sources in
German archives.　Those from the Electoral Oberamt of Simmern,
representing villages in the Hunsrueck area, come from the Census
of the Electoral Oberamt of Simmern for the year 1750, in the State
Archives of Coblenz (Abt. 4, Nr. 3319); those from Hueffelsheim
from the Lutheran Church Register of Hueffelsheim; the remainder
from various official acts in the Palatine State Archives at
Speyer.　The names have been checked against Strassburger and
Hinke's *Pennsylvania German Pioneers*.

From the Electoral Oberamt of Simmern

1.　Jungker, Johann Nicklas—of Moerschbach (Kreis Simmern), "who
has gone to the Island of Pensylphanien," pays in taxes two florins
for the tithe.

2.　Muehleissen, Johann Jacob—of Pleizenhausen (Kreis Simmern),
"intends to go with wife and child to the New Land."　He is, with
his wife and child, freed from vassalage on payment of a manumission tax of 16 florins and a further tax of 15 florins for the
tithe.　[Jacob Muehleysen, Ship Patience, August 11, 1750.]

3.　Stiehl, Abraham—of Steinbach (Kreis Simmern), "has made up
his mind to go to Pennsylvania"; is, with wife and four children,
freed from vassalage on payment of 32 florins for manumission and
29 florins for the tithe.　[Johann Abraham Stiehl, Ship Patience,
August 11, 1750.]

4. Doerter (Dorten), Johann Anton—of Laubach (Kreis Simmern), "who has gone to the Island of Pensylphania," pays, with wife and six children, 59 florins for manumission and 53 florins tithe.

5. Brach, Nickel—of Ravensbeuren (Kreis Zell, Mosel), "who went to Pensylphania," pays 20 florins for the tithe.

6. Cuntz, Nickel—of Unzenberg (Kreis Simmern), "who has gone to the Island of Pensylphania," pays 100 florins for the tithe. [Johann Nickel Cuntz, Ship Patience, August 11, 1750.]

From Hueffelsheim (Kreis Kreuznach)

7. Wolffskehl, Anna Margaretha—born 11-18-1735 at Hueffelsheim, daughter of Johannes Wolffskehl and wife Anna Maria, "went with her father to the New Land." Elisabetha Wolffskehl, born 12-28-1733 at Hueffelsheim to the same parents, "went with her father in 1742 to the New Land." Maria Agnes Wolffskehl, born 1-27-1738 of the same parents, "went with her father to the New Land." [Johannes Wolffskehl, Ship Loyal Judith, September 3, 1742.]

8. Reitzel, Maria Wilhelmina—born 9-2-1734 at Hueffelsheim, daughter of the shoemaker Johann Georg Reitzel and wife Sybilla, "went with her father to the New Land in 1741." Johann Peter Reitzel, born at Hueffelsheim 10-28-1737 to the same parents, "went with his parents to the New Land in 1741." [Johann Georg Reutzel, Ship Molly, 10-17-1741.]

From Eisenbach (Kreis Kusel)

9. Pfaff, Theobald—"who disappeared eight years ago from Eisenbach and emigrated to America, leaving nine children behind, of whom three are at present housed in the prince's orphanage at Homburg" (Document dated 1-29-1777). [Theobalt Pfaff, Ship Betsy, 10-26-1768.]

From Hornbach (Kreis Zweibruecken)

10. Stribeck, Johann Georg und Christian—sons of Conrad Stribeck, citizen and woolspinner at Hornbach from his first marriage with Elisabetha Schaeffer, "who both after their mother's death went to the New Land in 1735 with their grandmother Elisabetha Schaeffer and their mother's brother, with the knowledge and permission of the most gracious authorities, and since the grandparents were still alive [and] said children consequently had nothing yet of their maternal inheritance, they have taken the grandmother's inheritance along." [Elizabeth Shever, Jerich Strebeck, Christian Strebeck, Ship Pensilvania Merchant, September 18, 1733.]

11. Bley, Philipp—son of the citizen and master cooper, Werner Bley of Hornbach, "who married here (i.e., Hornbach), but ten years ago went to the District of Kleeburg in Alsace and later on, with the permission of the most gracious authorities, went to America." (The emigration to America took place around 1748-9.) Werner Bley's wife was Elisabetha Huber.

12. Maus, Samuel—son of Friderich Maus, councilor of Hornbach and his wife Susanna Mueller, "went to America" around 1754. [Samuel Maus, Ship Edinburg, 9-14-1753.]

13. Henge, Catharina—daughter of Samuel Mueller, citizen and tanner at Hornbach, and his wife Maria Margaretha Maus, "who was divorced on the grounds of adultery from her husband Georg Henge, to whom she had a son named Philipp, and afterwards went to America, where, according to a letter which reached here, she married a man named Fischer." (The emigration took place around 1766.) According to another document her son is also said to have gone to America.

14. Leiner, Ludwig—of Hornbach, "went abroad as woolenweaver," and "is reported in 1784 to have died in America."

15. Zutter, Daniel and Balthasar—sons of Benedict Baltzer Zutter, woolspinner at Hornbach, "secretly disappeared and went away to America" (Document dated 6-7-1763). [Daniel Zutter, Balthazar Zutter, Ship Chance, 12-1-1763.]

From Brenschelbach (Kreis Homburg, Saar)

16. Hochstraser, Paul—son of Samuel Hochstraser of Brenschelbach and his wife Elisabetha, "who has now established himself as master tailor in Philadelphia" (Document dated 4-18-1761). But according to a Letter of Attorney dated 1-23-1764, Paul Hochstraser, breeches maker, with his sister Catharina, was resident in the city of Albany, province of New York. [Paulus Hochstrasser, Ship Edinburg, 9-14-1753.] The Jacob Hochstrasser who emigrated in 1767 was perhaps a brother of Paul's since the latter had a brother by that name.

From Walsheim on the Blies (Kreis Homburg, Saar)

17. Schunk, Johannes, Catharina, Elisabetha, Maria and Simon—children of Wilhelm Schunk of Walsheim and wife Catharina Schwarz, "have been for nine or ten years in America" (Document dated 10-18-1781).

Albisheim (Kreis Kirchheimbolanden)

1. Johann Engel Morgenstern, born at Albisheim September 20, 1726—son of Johann Philipp Morgenstern and wife Maria Rosina—"residing in Pennsylvania." [Johann Engelbert Morgenstern, Ship St. Andrew, September 9, 1749.]

2. Abraham Brubacher—son of Jacob Brubacher from his first marriage—"in Pennsylvania" (Document dated 1763). The Brubacher family, of Mennonite background, was in the 18th century located in the region of Albisheim, also in the Mennonite settlement of Ibersheim, near Worms.

Altenkirchen (Kreis Kusel)

3. Jacob Berg—son of Jacob Berg of Altenkirchen and wife Anna Margaretha Wagner—blacksmith by trade, went to Pennsylvania without manumission, along with Johann Theobald Schramm—son of George Schramm of Altenkirchen—in the year 1769. The property of both of them, namely an inheritance which came to them later, was on that account confiscated by the Government of the Duchy of Zweibruecken, since they no longer intended to return to their homeland. Jacob Berg was referred to in the documents as a blacksmith at Middle-

town, near Frederick, Maryland, while of Theobald Schramm is known
only that after his arrival in America he worked as a hostler in
Philadelphia. [Jacob Berg, Theobald Schramm, Ship Minerva, October
13, 1769.]

Appenhofen (Kreis Bergzabern)

4. Margretha and Sibilla Wintz—daughters of Georg Wintz of
Appenhofen—"who are by this time living in the New Land" (Document
dated February 10, 1752). One of them was married to Thomas Schley
of Frederick, Maryland.

5. Margretha Kuhn—daughter of Nicklaus Kuhn, citizen of Appen-
hofen, and his wife Elisabetha Nickler—was, according to official
declarations, married at Billigheim to Friedrich Wuerthsbacher (or
Wirthsbacher), who was a physician born in the region of Heilbronn
(Wuerttemberg), and went with him to America in 1764. [Friderich
Wurtzbacher, Ship Hero, October 27; 1764.]

6. Georg Michel Banz, tailor by trade, and his sister Catharina
Banz, both from Appenhofen, the former single, the latter married
to Peter Brunner of Klingen, went to Pennsylvania without issue
about 1748. A letter still extant in the Speyer Archives describes
Georg Michel Banz as settled in Frederick County, Maryland, Johann
Peter Brunner in the neighborhood of the town of Frederick. [Peter
Brunner, Ship Albany, September 2, 1749.]

Assenheim (Kreis Ludwigshafen)

7. Franz Balthasar Schalter—son of Johann Georg Schalter (died
1754) of Assenheim and his wife Elisabeth—went to Pennsylvania
shortly after his father's death, in order to inherit here the
property of a brother of his father, who had already been a long
time resident of Pennsylvania. After the death of his uncle he
stayed in Pennsylvania. On November 16, 1767, he wrote from Alsace
Township, Berks County, to his relatives, that he renounced his
share of the inheritance, which he would have had a claim on from
home, and wishes only that a clock and a Bible be sent over to him.
With him went Johann Georg Boerstler, likewise from Assenheim, to
America, but later returned home again. [Frantz Baltzer Schalter,
Jorg Boerstler, Ship Edinburgh, September 30, 1754.]

8. Jacob Neff—son of the Anabaptist (Mennonite) Peter Neff of
Assenheim and his wife Veronika Roesch—"absent in America" (Document dated May 27, 1789). [Jacob Neff, Brig Betsy, October 15,
1785.]

Billigheim (Kreis Bergzabern)

9. Bernhard Kney—son of Philipp Kney of Billigheim and his wife
Maria Margaretha Hutmacher—"who has gone to the so-called New
Land" (Document dated May 10, 1755).

10. Anna Margaretha Degreiff—daughter of the councilor Jacob
Degreiff of Billigheim—"is married in the New Land" (Document
dated May 12, 1755).

Boeckweiler (Kreis Homburg, Saar)

11. Johannes Keller—son of Daniel Keller, of Boeckweiler—
"established and married in the New Land" (Document dated October

19, 1776).

12. Henrich Kunz—"son of the deceased citizen of the same name, of Boeckweiler and wife Maria Margaretha Hock—removed himself from this country in 1764 and according to report that has reached here went to America without permission, contrary to the present governmental order" (*Frankfurter Kayserl. Reichs-Ober-Amts-Postzeitung*, 2-13-1787). According to the documents Henrich Kunz was a cartwright and from a letter dated August 21, 1768 we learn that he was living with Jonathan Heger in Canageschick in Maryland.

Breitfurt (Kreis Homburg, Saar)

13. Jacob Welker—son of Wilhelm Welker of Breitfurt—"who according to report, has gone to America" (Document dated December 4, 1777). [Either Jacob Welcker, Ship Minerva, September 17, 1771, or Jacob Welcker, Ship Crawford, October 26, 1768.]

14. Anna Appolonia Vogelgesang—daughter of Nickel Gentes, magistrate and citizen of Breitfurt—"married to Georg Vogelgesang, Jr. (evidently also from Breitfurt), resident in America" (Document dated May 6, 1765). [Georg Vogelgesang, Ship Squirrel, October 21, 1761.]

15. Matheiss and Georg Schmidt—children of Abraham Schmidt, citizen and magistrate of Breitfurt—"in America" (Document dated October 7, 1760).

16. Joseph Neu—son of Georg Neu, resident of Breitfurt and his wife Christina Margaretha Gentess—"went to America" around 1740. His brother Peter Neu, "went to America" around 1753.

17. Johann Otto Neu—son of Wilhelm Neu of Breitfurt and his wife Anna Margaretha—"now residing in the New Land" (Document of May 19, 1767). His brother Johann Simon Neu, "also residing in the New Land" (Document of May 19, 1767).

Dannstadt (Kreis Ludwigshafen)

18. About the year 1748 Rudolph Drach and his sister Anna Maria Drach from Dannstadt, both single, went to America, where they married and had children. In the year 1768 they requested, through a power of attorney, the surrender of their property on payment of the tithe. Their property was, however, not surrendered, but confiscated according to the Emigration Edict of the Electoral Palatinate.

Edenkoben

19. Philipp Carl Haas—son of Johann Georg Haas—intended in the year 1748, to go, with his wife and five children, to the New Land "on account of a better fortune." [Philipp Carel Haas, Ship Patience, September 16, 1748.]

20. Anna Elisabetha Seyffert—daughter of Johann Gottfried Seyffert of Edenkoben—"married to David Delater, who went to Pennsylvania" (about 1740). [David Delater, Ship St. Andrew, October 2, 1741.]

21. Anna Catharina Gleich—daughter of the master miller Henrich Gleich of Edenkoben—"went to Pennsylvania" (about 1756).

22. Johann Georg Croissant and his sister Anna Catharina Crois-

sant—children of Jacob Croissant of Edenkoben—"who went to Pennsylvania." (about 1756).

Ellerstadt (Kreis Neustadt)

23. In a Property Inventory of Ellerstadt from the year 1781 it
is reported of Johann Caspar Huber—son of Michael Huber of Ellerstadt and his wife Anna Barbara—"living in Philadelphia and 44
years old; he has been absent from here 18 years." [Casper Huber,
Ship Chance, November 1, 1763.]

Elschbach (Kreis Kusel)

24. Johann Georg Jung—son of Hermann Jung of Elschbach and his
wife Anna Margaretha—"living in the New Land" (Document dated
1754).

Freckenfeld (Kreis Germersheim)

25. Johann Hahn—son of Jacob Hahn of Freckenfeld and his wife
Ottilia Eichenlaub—"went to the New Land." Conrad Hahn, brother
of the preceding, single, "to the New Land." Johann Jacob Hahn,
brother of the two preceding emigrants, "in the New Land." The
later was baptized at Freckenfeld February 9, 1727. An Inventory
of September 11, 1754, lists all three persons as emigrated before
that date.

26. Georg Dierwaechter, baptized at Freckenfeld, February 13,
1724, and Johann Erhard Dierwaechter—sons of Peter Dierwaechter of
Freckenfeld and his wife Anna Catharina Hummel—"who both went to
the so-called New Land or Pennsylvania" (about 1751). [Ehrhardt
Thuerwaechter, Ship Janet, October 7, 1751.]

27. Margaretha Apfel—daughter of Georg Apfel of Freckenfeld and
his wife Anna Catharina Gruber—"wife of Michael Herrman, former
citizen at Candel, who went to the New Land" (Document dated 1755).
[Presumably Michel Hermann, Ship Richard & Mary, September 30,
1754.]

28. Georg Baur—son of the citizen and beadle Jacob Baur of
Freckenfeld and his wife Anna Catharina Klein—"who went to the New
Land" (Document dated June 10, 1761).

Freinsheim (Kreis Neustadt)

29. Michel Rezer—son of the cooper Theobald Rezer of Freinsheim
and his wife Anna Maria Held—"who went away in the year 1756 to
Pennsylvania."

30. Johann Niclaus Bach—son of Sebastian Bach, who died at
Freinsheim in 1753—"who is now, however, in Pennsylvania" (Document dated June 25, 1768). Niclaus Bach was a resident of the city
of New York, as appears from a letter written from there. [Possi-
bly Nickel Bach, Ship Adventure, September 25, 1754.]

31. Johann Peter Weilbrenner—son of Georg Daniel Weilbrenner,
citizen and master butcher at Friensheim and his wife Catharina Hib
—went to America in 1753 and settled at Boucherville near Montreal. In a document dated at Montreal, June 12, 1781, he
renounced his share of the property that had fallen to him, in
favor of his brothers and sisters. At the same time there was in
Montreal Johann Jacob Maurer, born at Kriegsfeld in the Palatinate,

Captain of the Second Battalion of the King's Royal Regiment, of New York. In a letter of his brother, from Heidelberg, he is "described as overseer of the Royal British ships in Canada."

Freisbach (Kreis Germersheim)

32. Johann Thomas Kern, baptized at Freisbach, September 19, 1700, son of Peter Kern of Freisbach—"went to Pennsylvania"—married at Freisbach, February 17, 1733, Maria Margaretha, daughter of Michel Jopp of Ottersheim. Children, born at Freisbach: 1. Johann Christoph, born January 25, 1736—"to Pennsylvania." 2. Anna Elisabeth, born November 20, 1733—"to Pennsylvania." [Johann Thomas Kern, Ship Samuel, August 30, 1737.]

33. Jacob Peter Muench, born at Freisbach June 28, 1733, son of Peter Muench and wife Christina—"to Pennsylvania." Johann Georg Muench, born at Freisbach September 27, 1731, son of the same parents—"to Pennsylvania." Philipp Simon Muench, born August 25, 1728 at Freisbach, son of the same parents—"to Pennsylvania." [Presumably Hans Georg Muenig, Ship Jacob, October 2, 1749; Simon Minch, Ship Brotherhood, November 3, 1750.]

Grossbundenbach (Kreis Zweibruecken)

34. Georg Deller, son of Georg Deller of Grossbundenbach—"who went to the New Land" (Document dated April 4, 1761). [Johann Georg Deller, Ship Dragon, September 26, 1749.]

35. Peter Lugenbiehl, son of Kilian Lugenbuehl of Grossbundenbach—"who emigrated to America in the year 1750." [Peter Lugenbuehl, Ship Brotherhood, November 3, 1750.]

36. Georg Peter Eckel, son of Michael Eckel of Grossbundenbach and his wife Anna Catharina Keller—"in America" (Document dated March 22, 1764). [Georg Peter Eckel, Ship Richard & Mary, September 26, 1752.]

37. Juliana Bach, daughter of Albrecht Bach, Sr., of Alststadt— "who was married to Johann Georg Eckel at Grossbundenbach, who went to the New Land" (Inventory of 1756).

Hassloch (Kreis Neustadt)

Jacob Treibelbiss from Hassloch, "went away to the New Land some thirty years ago" (Inventory of 1764). Johann Jacob Treibelbiss was born April 10, 1709, at Hassloch, son of the carpenter Jacob Treibelbiss and his wife Anna Margaretha. [Johann Jacob Dreibelbiss, Ship Mary of London, September 26, 1732.]

Hessheim (Kreis Frankenthal)

Carl Ludwig Bardier—son of Adam Bardier of Hessheim and his wife Sibilla—"at present in Pennsylvania" (Document dated June 26, 1772).

Heuchelheim (Kreis Bergzabern)

Anna Barbara Decker, daughter of Philipp Strohschneider of Heuchelheim and his wife Anna Barbara, wife of Georg Decker from Wollmesheim, "now in the New Land" (Document dated March 11, 1754). [Johann Joerg Decker, Ship Two Brothers, September 21, 1751.]

Michael Roehmell ("in the New Land") and Georg Roehmell ("there too"), sons of Martin Roehmell of Heuchelheim and his wife Catha-

rina Ullrich (Document dated June 12, 1756). [G. Michael and Hans
George Rommigh, Ship Two Brothers, September 24, 1750?]
    Georg Jacob Kaeufer, son of Johannes Kaeufer of Heuchelheim and
his wife Catharina Elisabetha, "in Pennsylvania" (Document dated
May 4, 1757). Cf. the Weiss family, under Muehlhofen.

Horbruch (Kreis Bernkastel)

According to a report of the Village-Mayor of Irmenach, dated
March 11, 1746, to the Government of Trarbach, Johann Peter Hehn
(or Henn), son of Nicol Hehn of Horbruch, had "gone away in the
year 1741 to the so-called New Land."

Hornbach (near Zweibruecken)

Samuel Maus, son of the councilor Friedrich Maus of Hornbach and
his wife Susanna Mueller, "former citizen of Zweibruecken, but went
ten years ago to America" (Inventory of 1763). [Samuel Maus, Ship
Edinburg, September 14, 1753.] See Dutchman, Winter 1954.

Hueffelsheim (Kreis Kreuznach)

Anna Maria Reutzele, born at Hueffelsheim August 2, 1720, daughter of the shoemaker Johann Georg Reutzele and wife Anna Sybilla,
"This child of the parish has gone to the New Land."
    Johann Jacob Viel, born at Hueffelsheim November 22, 1718, son of
Theobald Viel, "went on May 17, 1767, to the New Land."
    Maria Wolffskehl, born at Hueffelsheim February 28, 1711, daugh-
ter of Theobald Viel and wife Anna Margaretha, married, at Hueffelsheim, November 19, 1730, Johannes Wolffskehl, and "went to the
New Land in 1742."
    Johann Michel Rech, born at Hueffelsheim March 1, 1751, son of
Johann Conrad Rech and wife Anna Margaretha, "parents and children
went to the New Land."

Hundsbach (Kreis Kreuznach)

Elisabetha Catharina Heyl, born at Hundsbach January 4, 1733,
daughter of Johann Peter Heyl, citizen at Hundsbach and wife
Susanna Catharina, "this child's father has gone to Pennsylvania"
(Reference in Lutheran Church Book of Hundsbach).

Ilbesheim (Kreis Landau)

Catharina Medart, daughter of Johann Adam Medart of Ilbesheim and
his wife Margaretha Kuntz, widow of Georg Clementz of Ilbesheim,
"who (the widow) went to the so-called New Land" (about 1753).
Carl Medart, her brother, "who also (about this same time) went to
America"; Valentin Medart, brother of the two preceding, "who also
went to the New Land" (Document dated May 19, 1758).
    Johann Valentin Clementz, son of Sebastian Clementz of Ilbesheim
(died 1760), "who went to the so-called New Land" (about 1754).
[Valentine Clementz, Ship Neptune, September 30, 1754.]
    Bernhard and Johann Adam Wuertenbecher, son of Johannes Wuerten-
becher of Ilbesheim and his wife Anna Maria, "went to the so-called
New Land" in May, 1753.
    Hanss Georg Kast, son of Hans Georg Kast of Ilbesheim and his
wife Margaretha Doerner, "who traveled to America already in the
year 1753." The Manumission Protocols of the Duchy of Zweibruecken

give the year of emigration as 1749. However, the emigrant is presumably Hans Jerg Kast, Ship Edinburgh, September 16, 1751.

Anna Barbara Klund, daughter of Johann Adam Klund, master shoemaker at Impflingen, "who went to the New Land" (about 1753).

Adam Hahn, linenweaver, "who already in the year 1753 went to the so-called New Land." He was the son of Johann Niclaus Hahn and his wife Anna Catharina Heb.

Juliana Clementz, daughter of Johann Adam Clementz of Ilbesheim and his wife Anna Maria Knoll, and wife of Valentin Zahneissen, "who went to the so-called New Land" (about 1754). According to the ship lists her husband came along: Vallentin Zaneichel, Ship Barclay, September 14, 1754.

Maria Catharine Doerner, daughter Bernhard Doerner, citizen and master shoemaker of Ilbesheim and his wife Catharina Pfuster, "who was married to Niclaus Fass and is in the New Land." [Nickel Fass, Ship Royal Union, August 15, 1750.] Jacob Doerner, her brother, "who likewise went to the so-called New Land." [Jacob Dorner, Ship Phoenix, November 2, 1752.]

Peter Frutschy, of Ilbesheim, after the death of his wife Anna Regina Obert, went, with his daughter Elisabeth (born at Ilbesheim April 11, 1747), "secretly, and contrary to the governmental prohibition, to the New Land." [Johann Peter Frutzuy, Ship Neptune, October 7, 1755.]

Wilhelm Michael, master shoemaker of Ilbesheim, "went to the so-called New Land" (about 1754).

Sebastian Doerr, son of Jacob Doerr of Ilbesheim and his wife Maria Catharina, "who learned the cooper trade and became a journeyman in the year 1749 and from here traveled to America."

Impflingen (Kreis Landau)

Margaretha Bossert, daughter of Johannes Bossert of Impflingen and his wife Margaretha, "who went from here (Impflingen) to America" (Document dated February 19, 1755).

Kandel (Kreis Germersheim)

Ludwig Einsel, baker, born at Kandel June 28, 1726, "at this time established in America, in the Province of New York, at Rhinebeck." [Johann Ludwig Einsel, Ship Duke of Bedford, September 14, 1751.]

Johann Diether Beyerle, son of the blacksmith Simon Beyerle of Kandel and his wife Anna Catharina Einsel, "who has been now for some years in America" (Document of 1782). [Dieter Beyerle, Ship Crawford, October 14, 1769.]

Georg Leonard Zoller, son of Leonard Zoller, citizen of Kandel and his wife Maria Odilia Weiss, "now 19 years absent and in America" (Property Inventory of 1784). [Geo. Leonard Zoller, Ship Hamilton, October 6, 1767.]

Friedrich Beyerle, son of Johannes Beyerle of Kandel and his wife Anna Maria Stoll, "now (1789) 16 years absent and his residence unknown." This is presumably Frederick Beyerle, Ship Union, September 30, 1774.

Anna Elisabetha Faubell, daughter of Niclaus Bald, citizen of

Kandel, and his wife Anna Maria Jooss, "wife of Johannes Faubell, former citizen here (at Kandel), who went together to the New Land" (Document dated May 17, 1756).

Johann Dieter Roedel, son of Georg Simon Roedel of Kandel and his wife Anna Apollonia, "now in America" (Document dated 1789). His brother Georg Friedrich Roedel was "also in America."

Of the six children of Jacob Burg, shoemaker at Kandel and his wife Apollonia Einsel, a document dated August 8, 1792, reports them all "absent in America." Their names were Philipp Jacob Burg, Elisabetha Margaretha Burg, Maria Elisabetha Burg, Johann Georg Burg, Maria Catharina Burg, and Maria Margaretha Burg.

Kleinbundenbach (Kreis Zweibruecken)

Maria Catharina Gerlinger, daughter of Philipp Jacob Gerlinger of Kleinbundenbach and his wife Agnes Kaercher, married to Andreas Greiner (born at Diemeringen in Alsace), emigrated (before 1752) to America. Both were living in Whitemarsh Township, Philadelphia County, Pennsylvania. [Andreas Creiner, Ship Phoenix, September 15, 1749.]

Nickel Kaercher of Kleinbundenbach, "has gone to America now many years ago" (Document dated 1796). Presumably John Nicklas Kargher, Ship Richard & Mary, September 26, 1752.

Kleinich (Kreis Bernkastel)

Johann Nickel Beyer, son of Matthias Beyer of Kleinich, along with Johann Georg Baertges, son of Matthias Baertges from the same place, are permitted by the Sponheim Government of Trarbach, April 27, 1748, to go away to Pennsylvania, "in order to perfect themselves in their chosen trade." Yet in case they do not return within three years, they must buy themselves free of vassalage, toward which end their coming inheritance is sequestrated. Under the same conditions, with a permit dated May 14, 1748, Michael Baertges, brother of the above Georg Baertges, tanner by trade, was able to emigrate to Pennsylvania. [Michael Baertges, Ship Two Brothers, September 15, 1748.]

On the same proviso, with permit dated March 18, 1748, Johann Nickel Neu, son of Christoffel Neu of Kleinich, weaver by trade; likewise Johann Petter Velten (Fehlten), son of Conrad Velten of Kleinich, shoemaker by trade, were permitted to emigrate to America. [Peter Felte, Ship Two Brothers, September 15, 1748.]

According to a permit from the Trarbach Government, dated April 26, 1741, Johann Conrad Lahm, tailor, son of the turner Peter Lahm of Kleinich; likewise the linenweaver Johann Michel Neu, son of Philps Neu from the same place; and Johann Matthias Bayer, son of the mason Matthias Bayer of Kleinich, were permitted to emigrate to Pennsylvania. Yet in case they did not return in two years, their manumission had to be paid (cf. above). The emigration of all three persons is documented in the official records. Matthias Bayer and Johann Michel Neu are said, however, to have died soon after their arrival in America. [Johann Konradt Lahm, Ship Europa, November 20, 1741.]

Klingen (Kreis Bergzabern)

Andreas Frohnhaeuser, son of Mathes Frohnhaeuser and his wife Maria Catharina Altschuh, "who has been in the New Land 25 years" (Inventory of 1774).

Michel Stuebinger, son of Andreas Stuebinger of Klingen, is "now in the so-called New Land" (Document dated September 15, 1756).

Georg Fischer, son of Philipp Fischer of Klingen and wife Anna Barbara Paul, "is in the New Land" (Document dated July 15, 1786).

Kuebelberg (Kreis Kusel)

Johann Adam Wagner, son of Theobald Wagner of Kuebelberg and wife Barbara, "married at Schmittweiler," is "in the New Land" (Document dated 1758).

Lachen (Kreis Neustadt)

Jacob Trueb, son of David Trueb of Lachen and his wife Catharina Elisabetha Hammann, "residing in Pennsylvania" (Document dated September 29, 1772). Anna Barbara Trueb, sister of Jacob, "likewise residing in Pennsylvania" (Document dated September 29, 1772).

Maria Catharina Theobald of Lachen, daughter of Johannes Theobald of Lachen, widow of Peter Hammann, went to Pennsylvania in 1764 with her second husband Jacob Sauerheber from Hassloch and the children of her first marriage. Johann Jacob Sauerheber was a resident of Maiden Creek Township, Berks County, Pennsylvania. [Jacob Sauerheber, Ship Hero, October 27, 1764.]

Maria Elisabetha Schuster, of Lachen, left her homeland unmarried at the age of 20 years, "now for thirty or more years away from Lachen and gone to America" (Property Inventory of 1784).

Andreas Jaeger went from Lachen to America in the year 1764 and took his niece Catharina Kircher (or Kercher) with him. The latter married in America Johannes Brunner of Passyunck near Philadelphia. Andreas Jaeger lived in Upper Paxtang, Lancaster County. [Andreas Jaeger, Ship Britannia, September 26, 1764.]

Lambsborn (Kreis Zweibruecken)

Maria Eva Trautmann (married) and Georg Trautmann, children of Henrich Trautmann of Lambsborn and his wife Susanna Heinz of Langwieden, "have gone to the New Land" (Document dated April 9, 1749). [Hans George Drautman, Ship Princess Augusta, September 16, 1736.]

Lambsheim (Kreis Frankenthal)

Jacob Hoenich of Lambsheim, former resident (but non-citizen) of Lambsheim, who wants to go to Pennsylvania or to the New Land, is, on account of his meagre property, manumitted gratis, likewise his stepdaughter Anna Maria Hauck, yet the latter must pay 12 florins to buy herself out of vassalage and 10 florins for the tithe (Protocols of the Oberamt of Neustadt, 1764). [Jacob Hoenick, Ship Hero, October 27, 1764.]

Limbach (Kreis Homburg, Saar)

Jacob Leibrock, son of Johann George Leibrock of Limbach, "who had resided at Bischweiler (Alsace), but has now gone to Pennsylvania" (Document dated March 13, 1752). [Jacob Leibrock, Ship Patience, September 9, 1751.]

Philipp Carl Koch, son of the Reformed pastor Georg Friedrich Koch of Limbach, "who has learned the bookbinder's trade and has been about 14 years in America" (Inventory of 1790, which places his emigration therefore about 1776).

Johann Henrich Oberkircher, son of Wilhelm Oberkircher of Limbach and his wife Maria Margaretha Keller, "who about 12 years ago left his wife and children behind and secretly escaped from here" (Inventory of 1783). [Presumably Henrich Oberkircher, Ship Sally, October 31, 1774.]

Loetzbeuren (Kreis Zell, Mosel)

Catharina Elisabetha Schnee, born at Loetzbeuren August 27, 1730, daughter of Johannes Schnee and wife Maria Margaretha, "went away to Pennsylvania in 1751." (Reference in Lutheran Church Book of Loetzbeuren).

Anna Margretha Dieterich, born at Loetzbeuren October 4, 1730, daughter of Johann Nicol Dieterich and wife Susanna Elisabetha, "this person has gone to Pennsylvania with her husband" (Ibid).

Maria Catharina Hoff, born at Loetzbeuren May 26, 1732, daughter of Frantz Hoff and wife Anna Elisabetha, "went to Pennsylvania" (Ibid).

Johann Willhelm Luetz, born at Loetzbeuren September 12, 1732, son of Matthess Luetz and wife Elisabetha Catharina, "went away to Pennsylvania in 1751" (Ibid.).

Anna Elisabetha Frantz, born at Loetzbeuren March 25, 1735, daughter of Johann Nicol Frantz and wife Maria Elisabetha, "went to Pennsylvania in 1751" (Ibid.).

Mannweiler (Kreis Rockenhausen)

Valentin Froellich, son of Johann Henrich Froellich of Mannweiler and wife Anna Margaretha, "now absent and with his wife Apolonia nee Rapp as well as two children gone away to the New Land" (Document dated May 22, 1723).

Mauschbach (Kreis Zweibruecken)

Daniel, Georg and Jacob Weber, sons of Philipp Weber of Mauschbach, "went to America" around the year 1750, "without previously being manumitted from vassalage by our most gracious authorities." [Possibly Johann Daniel Weber, Ship Isaac, September 27, 1749.]

Minderslachen (near Kandel)

Anna Barbara Bohlander, daughter of Georg Beyerle, citizen of Minderslachen, and his wife Anna Catharina Roth, married to Johann Adam Bohlander of Minderslachen, "who went together to the New Land" (about 1755). [Johannes Bohlander, Ship Good Intent, October 3, 1754.]

Joseph Fetsch, son of Christian Fetsch of Minderslachen and his wife Barbara Himmler, "who is said actually to be residing in Philadelphia" (about 1774). [Joseph Foetsch, Ship Union, September 30, 1774.]

Minfeld (Kreis Germersheim)

Georg Michael Gross, unmarried, and Anna Maria Gross, children of Frantz Gross of Minfeld, "went to the New Land" (about 1751).

Hanss Erhard Fosselmann, son of Ludwig Fosselman of Minfeld and
wife Maria Margaretha Schaeffer, "who now thirty years ago went to
the so-called New Land" (Inventory of 1762). [Hans Erhart Vossel-
man, Ship John and William, October 17, 1732.]

Maria Elisabetha Kauffmann, sister of Erhard Fosselmann, married
to the mason Johannes Kauffmann, "who (about 1750) went to Zweibruecken and (about 1756) to America."

Maria Koenig and Abrahamb Koenig, children of Frantz Koenig,
farm-steward of the cloister at Minfeld, "went to the New Land"
about 1752.

Rachell Bouquet, daughter of the citizen and farm-steward of the
cloister at Minfeld, "who went off single to the West Indies."
Rosina Bouquet, sister of Rachell, wife of Hanss Georg Hoffman,
"who likewise went to America." Matheus Bouquet, brother of the
two preceding, "who likewise went away, single, and in common with
the above mentioned, to America." The emigration of all three is
posited in a document dated February 26, 1762.

Jacob Haen of Minfeld, "went to the New Land" (Document dated
1761). [Jacob Haen, Snow Ketty, October 16, 1752.]

Niclaus Oth, son of Michael Oth of Minfeld and wife Maria Margaretha Fosselmann, "in New England or America" (emigration about
1754). [Presumably Johann Nickolaus Ott, Ship Phoenix, November 2,
1752.]

Moersback (Kreis Zweibruecken)

Michael Binckle (Benckle), son of Hanss Binckli of Moersbach,
"went to America" (about 1734). The family was of Swiss origin—
the official papers mention an aunt of the emigrant who died in
Canton Berne. [Hans Michel Bingley, Ship Oliver, August 26, 1735.]

Johann Adam Traub and Jacob Traub, sons of Heinrich Traub of
Muehlhofen and his wife Maria Catharina Roeller, "who both went to
the so-called New Land a year ago (1754)". [J. Adam Traub, Jacob
Traub, Ship Barclay, September 14, 1754.]

Valentin Jung, son of Peter Jung, citizen resident at Muehlhofen
and his wife Magdalena Fine, "who went to the so-called New Land"
(about 1736). [Valentine Young, Ship Charming Nancy, October 8,
1737.] Johann Jacob Jung, brother of Valentin, "who also went
there" (about 1749). Maria Catharina [Jung], their sister, "married Caspar Baer, and afterwards went there (i.e., America) with
him" [Casper Ber, Ship Restauration, October 9, 1747.] Johann Adam
Jung, brother of the preceding, "who went there too" (Document
dated September 15, 1756). [Johann Adam Jung, Ship Two Brothers,
September 14, 1749.]

Benedict Forster, son of the citizen and master miller Ludwig
Forster of Muehlhofen and his wife Anna Juditha Reuther, "to the
New Land" (after 1746). [Benedict Forster, Ship Neptune, September
30, 1754.]

Frantz Weiss, Abraham Weiss, Hanss Peter Weiss, and Daniel Weiss,
son of Jacob Weiss of Muehlhofen and his wife Margaretha Kessler,
"which four children went one after the other to America; news of

them received now and then" (Property Inventory of March 16, 1763).
According to official declarations of the end of April, 1750, Abraham Weiss is said to have gone with wife and children to America,
from Moerzheim, where he was working as a farmer. Frantz Weiss "is
reported to have gone away, a single man, with his brother Abraham
Weiss, to America." According to the Acts he was born April 9,
1705, at Barbelroth in the Palatinate. For Hanss Peter Weiss (born
May 5, 1712, at Barbelroth) the same emigration data apply as for
his brother Frantz. [Johann Peter Weis, Ship Anderson, August 21,
1750.] Daniel Weiss (born October 6, 1715, at Muehlhofen), "went
to America from here (Muehlhofen) with his wife and four children
in the year 1754." [Daniel Weiss, Ship Barclay, September 14,
1754.] Margaretha Weis, daughter of Matheis Mans of Muehlhofen and
his wife Eva, "wife of Daniel Weis, who went off the beginning of
1754 to New England." "Daniel Weis's wife, who left Muehlhofen in
the year 1754 and went to America" (cf. Daniel Weis). Catharina
Weiss (born October 10, 1709, at Barbelroth), "went to America with
her husband (Kaeufer of Heuchelheim, q.v.) and Frantz and Abraham
Weiss to America.
     Barbara Hauswirth, daughter of Adam Zimpelmann, assistant judge
of Muehlhofen, "wife of Christian Hauswirth from here (Muehlhofen),
who went with her husband to America in the year 1753." [Christian
Hauswirth, Ship John and Elizabeth, November 7, 1754.]
     Johann Jacob Koehler, son of the assistant judge and citizen
Andreas Koehler at Muehlhofen and his wife Anna Catharine Zimmer,
"who now over fourteen years ago traveled to the so-called New
Land" (Property Inventory of 1765). [Jacob Koehler, Ship Phoenix,
September 25, 1751.]
     Anna Elisabetha Meister, daughter of Peter Meister of Muehlhofen
and his wife Anna Maria Kesseler, "went away single from Muehlhofen
to America" (Document dated June 18, 1754).
                    Mutterstadt (Kreis Ludwigshafen)
     Balthasar Reymer of Mutterstadt is permitted to go to the New
Land with wife and children, but must pay the tithe on his property
that he is taking out of the country (Protocols of the Oberamt of
Neustadt, 1753). [Balthaser Reimer, Ship Brothers, September 30,
1754.]
                    Niederlustadt (Kreis Germersheim)
     Peter Roch, son of the blacksmith Peter Roch of Niederlustadt and
his wife Maria Barbara Stadler, "who went to Pennsylvania in the
year 1753 and left in this neighborhood at Offenbach his wife,
Margaret nee Lutz, besides a little son, Friedrich Roch, aged eight
years." [Johann Peter Roch, Ship Rowand, September 19, 1753.]
     Andreas Ott, son of Georg Ott of Niederlustadt and his wife Cath-
arina Groh, "went to the New Land" (about 1750).
                    Niedermiesau (today Miesau, Kreis Kusel)
     Gertrud Franck, daughter of Johannes Franck of Niedermiesau and
his wife Anna Catharina Rheinberger of Otterberg, "married to Henrich Kohl in the New Land"; her sister Anna Maria was "married to

Valentin Hoffmann in the New Land" (Document dated April 1, 1762).

Oberkleinich (Kreis Bernkastel)

According to a report of the Village-Mayor of Kleinich to the Government of Trarbach, dated May 8, 1741, Maria Catharina and Nickel Lahm, children of Matthias Lahm of Oberkleinich, want "to go to the New Land." [Johann Nicklaus Lahm, Ship Lydia, September 29, 1741.] In a report to the Sponheim Government, dated May 12, 1741, the Village-Mayor of Irmenach wrote: "I wish herewith to report that in the past year, as I recently learned, two young apprentices have gone to the so-called New Land under the pretense of completing their apprenticeship. One of them, by the name of Johann Peter Lorentz, was born in the village of Hoschidt (=Hochscheidt), the other, Johan Petter Lahm, was a native of Oberkleinich." According to an entry of the Government of Trarbach, dated 1740, they were both described as actually emigrated "to the New Land". [Peter Lorentz, Peter Laam, Ship Lydia, September 27, 1740.]

Oberlustadt (Kreis Germersheim)

Daniel Hoffmann, son of Jacob Hoffman of Oberlustadt and Christina Brueckner, his second wife, "who went to the New Land" (Document dated August 30, 1758). [Either Daniel Hoffman, Ship Neptune, September 30, 1753, or Daniel Hoffman, Ship Robert and Alice, September 3, 1739.]

Johann Jakob Fauth, son of Bernhard Fauth of Oberlustadt and wife Katharina Haf, "went to America" (about 1765). [Jacob Faut, Ship Polly, August 24, 1765.] See next entry.

Catharina Heintz, daughter of Johann Adam Theiss of Oberlustadt and wife Magdalena Schmitt, "who married Georg Jakob Heintz of Roth (Rhodt u. Rietburg, Kreis Landau) and went with him to Pennsylvania." Louisa, her sister, "married Jacob Fauth from here and likewise went to Pennsylvania."

Georg Adam Horter, son of Jacob Horter of Oberlustadt and Agnes Sohland his wife, "who now 12 years ago went to Pennsylvania" (Property Inventory of 1768, which places the date of emigration about 1756).

Basic to genealogical research in this country are the eighteenth century immigrant lists being assembled by scholars abroad. Dr. Friedrich Krebs, one of the principal researchers in Germany today, here concludes an article which was begun two issues back. The source materials are the state and municipal archives covering the areas from which so many thousands emigrated two centuries ago.

Oberlustadt (Kreis Germersheim)

Barbara Horter, "widow of Georg Horter, deceased citizen at Oberlustadt, left here about a year ago for the so-called New England with her son Velten Horter. Also there was a son of hers by the name of Georg Jacob Horter who went to the above-mentioned New England several years ago" (Inventory of 1765). [Johann Valtin Horter, Ship Britannia, September 26, 1764.]

Georg Adam Jahraus, son of Andreas Jahraus of Oberlustadt and his

wife Margaretha Schmid, "residing in America" (Document dated
October 30, 1786).

Anna Elisabetha Schmitt, daughter of Andreas Schmitt of Oberlustadt and his wife Catharina Jahraus, "wife of Friedrich Doll,
inhabitant of Pennsylvania" (Document dated March 30, 1770).

Anna Apolonia Sigrist, daughter of Martin Sigrist of Oberlustadt
and wife Catharina Boehm, "went to Pennsylvania" (about 1744).

Obermiesau (today Miesau, Kreis Kusel)

Nickel Lang, son of Johannes Lang of Obermiesau and wife Anna
Catharina, "went to the New Land" (about 1735) with wife and child-
ren, from Waldmohr, where he was then residing. His step-sister
Eva Rosina Jacobi, daughter of Martin Jacobi of Obermiesau, went to
America at the same time, presumably with her brother, and was
there married to Friedrich Steffinger. Her sister Catharina Jacobi
went "to the New Land" with her, along with her husband Valentin
Neu. [Fallendin Neu, Nickel Lang, Ship Harle, September 1, 1736.]

Christian Hammel, son of Bernhard Hammel of Obermiesau, "went to
the New Land in 1734 as an apprentice butcher."

Obersuelzen (Kreis Frankenthal)

Paul Fried, son of the Anabaptist (Mennonite) Peter Fried of
Obersuelzen, "went to the New Land" (Document dated June 6, 1747).

Johann Jacob Fuchs, son of Georg Henrich Fuchs of Obersuelzen,
"who is in the New Land" (Document dated June 17, 1758).

Lorentz Beck, of Obersuelzen, "in the New Land" (Document dated
1771). [Johan Loretz Beck, Ship Hero, November 27, 1764.]

Ottersheim (Kreis Kirchheimbolanden)

Henrich Lebkuecher, son of Johann Adam Lebkuecher of Ottersheim,
"last summer (1753) for the second time went to the New Land, without paying the tithe." [Henrich Lebkucher, Ship Lydia, September
20, 1743.]

Ottersheim (Kreis Germersheim)

Conrad Doll, son of Georg Doll of Ottersheim and wife Anna Margaretha Weinheimer, "this man is in America" (Document dated March
21, 1753).

Georg Kuhn, son of Valentin Kuhn of Ottersheim, "is said to
reside in the New Land, according to a letter written April 26,
1747 from 'Carlsdaun' (Charleston) in South Carolina."

Rohrbach (Kreis Bergzabern)

Philipp and Andreas Boudmond, sons of Philipp Boudmond, citizen
of Rohrbach (died 1762), "who both are in the New Land for the 12th
year" (Inventory of 1762). [Andre Baudemont, Ship Osgood, September 29, 1750.]

Peter Dorst, son of Peter Dorst of Rohrbach and his wife Maria
Catharina, "who is in the New Land" (Document dated May 12, 1762).

Hanss Georg Hoffmann, son of Georg Bernhardt Hoffmann of Rohrbach
and his wife Maria Elisabetha, "married in the New Land" (Document
dated January 14, 1765).

Adam Beckenhaub, son of Jacob Beckenhaub of Rohrbach and wife
Anna, "who went about 15 years ago to the New Land" (Property

Inventory of 1766). [Hans Adam Beckenhaub, Ship Neptune, September 30, 1754.]

Hanss Peter Hoffmann, son of Hans Georg Hoffmann of Rohrbach and wife Margaretha, "who has now been living in the New Land over nine years" (Inventory of 1742). [Presumably Johann Peter Hofman, Ship Dragon, September 30, 1732.]

Rumbach (Kreis Pirmasens)

Margaretha Catharina Bley, daughter of Jacob Neuhard, assistant judge at Rumbach and his wife Anna Barbara, "married to Adam Bley, citizen here (at Rumbach) and in the Spring (1753) emigrated to America with her husband Adam Bley."

Georg Michael Schaeffer, son of Heinrich Schaeffer, citizen at Rumbach and his wife Anna Maria Schneider, "who has been a citizen here at Rumbach and emigrated secretly to America in the year 1766."

Susanna Catharina Schaub, Heinrich Schaub, Maria Dorothea Schaub, children of Balthasar Schaub of Rumbach, "emigrated to America" (Document dated June 23, 1770). [Henry Schaub, Ship Sally, November 10, 1767.] Of Susanna Catharina Schaub the records report, "now married to Jacob Neuhard the blacksmith, citizen at Rumbach, and several years ago emigrated to America (Document dated 1770). Of Maria Dorothea: "Now married to Georg Michael Schaeffer, citizen here and likewise gone to America with the above mentioned."

St. Julian (Kreis Kusel)

Johann Henrich Allmann, mason, son of Henrich Allmann of Sienhachenbach, married at St. Julian, January 18, 1746, to Maria Barbara Soffel, born at St. Julian October 5, 1723, daughter of Bernhardt Soffel of St. Julian and wife Maria Engel, "both emigrated to Pennsylvania with six children May 15, 1764." Children, born at St. Julian: 1. Maria Sara, born July 6, 1747. 2. Anna Margretha, born November 20, 1749 ("died on the way to America in 1764"). 3. Maria Elisabetha, born August 14, 1752. 4. Maria Catharina, born December 11, 1754. 5. Johann Nicol, born March 3, 1764 ("died on the way to America in the same year"). 6. Anna Elisabetha, born August 27, 1760. All references from the Lutheran Church Book of St. Julian.

Johann Friedrich Hirschfeld(t), born at St. Julian October 12, 1728, son of Johann Philipp Hirschfeld and wife Maria Margretha, "turner by trade—emigrated to Pennsylvania with wife and three children [May 15,] 1764" (Reference in Lutheran Church Book of St. Julian). Friedrich Hirschfeld married at St. Julian, February 10, 1756, Maria Margretha Neu, born at Obereisenbach (Kreis Kusel), September 25, 1728, daughter of Johann Jacob Neu and wife Maria Elisabetha. Children, born at St. Julian: 1. Maria Elisabetha, born December 22, 1756. 2. Johann Henrich, born June 13, 1759. 3. Maria Margaretha, born August 14, 1762. [Henrich Allman, Friedrich Hirschfeldt, Ship Richmond, October 20, 1764.]

Johann Jacob Jeckel, born at St. Julian April 5, 1722, son of Johann Christoph Jeckel and wife Anna Maria, "emigrated to Pennsyl-

vania April 24, 1752" (Reference in Lutheran Church Book of St.
Julian).

Georg Abraham Jacob, blacksmith by trade, born at Eschenau (Kreis
Kusel) December 31, 1723, son of Johann Peter Jacob of Eschenau and
wife Anna Margretha, married at St. Julian, June 16, 1750, to Maria
Dorothea Grill, born at St. Julian February 22, 1731, daughter of
Johann Georg Grill of St. Julian, "both emigrated to Pennsylvania
with five [four] children, May 15, 1764" (Reference in Lutheran
Church Book of St. Julian). Children, born at St. Julian: 1. Jo-
hann Georg, born March 11, 1760. 2. Maria Magdalena Elisabetha,
born November 25, 1762. 3. Johann Peter, born November 10, 1757.
[Abraham Jacob, Ship Richmond, October 20, 1764.]

Johann Nicol Grimm, widower, married (1st) at St. Julian November
27, 1736, to Anna Elisabetha, widow of Adam Jeckel; married (2d) at
St. Julian May 25, 1751, to Maria Magdalena, daughter of Johannes
Dickes of Baumholder, "both migrated to Pennsylvania with [——]
children, May 15, 1764" (Reference in Lutheran Church Book of St.
Julian). Children, born at St. Julian: 1. Friderich Jacob, born
November 2, 1758, "died at Portsmouth in England on the way to
America, 1764." 2. Maria Dorothea, born February 17, 1756.

Steinweiler (Kreis Germersheim)

Johannes Lingenfelder, son of the master baker Peter Lingenfelder
of Steinweiler, "who is staying in the so-called New Land" (emigrated about 1753).

Stetten (Kreis Kirchheimbolanden)

Michel Niederauer, son of Jost Fritz Niederauer of Stetten, "who
is in the New Land" (Document dated 1752). [Michel Niederauer,
Ship Two Brothers, October 13, 1747.]

Waldmohr (Kreis Kusel)

Johannes Heill, son of Michael Heill, resident and citizen at
Waldmohr and his wife Maria Catharina Schaeffer, "went to the New
Land" (Document dated March 10, 1745).

Philipp Nickel Balbierer, son of Henrich Balbierer of Waldmohr
and his wife Maria Barbara, baptized March 22, 1712, at Kleinott-
weiler, went to America in 1750 with the family of Franz Kunz.
[Philliebs Balbirer, Ship Edinburgh, August 13, 1750.]

Valentin Blum, blacksmith, "by trade a nailsmith, in the New
Land," likewise his sister Eva Elisabetha, who was married to
Nickel Lang (q.v.) of Waldmohr. Emigration about 1736.

Walshausen (Kreis Zweibruecken)

Heinrich Haller, son of the citizen and master tailor Jacob Haller of Walshausen, from his first marriage with Elisabetha Moser,
"deserted from the old Ducal Body Guard and emigrated to Pennsylvania." This emigration took place around 1748. His property,
specifically an inheritance which later fell to him, a sum of 102
florins 11 batzen and 6 pfennig, was therefore confiscated by the
Zweibruecken authorities, since his emigration took place without
manumission. [Henrich Haller, Ship St. Andrew, August 18, 1750.]

Weingarten (Kreis Germersheim)

Paul Bauersachs, born September 29, 1744, at Weingarten, son of
David Bauersachs, citizen of Weingarten and wife Anna Maria Damian
of Boebingen, "who in the beginning settled himself as a citizen of
Freisbach, but from there went away to America" (Document dated
August 5, 1784). [Paulus Bauersachs, Brig Betsey, December 4,
1771.]

Peter Brunnemer, baptized at Weingarten April 28, 1726, son of
Johannes Brunnemer and wife Anna Margaretha, "went away to Pennsylvania without previous permission" about 1749. According to a
power of attorney authorized by him, dated August 15, 1766, Peter
Brunnemer was settled in Augusta County in the Province of Virginia.

Weisenheim am Sand (Kreis Neustadt)

Anna Barbara Reitenbach, daughter of Jacob Reitenbach of Weisenheim am Sand and his wife Gertraud Keller, was taken along to
America in the year 1764 by the brother of her father Michel Reidenbach of Weisenheim. In America she married Michel Lauer.
Michel Reidenbach's first emigration took place about 1744. In the
year 1764 he returned to Weisenheim, to receive an inheritance for
the two children of his brother Johann Nicolaus Reidenbach who had
died in Pennsylvania. [Johann Nickel Reidenbach, Johann Michel
Reidenbach, Ship Lydia, September 20, 1743; Michel Reidebach, Ship
Richmond, October 20, 1764.]

Lorentz and Johann Christian Lauffer, from Weisenheim am Sand,
"went to the New Land" (about 1728).

Johannes Quast of Weisenheim am Sand, "vassal, staying in Pennsylvania" (Document dated 1775). [Joh. Quast, Ship Crawford,
October 16, 1772.]

Westheim (Kreis Germersheim)

Valentin Batteiger, son of Peter Batteiger of Westheim and wife
Maria Eva, "absent, staying in America" (Document dated 1777).
[Johann Valentin Batteiger, Ship Minerva, October 29, 1767.]

Georg Adam Schwab, son of Andreas Schwab of Westheim and wife
Rosina Barbara, "residing in Pennsylvania" (Document dated March
17, 1765).

Wolfersheim (Kreis St. Ingbert, Saar)

Christian Brengel, son of Kilian Brengel of Wolfersheim and wife
Juliana, "having signified with the princely authorities his intention of returning, went to Maryland" (about 1754). His brother
Jacob Brengel, "went under the same provision to America." [Chris-
tian Brengel, Jacob Brengel, Ship Phoenix, October 1, 1754.]

Anna Catharina Brengel, sister of both, "followed her two
brothers Christian and Jacob Brengel to America" (about 1764).
Georg Brengel, brother of the above mentioned persons, "married in
America, whither he went (about 1764) as an apprentice linen-
weaver."

Wolfstein (Kreis Kusel)

Maria Margaretha Fuchs, daughter of Friedrich Fuchs of Wolfstein

and wife Anna Maria, "wife of Peter Doerr of Rossbach (Kreis
Kusel), who went with her husband to America" (Document dated
1781). [Peter Doerr, Ship Prince of Wales, November 5, 1764.]
    Johann Jacob Schmidt, son of the master blacksmith Sebastian
Schmidt of Wolfstein, went to America (before 1744). In a letter
written October 17, 1753, from Bethel Township on the Little Swatara, in Berks County, Pennsylvania, he mentions that Debalt Werner
from Wolfstein (emigrated 1744) and Wilhelm Dauwer from Baumholder
[Wilhelm Dauber, Ship (——), October 20, 1747] brought letters for
him to America. His brother Johann Henrich Schmitt went to America
in 1754. From him there is a letter from Philadelphia, received
November 21, 1754, which describes the sea voyage and trip across
to America.

Wollmesheim (Kreis Landau)

    Johann Michel Ungerer, son of Stephan Ungerer of Wollmesheim and
wife Anna Maria Sahner "living in the New Land" (Document dated
October 26, 1759). [Johann Michel Ungerer, Ship Beulah, September
10, 1753.]

Zeiskam (Kreis Germersheim)

    Philipp Jacob Geiss, farrier at Zeiskam, son of Henrich Geiss of
Freisbach, married at Zeiskam, May 4, 1745, to Anna Appolonia Guen-
ter, daughter of Andreas Guenter of Zeiskam, widow of the farrier
Conrad Maylaender of Zeiskam. Children, born at Zeiskam: 1. Aga-
tha Geiss, born September 29, 1747. 2. Johann Georg Geiss, born
December 27, 1748. 3. Maria Barbara, born October 5, 1750.
According to official records the family went to America about 1751
and according to a power of attorney of Philipp Jacob Geiss, dated
May 28, 1763, was settled in Bern Township, Berks County, Pennsylvania. [Philipp Jacob Geis, Ship Phoenix, September 25, 1751.]
    Andreas Eberhardt, born at Zeiskam June 4, 1733, son of Friderich
Eberhardt, master weaver, and his wife Elisabetha, at Zeiskam, "who
has gone away to America" (Document dated June 22, 1772). [Presum-
ably Andreas Ebehrth, Ship Bannister, October 21, 1754.]
    Lorentz Schmitt, surgeon and barber, son of Mathes Schmitt, citi-
zen at Billigheim, married at Zeiskam, May 14, 1748, Maria Helena
Guth, daughter of Johannes Guth of Zeiskam. After his marriage
Lorentz Schmitt was surgeon and barber at Zeiskam. Children, born
at Zeiskam: 1. Johann Jacob, born May 23, 1749, "has gone to the
New Land". 2. Philipp Peter, born September 22, 1750. Source:
Reformed Church Book of Zeiskam. According to governmental records
Maria Helena Schmitt, nee Guth, intended in 1751 to go with her
husband and two children to the "New Land" and on that account had
her inheritance paid out to her. According to another reference
dated 1757 they had "gone away to America about six years ago."
[Lorentz Schmitt, Ship Phoenix, September 25, 1751.]
    Johann Peter Zwicker, citizen at Zeiskam, married at Zeiskam
August 9, 1753, Maria Magdalena Haffner. Children, all born at
Zeiskam: 1. Johann Peter, baptized May 24, 1736, "went to the New
Land with his father and mother". 2. Magdalena, baptized August 4,

1739, same reference.   3. Georg Melchior, born November 9, 1743, same reference.   4. Johann Georg, born June 27, 1747, same reference.   5. Maria Barbara, born October 23, 1750, same reference. Source: Reformed Church Book of Zeiskam.

Samuel Sinn, master baker at Zeiskam, son of Peter Sinn, master baker at Zeiskam, married (at Zeiskam) January 31, 1747, Anna Barbara Trauth, daughter of Johann Georg Trauth of Offenbach (Palatinate). Of their son, Johann Friedrich, born at Zeiskam, November 23, 1751, the Reformed Church Book of Zeiskam reports, "went with his father to the New Land."

Friedrich Krebs. "Amerika-Auswanderer des 18. Jahrhunderts aus der Heutigen Pfalz und der Nahe- und Hunsrückgegend," *Mitteilungen zur Wanderungsgeschichte der Pfälzer (Beilage zu Pfälzische Familien- und Wappenkunde)*, folge 11-12 (1954), 62-66 [Lancour No. 152].

An English translation of this article is included in Lancour No. 141, above.

"Early Swiss Settlers," *Notes and Queries Historical, Biographical and Genealogical Relating Chiefly to Interior Pennsylvania.* Annual Volume 1900 (1901), 121-122 [Lancour No. 153].

This article contains the name of 48 Swiss emigrants who left Zürich in October 1734, and arrived in Philadelphia on board the ship *Mercury*, May 29, 1735. A complete list of these passengers and others on board the *Mercury* may be found in Lancour Nos. 144 and 145. The original source, found in the Swiss Archives, was a pamphlet entitled *Der Hinkinde Bott von Carolina*, by Ludwig Weber of Wallisellen (Zürich, 1735).

Ernst Steinemann, editor. "A List of Eighteenth-Century Emigrants from the Canton of Schaffhausen to the American Colonies, 1734-1752. With an Introduction by Dr. Don Yoder," *The Pennsylvania German Folklore Society Yearbook*, 16 (1951), 185-196 [Lancour No. 154].

The Genealogical Publishing Company will reprint this article in a volume of works previously published by The Pennsylvania German Folklore Society.

John W. Jordan. "Moravian Immigration to Pennsylvania, 1734-1765,"
  The Pennsylvania Magazine of History and Biography, 33 (1909),
  228-248 [Lancour No. 155].

This article has been reprinted together with others from the
same journal in *Emigrants to Pennsylvania, 1641-1819*, published in
1977 by the Genealogical Publishing Company of Baltimore.

———

Friedrich Krebs. "Die Amerikaauswanderung aus dem Kurpfälzischen
  Oberamt Heidelberg in den Jahren 1737, 1738, 1751, 1753 und
  1754," *Badische Heimat*, 38 (1958), 303-304 [Lancour No. 156].

The English translation of this article is included in Lancour
No. 141, above.

———

Harold E. Gillingham. "Philadelphia Arrivals, 1738," *Publications
  of the Genealogical Society of Pennsylvania*, 12 (1934), 150 [Lan-
  cour No. 157].

In the Reynell Papers, recently acquired by The Historical
Society of Pennsylvania, is an Invoice of goods shipped from London, July, 1738, on board the *Elizabeth*, Edward Kervell Master, for
account of Daniel Flaxney and consigned to John Reynell, a Philadelphia merchant, the following indentured passengers: Listed as
"7 servants"—

　　　　　　　Jnº. Cox, a Boy, 5 years
　　　　　　　John Richards, Gardner, 4 years
　　　　　　　Edw. Hancock, Butcher, 4 years
　　　　　　　Nth. Manton, Surgeon, 4 years
　　　　　　　Geº. Goodman, Butcher, 4 years
　　　　　　　Jnº. West, Wool-comber, 4 years
　　　　　　　Jnº. Kamb, Shoemaker, 4 years.
The passages, at £5. each, were charged on invoice at £35.0.0 and
the "Clothes &c." at £3. each, or £21.0.0, making a total of £56.
  This is the first instance which has come to my attention where
servants were entered on an Invoice; and I have examined hundreds
of such papers for the early eighteenth century.

———

Hugo Froehlich. "Pioneers from Staudernheim," *The Pennsylvania
  Dutchman*, 8 (Fall-Winter 1956-1957), 43-46 [Lancour No. 158].

The following article was translated from the original German by
Dr. Don Yoder.

The Lutheran Church Register of the village of Staudernheim, in the Nahe Valley near Bad Kreuznach in the Northern Palatinate, belongs in the rare category of Palatine church books which contain a notable number of references to 18th century emigrants.

In the case of emigration, the minister—in the classical Latin of the clergy and the university—added a note to the record of his lost parishioner's baptism—"*Americanus factus*"—"became an American."

Emigration from 18th century Staudernheim involved three destinations—America, Prussia, and Poland. Some ninety persons left the village for America in the years 1738-1750, with the high point coming in the years 1739 and 1741, when entire families left together for Pennsylvania.

But there was also emigration into Prussia, sponsored by the Hohenzollerns in their attempt to build up Brandenburg and Pomerania. This movement (30 persons) took place in 1747 and 1748 and other unlisted years, and the pastor designated his loss with the Latin phrase "*Borussus factus*"—"became a Prussian"; for this emigration see Otto Gebhard, *Friederizianische Pfalzerkolonien in Brandenburg und Pommern* (Stettin, 1939).

Emigration to Poland (Galicia), involving fifteen persons from Staudernheim, took place around 1783 and 1784. It is significant that there are in this list some cases of one member of a family heading westward across the Atlantic to Pennsylvania, another turning up later in the German-speaking settlements of Eastern Europe.

The Latin and German phrases given in parentheses are quotations from the original church register; the materials in brackets giving arrivals in Philadelphia are, as usual in our emigrant lists, from the colonial ship-lists as published in Strassburger and Hinke, *Pennsylvania German Pioneers* (Norristown, Pennsylvania: The Pennsylvania German Society, 1934) [Readers should note also that the emigrants are arranged by family, and that in not every case did the head of a family emigrate].

The materials have been translated from Hugo Fröhlich, "Auswanderer im lutherischen Kirchenbuch von Staudernheim an der Nahe," which appeared in *Mitteilungen zur Wanderungsgeschichte der Pfalzer*, edited by Dr. Fritz Braun of the *Heimatstelle Pfalz*, Kaiserslautern, and published as a supplement to *Pfalzische Familien- und Wappenkunde*, 1954, to whose editorial board we are grateful for the privilege of reprinting these unusual materials.

Barth, Johann Nikolaus, tailor, buried at Staudernheim, March 17, 1729, married at Staudernheim, January 23, 1714, Anna Maria Seiss, daughter of Michael Seiss and widow of Friedrich Lautenbach. The following children, born at Staudernheim, emigrated:

1. Anna Christina Barth, baptized March 19, 1718; emigrated to Prussia with her illegitimate son, born at Staudernheim, Johann Nikolaus, baptized January 6, 1746 (*Borussiana cum filio facta*).

2. Johann Nikolaus Barth, baptized August 11, 1720 (*Americanus factus*).
3. Johannes Barth, baptized October 22, 1724 (*Americanus factus*). [Perhaps Johannes Barth, who arrived Philadelphia on the ship *Lydia*, October 19, 1749.]

Beier, Johann Friedrich, son of Johann Wilhelm Beier, married Anna Elisabeth Ebert, daughter of Johann George Ebert. The following children, born at Staudernheim, emigrated to America [in 1741]:
1. Johann Kasimir Beier, baptized August 4, 1726...
2. Johann Nikolaus Beier, baptized January 4, 1730 (*anno 1741 Americana (!) facta*).
3. Johann Friedrich Beier, baptized December 15, 1732...
4. Anna Maria Beier, baptized January 27, 1737...
5. Johann Andreas Beier, baptized February 6, 1739...

Christian, Johann Peter, son of Johann Valentin Christian, linen-weaver, noted as dead at the confirmation of his son Philipp Jakob at Easter 1732, married at Staudernheim April 20, 1706, Maria Elisabeth Dorth, daughter of Johann Jakob Dorth at Pfalzisch-Weierbach. Children, born at Staudernheim, emigrated:
1. Johann Georg Christian, baptized April 11, 1707 [to Prussia with wife and children given in article].
2. Philipp Jakob Christian, baptized May 13, 1717 (*Americanus factus*).

Conradt, Johann Nikolaus, buried at Staudernheim June 1, 1736, married Anna Maria Wagner, daughter of Johann Sebastian Wagner at Gebroth; the widow married II. Simon Jakob Fey (q.v.). Child, born at Staudernheim:
1. Johann Konrad Conradt, baptized October 21, 1728 (*Americanus factus*). [Perhaps Connrad Conrath, who arrived at Philadelphia on the ship *Neptune*, October 25, 1746.]

Cron, Simon Jakob, baptized October 18, 1692, son of David Cron, married I. at Staudernheim, August 30, 1718, Anna Magdalena Rollauer, daughter of Ludwig Rollauer and widow of Johannes Schmidt, buried at Staudernheim September 11, 1734; married II. at Staudernheim, January 17, 1736, Susanna Martha Sponheimer, daughter of Johann Wilhelm Sponheimer at Waldböckelheim. Children born at Staudernheim—Nos. 1-4 of the first marriage, 5-6 of the second marriage [all emigrated to America in 1741]:
1. Johann Konrad Cron, baptized February 5, 1722...
2. Johann Philipp Cron, baptized November 19, 1723...
3. Anna Christina Cron, baptized December 12, 1725...
4. Anna Maria Cron, baptized September 14, 1730...
5. Johann David Cron, baptized December 6, 1736...
6. Anna Margarethe Cron, baptized August 16, 1739...
[Simon Jacob Cron (Croon), 48 years old, arrived at Philadelphia on the ship *Friendship*, October 12, 1741.]

Dietz, Johann Michel, son of Nikolaus Dietz, cartwright, buried February 9, 1727, married at Staudernheim, October 16, 1725, Maria Dorothea, daughter of Philipp Heinrich Cless, who possibly became the second wife of Johann Philipp Tesch (q.v.). Child, born at Staudernheim [emigrated to America in 1741]:
1. Johann Jakob Dietz, baptized October 19, 1726... [Possibly Johann Jacob Dietz (Ditts), 19 years old, who arrived at Philadelphia on the ship *Marlborough*, September 23, 1741.]

Ehrhard, Johann Peter, son of Johannes Ehrhard, married at Staudernheim, February 3, 1708, Anna Margarethe Becker, daughter of Nikolaus Becker. Children, born at Staudernheim:
1. Johann Heinrich Ehrhard, baptized November 19, 1713; according to the records arrived in America in 1739.
2. Maria Elisabeth Ehrhard, baptized November 30, 1716 (*Americana facta*).
3. Maria Christina Ehrhard, baptized August 17, 1721 (*anno 1741 Americana facta*).
[Johann Henrich Ehrhard (Erhart, Gerhard), 23 years old, arrived at Philadelphia on the ship *Samuel*, August 27, 1739.]

Ehrhard, Johann Philipp, son of Johannes Ehrhard, married at Staudernheim November 30, 1717, Elisabeth Dorothea Jung, daughter of Johannes Jung at Huffelsheim. Children, born at Staudernheim:
1. Anna Margarethe Ehrhard, baptized October 16, 1718 (*anno 1742 Americana facta*), married John Karl Schneider (q.v.).
2. Johannes Ehrhard, baptized August 11, 1720 (*anno 1741 Americanus factus*).
3. Anna Barbara Ehrhard, baptized April 29, 1723 (*anno 1741 Americana facta*).
4. Anna Maria Ehrhard, baptized May 9, 1726 (*anno 1741 Americana facta*).
[Johannes Ehrhard (Erhardt, Erhart), 21 years old, arrived at Philadelphia on the ship *Friendship*, October 12, 1741; with him in the same ship list is Wilhelm Erhard, 20 years old.]

Fey, Johann Ludwig, son of Johannes Fey, buried at Staudernheim September 9, 1759, married I. Anna Barbara, buried at Staudernheim January 26, 1735; married II. at Staudernheim, January 8, 1737, Anna Katharina Graff, daughter of Kaspar Graff at Huffelsheim, buried at Staudernheim November 25, 1787. Children of the first marriage, born at Staudernheim:
1. Simon Jakob Fey, baptized January 22, 1708, buried at Staudernheim, March 22, 1787; married I. Staudernheim, November 13, 1736, Anna Maria, widow of Johann Nikolaus Conradt (q.v.); married II. Staudernheim, December 27, 1743, Maria Christina Kratzmann, daughter of Johann Nikolaus Kratzmann. His son Johann Peter Fey, of the second marriage, born 1755, married 1784 to Maria Magdalena Spiess, settled in

Dornfeld, Galic[i]a, Poland; the emigrant's son Peter Fey
was a schoolmaster at Reichenbach in Dornfeld.
2. Johann Tobias Fey, baptized July 6, 1724 (*Americanus factus
    1750*). [Tobias Fey arrived at Philadelphia on the ship
    Dragon, September 26, 1749.]

Fey, Johann Wilhelm, son of Johann Nikolaus Fay, cooper, baptized
January 9, 1687 (*Americanus factus*), married at Staudernheim,
November 26, 1715, Maria Barbara Dietz, daughter of Nikolaus Dietz.
Children, born at Staudernheim [all to America in 1741]:
1. Anna Katharina Fey, baptized December 12, 1718...
2. Anna Margarethe Fey, baptized January 15, 1723...
3. Johann Michael Fey, baptized January 31, 1725...
4. Johann Simon Fey, baptized January 6, 1727...
5. Susanna Barbara Fey, baptized September 28, 1730...
6. Johann Nikolaus Fey, baptized September 23, 1734....
[Johann Wilhelm Fey, 53 years old, and Johann Michel Fey, 17
years old, arrived at Philadelphia on the snow *Molly*, October 26,
1741.]

Finck, Hans Georg, son of Heinrich Finck, buried at Staudernheim,
October 15, 1742, married I. Anna Maria, died at Staudernheim September 17, 1700; married II, at Staudernheim, April 5, 1701, Anna
Maria Hoffmann, daughter of Konrad Hoffman at Abtweiler. Child of
the second marriage, born at Staudernheim:
1. Johann Nikolaus Finck, baptized February 13, 1707 (*anno 1738
    Americanus factus*). [Possibly Johann Nickel Finck, 33
    years old, who arrived at Philadelphia on the ship *Samuel*,
    August 30, 1737.]

Fuchs, Johann Peter, hired man on the Klosterhof, married Anna
Margarethe; children, born at Staudernheim [all to America, 1741]:
1. Elisabeth Katharina Fuchs, baptized March 31, 1730...
2. Maria Magdalena Fuchs, baptized March 16, 1732...
3. Maria Margarethe Fuchs, baptized February 28, 1734...
4. Johann Nikolaus Fuchs, baptized May 16, 1736...
5. Anna Katharina Fuchs, baptized September 28, 1738...
6. Johann Jacob Fuchs, baptized July 22, 1740....

Grimm, Johann Philipp, son of Johann Peter Grimm, married at
Staudernheim, May 7, 1720, Anna Margarethe Weber, daughter of
Sebastian Jakob Weber.
Children, born at Staudernheim [all to America in 1739]:
1. Maria Elisabeth Grimm, baptized March 11, 1721...
2. Johann Peter Grimm, baptized May 14, 1723...
3. Johann Jakob Grimm, baptized August 23, 1726...
4. Anna Margarethe Grimm, baptized October 9, 1729...
5. Johann David Grimm, baptized August 28, 1737....

Haspelhorn, Johann Peter, son of Hans Michael Haspelhorn, buried at Staudernheim February 10, 1762, married I. Sabina Katherina, buried at Staudernheim, September 25, 1748, Anna Barbara Janson, daughter of Johann Michael Janson at Neubamberg [sic—has something been omitted?]. Children, born at Staudernheim:
1. Johann Ludwig Haspelhorn, baptized February 4, 1726 (Americanus factus).
2. Anna Sara Haspelhorn, baptized September 1, 1738; went to Poland in March of 1784.
[Ludwig Haspelhorn arrived in Philadelphia on the ship Dragon, September 26, 1749.]

Heblich, Christmann, from Ebernburg, buried at Staudernheim, July 19, 1750, married at Staudernheim, November, 1708, Anna Christina, buried at Staudernheim, January 9, 1743. Children, born at Staudernheim [both emigrated to America]:
1. Anna Margarethe Heblich, baptized September 24, 1713...
2. Anna Elisabeth Heblich, baptized February 16, 1716...; married Johann Peter Kistner (q.v.).

Kistner, Johann Peter, son of Johann Simon Kistner at Uberhochstetten, buried at Staudernheim, January 25, 1740, Anna Elisabeth Heblich (see above), who went to America with her son, born at Staudernheim: Simon Jakob Kistner, baptized January 27, 1743 (cum matre Americanus factus).

Klein, Johann Georg, cabinet-maker, from Borrstadt on the other side of the Rhine in the territory of Idstein, buried at Staudernheim, July 20, 1770, married I. at Staudernheim, February 15, 1715, Maria Margarethe Schappert, daughter of Johannes Schappert, buried October 15, 1726; married II, at Staudernheim, after proclamation on the 20th, 21st, and 22nd Sundays after Trinity 1727, N.N.; married III, at Staudernheim around 1730 Anna Magdalena, buried at Staudernheim January 20, 1739; married IV, at Staudernheim, June 2, 1739, Anna Maria Kaul, daughter of Johann Peter Kaul at Waldböckelheim, buried September 25, 1781. (The marriage of 1739 is expressly designated as the fourth marriage. It is possible that the second and third marriages above are identical; in that case the first marriage would have taken place before 1715.) Children, born at Staudernheim:
1. Johann Jakob Klein, baptized May 4, 1721 (anno 1741 Americanus factus).
2. Johann Peter Klein, baptized July 25, 1745 emigrated to Poland (den 25. August 1784 Polonius factus); cabinet-maker, married at Staudernheim, February 8, 1774, Anna Margarethe, widow of Philipp Freund at Kreuznach. Only one child appears to have been born at Staudernheim, Johann David Klein, born November 1, 1774, died September 11, 1781....

[Jacob Klein (Kleyn), 20 years old, arrived at Philadelphia, on
the ship *St. Andrew*, October 2, 1741.]

Lautenbach, Johannes, buried at Staudernheim May 16, 1736, married at Staudernheim, January 12, 1706, Anna Margarethe Gratzmann,
daughter of Peter Gratzmann, buried at Staudernheim, February 27,
1746. Children born in Staudernheim:
1. Maria Katharina Lautenbach, baptized December 4, 1712, emigrated to Pomerania with her husband...; married at Staudernheim, November 19, 1737, Johann Nikolaus Holzapiel, son
   of Johann Martin Halzapfel at Kirn, shoemaker.
2. Johann David Lautenbach, baptized January 25, 1717 (*anno 1739
   Americanus factus*).
3. Johannes Lautenbach, baptized February 17, 1724 (*Americanus
   factus*).
[Johann David Lautenbach (Laudenback, Loudinback), 23 years old,
arrived at Philadelphia, on the ship *Samuel*, August 27, 1739.]

Litzenburger, Theobald, son of Philipp Litzenburger, married at
Staudernheim, May 10, 1718, Maria Barbara Seiberlein, daughter of
Hans Konrad Seiberlein, School porter (*Schuldiener*) at Hennweiler.
Child, born at Staudernheim: Maria Christina, baptized July 28,
1720 (*Americana facta*).

Maurer, Johann Jakob, son of Paul Maurer at Sobernheim, married
Anna Elisabeth. Children, born at Staudernheim:
1. Katharina Barbara Maurer, baptized December 6, 1730 (*Americana cum patre*).
2. Anna Eva Maurer, baptized October 29, 1736 (*Americana cum
   patre*).
[Jacob Maurer (Mower), 32 years old, arrived at Philadelphia on
the ship *Samuel*, December 3, 1740.]

Otto, Johann Friedrich, son of the village mayor (*Schultheiss*),
dead before 1742, married at Staudernheim, February 23, 1706, Anna
Katharina Schmidt, daughter of Johann Thielmann Schmidt, buried at
Staudernheim, November 18, 1759. Children, born at Staudernheim:
1. Maria Katharina Otto, baptized March 7, 1709; lived at
   Sobernheim, married Johannes Melchior and both came to
   America (*Americani facti*).
2. Johann Tobias Otto, baptized June 8, 1726 (*anno 1741 Americanus factus*).
[Johannes Melchior (Melchier), 28 years old, arrived at Philadelphia on the ship *Friendship*, October 12, 1741.]

Ritter, Johann Peter, Village Mayor (*Schultheiss*), son of Matthias Ritter, married Maria Elisabeth. Children, born at Staudernheim:
1. Johann Heinrich Ritter, baptized July 27, 1732 (*Americanus
   cum patre factus*).

2. Johann Michael Ritter, baptized September 8, 1734 (*anno 1741 Americanus factus*).
3. Johannes Ritter, baptized March 7, 1737 (*anno 1741 Americanus factus*).

Rollard, Johann Peter, son of Ludwig Rollard, buried at Staudern-heim, March 4, 1733, married at Staudernheim, April 26, 1718, Anna Christina Muhlberger, daughter of George Muhlberger at Oberhausen, Oberamt Meisenheim; the widow married II, at Staudernheim, December 8, 1733, Matthias Wirth, son of Johann Philipp Wirth of Weiden. Child, born at Staudernheim: Johann Peter Rollard, baptized May 29, 1730 (*Americanus factus*).
[Johann Peter Roller (Rollar), arrived at Philadelphia on the ship *Richard and Mary*, September 26, 1752.]

Schappert, Johann Michael, son of Johannes Schappert, buried at Staudernheim, January 28, 1753, married I. at Kirschroth (Church Register Staudernheim), January 25, 1707, Anna Katharina Gutheil, daughter of Konrad Gutheil at Kirchroth, buried at Staudernheim, March 22, 1721; married II, at Staudernheim, February 3, 1722, Anna Katharina Grimm, daughter of Johann Simon Grimm, buried at Stau-dernheim, December 22, 1725; married III, at Staudernheim, January 8, 1732, Anna Barbara Seiss, daughter of Johannes Seiss. Children, born at Staudernheim:
1. Anna Barbara Schappert, baptized November 28, 1725, emigrated to Prussia (*Borussiana facta*).
2. Johann Nikolaus Schappert, baptized September 21, 1746, was married in Switzerland, at Bern, and went from Switzerland to America (*Ist in der Schweiz zu Bern verheiratet, aus der Schweiz in Amerika*).
[Nicolaus Schapperdt arrived at Philadelphia on the ship *Chance*, November 1, 1763. Before his name in the ship's list there appears the name of "Filb Schabbert". Possibly this was the brother of Jo-hann Nikolaus Schappert, Johann Philipp Schappert, baptized at Staudernheim, February 25, 1739.]

Schneider, Johann Karl, stone-mason, son of Heinrich Schneider at "Fremersheim," married at Staudernheim, May 31, 1740, Anna Mar-garethe Ehrhard (q.v.). Twins, born at Staudernheim:
1. Johannes Schneider.
2. Anna Barbara Schneider, baptized March 3, 1741 (*cum parenti-bus Americani facti*).
[Carl Schneyder (Snyder), 23 years old, arrived at Philadelphia on the ship *Friendship*, October 12, 1741.]

Seiss, Johann Jakob, son of Matthias Seiss, musician, buried at Staudernheim, November 3, 1744, married I. Johannetta; married II. Maria Barbara, buried at Staudernheim, October 20, 1785. Child of the first marriage, born at Staudernheim:

1. Johann Andreas Seiss, baptized December 15, 1720 (*Americanus factus*). [Joh. Andreas Seysen arrived in Philadelphia on the ship *Edinburgh*, August 13, 1750.]

Seiss, Johannes, son of Antonius Seiss, buried at Staudernheim, May 8, 1728, married I. Anna Elisabeth, died at Staudernheim, August 19, 1700; married II. at Staudernheim, June 7, 1701, Sabine Cron, daughter of Hans Simon Cron and widow of Johann Nikolaus Fey, buried at Staudernheim, June 4, 1751. Child of the second marriage, born at Staudernheim: Johann Adam Seiss, baptized August 18, 1710 (*anno 1740 Americanus factus*). [Possibly Johann Adam Syce (Seysen), 25 years old, who arrived at Philadelphia on the ship *Friendship*, October 12, 1741.]

Sponheimer, Johann Peter, son of Johann Wilhelm Sponheimer, buried at Staudernheim, January 11, 1759, married I. at Staudernheim, May 14, 1706, Anna Christina Damgen, daughter of Christian Damgen at Sobernheim, buried at Staudernheim November 26, 1710; married II. at Staudernheim, November 17, 1711, Anna Maria Fey, daughter of Johannes Fey. Children, of the first and second marriages, born at Staudernheim:
1. Anna Margarethe Sponheimer, baptized October 23, 1707 (*anno 1741 Americana facta*).
2. Johann Nikolaus Sponheimer, baptized September 4, 1712; served in Potsdam among King Frederick William's Giant Guards and was married there (*dieser ist in Potsdam unter den grossen Granadieren und auch verheiratet*).

Tesch, Johann Philipp, son of Paul Tesch, married I. at Staudernheim, April 30, 1726, Anna Christina Schappert, daughter of Johannes Schappert, buried at Staudernheim, January 4, 1733; married II. at Staudernheim, April 15, 1733, Maria Dorothea, widow. Children of the first and second marriages, born at Staudernheim:
1. Johann Michel Tesch, baptized May 31, 1731 (*anno 1741 Americanus factus*).
2. Johann Peter Tesch, baptized December 20, 1733 (*anno 1741 Americanus factus*).
3. Simon Philipp Tesch, baptized July 25, 1737 (*anno 1741 Americanus factus*).
[Johann Philipp Desch (Tash), 40 years old, arrived at Philadelphia on the snow *Molly*, October 26, 1741.]

Textor, Hieronymus, gunsmith, married Anna Margarethe. Child, born at Staudernheim: Christina Elisabeth Textor, baptized August 8, 1748 (*anno 1751 Americana cum parentibus facta*). [Hieronimus Textur arrived at Philadelphia on the ship *Edinburgh*, September 16, 1751.]

Wander, Simon Jakob, son of Johann Philipp Wander, died at Staudernheim, October 25, 1742 (reference in Baptismal Register), married Anna Maria. Child, born at Staudernheim: Anna Christina Wander, baptized October 29, 1717 (*anno 1742 Americana facta*).

Wander, Johann Tobias, son of Heinrich Wander, buried at Staudernheim, September 22, 1735, married at Staudernheim, September 17, 1720, Anna Eva Seiss, daughter of Michel Seiss; the widow married II. at Staudernheim, April 3, 1736, Johann Nikolaus Lang. Child, born at Staudernheim: Johann Heinrich Wander, baptized October 28, 1723 (*Americanus factus*).

————

Friedrich Krebs. "Auswanderer nach den Nordamerikanischen Kolonien im Lutherischen Kirchenbuch von Thaleischweiler," *Mitteilungen zur Wanderungsgeschichte der Pfälzer (Beilage zu Pfälzische Familien- und Wappenkunde)*, folge 3-4 (1952), 21-24 [Lancour No. 159].

Vorliegende kurze Zusammenstellung gibt ein Verzeichnis der Auswanderer nach Nordamerika (Pennsylvanien) an Hand der Einträge und Marginalien im lutherischen Kirchenbuch von Thaleischweiler.

Solche Auswanderungsvermerke sind besonders wertvoll, weil sie in den Kirchenbüchern nur selten anzuteffen sind, jedoch eine sehr wesentliche Quelle für die Erfassung der Auswanderung des 18. Jahrhunderts bilden. Die betr. Kirchenbücher enthalten sowohl im Heirats- wie im Taufregister Einträge; leider weist jedoch das Heiratsregister gerade für die wichtigen Jahre 1751/53 eine Lücke auf. Die Kinder der Auswanderer wurden versuchsweise auch mit aufgenommen, wenn nicht im Kirchenbuch bis zur Auswanderung ihr Todesdatum nachgewiesen werden konnte. Wie in den Veröffentlichungen Gerbers über die Auswanderung aus Württemberg aus Kirchenbüchern des 18. Jahrhunderts stellen auch hier die Handwerker einen erheblichen Prozentsatz der Auswanderer, da diese in Amerika in jener Zeit sehr gesucht waren. Dass Eheleute wegen verfrühter Konkubation oder Mütter mit unehelichen Kindern auswanderten, ist ebenfalls nicht selten. (Vgl. auch Gerber: „Beiträge z. Auswanderung nach Amerika im 18. Jahrhundert". Stuttg. 1928 S. 4).

Was die zeitliche Gliederung der Auswanderung betrifft, so kann man eine kleine Wanderung um 1738/39 und zwei grössere um 1749/50 und 1763/65 (dies die Hauptauswanderung) unterscheiden.

Die Angabe der Ankunftszeit in Philadelphia und der betr. Schiffe erfolgte an Hand von Strassburger-Hinke, „Pennsylvania German pioneers" Norristown 1934. Für einzelne Auskünfte bin ich Herrn Prof. Biundo, dem Geschichtsschreiber Thaleischweilers zu Danke verpflichtet.

Allenbach, Friedr., Schütze zu Thaleischweiler, Sohn von Andreas Allenbach, Schirmsverwandten zu Thaleischweiler, ∞ 30. 1. 1742 zu Thaleischweiler Eva Catharina Helli, Tochter des Matthäus Helli

aus der Schweiz. (sind in Pennsylvan. gezogen 1750).
Kinder zu Th. geboren:
1. Anna Maria, * 10. 3. 1744.
2. Elisabetha Catharina, * 27. 11. 1746.
[Friedrich Almbach, 18. August 1750, Schiff: „St. Andrew".]
Allenbach, Anna Maria, * 29. 3. 1726 zu Th. als Tochter des Andreas
Allenbach und seiner Gattin Anna Barbara (ist in Pennsylvaniam
gezogen 1752 den 20ten Maji).
Alspach, Reinhardt von Fröschen, ∞ 29. 3. 1737 zu Th. Anna Magda-
lena Brandstätter, „musste nach der Copulation das Land räumen.
Er ward wieder angenommen, zog aber in Pennsylvan.". [Reinhart
Altspach 11. Sept. 1738, Schiff: „Robert and Alice".] Reinhart
A. scheint wieder in die Heimat zurückgekehrt zu sein; denn ab
1760 erscheinen wieder Taufen seiner Kinder in den Kirchenbüchern
von Thaleischweiler.
Alspach, Johannes, * 12. 2. 1748 zu Oberfröschen (Höhfröschen) als
Sohn des Johannes Alspach und der Anna Ottilia. Eintrag bei der
Geburt: (gieng in Pennsylv. 1763). Von denselben Eltern stammen
Johann David Alspach, * 22. 9. 1735 zu (Ober)fröschen (ist in
Pennsylvanien gangen). sowie Georg Heinrich Alspach, * 24. 3.
1746 zu Oberfröschen (Höhfröschen), (ist in Pennsylv. 1763) und
Anna Barbara Alspach, * 25. 9. 1737 (ist in Pennsylv. 1763)
[Henrich Alsbach, 1. November 1763, Schiff: „Chance"]. Möglich-
erweise zogen auch die Eltern dieser 3 Söhne nach Pennsylvanien.
Bockrickert, Israel, Schmied, Sohn des Hanss Leonhardt Bockrickert,
Bürgers und Leinewebers zu Pfaffenhofen (Württemberg), ∞ 9. 2.
1745 zu Th. mit Anna Margaretha Dauenhauer, Tochter des Andreas
Dauenhauer von Thaleischweiler (zog mit Frau und 2 Kindern in
Penns. 1765 den 7ten Maj).
Kinder zu Th. geboren:
1. Anna Maria, * 10. 5. 1748.
2. Israel, * 18. 11. 1761.
[Israel Bockreiker, 9. September 1765, Schiff: „Chance".]
Balssel, Peter, Bürger zu Th., ∞ (II.) zu Th. 12. 5. 1744 Anna
Maria Dorn, Tochter des Theodor Dorn von Mühlbach (Höhmühlbach,
Krs. Pirmasens, Pfalz). (sind a Pennsylv. gezogen 1750).
Kinder zu Th. geboren:
1. Johann Jacob, * 10. 9. 1745.
2. Elisabetha Barbara, * 24. 9. 1748.
[Peter Balsam, 18. 8. 1750, Schiff: „St. Andrew".]
Brandstetter, Johann Friedrich, Grenadier zu Pirmasens, * 23. 11.
1724 zu Fröschen als der Sohn des Zimmermanns Michael Brandstetter und der Maria Catharina. ∞ 18. 2. 1749 zu Th. Anna Barbara
Mag, Tochter des Peter Mag von Krickenbach. (diese zogen in Pennsylv. 1764 den 14. Maji).
Kinder zu Fröschen geboren:
1. Anna Esther, * 2. 2. 1754.
2. Johann Friedrich, * 18. 10. 1755.
3. Dorothea Barbara, * 26. 3. 1757.

4. Johann Michael, * 26. 4. 1759.
5. Johannes, * 19. 9. 1761.
6. Maria Elisabetha, * 27. 7. 1763.
[Friedrich Brandstetter, 20. Sept. 1764, Schiff: „Sarah".]
Brandstätter, Matthias, Sohn des Andreas Brandstätter von Aachen,
Markgrafschaft Ansbach, was sich schwer bestimmen lässt. (Nach
einer Mitteilung von Prof. Dr. Biundo ist er von Meierndorf in
Mittelfranken. Im Kirchenbuch ist vielleicht ein Zettel verloren
gegangen?), ∞ 7. 11. 1741 zu Thalfröschen Marie Magdalene Schaar,
Tochter des Konrad Schaar von Fröschen. (sind ins Neuland gezogen
1749 den 1ten Maji).
Kinder zu Oberfröschen (Höhfröschen) geboren:
1. Anna Barbara, * 19. 12. 1744.
2. Andreas, * 15. 8. 1747.
Bruder, Johann Heinrich, * 18. 6. 1730 zu Oberfröschen (Höhfröschen), als Sohn des Michael Bruder und der Anna Eva (Ist in
Pennseylvanien gangen anno 1749 den 1ten Maji).
Daude, Johann Heinrich, Wagner, Sohn des Heinrich Daude, Wagner zu
Fröschen, ∞ 8. 5. 1742 zu Thalfröschen Anna Elisabeth Brandstetter, Tochter des Michael Brandstetter, (gieng mit Frau und Kindern und dem Tochtermann, auch dessen Frau und Kindern in Pennsylv. 1765 den 7ten Maji).
Kinder zu Fröschen geboren:
1. Marie Magdalena, * 8. 8. 1742 (zog mit ihren Eltern, Mann
    und Kindern in Pennsylv. 1765 den 7ten Maji).
2. Anna Catharina, * 14. 8. 1748.
3. Anna Elisabetha, * 15. 12. 1751.
4. Elisabetha Margaretha, * 22. 9. 1756.
Fischer, Hanss Adam, blind, * 27. 10. 1720 zu Fröschen als der Sohn
des Johann Diebold Fischer und der Maria Elisabeth (ist ins neue
Land gezogen), ∞ 9. 2. 1745 zu Th. Maria Barbara Brenner, Tochter
des Andreas Brenner, Hirten von der Mäusmühle (sind in Pennsylv.
gezogen 1743).
Kinder: Johann Jacob, * 22. 5. 1747 zu Th.
Gänssel, Johann Adam, * 23. 7. 1758 zu Fröschen als der Sohn von
Johann Valentin Gänssel und der Catharina (ist mit s. Eltern in
Pennsylvan. 1763 im Maji). Johann Valentin G., der Sohn von
Jacob G., Hintersassen zu Fröschen, hatte 15. 2. 1758 zu Th.
Maria Catharina Tochter des Ludwig Petri von Krikkenbach (Krs.
Kaiserslautern) geh. [Vallentin Gänsel, 1. November 1763,
Schiff: „Chance".]
Grob, Maria Catharina, Tochter des Matthias Bayritsch von Th., ∞
19. 1. 1734 zu Th. Nicolaus Grob, Sohn des Heinrich Grob von
Heltersberg. Nach dem Tode ihres Gatten († 5. 8. 1764 zu Th.)
zog seine Witwe mit ihrem Bruder Peter Bayritsch und ihren Kin-
dern nach Pennsylvanien (Diese Witwe zog mit ihrem Bruder Peter
Bayritschen und ihren Kindern in Pennsylvanien 1765). [Peter
Belritsch, 9. Sept. 1765, Schiff: „Chance".]
Kinder zu Th. geboren:

1. Anna Elisabetha, * 29. 4. 1737 (gieng in Penns. 1765 mit ihrem Mann, ihrer Mutter, dem Bayritsch u. ihren 3 Kindern und ihren Geschwistern).
2. Anna Susanna, * 27. 8. 1739.
3. Maria Ottilia, * 13. 5. 1742 (gieng in Pennsylvan. 1764).
4. Israel, * 27. 3. 1745 (gieng in Pennsylvan. 1764).
5. Maria Catharina, * 2. 10. 1747.
6. Johann Peter, * 7. 6. 1751.
7. Anna Maria, * 23. 1. 1754.
8. Johann Michael, * 24. 9. 1757.
9. Anna Margaretha, * 19. 11. 1760.
[Israel Grob, 20 Sept. 1764, Schiff: „Sarah".]
Herdt (Hirt), Georg, Sohn des katholischen Wasenmeisters von Th., ∞ 24. 11. 1738 zu Th. Maria Magdalena, Tochter des Bernhardt Dreher, Schuhmachers zu Th. (sind in Pennsylvanien gezogen).
Kinder: Johann Nicolaus, * 26. 7. 1739 zu Th.
[Jurgen Hert, 12 Okt. 1741, Schiff: „Friendship".]
Ilgis (Ilges), Paul, Küfer und Hintersass auf dem Meisenbacher Hof, ∞ (II.) zu Th. 23. 2. 1745 Maria Catharina, Tochter des Nicolaus Blau, eines Friesen (Friese bedeutet hier einen Handwerksnamen [Gräber], nicht Angehörigen des Volksstamms der Friesen). (sind in Pennsylv. gezogen 1750).
Kinder aus der ersten Ehe mit Anna Margaretha:
1. Anna Elisabetha, * 29. 6. 1731.
2. Maria Ottilia, * 30. 7. 1736.
3. Anna Catharina, * 4. 8. 1741 auf dem Meisenbacher Hof.
Kinder der zweiten Ehe auf dem Meisenbacher Hof geboren:
1. Johann Georg, * 23. 11. 1745.
2. Maria Barbara, * 27. 10. 1747.
[Johann Paul Ilges, 18. August 1750, Schiff: „St. Andrew".]
Ilgis, Johann Paul, * 19. 7. 1749 zu Maisebach (Meisenbacher Hof) als der uneheliche Sohn der Christina Margaretha, Tochter des Paul Ilges vom Meisenbacher Hof, und des Hanss Adam Seidler, Müllers, gebürtig von Herschberg als der Sohn des Johann Seidler. (sind miteinander in Pennsylv. gezogen 1750) [Hans Adam Seydler, 18 August 1750, Schiff: „St. Andrew"].
Kastner, Christian, Weber, Sohn des Zimmermanns und Holzhauers Christian Kastner zu Neufröschen (Höhfröschen), aber gebürtig von Lauf b. Nürnberg und seines Weibes Utilia (Ottilia), ∞ 3. 12. 1748 zu Th. mit Susanna, Tochter des Georg Mattinger, Bürgers von Neufröschen (Höhfröschen), (sind in Pennsylvan. gezogen 1750).
Kinder: Maria Barbara, * 4. 11. 1749 zu Fröschen. (Ist von seinen Eltern in Pennsylv. mitgenommen worden 1750).
Kastner, Philipp Peter, Kuhhirt zu Unterfröschen (Thalfröschen), * 9. 4. 1732 als der Sohn des Zimmermanns Christian Kastner und der A. Ottilia, also Bruder von Vorstehendem, (zog in Pennsylvan. den 16ten Maji 1763). Philipp Peter K. war zweimal verheiratet:
I. ∞ 30. 10. 1759 zu Th. Catharina Elisabetha Klein, Tochter des Hanss Adam Klein, Pattaschebrenners zu Burgalben.

Kind: Johann Jacob, * 1. 8. 1760 zu Fröschen.
II. ∞ 27. 4. 1762 zu Th. Anna Catharina Roth, Tochter des Hirten
Friedrich Roth zu Höheinöd.
Kind: Eva Elisabetha, * 5. 2. 1763 zu Fröschen. (sind beyde in
Pennsylv. gezogen 1763). [Philipp Casner, 1. November 1763,
Schiff: „Chance".]
Kieffer, Heinrich, Schneider, Sohn des Johannes K. von Herschberg,
∞ 20. 8. 1737 zu Th. Maria Catharina, Tochter des Bartholomäus
Jesrang von Th. und dessen Ehefrau Anna Maria (sind mit den
Eltern in Pennsylvanien gezogen).
Kind: Catharina Elisabetha, * 18. 9. 1738 zu Th.
[Bartholome Jesran, Henrick Kifer, 3 Sept. 1739, Schiff: „Loyall
Judith".]
Krieger, Jacob, Weber zu Fröschen, Sohn des Schuhmachers Gottlieb
Krieger, ∞ 10. 8. 1745 zu Th. Maria (Anna) Barbara, * 21. 3. 1723
zu Fröschen als Tochter des Michael Brandstetter, Zimmermanns zu
Fröschen und seines Weibes Maria Catharina (ist mit Frau und Kin-
dern in Pennsylv. gezogen 1765 den 7ten Maji).
Kinder zu Fröschen geboren:
   1. Heinrich Jacob, * 7. 11. 1745.
   2. Johann Georg, * 9. 12. 1751.
   3. Eva Catharina, * 16. 6. 1757.
   4. Hanss Theobald, * 31. 1. 1762.
   5. Johann Michael, * 31. 1. 1762.
   6. Anna Margaretha, * 15. 1. 1764.
[Jacob Krieger, 9. Sept. 1765, Schiff: „Chance".]
Lambert, Johann Heinrich, Wagner von Otterberg, Sohn des Johann
Nicolaus Lambert von Otterberg, ∞ 6. 12. 1760 zu Th. Maria Magdalena Daude, Tochter des Heinrich Daude, Wagners zu Fröschen (ist
mit Frau und Kindern in Pennsylv. gezogen 1763 den 7ten Maji).
Kinder zu Fröschen geboren:
   1. Maria Catharina, * 5. 12. 1760 (unehelich).
   2. Maria Charlotta, * 23. 10. 1763.
[Henrich Lambert, 9. Sept. 1765, Schiff: „Chance".]
Ludi, Johann Nicolaus, Schuhmacher, Sohn des Daniel Ludi von Th., ∞
30. 11. 1756 zu Th. Anna Elisabetha, Tochter des Nicolaus Grob
von Th. (ziehen in Penns. 1765).
Kinder zu Th. geboren:
   1. Philipp Jacob, * 10. 5. 1760.
   2. Nicolaus Peter, * 22. 8. 1762.
   3. Jacob Peter, * 8. 3. 1765.
[Nicklaus Ludi, 9. Sept. 1765, Schiff: „Chance".]
Ludi, Johann Peter, Sohn des Müllers Hanss Peter Ludi von Th., ∞
(I.) 21. 8. 1731 zu Th. Maria Apollonia Heyd, Tochter des Rudolph
Heyd von Rieschweiler, ∞ (II.) 29. 7. 1732 zu Th. Anna Apollonia,
Tochter von Andreas Allenbach von Th. (ist in Pennsylv. gezogen).
[Vermutlich: Johann Peter Locke (Lough), 3. 9. 1751, Schiff:
„Loyal Judith".]
Mang, Gottfried, Weber von Trippstadt, Sohn des Webers Theobald

Mang von Trippstadt, ∞ 18. 1. 1735 zu Th. Maria Barbara, Tochter
des Bartholomäus Jessrang von Th. (ist in Pennsylv. gezogen).
[Gothfrid Mang, 3. Sept. 1739, Schiff: „Loyal Judith".]
Ohlinger (Ollinger), Johann Georg, Weber, Sohn des Hanss Georg
Ohlinger, ∞ 4. 4. 1741 zu Th. Maria Barbara Dauenhauer, Tochter
des Hanss Georg Dauenhauer zu Fröschen und der Anna Magdalena
(sind gleich in Pennsylvan. gezogen).
[Hans Jorg Ollinger, 12. Oktober 1741, Schiff: „Friendship".]
Schultz, Valentin, zu Fröschen und Ehetrau Kunigunde,
   Kinder zu Fröschen geboren:
   1. Johann Peter, get. 24. 6. 1729.
   2. Georg Henrich, * 6. 3. 1727.
   3. Anna Barbara, * 7. 1. 1732.
   4. Anna Magdalena, * 11. 1. 1737.
   (Die Eltern sind in Pennsylvan. gezogen). [Valentine Schults,
   11. Sept. 1738, Schiff: „Robert and Alice".]
Veiogkt, Georg Jacob, * 18. 12. 1741 zu Fröschen als Sohn des
Thomas V. und der Anna Ottilia (gieng in Pennsylvanien 1764 im
Maji). (Joh. Thomas Veyock, Sohn von Peter Veyock, Einwohners zu
Weidenthal, ∞ 27. 1. 1739 zu Th. Anna Ottilia Schwab, Tochter des
Johannes Schwab, Bürgers zu Fröschen.) [Jacob Felock, 20. Sept.
1764, Schiff: „Sarah".]
Zaun, Joh. Martin, Schuhmacher zu Th., Sohn des Schuhmachers Hanss
Jacob Zaun von Monnernheim (vermutlich Mommenheim, Rheinhessen,
Kr. Oppenheim), ∞ 2. 10. 1736 zu Th. Susanna Margaretha, Witwe
des Peter Siber (sind in Pennsylvan. gezogen).
   Kinder: Peter Jacob, * 26. 5. 1737 zu Th.

———

Louis F. Middlebrook. "The Ship *Mary* of Philadelphia, 1740," *The
Pennsylvania Magazine of History and Biography*, 58 (1934), 127-
151 [Lancour No. 160].

This is a general account of the building and early history of
the ship *Mary*. Page 150 of the article contains one passenger list
pertaining to the Hagenbuck, Rebsamen, Rueg, Epprecht and Angst
families arriving in Philadelphia in 1740. This list has been
reprinted on page 262 of *Emigrants to Pennsylvania* (Baltimore:
Genealogical Publishing Company, 1977).

———

"Persons Naturalized in the Province of Pennsylvania," *Pennsylvania
Archives*, 2nd series, 2 (1876), 293-415 [Lancour No. 161].

This list is omitted here because it is widely available in
libraries, particularly those of universities, because it is book
length, and because it is slightly more complete and more time-

inclusive, in the words of Lancour, than Giuseppi's *Naturalizations of Foreign Protestants* [Lancour No. 19], reprinted by the Genealogical Publishing Company.

Friedrich Krebs. "Zur Amerikaauswanderung aus dem Kurpfälzischen Oberamt Heidelberg 1741-1748," *Zeitschrift für die Geschichte des Oberrheins*, 106 (neue folge 67) (1958), 485-486 [Lancour No. 162].

The English translation of this article is included in Lancour No. 141, reprinted above.

Friedrich Krebs. "Amerika-Auswanderer aus dem Oberamt Oppenheim 1742-49," *Hessische Familienkunde*, 3 (1954-1956), 342-343 [Lancour No. 163].

The English translation of this article is included in Lancour No. 141, reprinted above.

John W. Jordan. "A Register of Members of the Moravian Church Who Emigrated to Pennsylvania, 1742-1767," *Notes and Queries: Historical, Biographical and Genealogical: Relating Chiefly to Interior Pennsylvania*, 4th series, I (1893), 162-163, 167-168, 169-170, 174-175, 208-211, 303-304; 2 (1895), 1-3 [Lancour No. 164].

These lists of Moravian arrivals at Philadelphia and New York, from which most migrated to Bethlehem and a few to North Carolina, are readily available in many libraries in the original edition. A twelve volume reprint, plus an index volume, is available from the Genealogical Publishing Company.

George W. Neible. "Servants and Apprentices Bound and Assigned before James Hamilton Mayor of Philadelphia, 1745," *The Pennsylvania Magazine of History and Biography*, 30 (1906), 348-352, 427-436; 31 (1907), 83-102, 195-206, 351-367, 461-473; 32 (1908), 88-103, 237-249, 351-370 [Lancour No. 165].

This article has been reprinted in full in pages 54 to 179 of *Emigrants to Pennsylvania, 1641-1819* (Baltimore: Genealogical Publishing Co., Inc., 1977).

"List of Servants Who Sailed from Dublin February 25th 1746/7 on the Euryal, and Arrived at Philadelphia April 11th.," *The Pennsylvania Magazine of History and Biography*, 26 (1902), 287 [Lancour No. 166].

This list of twenty women, giving only their names, has been reprinted on page 262 of *Emigrants to Pennsylvania, 1641-1819* (Baltimore: Genealogical Publishing Co., Inc., 1977).

Friedrich Krebs. "Einige Amerika-Auswanderer des 18. Jahrhunderts," *Senftenegger Monatsblatt für Genealogie und Heraldik*, 4 (1956-1959), 195-198 [Lancour No. 167].

The English translation of this article is included in Lancour No. 141, reprinted above.

Friedrich Krebs. "Einige Amerika-Auswanderer des 18. Jahrhunderts," *Senftenegger Monatsblatt für Genealogie und Heraldik*, 5 (1960-1963), 123-126 [Lancour No. 168].

The English translation of this article is included in Lancour No. 141, reprinted above.

Friedrich Krebs. "Pennsylvania Pioneers from the Neckar Valley, 1749-1750," *The Pennsylvania Dutchman*, 5 (June 1953), 13 [Lancour No. 169].

Again we turn to the local government records of Germany for information on eighteenth-century emigrants to Pennsylvania. The source of the present emigrant list is the Protocols of the Districts (*Oberämter*) of Heidelberg and Mosbach, which in the eighteenth century were part of the dominions of the Electors of the Palatinate, but today form part of the state of Württemberg-Baden.
These emigrants from the Electoral Palatinate had to pay a fee for their manumission from vassalage, besides the additional tax of the "Tenth Penny" or Tithe, (*Zehnten Pfennig*)—the tenth part of their property. Those without property were however manumitted gratis.
We have included in this List persons whose destination was not expressly stated as "America," if their names could be found in the Pennsylvania Ship Lists of the particular year involved. As far as

the names of the emigrants could be identified in these Ship Lists
—the Strassburger-Hinke *Pennsylvania German Pioneers* (Norristown,
Pa.: The Pennsylvania German Society, 1934)—they have been added
in brackets. The List has been published in German in *Badische
Heimat* (Freiburg, May, 1953).

District of Heidelberg (1749)

Johannes Euler, citizen and master blacksmith at Hohensachsen
(Kr. Mannheim), is manumitted upon payment of 10 florins (gulden)
for the Tenth Penny. [Johannes Eulers, Ship *Patience*, September
19, 1749.]

Leon[h]ard Eberle, of Eiterbach (Kr. Heidelberg), may go to the
"New Land"...with his wife and three children, with the permission
of the Electoral government, upon payment of 4 florins to buy himself out of vassalage, and 40 florins for the additional tax.

Jacob Grauss [Krauss], inhabitant of Daisbach (Kr. Sinsheim), is,
on account of his poverty and propertyless state, manumitted gratis
in order to go to the New Land with his wife and children. [Jacob
Krauss, Ship *Dragon*, September 26, 1749.]

Philipp Georg Mueller, of Meckesheim (Kr. Heidelberg), is permitted to go to the New Land with wife and two children, upon payment
of 10 florins for the additional tax. [Pips Georg Müller, Ship
Chesterfield, September 2, 1749.]

Johann Michael Mueller, of Meckesheim (Kr. Heidelberg), leaving
behind the Tenth Penny on his Property, may go to Pennsylvania in
the hope of better luck.... [Johann Michael Müller, Ship *Speed-
well*, September 26, 1749.]

Jacob Frey, of Wieblingen (today part of Heidelberg), may go free
upon payment of the Tenth Penny. [Jacob Frey, Ship *Dragon*, September 26, 1749.]

George Linz, Philipp Brenner, and Georg Kumpff, from Asbach (Kr.
Mosbach), receive permission to emigrate to the New Land, upon payment of the Tenth Penny. Georg Linz must also pay 10 florins for
his manumission. [Jerg Linz, Hans Philipp Brenner, Ship *Patience*,
September 19, 1749.]

District of Mosbach (1749)

Wilhelm Besch, from Mittelschefflenz (Kr. Mosbach) may go to
Pennsylvania.

Jacob Behr and Martin Treibel, from Eberbach (Kr. Heidelberg),
may go to [New] England upon payment of the Tenth Penny. [Johann
Jacob Behr, Martin Treibel, Ship *Jacob*, October 2, 1749.]

Peter Ehret, from Mittelschefflenz, may emigrate to New England
upon payment of the Tenth Penny.

Adam Ludwig and Jacob Bender, from Burcken (Neckarburken),
receive permission to emigrate to New England. [Hans Adam Ludwig,
Ship *Patience*, September 19, 1749.]

Peter Spohn, from Schollbronn (Schollbrunn, Kr. Mosbach), may go
to New England upon payment of 14 florins for manumission from vas-

salage and 14 florins for the Tenth Penny. [Petter Spohn, Ship
Patience, September 19, 1749.]

Michel Zilling, from Mittelschefflenz, wants to emigrate to New
England. [Michel Zilling, Ship *Patience*, September 19, 1749.]

District of Heidelberg (1750)

Johann Battenfeld, from Michelbach (Kr. Mosbach), receives per-
mission to go with his wife, two sons and three daughters, to the
New Land, upon payment of the Tenth Penny at 30 florins. [Johannes
Battefeldt, Ship *Two Brothers*, August 28, 1750.]

Johann Adam Eberle, from Eiterbach (Kr. Heidelberg), is manumitted upon payment of 10 florins for manumission and 9 florins additional tax. [Adam Eberle, Ship *Brothers*, August 24, 1750.]

Johann Georg Gansshorn, from Bammental (Kr. Heidelberg), baker,
may emigrate gratis. [Hans Jörg Ganshorn, Ship *Two Brothers*,
August 24, 1750.]

Johann Mathias Gerner, of Helmstadt (Kr. Sinsheim) wants to go to
the so-called New Land. [Johan Matthes Gerner, Ship *Two Brothers*,
August 28, 1750.]

Johann Georg Koberstein and Johann Georg Ludwig, of Zuzenhausen
(Kr. Sinsheim), are permitted to go to the so-called New Land with
their wives, Anna Catharina and Maria Margaretha; yet the former
must pay 3 florins, the latter 2 florins 36 kreuzer Manumission
Tax. [Hans Gorg Koberstein, Johan George Ludwig, Ship *Osgood*,
September 29, 1750.]

Johann Friedrich Mueller, of Meckesheim (Kr. Heidelberg), is permitted to go to the so-called New Land, upon payment of 2 florins
on his property of 20 florins.

Johann Adam Wollfarth, an orphaned citizen's son from Spechbach
(Kr. Heidelberg), is released from vassalage upon payment of 20
florins and granted the right of emigration on payment of 18
florins additional tax. [Johann Adam Wolfart, Ship *Brothers*,
August 24, 1750.]

———

Friedrich Krebs. "Einige Amerika-Auswanderer des 18. Jahrhunderts
aus Württemberg," *Südwestdeutsche Blätter für Familien- und Wappenkunde*, 9 (1957), 442-443 [Lancour No. 170].

The English translation of this article is included in Lancour
No. 141, reprinted above.

———

Friedrich Krebs. "Emigrants from Baden-Durlach to Pennsylvania,
1749-1755," *National Genealogical Society Quarterly*, 45 (1957),
30-31 [Lancour No. 171].

During the years 1749-1755, emigration from southwestern Germany was at its height, as is evident from the number of ships which arrived in the harbor of Philadelphia (see Hinke-Strassburger: "Pennsylvania Pioneers," Vol. 1, p. xxix). A considerable number of persons must have migrated to the "New Land" at this time from the tiny district of Baden-Durlach, judging by the great number of petitions for permits to depart that are preserved in the court archives. These petitions were first taken up by the Court Council, then passed on to the Revenue Office, which made a formal proclamation of the manumission of the parties concerned and fixed the amount of tax to be paid. The council and revenue records of Baden-Durlach are, for this reason, the chief source for research into the emigration from the region at that time.

In the list below, whenever the emigrant can be identified in the Hinke-Strassburger ship lists from the port of Philadelphia, this is indicated in a following parenthesis.

Hunold, Matthäus, Reformed, charcoal-burner, from Weiler bei Pforzheim, permitted to go to Pennsylvania with wife and child (Ship *Two Brothers*, Sept. 21, 1751).

Loble, Georg, aged 70, from Wössingen, permitted to travel with his wife to join his four children already settled in Pennsylvania.

Winther, Samuel, also from Wössingen, to Pennsylvania with wife and children.

Schickle, Georg, the younger, from Bauschlott, with wife and four children.

Rossle, Gabriel, from Wössingen, with wife and three children (*Shirley*, Sept. 5, 1751).

Durr, Johann Georg, from Nöttingen, cooper, unmarried (*Duke of Wirtenberg*, Oct. 16, 1751).

Schmelzle, Rudolph, from Obermutschelbach.

Wildemann, Jacob, also from Obermutschelbach.

Meyer, Hanss Jerg, from Obermutschelbach, with wife and four children (the last two on *Duke of Wirtenberg*, Oct. 16, 1751).

Worlich, Michael, nail-maker at Stein.

Heyd, Jacob, from Grötzingen.

Frantz, Jacob, also from Grötzingen, single.

Nagel, Sebastian, from Blankenloch.

Hemperl, Elisabetha, from Blankenloch. (Nagel, Frantz and Heyd on ship *Brothers*, Sept. 16, 1751).

Groner or Kroner, Jacob, a youth from Bauschlott.

Augenstein, Christian, Anna Maria, Caspar and Hannss Georg, four unmarried children of Abraham Augenstein, widower, a citizen of Auerbach (see *Two Brothers*, Sept. 21, 1751, and *Duke of Wirtenberg*, Oct. 16, 1751.)

Hauer, Bernhardt and Christoph, from Blankenloch, destination not recorded (*Brothers*, Sept. 16, 1751).

Reich, Mattheus, a citizen of Singen, to go to Pennsylvania (*Duke of Wirtenberg*, Oct. 16, 1751).

Nagel, Joachim, a former grenadier, born at Blankenloch, requested
manumission for himself and wife to go to Pennsylvania (*Brothers*,
Sept. 16, 1751).
Bossert, Michael, unmarried, from Bauschlott.
Kaucher, Michael, unmarried, from Göbrichen (both above on *Phoenix*,
Sept. 25, 1751).
Kaucher, Jacob the younger, of Göbrichen, manumitted with wife and
children.
Worner, Philipp Jacob, a citizen of Wössingen (*Duke of Wirtenberg*,
Oct. 16, 1751).
Hauss, Michael of Knielingen, manumitted with his wife (*Brothers*,
Sept. 16, 1751).
Hauss, Johannes of Knielingen, wife and children. Found only in
the council records (*Anderson*, Aug. 25, 1751).
Schlickers, Ludwig of Knielingen, with wife and stepson.
Mussnung, David, of Grötzingen (*Brothers*, Sept. 16, 1751).
Decker, Johann Jacob, unmarried, from Weissenstein (*Kitty*, Oct. 16,
1752).
Dillmann, Georg of Teutscheneureuth, with wife and two children.
Meinzer, Martin of Knielingen, with wife and two children (*Bro-
thers*, Sept. 16, 1751—both the foregoing).
Graf (Gravin), Barbara, unmarried, from Ispringen.
Meinzer, Johannes from Hagsfelden, with wife and two children
(*Brothers*, Sept. 16, 1751).
Schwarz, Matthias, from Auerbach.
Mayer, Michael, from Bauschlott.
Binder, Jacob, from Bauschlott, with wife and children.
Loffler, Dietrich, from Grötzingen, with wife and 4 children, a
tenant farmer (*Phoenix*, Sept. 25, 1751).

Friedrich Krebs. "18th Century Emigrants from Edenkoben in the
Palatinate," *The Pennsylvania Dutchman*, 4 (Jan. 1, 1953), 9 [Lan-
cour No. 172].

[Pennsylvania's genealogists are always glad when a new list of
German emigrants to Pennsylvania or other American colonies turns
up in 18th Century sources. During our 1952 Tour of the Palatin-
ate, in connection with our formal visit to the "wine-happy" town
of Edenkoben in the Palatinate, the *Geschäfts Anzeiger* (Edenkoben,
August 2, 1952) published the following article by Dr. Krebs,
Archivist in Speyer, who has unearthed other names of Pennsylvania
Dutch emigrant pioneers which will be published in the forthcoming
Yearbook of the Pennsylvania German Folklore Society. The present
article was translated by the Editor.—D(on) Y(oder).]
That the longing for the "Land of Unlimited Possibilities" has
not abated up until the present day, is proved by a report of Dr.
Friedrich Krebs, of the State Archives in Speyer, which throws

light on the difficulties faced by the Palatine serfs of the 18th
Century when it came to emigration.

In many respects, the emigrants of those earlier times had, even
from the side of the authorities, to struggle with much greater
difficulties than the emigrants of the present day, whose departure
is rather encouraged by the state. For their release from bondage
as subjects and their manumission from serfdom, a special duty had
to be paid, besides the so-called "Tenth Penny," a sum to the
extent of 10% of the emigrant's property. Yet emigrants with no
means were "manumitted" anyway. But for secret emigration, the
penalty was mostly the confiscation of the property. There are
these facts to be noticed in the following.

From Edenkoben, then under the rule of the Electoral Palatinate,
there emigrated in the 18th Century, according to the Protocols of
the Bailiwick of Neustadt, a comparatively large number of persons.
Actually the number may have been still higher, due to secret emigration. Many of these emigrants' names can be located in the
Pennsylvania Ship Lists.

For instance, in 1750 Jacob Körner of Edenkoben, who was going to
Pennsylvania with his wife, was released from serfdom gratis, likewise in 1751 George Krauss, with wife and two children. In 1752
Niclas Leonhard, who had secretly emigrated around 1749, requested
manumission so that his inheritance could be handed over to him.
His request was granted, yet he had to pay 35 florins (guldens) for
his manumission, for the "Tenth Penny" 31 florins, and for the
Military Treasury, in lieu of military service unrendered, 7 florins. His brother Wilhelm Leonhard, who later also wanted to emigrate, was described as an "ill-behaved and dissolute petitioner"
(ohnartiger und liederlicher Supplicant), so that his request for
emigration could be granted with no difficulties at all.

In 1752 Martin Grün, Heinrich Schenkel, and Christoph Müller went
to "Pennsylvanien." They had to pay all the aforementioned duties,
except Martin Grün who, because of his having no property, was
manumitted without charge. But the request for emigration met with
great difficulties in the case of the three stepdaughters of Martin
Grün—Anna Barbara, Maria Elisabetha, and Maria Catharina Frank—
who were such good workers, at the best age for working, and so
plainly valued by the Electoral Government that they received manumission reluctantly and only after long struggles.

For the same year, 1752, a great emigration year, Philipp Carl
Schenkel and Jacob Welde of Edenkoben also went as emigrants to
North America, all manumitted gratis on account of their poverty.
Likewise in 1752 came the departure from Edenkoben of Jacob Schuster and the wife of Johann Philipp Schenkel, both serfs of the
Zweibrücken Government, with the husband of the latter. The departure of other persons, Abraham Sonntag and Jacob Schenkel, occa-
sioned serious apprehensions on the part of the Electoral Government, on account of the competition with Pfalz-Zweibrücken, which
also possessed serfs in Edenkoben.

But when the Mayor of Edenkoben reported that the Electoral Palatinate possessed 315 men and 377 women as serfs in Edenkoben, while
Zweibrücken could muster only 36 men and 40 women, the right of departure was granted the petitioners for the payment of a small
duty, or even gratis, "because they have so little property and
cannot make a good living in Edenkoben."
Johann Adam Hartmann took the shortest road—he left the land
very suddenly, for he had killed a stag on the government preserves
and faced a heavy penalty! In 1764 he sailed under a false name on
the Ship *Boston*, and so after his landing in Philadelphia, escaped
legal prosecution!

Fritz Braun. "18th Century Palatine Emigrants from the Ludwigshafen Area," *The Pennsylvania Dutchman*, 5 (March 1, 1954), 13
[Lancour No. 173].

Following our interest in determining the European homes of our
Pennsylvania emigrant pioneers, we publish here a list of Palatine
emigrants who came to Pennsylvania in the 18th Century, translated
from Dr. Fritz Braun, "Auswanderung aus dem heutigen Stadtgebiet
von Ludwigshafen am Rhein im 18. Jahrhundert," from *Landsleute
drinnen und draussen—Heimatstelle Pfalz—Mitteilungen zur Wanderungsgeschichte der Pfälzer*, series 5 (1953), pp. 25-31. We have
not included in this list the emigrants who moved eastward into
Eastern Europe into the German settlements in Galicia, the Banat,
the Batschka, nor the few who came to French Guiana.—D. Y.

1. Bayer, Catharina, daughter of Adam and Marie Bayer of Oppau,
married April 1729, Conrad Wetzel, born 1697 in "Waldsiefer," emigrated 1720 or earlier to Pennsylvania.
2. Beroth, Franz Ludwig, from Oppau, born *circa* 1699, died York
County, Pennsylvania, August 1778, married before 1732, Susanna
[—], Reformed, came to Pennsylvania on the Ship *Winter Galley*,
September 5, 1738. The family were Moravians and lived for awhile
at Bethlehem, Pa., with branches in York County and North Carolina.
3. Buettner (Bittner), (Johann) Caspar, Lutheran, married at
Maudach, June 14, 1729, Maria Elisabetha Münch, daughter of Jean
Noe Münch of Dannstadt and wife Johanna. Arrived at Philadelphia
on the Ship *Thistle of Glasgow*, August 29, 1730. On the same ship
was Johannes Munch (Hans Minigh), the father-in-law. In 1763-4
Peter Büttner of Maudach emigrated to Cayenne in French Guiana.
From the Dannstadt Church Registers, furnished by Dr. Eyselein.
4. Eichert, Christian, from Oppau, a Mennonite, received permission gratis in 1752 to emigrate to Nova Scotia, with wife and two
children. From the *Neustadter Oberamtsprotokolle* (Protocols of the
District of Neustadt), Palatine State Archives, Speyer, furnished
by Dr. Friedrich Krebs.

5. Glatz, Henrich, of Oppau, who appears in records of 1752 as wanting to go to Pennsylvania, was "manumitted gratis on account of his having no property." From the *Neustadter Oberamtsprotokolle*.

6. Herget (Hergedt), Johann Peter, citizen of Oggersheim, received in 1750 permission to emigrate to Pennsylvania, with his wife and children. This was granted upon payment of 60 florins tax plus 30 florins for his step-son, Christoph Braun. They arrived at Philadelphia on the Ship *Two Brothers*, August 28, 1750. On the same ship was Balthasar Löffel (Löffler), q.v., also of Oggersheim. From the *Neustadter Oberamtsprotokolle*.

7. Joachim, Friedrich, and wife, of Edigsheim, received permission in 1764, upon payment of the "Tenth Penny or Tithe," to emigrate to Pennsylvania, and arrived at Philadelphia on the Ship *Britannia*, September 26, 1764. From the *Neustadter Oberamtsprotokolle*.

8. Keppler, Simon, of Oggersheim, emigrated to America in 1754, arriving in Philadelphia on the Ship *Nancy*, September 14, 1754. In 1773 he petitions for the remittance of his inheritance, which was granted after paying a double portion of the Tithe. From the *Neustadter Oberamtsprotokolle*.

9. Loeffel (Loeffler), Balthasar, of Oggersheim, received permission in 1750 to emigrate to Pennsylvania, on paying 19 florins for the Tithe. He arrived at Philadelphia on the Ship *Two Brothers*, August 28, 1750, with Johann Peter Herget (q.v.). From the *Neustadter Oberamtsprotokolle*.

10. Niecke (Nick), Anna Regina, born at Rheingönnheim, April 22, 1737, died at Lititz, Pennsylvania, March 10, 1768. For seven years she was in service in the Fenstermacher Family (from Meisenheim) in Lititz, Pennsylvania.

11. Reuther, Anna Margaretha, of Oppau, daughter of Hans Jacob Reuther, married Abraham Reiber of Sandhofen, arrived at Philadelphia on the Ship *Dragon*, October 17, 1749. The Reiber Family settled in Goshenhoppen, Pennsylvania, in the house of Hans Bauer, and inquired after the family of Franz Ludwig Beroth (q.v.), according to Anita L. Eyster, "Notices by German Settlers in German Newspapers," *Pennsylvania German Folklore Society*, Volume III (Allentown, 1938). According to the *Oppauer Nahrungszettel* for June 12, 1718, Hans Jakob Reuther, aged 47, had the following family: (1) Mathes, aged 19; (2) Catharina, aged 15; (3) Susanne, aged 11; (4) Anna Margaretha, aged 9; and (5) Hans Stefan, aged 3, baptized January 27, 1715. Anna Margaretha was therefore 40 years old at the time of her emigration.

12. Sachs, Daniel, of Oggersheim, received permission in 1751 to emigrate to Pennsylvania, with wife and children, upon payment of a Tithe of 16 florins. From the *Neustadter Oberamtsprotokolle*.

Friedrich Krebs. "Palatine Emigrants from the District of Neustadt, 1750," *The Pennsylvania Dutchman*, 5 (May 1953), 9 [Lancour
No. 174.]

This short new list of Palatine emigrants of the eighteenth century is derived from an extract from the Protocolls of the District
of Neustadt in the Electoral Palatinate for the year 1750. Since
these government protocols contain only the record of permission to
emigrate, and, strictly speaking, do not prove emigration itself,
it is quite necessary for the historian and genealogist to search
the respective church registers, to determine whether the supposed
"emigrant" actually left the community or not.

In the present instance this further research has been omitted,
since most of the persons who applied for permission to emigrate
actually do appear in the ships' lists of emigrants landing at
Philadelphia. Our references to ships and dates appended in
brackets after almost every item, are naturally from Strassburger-
Hinke, *Pennsylvania German Pioneers* (Norristown, Pa.: The Pennsylvania German Society, 1934).

The few persons whose names do not appear in these official
lists, can be assumed also to have emigrated, yet the cautionary
statement is always necessary. The Protocols of the District of
Neustadt are part of the holdings of the Palatine State Archives at
Speyer.—F. K.

1. Jacob Ackermann, citizen at Weidenthal, is permitted, along
with his wife and three children, and upon payment of 10 florins
for the "Tenth Penny" [*Zehnten Pfennig*], to go to Pennsylvania.
[Jacob Ackermahnn, Ship *Anderson*, August 21, 1750.]

2. Peter Franck and Jacob Brickert, inhabitants of Lachen, are
permitted along with their wives and children, and upon payment of
the "Tenth Penny"—which amounts to 27 florins for the former and
5 florins 30 kreuzer for the latter, to go to Pennsylvania. [Jacob
Bricker, Ship *Sandwich*, November 30, 1750.]

3. Mathias Brickert, of Lachen, is permitted to go to Pennsylvania gratis. [Matthäus Brückert, Ship *Brotherhood*, November 3,
1750.]

4. Philipp Rheinhard Gassmann, the citizen of Winzingen [today
part of the City of Neustadt], is permitted, along with his wife
and three children, to go to Pennsylvania. [Philipp Gassmann, Ship
Sandwich, November 30, 1750.]

5. Johannes Guschwa, of Weidenthal, is permitted, along with his
wife and two children, to go to Pennsylvania gratis.

6. Peter Herget, the citizen of Oggersheim, is permitted, along
with his wife and children, upon payment of 60 florins supplementary tax and 30 florins for his stepson Christoph Braun, to go to
Pennsylvania. [Petter Hergedt, Ship *Two Brothers*, August 28,
1750.]

7. Balthasar Loeffel, of Oggersheim, is permitted, upon payment
of 19 florins for the "Tenth Penny," to emigrate with his wife to

Pennsylvania. [Balsasar Löffler, Ship *Two Brothers*, August 28, 1750.]

8. Andreas Muehlschlaegel, the Reformed schoolmaster [*Schuldiener*] of Weidenthal, is permitted to go to Pennsylvania, but must first pay the supplementary tax (Tenth Penny) upon his property of 300 florins. [Johann Andreas Mühlschlägel, Ship *Patience*, August 11, 1750.]

9. David Schmitt, of Weidenthal, is permitted, upon payment of 5 florins supplementary tax (Tenth Penny), to emigrate with his wife and three daughters to Pennsylvania. [David Smith, Ship *Patience*, August 11, 1750.]

10. Johann Adam Wetzel, of Weidenthal, is permitted, upon payment of 8 florins, 30 kreuzer for the "Tenth Penny," to go to Pennsylvania. [Possibly Johann Adam Wentzell, Ship *Patience*, August 11, 1750.]

11. Lorentz Laxgang, of Dannstadt, is granted free permission to leave for Pennsylvania, along with his wife and stepchildren.

12. Jacob Koerner, of Edenkoben, who wants to go to Pennsylvania, is, along with his wife, released gratis from serfdom. [This is possibly Jacob Karner, Ship *Royal Union*, August 15, 1750.]

13. Maria Catharine Hammann, of Lachen, is permitted to emigrate to Pennsylvania gratis.

———

Friedrich Krebs, ed. "A List of German Immigrants to the American Colonies from Zweibruecken in the Palatinate, 1750-1771. With an Introduction by Dr. Don Yoder," *The Pennsylvania German Folklore Society Yearbook*, 16 (1951), 171-183 [Lancour No. 175].

Taken from a manuscript in the Kirchschaffnei Archiv in Zweibrücken, this list of 152 emigrants to Pennsylvania and Carolina, of whom 45 are identified in Strassburger and Hinke [Lancour No. 146], this article was originally published in English, then in German as "Eine Liste Deutscher Auswanderer nach den Amerikanischen Kolonien aus Zweibrücken in der Pfalz 1750-1771," in *Familie und Volk*, 1 (1952), 29-32.

The passenger lists from the Pennsylvania German Folklore Society are being prepared for publication by Genealogical Publishing Company of Baltimore.

———

Friedrich Krebs. "Zur Amerika-Auswanderung des 18. Jahrhunderts aus Altwürttemberg hauptsächlich aus dem ehemaligen Oberamt Urach," *Südwestdeutsche Blatter für Familien- und Wappenkunde*, 9 (1957), 464-465 [Lancour No. 176].

Bei Durchsicht der württembergischen Oberratsprotokolle und des

Akts A 413 Bü 133, beide im Staatsfilialarchiv Ludwigsburg, fand
ich bis jetzt noch einige, bisher noch nicht bekannte Amerika-Auswanderer.

Andreas Messerschmid et cons. von Ofterdingen (Krs. Tübingen)
bitten „in Americam ziehen zu dürfen" (Oberratspr. 1751 S. 226)
(Andreas Messerschmid, Ankunft Philadelphia 16. 9. 1751, Schiff
Nancy).

Gallus Schliechter et. cons. von Ehningen (Krs. Böblingen) bitten
um dasselbe (Oberratspr. 1751 S. 219). (Gallus Schlichter, Ankunft
Philadelphia, 25. 9. 1751, Schiff Phönix).

Die folgenden Namen sind dem oben genannten Akt A 413 Bü 133
(Auswanderung aus dem Oberamt Urach) entnommen. Teilweise sind die
Namen aus genannten Akt schon in der Abhandlung von Donald Herbert
Yoder „Emigrants from Württemberg. The Adolf Gerber lists. The
Pennsylvania German Folklore Society" Bd. 10 (1945) publiziert, wobei allerdings nicht der obige Akt, sondern die Oberratsprotokolle
als Quelle dienten. (Soweit die Namen in der Abh. von Yoder schon
publiziert sind, wurden sie hier natürlich nicht berücksichtigt.)
Der genannte Akt enthält die Namen einer grösseren Anzahl von Personen, die in den Jahren 1738/54 die Erlaubnis zur Auswanderung
nach Amerika erhielten. Nicht alle, die diese Erlaubnis erhielten,
erscheinen in den Schiffslisten des Hafens von Philadelphia, sei
es, dass sie überhaupt nicht auswanderten, was nur durch mühevolle
Nachforschungen in den Kirchenbüchern festgestellt werden könnte,
sei es, dass sie unterwegs umkamen und Amerika gar nicht erreichten, sei es, dass sie in einem anderen Hafen als dem von Philadelphia landeten. Aber auch selbst die von Hinke und Strassburger
herausgegebenen Schiffslisten des Hafens von Philadelphia sind
nicht vollständig und verzeichnen nicht alle dort gelandeten
Schiffe.

Auf ihr Bürgerrecht mussten die Auswanderungswilligen beim Verlassen der Heimat verzichten. Ausserdem wurde ihnen mitgeteilt,
dass der regressus in patriam (Rückkehr ins Vaterland) ihnen nicht
mehr gestattet würde. Als Motiv für die Auswanderung, soweit dies
überhaupt angegeben ist, erscheint immer die materielle Not. Für
eine Massenauswanderung aus Altwürttemberg nach Amerika im Zeitraum von 1749/55 spricht die Tatsache, dass nach einem Bericht des
Oberamts Urach v. 31. 3. 1751 allein 39 Personen aus dem Ort Dettingen „entschlossen waren, nacher Neu-Engelland zu ziehen, in der
Hoffnung ihre bessere Nahrung und Versorgung allda zu finden, weil
sie meistenteils arme Leuth und wenig im Vermögen haben", und diese
Erlaubnis unter den oben genannten Bedingungen auch erhielten.

Zu diesen Personen, die 1751 die Auswanderungserlaubnis nach
Amerika erhielten und von Dettingen (Dettingen/Erms, Krs. Reutlin-
gen) auswandern wollten, zählte der aus Neuffen gebürtige Weber
Jacob Waltz mit Ehefrau Maria Agnes geb. Berger von Dettingen,
beide ungef. 30 J., mit den Kindern Maria Elisabetha (10 J.) und
Georg Christoph (3 J.). (Jacob Waltz, Ankunft Philadelphia, 25. 9.
1751, Schiff Phönix), ferner der von Linsenhofen gebürtige Weber

Johannes Löffler (30 J.) mit Ehefrau Elisabetha und Töchtern Maria
Regina und Maria Catharina, des weiteren Ursula Barbara, Witwe des
Jacob Haas, von etl. 40 J., die mit ihren 6 Kindern Johannes,
Jacob, Christoph Adam, Georg Adam, Joseph zu ihrer Schwester nach
Pennsilvanien auswandern wollte, ebenso Maria Agnes (24 J.), T. des
Webers Marx Würtz, Anna; Witwe des Johannes Veyl, v. 50 J., Joseph
Lehmann, ein Taglöhner von etl. 30 Jahren, mit Ehefrau Ursula Ran-
decker und zwei Kindern Magdalena (10 J.) und Christian (6 J.)
(vermutl. Joseph Lehmann, Ankunft Philadelphia, 24. 9. 1751, Schiff
Neptune), Tobias Daumüller, ein Metzger von ca. 30 J., mit Ehefr.
Barbara und 3 Kindern Maria Catharina (10 J.), Maria Agnes (8 J.)
und Johann Christoph (5 J.) (Tobias Daumiller, Ankunft Philadelphia, 24. 9. 1751, Schiff Neptune), Hanss Jerg Bader, ein von Neuffen gebürtiger Weber von ca. 40 J., mit Ehefrau Magdalena und Tochter Maria Barbara, Johann Adam Randecker, ein lediger Maurergesell
("läuft immer auf dem Land herum und führt einen bösen Wandel, ist
in der alten und neuen Welt nichts nutz"), Johannes Müller, ein
Salpetersieder v. 34 J., "mit gediegenem Gemüt und ordentlichem
Wesen", mit Ehefrau Regina und 2 Töchtern Regina und Franziska Magdalena, Johannes Spitz, Weber, und Ehefrau Catharina mit 2 Töchtern
Maria Catharina und Rosina ("sehr schlecht unordentliche Leute,
welche man den Flecken hat gern räumen sehen"). (Die Personalanga-
ben mit den Stellungnahmen entstammen einem Bericht des Pfarrers
Friedr. Christoph Steinhofer v. Dettingen vom 29. 3. 1751).
    1751 durfte Hanss Jerg Spohn von Hülben mit Familie nach Pennsil-
vanien ziehen (Hans Jerg Spohn, Ankunft Philadelphia, 24. 9. 1751,
Schiff Neptune), desgleichen Hanss Jacob Schweller, Schuhmacher zu
Metzingen, mit Weib und Tochter ebenfalls nach Amerika (Neuschott-
land) (vermutl. Jacob Schweller, Ankunft Philadelphia, 19. 9. 1752,
Schiff Edinburgh); 1752 durften endlich der Schulmeister Jacob
Kohler (66 J.) mit Weib (68 J.) und einer Tochter und dem Sohn
Johann Georg, Jacob Mack, Christoff Pfaff, Heinrich Schindler, Jo-
hannes Müller, alle von Donnstetten, und der Küfer Balthasar
Schmied von Feldstetten ("kann mit seinem Küferhandwerk auf der Alp
nichts verdienen") zu den üblichen Bedingungen nach Amerika auswandern.
    1753 durfte Josias Wild, Einwohner zu Dettingen, mit Weib und
Stieftochter Barbara nach Pennsilvanien ziehen. Doch wurde das
mütterliche Vermögen seiner Stieftochter Barbara im Betrage von 150
fl. bis zu deren Volljährigkeit in der Heimat verwaltet. (Josias
Wild, Ankunft Philadelphia, 17. 9. 1753, Schiff Richard and Mary).
    1754 erhielten Gottfried Rattenauer und Jacob Salzer, beide von
Dettingen, die Auswanderungserlaubnis nach Amerika; aber obwohl
beide vor dem zug nach Amerika dringend gewarnt wurden, "weil sie
sich dadurch in das äusserste Elend setzen würden", landete doch
Jacob Saltzer mit dem Schiff Richard and Mary am 30. 9. 1754 in
Philadelphia. Ebenso durfte im gleichen Jahre Hannss Martin Schäffer von Sondelfingen mit den Seinigen abziehen (Hans Martin Schäffer, Ankunft Philadelphia, 30. 9. 1754, Schiff Richard and Mary).

Friedrich Krebs. "Pennsylvania Dutch Pioneers from Baden-Durlach: 1752," *The Pennsylvania Dutchman*, 8 (Summer-Fall 1957), 48 [Lancour No. 177].

The Protocols of the Council and Revenue Chamber of Baden-Durlach, preserved in the General State Archives of Baden, at Karlsruhe, are the source for the present list of persons who received permission to emigrate.

The petitions for emigration were handled in the sessions of the Council and then referred to the Revenue Chamber, which formally pronounced the manumission and fixed the emigration taxes.

As far as the identity of the emigrants cited in the protocols is established with certainty, or probability, the dates of their arrival in Philadelphia have been noted from the ship lists published by Hinke and Strassburger and the number of the relevant list cited in parentheses under the abbreviation HS.

1. Armbruster, Jacob, from Söllingen, with wife and three children (Pr. 853 Nr. 936, Pr. 1336 Nr. 1058), September 27, 1752 (HS 186 C).

2. Bertsch, Georg, citizen at Königsbach, went to the "New Land" with his second wife and the youngest child of his first marriage, on account of continual quarreling with the children of the first marriage (Pr. 854 Nr. 1198), September 25, 1751 (HS 173 C).

3. Beitighoffer, Philipp, from Söllingen, without specifying goal of emigration (Pr. 854 No. 1303, Pr. 1336 Nr. 1670), September 27, 1752 (HS 186 C).

4. Cammerer, Joseph, of Stein, with wife and children (Pr. 853 Nr. 576, Pr. 1335 No. 769).

5. Dahlinger, Caspar, from Weiler, had the Tithe (Tenth Penny) to pay (Pr. 1336 Nr. 1522).

6. Eurich, Hanss (Georg), of Königsbach, manumitted on account of poverty, goal of emigration: Pennsylvania (Pr. 854 No. 1196, Pr. 1336 No. 1427).

7. Finck, Friedrich, of Königsbach, goal of emigration: Carolina (Pr. 854 No. 1197, Pr. 1336 No. 1428).

8. Graeb[n]er, Emanuel, of Königsbach, goal of emigration: Carolina (Pr. 854 No. 1194, Pr. 1336 No. 1430).

9. Haushalter, Lorentz, of Söllingen, without specifying goal of emigration (Pr. 1335 No. 956), October 23, 1752 (HS 191 C).

10. Mussgnug, Jacob, of Söllingen, without specifying goal of emigration (Pr. 853 No. 996, Pr. 1336 No. 1084), September 27, 1752 (HS 186 C).

11. Reiser (Reister?), Jacob, day-laborer, of Stein, had the Tithe to pay, goal of emigration: Carolina (Pr. 853 Nr. 1, Pr. 1335 Nr. 258), September 27, 1752 (HS 184 C).

12. Schneidemann, Georg Friedrich, day-laborer, of Stein, had the Tithe to pay, goal of emigration: Carolina (Pr. 853 Nr. 2, Pr. 1335 Nr. 259).

13. Seiz, Johannes, from Russheim, with wife and 3 children to Pennsylvania, had to pay no emigration taxes, "on account of their extreme proverty" [*„um deren äusserster Armut willen"*] and "since they are leaving the country really as beggars" [*„da sie als pure Bettler aus dem Lande ziehen"*] (Pr. 853 Nr. 951, Pr. 1336 Nr. 1054), October 23, 1752 (HS 191 C).

14. Spatz, Georg Michael, of Söllingen, was with his family manumitted without payment of taxes for emigration to America, "on account of great poverty" [*„um grosser Armut willen"*] (Pr. 854 Nr. 1200, Pr. 1336 Nr. 1434), September 27, 1752 (HS 186 C).

15. Steinwender, Daniel, of Stein (Pr. 853 Nr. 577, Pr. 1335 Nr. 770).

16. Tiefenbach, Mrs., the wife of Caspar Tiefenbach, who has already gone from Graben to America (August 13, 1750, HS 184 C), with her children, who were so poor, that the community declared itself ready to advance the travel money (Pr. 853 Nr. 952, Pr. 1336 Nr. 1429).

17. Vetter, Adam, of Königsbach, manumitted gratis on account of poverty, goal of emigration: Carolina (Pr. 854 Nr. 1195, Pr. 1336 Nr. 1429).

18. Weiss, Conrad, of Söllingen, without specifying goal of emigration (Pr. 1336 Nr. 1670), September 27, 1752 (HS 186 C).

19. Woessinger, Mattheus, of Darmsbach, with wife and 4 children (Pr. 853 No. 575, Pr. 1335 Nr. 823), October 20, 1752 (HS 190 C: Wessener).

20. Xander, David, of Söllingen, with wife and children (Pr. 853 Nr. 935, Pr. 1336 Nr. 1059), September 27, 1752 (HS 186 C).

21. Zimmermann, David, of Berghausen, with wife and 5 children, without specifying goal of emigration (Pr. 1336 Nr. 1081), November 22, 1752 (HS 195 C).

Friedrich Krebs. "Beiträge zur Amerikaauswanderung des 18. Jahrhunderts aus Altwürttemberg," *Südwestdeutsche Blätter für Familien- und Wappenkunde*, 11 (1959-1962), 186-189 [Lancour No. 178].

Nach einem um 1775 entstandenen Aktenstück war Jacob Geigle, Sohn des Johann Jacob Geigle von Lienzingen, Oberamt Maulbronn, (heute Lienzingen, Krs. Vaihingen/Enz) vor ungefähr 24 Jahren als lediger Bursch mit der Magd des Hirschwirtes von L., einer Anna Juditha Drexler, mit der er sich unterwegs trauen liess, von seinem Heimatort nach Pennsylvanien ausgewandert. Zuhause soll er eine Bürgerstochter namens Stumpf(in) unehelich geschwängert haben, weshalb er zu einer Gefängnisstrafe verurteilt wurde. In der Tat landete Jacob Geigle im Jahre 1751 mit dem Schiff Phoenix im Hafen von Philadelphia und leistete dort am 25. September 1751 der englischen Regierung den Treueid. Als der Ausgewanderte dann später (um 1775)

durch einen Bevollmächtigten die Herausgabe des elterlichen Vermög-
ensanteils verlangte, weigerten sich seine Schwäger, Conrad Munzin-
ger von Lienzingen und Friedrich Link von Schmie, die das betr.
Erbteil bisher verwaltet hatten es nach Amerika verabfolgen zu lassen, weil die Erbschaft (an 1000 fl.) zu gross und die Vollmacht
durch mehrere Hände gelaufen sei. Auch befürchteten sie, dass das
Geld, da in Amerika bereits Kriegszustand herrsche, in Feindeshand
fallen könne. In der Tat sistierte die württembergische Regierung
die Herausgabe des Vermögens bis zu einem späteren Zeitpunkt. Aus
den Akten ist leider nicht mit Sicherheit zu entnehmen, ob der Ausgewanderte nicht schliesslich doch noch zu seinem Rechte kam. Nach
Aussage des betr. Aktenstücks (Staatsfilialarchiv Ludwigsburg, A
213, B 320) wohnte Jacob Geigle in Middletown township, Grafschaft
Cumberland, Pennsylvanien.

Auf eine Massenauswanderung nach-Pennsylvanien aus der Stadt und
Amt Freudenstadt im Jahre 1752 kann aus einem Aktenstück des
Staatsfilialarchivs Ludwigsburg (A 343/344 B 14) geschlossen wer-
den; denn am 7. Mai 1752 berichtete Vogt Brastberger von Freuden-
stadt an die württembergische Regierung, dass in der ihm vertrauten
Stadt mit Amt sich 18 Haushaltungen „resolvirt" hätten, mit all den
Ihren aus ihrem Vaterlande hinweg nach Pennsylvanien zu ziehen.
Die Seelenzahl der Emigranten wurde mit 111, ihr Vermögen, das sie
mitnehmen wollten, mit 2180 fl. angegeben.

Im einzelnen wollten nach Pennsylvanien abziehen: aus dem Ort
Freudenstadt der Metzger Ludwig Uber (30 J.) mit seinem Weib Mar-
garetha Barbara (30 J.) und den 3 Kindern Johann David (7 Jh.),
Johannes (5 J.) und Johannes Ludwig (3 J.), Johann Philipp Artz
(Artzt) von Beruf Nagelschmied, (29 J.) mit Ehefrau Maria Barbara
(26 J.) und den Kindern Sophia Dorothea und Catharina Christina (4
Wochen alt), der Taglöhner Tobias Finckbeiner (30 J.) und Ehefrau
Esther (46 J.) und 4 Kindern aus der 1. Ehe der Ehefrau Maria Agnes
(14 J.), Anna Maria (11 J.), Philipp Andreas (7 J.), Ludwig Heinrich (5 J.), der Zimmermann Jacob Bosch (46 J.) mit Ehefrau Barbara
(37 J.) und den Kindern Johann Jacob (15 J.), Johannes (10 J.),
Anna Maria (6 J.), Joseph (4 J.) und Johann Friedrich, der Buchbin-
der Johann Georg Ott, ein Proselyt, (32 J.), mit Ehefrau Anna Maria
(26 J.) und den Kindern Rosina Barbara (2 J.) und Johannes (1/2
J.), ferner Eva, Witwe des Jerg Schmätzlen (49 J.) mit den Kindern
Barbara (19 J.), Simon (14 J.) und Agatha (11 J.), der Obertorwart
und Schuhmacher Andreas Schneider (53 J.) mit Ehefrau Anna (51 J.)
und dem Kind Anna Elisabetha (18 J.), der Schreiner Tobias Bub, (42
J.) mit Ehefrau Barbara (40 J.) und den Kindern Jerg Friedrich (7
J.), Tobias (5 J.), Johannes (3 J.) und Sophia Dorothea (1 J.), der
Weber Georg Ziegler (43 J.) mit der Ehefrau Jacobina (42 J.) und 6
Kindern: Anna Maria (15 J.), Georg Jacob (11 J.), Christiana Mar-
garetha (7 J.), Agnes Catharina (5 J.), Magdalena (3 J.), Georg
Bernhard (1/2 J.), der Bäcker Jacob Bernhard Schwab (52 J.) mit
Ehefrau Elisabetha (45 J.) und den 6 Kindern Christina Barbara (22
J.), Johann Adam (20 J.), Johann Friedrich (18 J.), Jacob Bernhard

(16 J.), Dorothea (14 J.), Elisabetha Catharina (8 J.), Emanuel
Friedrich Weckerlen, (24 J.), von Beruf Kannegiesser, mit Ehefrau
Maria Elisabetha (32 J.) und den 3 Kindern: Sabina Margaretha (4
J.), Jeremias Friedrich (3 J.) und Juliana Dorothea (1/2 J.). Die
Schwester der Ehefrau, Anna Barbara Heinzelmännin (24 J.), ledigen
Standes, wollte auch mitziehen. Der Bäcker Georg Christoph Westlen
aus Freudenstadt (42 J.), der mit der Ehefrau Rosina Margaretha
auch mitziehen wollte, blieb zuhause.

Aus dem Amt Freudenstadt wollten nach Pennsylvanien abziehen:
aus Neuneck (Württemberg, Krs. Freudenstadt) der Bäcker Bernhard
Kauffmann (40 J.) mit Ehefrau Agatha (32 J.) und den Kindern Johannes (13 J.), Bernhard (8 J.) und Johanna (3 J.), der Tagelöhner Johannes Flait (32 J.) mit Ehefrau Margaretha (30 J.), der noch eine
Verwandte namens Anna (10 J.) mitnehmen wollte, die gebrechlich und
geistig zurückgeblieben war, ferner der ledige Schneider Johann
Friedrich Pfefferlen, (20 J.) Schwager von Flait, und schliesslich
noch eine weitere Verwandte von Flait, namens Anna Maria (16 J.),
Hanss Jerg Lockmayer (52 J.), mit Ehefrau Magdalena (50 J.) und den
Kindern Christina (25 J.), Hanss Michel (22 J.), Johannes (16 J.)
und endlich Hannss Jerg Geyser (51 J.) und der Ehefrau Barbara
(50 J.) mit den Zwillingen Anna Maria und Johannes (beide 18 J.),
ferner aus Unteriflingen Hanss Martin Schwarz, Maurer (40 J.) mit
Ehefrau Catharina (40 J.) und den Kindern Agnes (9 J.), Elisabetha
(4 J.) und Maria, auch der Bruder Jacob Schwarz von Johann Martin
Schwarz wollte mit, der Beisitzer Mattheus Brechtlen (38 J.) mit
Ehefrau Elisabetha (32 J.) und dem Kind Barbara (10 J.), der ledige
Michel Bach (Baach) mit der Verlobten Anna Kauffmann (28 J.),
schliesslich noch Elisabeth Frick (26 J.), die sich mit Michel Marquart von Dornstetten verheiraten wollte. Aus Böffingen (Württemberg, Krs. Freudenstadt) wollten der Tagelöhner Hannss Jerg Späth,
(56 J.) mit der Ehefrau Barbara (50 J.) und den Kindern Eva Margaretha (26 J.), Anna (22 J.), Catharina (20 J.), Magdalena (18
J.), Hannss Jacob (17 J.), Christian (14 J.), Hannss Jerg (12 J.)
und Hannss Martin (7 J.), aus Rodt bei Lossburg (Württ., Krs. Freudenstadt) Franz Anton Sinn, ein Tagelöhner (50 J.) mit Ehefrau
Christina (46 J.) und den Kindern 1. Ehe Catharina (23 J.), Anna
Maria (22 J.), Eva (19 J.) und 2. Ehe Elisabetha (15 J.), Jacob (14
J.), Michel (10 J.), Hanss Jerg (6 J.), Barbara (2 J.).—

Die württembergische Regierung hatte gegen die Auswanderung der
Betreffenden wenig einzuwenden, alle durften nach Aufkündigung
ihres Bürger- und Untertanenrechtes für sich und ihre Kinder abziehen, wenngleich die Rückkehr in die Heimat (regressus in patriam)
nicht mehr gestattet wurde. (Erl. v. 13. 5. 1752). Nur bei den
Kindern 1. Ehe des Tobias Finckbeiner wurde einschränkend verordnet, dass diese, falls sie ein beträchtliches Vermögen besässen,
dieses nicht ohne besondere Erlaubnis mitnehmen könnten und bei
Johannes Flait, dass er seine geistig zurückgebliebene Verwandte
Anna besser anderweitig versorge als sie auf die Reise nach Amerika
mitzunehmen.

In den Schiffslisten des Hafens von Philadelphia finden wir einen grossen Teil der Auswanderungslustigen als Passagiere des Schiffes Duke of Wirtenburg wieder, das im Jahr 1752 dort landete (Hinke-Strassburger „Pennsylvania German pioneers" Liste 190 C) nämlich Johann Ludwig Uber, Jacob Bosch, Johann Georg Ott, Georg Ziegler, Jacob Bernhardt Schwab, Johann Adam Schwab, Immanuel Friderich Weckerlin, Tobias Baub (wohl für Bub), Johannes Flait, Johann Lockmir (für Lockmayer), Johann Georg Jayser, Michel Bach; die übrigen Auswanderungslustigen werden wohl, falls sie nicht unterwegs zugrunde gingen, in anderen Häfen Amerikas gelandet sein, worüber keine Schiffslisten vorliegen.

Die Ursache der Auswanderung ist fast immer wirtschaftliche Not und Überbevölkerung des Landes; so sagt das betr. Aktenstück wörtlich: „Sie (die Ausw.) seynd mehist arme Leuthe, welche bey gegenwärttigen hardten und geldlosen Zeiten sich sehr kümerlich nähren müssten, ja bey erhöheten Steuern u. Anlagen vilen herrsch. Gelder, auch sonst allerhand Beschwehrden, bey hausslichen Ehrn sich fast nicht mehr conserviren wusten, welches Sie auch vor die Ursach ihrer emigration angeben." Bernhard Kaufmann, Bäcker aus Neuneck, gab an, es seien zuviele Bäcker in Neuneck, die nebeneinander das Handwerk nicht „treiben" könnten. Grundbesitz habe er nicht, er sei auch kein Tagelöhner, so dass er nicht wisse, wie er sich mit Weib und Kind durchbringen und erhalten könne. Der Nagelschmied Johann Philipp Artzt gab an, man könne sich in Freudenstadt unmöglich ernähren, da Eisen und Kohle jedes Jahr teurer würden und er nicht mit den ausländischen Handwerkern seiner Branche konkurrieren könne, welche infolge billigerer Rohstoffe (Eisen und Kohle) billiger produzieren könnten und auf dem Land und den Märkten die Einheimischen unterböten. Ähnlich klagte auch der zu Hause verbleibende Georg Christoph Westlen, ihn treibe zum Wegzug die höchste Not, da er auf seinem Bäckerhandwerk keine Arbeit und kein Auskommen finde.

(Anschrift des Verfassers: Dr. Friedr. Krebs, Archivar, Speyer, Postf. 65)

"Moravian Pioneers in the Swatara Valley, 1752," *The Pennsylvania Dutchman*, 2 (Dec. 15, 1950), 6 [Lancour No. 179].

Undoubtedly the Moravians were the best record-keepers of all the Pennsylvania Dutch church groups. For when they established a congregation, they prepared family registers of all their members, giving vital statistics of parents and children, and, most valuable of all, telling where in the old homeland the emigrant had come from.

We print here these lists, the *Catálogus der Geschwister in Swatara den 25. Oct. 1752* (Catalogue of the Brethren and Sisters in Swatara, October 25, 1752). It was painstakingly transcribed from the original document in the Moravian Archives at Bethlehem by the late Rev. Dr. William J. Hinke.—D. Y.

1) Ludwig Born, a tailor, from Rimschweyler in Zweybruecken, b. 1702, Reformed. Wife: Anna Marie, from Wuenschberg, b. 1705, Reformed. Husband received into Moravian membership, 1749; wife, 1750. Children: (a) Johann Daniel, b. September 18, 1726; (b) Maria Barbara, b. December 15, 1731; (c) Anna Catharina, b. 1735; (d) Christina Margaretha, b. 1738; (e) Anna Maria, b. January 28, 1741; (f) Johannes, b. March 28, 1747; and (g) Samuel, b. December 7, 1749.

2) Johannes Spittler, from Pennwihl, born December 7, 1690, Reformed. Wife: Catharina, from Ebding, Basel, born 1700, Reformed. Husband received into Moravian membership, 1749. Children: (a) Johannes, b. September 24, 1717; (b) Verona, b. November 3, 1720; (c) Jacob, b. August 30, 1722; (d) Barbara, b. April 4, 1728.

3) Friedrich Weiser, from Schohari, born November 3, 1714, Lutheran. Wife: Anna Catharina, from Hagenburg, born February 26, 1718, Reformed. Husband received into Moravian membership, 1750. Children: (a) Friedrich, b. May 21, 1740; (b) Jacob, b. August 5, 1742; (c) Rebecca, b. April 5, 1748; and (d) Philippus, b. August 21, 1750.

4) Robert Laer, from London, born 1697, Anglican. Wife: Margaretha, from Erthon in Ireland, born 1699, Catholic. Husband received into membership, 1749. Children: (a) Henrich, b. March, 1725; (b) Robert, b. July, 1728; (c) Thomas, b. August 19, 1731; and (d) Joseph, b. March 1, 1743.

5) Casper Corr, from Nassau, born 1725, Lutheran. Wife: Barbara, from Siegen, born 1728, Reformed. Husband received into Moravian membership, 1750. Children: (a) Christian, b. January 7, 1747.

6) Philip Mies, a cabinetmaker, from Altenhausen in Wittgenstein, born 1712, Reformed. Wife: Louisa, from Kiselberg in Freudenberg, born 1721, Reformed. Husband received into Moravian membership, 1749. Children: (a) Johann Georg, b. February 7, 1740; (b) Christiana, b. November, 1742; (c) Anna Barbara, b. August 26, 1745; (d) Casper, b. June 7, 1748; and Philippus, b. September, 1750.

[No number seven is given.]

8) Christian Ohrendorf, widower, from Kiselberg in Freudenberg, born 1692, Reformed. Received into Moravian membership, 1749. Children: (a) Louisa, b. 1721; (b) Anna Margaretha, b. 1724; (c) Johann Christian, b. 1727; (d) Barbara, b. 1728; (e) Magdalena, b. 1731; and Johann Heinrich, b. 1733.

9) Georg Miss, from Berghausen, born 1704, Reformed. Wife: Anna Juliana, from Ambthausen in Wittgenstein, born 1714, Reformed. Husband received into Moravian membership, 1750. Children: (a) Maria Christina, b. December 16, 1736; (b) Johann Georg, b. September 28, 1739; (c) Catharina, b. May 10, 1749; (d) Johann Gerhard, b. November 1747; and (e) Johann Heinrich, b. January 24, 1752.

10) Christian Birme, from Guggisberg in Schwartzenburg, Reformed. Wife: Maria Sara, from Tulpehocken in Pennsylvania, born 1724, Lutheran. Both received into Moravian membership, 1751. Children: (a) Anna Maria, b. January 9, 1746; (b) Anna Barbara, b. March 22, 1749; and (c) Christian, b. April 23, 1751.

"Moravian Brethren in Heidelberg, 1752," *The Pennsylvania Dutchman*, 2 (Jan. 1, 1951), 6 [Lancour No. 180].

The following list of emigrant pioneers comes from the *Catalogus der Geschwister in Heidelberg Oct. 1752* (List of the Brethren and Sisters in Heidelberg, October, 1752). This transcription is from the William J. Hinke Collection in the Historical Society of the Evangelical and Reformed Church, at Franklin and Marshall College, Lancaster, Pa., and was made from the original in the Moravian Archives at Bethlehem, Pa.—D. Y. [Don Yoder].

1) Tobias Boeckel, from Kallstadt in the County of Leiningen, born November, 1711, Lutheran. Wife: Christiana, from Muckstein (?), born May, 1714, Reformed. Husband received into Moravian membership, 1745. Children: (a) Johann Nicolaus, b. October 20, 1741; (b) Friedrich, b. November 9, 1743; (c) Maria, b. November 19, 1745; (d) Johannes, b. March 26, 1750; and (e) Magdalena, b. April 28, 1752.

2) George Brendel on the Muddy Creek, from Lorraine, born April 18, 1713, Lutheran. Wife: Eva Catharina, from Lorraine, born September 11, 1717, Lutheran. Children: (a) Anna Maria, b. August, 1741; (b) Johann Georg, b. August 12, 1743; (c) Eva Catharina, b. February 20, 1745; (d) Johannes, b. June 22, 1746; (e) Heinrich, b. March 3, 1748; (f) Elisabeth, b. January 31, 1750; and (g) Maria Barbara, b. February 19, 1752.

3) Jacob Conrad, from Miedesheim [Miekesheim?] in Alsace, born February 3, 1717, Lutheran. Wife: Maria Catharina, from Behl near Landau in the Palatinate, Reformed. Husband received into Moravian membership, 1746. Children: (a) Christian, b. December 13, 1744; (b) Johannes, b. January 15, 1747; and (c) Johan Jacob, b. September 7, 1751.

4) Johannes Fischer, from Eckartshausen, born December, 1693, Reformed. Second wife: Anna Sybilla, from Creuznach, born 1701, Lutheran. Both received into Moravian membership, 1745. Children: (a) [----]; (b) Catharina Barbara, b. September 22, 1740; and (c) Anna Maria, b. February 10, 1742.

5) Peter Foltz, a cooper, from Guntershofen in Alsace, born July 25, 1726, Lutheran. Wife: Eva Elisabeth, from the same place, Lutheran. Husband received into Moravian membership, 1752. Children: (a) Johann Stephan, b. March 25, 1747; (b) Johann Peter, b. April 1, 1749; and (c) Andreas, b. March 6, 1751.

6) Peter Frey, from Wingan in Sickingen, born September 27,

1689, Lutheran. Wife: Anna Barbara, from the same place, born
April 5, 1696, Lutheran. Children: (a) Maria Margaretha, b.
November 20, 1716; (b) Anna Eva, b. December 30, 1718; (c) Johann
Valentin, b. March 9, 1721; (d) Anna Barbara, b. September 7, 1723;
(e) Johann Peter, b. November 13, 1729; (f) Christian, b. December
31, 1731; (g) Anna Maria, b. April 7, 1726; (h) Juliana, b. February, 1735; and (i) Johann Georg, b. December, 1740 [note dates out
of order].

7) Friedrich Gerhardt, from Langen Selbolt in Ysenburg, born
March 26, 1715. Reformed. Second wife: Barbara, from Birken in
Basel, born 1718, Reformed. Both received into Moravian membership, 1745. Children: (a) Peter, b. October 28, 1737; (b) Conrad,
b. November 11, 1740, baptized by Rieger; (c) Elisabeth, b. September 27, 1742; (d) Friedrich, b. September 12, 1744; (e) Johannes,
b. February 1, 1749; (f) Anna Maria, b. June 2, 1749; and (g)
Jacob, b. December 21, 1751.

8) Nicolaus Glat, from Waltersbach in Alsace, born November,
1713, Lutheran. Second wife: Elisabeth, from Bischweiler in
Alsace, born March 25, 1720, Lutheran. Husband received into Mora-
vian membership, 1745; wife, 1750. Children: (a) Elisabeth, b.
October 27, 1742; (b) Anna Maria, b. December 14, 1744, baptized by
Lischy; (c) Georg, b. November 4, 1746; and (d) Maria Catharina, b.
November 14, 1751.

9) Jacob Groeter, from Gumbartshofen in Alsace, born 1708,
Lutheran. Second wife: Barbara, from Breuschdorf in Alsace, born
May 18, 1703, Lutheran. Both received into Moravian membership,
1745. Children: (a) Johann Georg, b. September 22, 1739; and (b)
Abraham, b. January 22, 1745.

10) Johannes Keller, from Switzerland, born 1711, Reformed.
Second wife: Elisabetha Eva, from Neustadt on the Hardt, Reformed.
Husband received into Moravian membership, 1745; wife, 1746.
Children: (a) Johannes, b. September 21, 1743 [only one given].

11) Johannes Meyer, from Duerckheim on the Hardt, born June 29,
1715, Lutheran. Wife: Maria Margaretha, from Kallstadt in Alsace,
born September, 1714, Reformed. Both received into Moravian membership, 1745. Children: (a) Anna Catharina, b. November 30,
1738, baptized by Schmidt; (b) Tobias, b. September 21, 1740; (c)
Johannes, b. August 2, 1742; (d) Christina, b. June 19, 1745; (d)
Anna Maria, b. October 17, 1747; and (e) Johann Philip, b. November
1, 1749.

12) Jacob Mueller, from Erbach in Zweybruecken, born 1708, Mennonite. Wife: Anna Elisabeth, from Gumbiller in Zweybruecken,
born 1718, Reformed. Husband received into Moravian membership,
1748; wife, 1749. Children: (a) Johannes, b. July 24, 1741; (b)
Salome, b. February 12, 1743; (c) Joseph, b. August 21, 1747; (d)
Catharina, b. April 10, 1749; and (e) Friedrich, b. February 22,
1741.

13) Casper Ried, from Wallborn in the Westrich, born 1707,
Lutheran. Wife: Anna Margareth, from Zuzenhausen in the Palati-

nate, born 1707, Reformed. Both received into Moravian membership, 1748. Children: (a) Johann Georg, (b) Johann Michael, (c) Elisabetha Catharina, (d) Maria Barbara, (e) Johann Casper, (f) Maria Margaretha, b. May 20, 1747; (g) Johann Philip; (h) Christina, b. 1749; and (i) Friedrich, b. October 28, 1751.

14) Heinrich Schuchart, from Eckartshausen, born 1695, Reformed. Wife: Anna Catharina, from Istlinhoffen. Husband received into Moravian membership, 1745; wife, 1748. Children: (a) Johann Jost, b. February 7, 1731; (b) Johannes, b. August, 1733; (c) Anna Maria, b. March 9, 1735; (d) Margaretha Catharina, b. May 9, 1736; (e) Maria Christina, b. 1737; (f) Johan Heinrich, b. September 4, 1741; (g) Carl, b. 1744; (h) Tobias, b. February 8, 1747; and (i) Anna Elisabeth, b. December 4, 1749.

15) Heinrich Stoehr, shoemaker, from Langen Sulzbach in Alsace, born January 11, 1715, Lutheran. Wife: Maria Barbara, from same place, born June 16, 1715, Lutheran. Both received into Moravian membership, 1745. Children: (a) Anna Margaretha, b. August 2, 1740; (b) Philip, b. August 26, 1742; (c) Anna Maria, b. July 11, 1744; (d) Heinrich, b. November 25, 1746; and (e) Johannes.

16) Philip Stoehr, from Langen Sulzbach in Alsace, born February 18, 1716, Lutheran. Wife: Anna Maria, from Umckstein (?), born 1725, Lutheran. Both received into Moravian membership, 1747. Children: (a) Maria Barbara, b. August 31, 1743; (b) Anna Elisabeth, b. August 17, 1745; and (c) Maria Magdalena, b. September 11, 1751.

17) Heinrich Schmit, from Wingen in Alsace, born December 19, 1688, Lutheran. Second wife: Anna Maria, also married for the second time, from Preuschdorf in Alsace, Lutheran. Both received into Moravian membership, 1745. Children: (a) Johann Friedrich, b. April 11, 1722; (b) Balthasar, b. 1730; (c) Maria Eva, b. August 29, 1719; (d) Johann Jacob, b. June 15, 1736; and (e) Maria Dorothea, b. August, 1743.

18) Christoph Weiser, from Grossen Asbach, born February, 1699, born Lutheran but of late a "Presbyterian" [Reformed]. Wife: Elisabeth, from Neuwiek [Neuwied?], born 1702, born Lutheran, then "Presbyterian." Husband received into Moravian membership, August, 1746; wife, October, 1750. Children: (a) Johann Conrad, b. September 19, 1725; (b) Margaretha, b. September 28, 1728; (c) Elisabeth, b. April 19, 1730; (d) Christoph, b. November 18, 1731; (e) Jacob, b. September 22, 1736; (f) Anna, b. April 5, 1738; (g) Benjamin, b. March 8, 1740; (h) Jabez, b. August 4, 1742; and (i) Georg Friedrich, b. May 22, 1746.

Friedrich Krebs. "Amerika-Auswanderer aus Baden-Durlach im Jahre
1753," *Senftenegger Monatsblatt für Genealogie und Heraldik*, 4
(1956-1959), 79-80 [Lancour No. 181].

Die folgende Liste von Personen, die im Jahre 1753 die Erlaubnis
zur Auswanderung nach Amerika erhielten, ist wie die anderen bereits, veröffentlichten Listen, den Hofrats- und Rentkammerproto-
kollen von Baden-Durlach des Jahres 1753 im Generallandesarchiv in
Karlsruhe entnommen. Nähere Erläuterungen finden sich in Spalte
289 ff. des III. Bandes dieses Blattes.

Al(1)geyer, Jacob (Heinrich), der Junge von Ispringen (Kreis
Pforzheim) mit den Seinigen, wegen Armut gratis manumittiert. (Pr.
858 Nr. 294, Pr. 1339 Nr. 351). Auer, Johannes, Hintersass von
Singen (Krs. Pforzheim) mit Weib und Kind, manumittiert gegen 10%
Vermögensabgabe. Reiseziel: Insul Carolina. (Pr. 858 Nr. 762, Pr.
1339 Nr. 679), 14. IX. 1753 (HS 199 B, C). Gö(h)ringer, Johann
Georg, von Singen (Krs. Pforzheim) mit Weib und Kind, wegen Armut
gratis manumittiert. Nach dem Berichte des Amtes Stein bettelarm
und würde „die Willfahr der Gemeinde Singen zu grossem Troste
gereichen". (Pr. 858 Nr. 763, Pr. 1339 Nr. 680), 14. IX. 1753 (Jorg
Gähringer, HS 199 B, C). Hoch, Martin, Bürger und Nagelschmied von
von Königsbach (Krs. Pforzheim) mit Weib und 2 Kindern, wird gratis
manumittiert. (Pr. 859 Nr. 1178, Pr. 1340 Nr. 983). Jock, Elisabetha, ledige Bürgerstochter von Aue (heute Teil der Stadt Karlsruhe) gegen 10% Manumissionstaxe. (Pr. 859 Nr. 1177, Pr. 1340 Nr.
981). Lindemann, Burckhardt, von Eutingen (Krs. Pforzheim) mit
Weib und 7 Kindern, will sich „um seines besseren Glücks willen"
nach Amerika begeben. Manumissionstaxe 10% von seinem Vermögen,
das er ausser Landes bringt. (Pr. 859 Nr. 1163 u. 1236, Pr. 1340
Nr. 1019 u. 1376) 26. IX. 1753 (HS 205 A, B, C). Roser, Adam, von
Singen (Krs. Pforzheim) mit Frau und 3 Kindern gegen 10% Manumissionstaxe. Ohne Angabe des Reisezieles. (Pr. 859 Nr. 1337, Pr.
1340 Nr. 1207) 14. IX. 1753 (HS 199 B, C). Schneider, Michael, der
Alte, von Eutingen (Krs. Pforzheim) will „ungeachtet aller Vorstellungen" zu seinem Sohne nach Pennsilvanien ziehen und darf mit.
Sondergenehmigung des Fürsten schliesslich auch abziehen. (Pr. 858
Nr. 416 u. 764, Pr. 859 Nr. 918). 26. IX. 1753 (HS 205 A, B, C).
Seuberlich, Ulrich, von Ellmendingen (Krs. Pforzheim) mit Weib und
3 Kindern, gegen 10% Manumissionstaxe, ohne Angabe des Reisezieles.
Nach dem Berichte des Oberamtes Pforzheim überschuldet und ein
„liederlicher Haushälter". (Pr. 859 Nr. 1162, Pr. 1340 Nr. 923).
17. IX. 1753 (HS 201 A, B, C). Weiss, Philipp, von Söllingen (Krs.
Karlsruhe) mit Weib und 2 Kindern, gegen 10% Manumissionstaxe. (Pr.
860 Nr. 1495, Pr. 1340 Nr. 1497). Entweder: 15. IX. 1753 (HS 200
A, B, C) oder 24. IX. 1753 (HS 203 A, B, C).

Friedrich Krebs. "More 18th Century Emigrants from the Palatinate," *The Pennsylvania Dutchman*, 5 (March 1, 1954), 12 [Lancour
No. 182].

From the *Oberamtsprotokollen von Neustadt an der Weinstrasse
(Pfalz) 1754-68* [Protocols of the District of Neustadt on the Weinstrasse (Palatinate) 1754-68], come the following new names of
Pennsylvania pioneers of the 18th century:
   1. Renner, Johann Jacob, of Mutterstadt, permitted in 1754 to
emigrate to the "New Land" with wife and children, but had to pay
the tithe on property which he took out of the country. Jacob Renner is listed on the Ship *Edinburgh*, arriving at Philadelphia,
September 30, 1754.
   2. Moerschheimer, Henrich (Merschheimer), citizen of Lambsheim,
permitted 1764 to go to Pennsylvania, in return for the Tithe on
the property he was taking with him. Henrich Morschheimer, Ship
Britannia, September 26, 1764.
   3. Wernz, Jacob, with Jacob Braun and Andres Matheis, all of
Ellerstadt, "because they are not in condition to be able further
to support themselves there, they ask permission to go to the New
Land." Were granted permission to leave without further ado, in
case none of their property remains after satisfying their credi-
tors, otherwise an account is to be rendered. In the Ship Lists
only the name of Jacob Werns appears, on the Ship *Jeneffer*, November 5, 1764.
   4. Hirschberger, Henrich, of Eppstein, Mennonite (*Wiedertäufer*),
is permitted to go to the Province of Pennsylvania, upon payment of
30 florins for the Tithe. He was also permitted to take along the
property which is coming to his three brothers (obviously also in
America), upon payment of 156 florins. Henrich Herschberger, Ship
Crawford, October 26, 1768.
   From the *Protocols of the District of Heidelberg* (1751) we hear
of other emigrants from the Odenwald: The following citizens and
residents of Schoenau near Heidelberg, in the Odenwald, were, on
account of their poverty, manumitted gratis: Balthasar Koenig,
Joerg Happes, Johann Wagner, and Joerg Luecker. All four arrived
in Philadelphia on the Ship *Queen of Denmark*, October 4, 1751:
George Licker, Balzer Konig, Johanes Wagner, George Happes.

R. G. Smith. "German Families," *The Pennsylvania Magazine of History and Biography*, 33 (1909), 501-502 [Lancour No. 183].

Taken from a list in Henry Miller's *Staats Bote* of February 9,
1758, this list, containing names of German families arriving from
Holland, with their places of origin, has been reprinted on page
261 of *Emigrants to Pennsylvania* (Michael Tepper, ed.), published
by the Genealogical Publishing Company in 1977.

"Record of Indentures of Individuals Bound Out as Apprentices, Servants, Etc. and of German and Other Redemptioners in the Office of the Mayor of the City of Philadelphia, October 3, 1771, to October 5, 1773," *The Pennsylvania-German Society Proceedings and Addresses*, 16 (1905-1907), 325 pages [Lancour No. 184].

Reprinted in an indexed volume of 364 pages by Genealogical Publishing in 1973, this chronological list gives names of about 5,000 individuals arriving from British, Irish and Dutch ports, naming the port of embarkation and giving details of the term and conditions of indenture.

"Record of Servants and Apprentices Bound and Assigned before Hon. John Gibson, Mayor of Philadelphia, December 5th, 1772 — May 21, 1773," *The Pennsylvania Magazine of History and Biography*, 33 (1909), 475-491; 34 (1910), 99-121, 213-228 [Lancour No. 185].

This list, duplicating in part No. 184, has been reprinted in Tepper's *Emigrants to Pennsylvania, 1641-1819* (see No. 183).

"A List of German Emigrants, 1773," *The Pennsylvania Magazine of History and Biography*, 13 (1889), 113-115 [Lancour No. 186].

This list was printed in Lancour No. 142, above.

"List of Arrivals per 'Pennsylvania Packet,' 1775," *The Pennsylvania Magazine of History and Biography*, 18 (1894), 379 [Lancour No. 187].

This list has been reprinted on page 239 of Tepper's *Emigrants to Pennsylvania, 1641-1819* (see Lancour No. 183).

United States. Work Projects Administration. *Index to Records of Aliens' Declarations of Intention and/or Oaths of Allegiance, 1789-1880, in United States Circuit Court, United States District Court, Supreme Court of Pennsylvania, Quarter Sessions Court, Court of Common Pleas, Philadelphia. Compiled by Works Projects Administration, Project No. 20837. Sponsored by Pennsylvania Historical Commission*, 11 vols. [Harrisburg, 1940?]. [Lancour No. 188].

No attempt has been made to include any part of this valuable work because of the size of the project. An alphabetical index of applicants for naturalization in the courts of Philadelphia from 1789 to 1880, the entries include the name of the applicant, country of former allegiance, court of record, and the date of the declaration of intention and/or the oath of allegiance.

———

Luther R. Kelker. "List of Foreigners Who Arrived at Philadelphia, 1791-1792," *The Pennsylvania Magazine of History and Biography*, 24 (1900), 187-194, 334-342 [Lancour No. 189].

This article is supplementary to Rupp's work [Lancour No. 145], but the names are included in part in Strassburger and Hinke [Lancour No. 146]. The article has been reprinted in *Emigrants to Pennsylvania* (see Lancour 183, above), pages 240-256.

———

Don Yoder, editor. "Lehigh County Naturalization Records," *The Pennsylvania Dutchman*, 1 (May 5, 1959), 6; 2 (January 1950), 6 [Lancour No. 190].

In the editor's search for the European origins of our Pennsylvania German pioneers, he has turned to a rich and hitherto untapped source—the Naturalization Papers of Aliens, preserved at the County Courthouses in accordance with a federal law of 1798.

The immigrant alien who settled in Pennsylvania after the formation of the United States Government under the Constitution had to file several papers with the Court of Common Pleas of the County in which he had taken up residence. The first of these papers was the "Declaration of Intention to Become a Citizen," the second was the "Petition for Naturalization," which was acted upon by the court, resulting in favorable cases in the naturalization of the petitioner.

The value of such papers for those interested in Pennsylvania Dutch genealogy, is that for the most part, they give us the name of the village, or at least the province of Germany, from which the emigrant came. This first article in a lengthy series of "Naturalization Records" which the Editor plans to publish, comes from information copied from the original papers in the Prothonotary's Office of the Lehigh County Courthouse in Allentown.

Not all these immigrants landed on our shores before 1808—the traditional and arbitrary date after which no immigrant is considered "Pennsylvania German" by the Membership Committee of the Pennsylvania German Society. However, I have included all German immigrants who petitioned for naturalization up to the year 1820. Most of them settled among the Pennsylvania Dutch, intermarried

with them, and their descendants are indistinguishable from the
mass of descendants of the Eighteenth Century Pennsylvania German
Pioneers.

1)   Johann Friedrich Huebener (D1), on December 22, 1812, filed
the following "Affidavit & Declaration of John F. Hubner—Intention
to Become a Citizen of the United States": "State of Pennsylvania,
Lehigh County SS. John F. Hubner of the age of thirty eight years
and upwards, a subject of the Imperial City of Hamburg, in [the]
empire of Germany, now residing within the County of Lehigh afsd
under the Jurisdiction of the United States, doth upon his oath ad-
ministered according to law declare that it is bona fide his Intention to become a citizen of these United States and to renounce
forever all allegiance and fidelity to any foreign prince Potentate
State or Sovereignty whatsoever and particularly to the Government
of the Imperial City of Hamburg aforesaid to whom he is a subject
and also all orders & letters of Nobility to which he may be
entitled.   Sworn & Declared in open Court, Dec. 22, 1812.   Signed:
Joh Frid Huebener."

2)   David Thim (D2), on December 22, 1812, filed a Declaration of
Intention, stating that he was "of the age of thirty seven years &
upwards a subject of West Prussia in the Empire of Germany, now
residing within the County of Lehigh."

3)   Samuel Heilner (D3), on December 22, 1812, filed a Declaration of Intention, stating that he was "of the age of twenty four
years or thereabouts a Subject of the Principality of Wertzburg
[Wuerzburg] in the Empire of Germany," now resident in Lehigh
County.

4)   Johann Christoph Zaenglein (D4), on February 24, 1813, filed
a Declaration of Intention, stating that he was "of the age of
thirty seven years & upwards, a subject of Prussian Koningsberg in
the Empire of Germany," now resident in Lehigh County.   Sworn in
open court, August 31, 1813.

5)   Nicholas Dick (D5), on February 24, 1813, filed a Declaration
of Intention, stating that he is "of the age of twenty seven years
or thereabouts formerly inhabitant of West Prussia in the Empire of
Germany," now resident in Lehigh County, and offers to renounce his
allegiance to Frederick IV, King of Prussia.

6)   Jacob Guelich (D8), on February 2, 1814, filed a Declaration
of Intention, stating that he was "born in the year of our Lord one
thousand seven hundred & eighty four—in Hamburg in the Empire of
Germany—whence he migrated in the year of our Lord one thousand
eight hundred & seven and has selected the Commonwealth of Pennsylvania, as the place of his intended settlement."   The Prothonotary
spelled his name "Gillich."

7)   Michael Herlein (D10), on May 3, 1814, filed a Declaration of
Intention, stating that he was "born in the year of our Lord one
thousand seven hundred & fifty seven—in the County or Circle of
Franconia in the Kingdom of Bavaria in Germany whence he migrated
in the year of our Lord one thousand eight hundred and five."   He

offers to renounce the sovereignty of the King of Bavaria.

8) David Trexler (D11), on August 29, 1814, filed a Declaration of Intention, stating that he was "born in the year one thousand seven hundred and eighty three, in the Kingdom of Wirtemberg [Wuerttemberg], whence he migrated in the year A.D. 1805." He offers to renounce the King of Wuerttemberg. The alien signed his name in German, "David Drexler."

9) Jakob Wilhelm Dechant (P9), on February 2, 1814, filed the following Petition for Naturalization. This immigrant is of especial interest in that he was a Reformed minister in Pennsylvania and Ohio for many years. "To the honorable Robert Porter Esquire, President and his Associates Judges of the Court of Common Pleas of the County of Lehigh. The Petition of Jacob William Dechant a native of Oppenheim in the Electorate of Mentz [Mainz] in the Empire of Germany, respectfully sheweth, That your petitioner on the twenty second day of January in the year of our Lord one thousand eight hundred and ten, filed a declaration in the Court of Common Pleas of Northampton County in the State of Pennsylvania, stating an oath, that he was then of the age of twenty seven years and a native of Oppenheim in the Electorate of Mentz [Mainz] in the Empire of Germany, but then residing in the township of Upper Saucon in the County of Northampton & State aforesaid, & that it was bona fide his Intention to become a citizen of the United States & to renounce forever all allegiance & fidelity to any foreign prince, potentate state of sovereignty whatever & particularly to the Elector of Mentz to whom he is now subject. That more than three years are elapsed since the making and filing [of] the above declaration. That your petitioner hath never borne any hereditary title or been of any of the orders of nobility, and if any such should by means unexpected descend to him, he doth absolutely and entirely renounce the same; that he hath never been heretofore proscribed by any state, or been legally convicted of having joined the Army of Great Britain during the late [revolutionary] war. That he is now ready and desirous to take the necessary Oath required by the Act of Congress in such Cases provided. Your petitioner therefore prays your honorable Court to admit him to become a citizen of the United States & of the Commonwealth of Pennsylvania. And he will pray, &c. Jk. Wm. Dechant. February 2d, 1814."

In another document he swears he will support the Constitution and renounce allegiance to the Elector of Mentz and to Napoleon, Emperor of France and Protector to the Rhenish Confederation. He was resident in the United States on September 2, 1805.

An affidavit of Daniel Cooper declares that the petitioner has "behaved as a man of Good moral character attached to the principles of the Constitution of the United States."

Any of your ancestors in this list? We continue from *The Dutchman* for May 5, 1949, the list of German and Swiss emigrants who

applied for naturalization before the courts of Lehigh County,
Pennsylvania, up to the year 1830. If you recognize any of your
forefathers among them, write us. We would like further information on all of these families.—D. Y.

1) Henry Heinen (P12), on December 7, 1815, filed a Petition for
Naturalization, stating that he was "a native of East Friesland, in
Germany." On November 18, 1812, he had filed his first papers in
the Court of Common Pleas of Northampton County. He renounces the
King of Prussia, and denies having been in the British Army in the
late revolutionary war. He further states that he was resident in
the United States on or about July 30, 1804, and for nine years
past has lived in Pennsylvania. He renounces the King of Prussia
and the King of Hanover, "to whose Dominion East: Friesland has
lately been annexed." John Marx or Marck testifies as to his good
moral character. According to Preston Laury, *The History of the
Allentown Conference of the Ministerium of Pennsylvania* (Kutztown:
Kutztown Publishing Company, 1926), this immigrant was the Reverend
Heinrich Heine, who from 1808-1817 served the Zionsville-Western
Salisbury Parish, later removing to Gettysburg. The Prothonotary's
Index refers to these papers under the name "Rev. Henry Heinen."

2) Ansel Arnold (D13), on September 3, 1817, filed a Declaration
of Intention, stating that he was born March 2, 1797, in Ebenhousen
in the Kingdom of Wirtemberg [Wuerttemberg] in Germany, whence he
migrated on March 18, 1816, to the United States, selecting Pennsylvania as his home. Intends to renounce his allegiance to
Frederick II, King of Wuerttemberg. A second paper (DR13), a
Report Preparatory to the Declaration of Intention, states he now
resides in Berks County. He arrived at Baltimore on or about July
28, 1816. He has no parents, guardian, master or mistress.

3) Daniel Zacharias (DR45), in May Term 1818, filed a Report
Preparatory to Filing a Declaration of Intention, stating that he
was born in Witgenstein now in the Principality of Darmstadt in the
Empire of Germany, on April 22, 1783, and owes allegiance to Francis II, Emperor of Germany. He emigrated from Wittgenstein, May
22, 1805, arriving at Philadelphia, November 28, 1805. With no
parents, etc., he chooses Lehigh County, Pennsylvania, as his home.
In May Term 1818 he also filed his Declaration of Intention (D15),
stating the same information. On September 1, 1823, he filed his
Petition for Naturalization, renouncing the Emperor of Austria "of
whom I was born a subject." The printer, Charles L. Hutter,
vouches for his good character.

4) Henry Detweiler (D16), on May 6, 1818, filed his Declaration
of Intention, stating that he was born December 18, 1795, in Langenbruk, in the Canton of Basel, in Switzerland, whence he migrated
April 2, 1817, to the United States. He signs his name "Dr. Henry
Detwiller." He was therefore the Allentown physician, famous in
the annals of homeopathic medicine in America. His Report (DR16),
filed at the same time, states that he arrived at Philadelphia,
July 20, 1817, and having no parents, etc., has settled in Lehigh

County.   In September Term, 1823, "Henry Detwiller, M. D.," filed
his Petition for Naturalization (P42), and renounced the government
of the Canton of Basel in the Republic of Switzerland.   John Bahl
vouches for his good character.

5) Carl Friedrich Schaeffle (D17), on May 6, 1819, filed his
Declaration of Intention, stating that he "is a subject of the King
of Wirtemberg in Europe, that he belongs to the Wirtemberg Nation,
that he was born" August 29, 1796, "in the town of Durrmenz in the
County of Maulbrunn and Kingdom of Wirtemberg afores'd, whence he
migrated on" April 12, 1818, landing at Philadelphia, August 28,
1818.   He is now 22 years, 8 months, and 7 days old, and intends to
make Pennsylvania his residence.   In his Report (DR17), filed at
the same time, May Term, 1819, he offers to renounce his allegiance
to William I, King of Wuerttemberg.

6) Christoph Gottlieb Rettich (D18), in May Term, 1819, filed
his Declaration of Intention, stating that he was born July 13,
1796, in the town of Maehringen in the County of Tuebingen, in the
Kingdom of Wirtemberg, whence he migrated May 29, 1817, landing at
Philadelphia on October 10, 1817.   His age is 22 years, 9 months,
and 23 days.   In his Report (DR18) he offers to renounce William I,
King of Wuerttemberg.

7) John Caspar Pfeiffer (D19), on September 6, 1820, filed his
Declaration of Intention, stating that he was born at Klein Sach-
senheim, in the County or Oberambt of Vayhingen, in the Kingdom of
Wirtemberg.   His age is 34 years, and he intends to make his home
in Heidelberg Township, Lehigh County.

8) Thomas Meyer (D20) on September 4, 1820, filed his Declaration of Intention, stating that he was born at Neusylingen or Nes-
lyngen in the Kingdom of Bavaria.   His age is 48 years, and he intends to settle in the Borough of Northampton [i. e., Allentown].

9) George Ising (P21), on December 9, 1820, filed his Petition
for Naturalization, stating that he landed in the United States in
September, 1786, and has resided for the last seven years in Lehigh
County.   The foreign sovereignty which he renounces in particular
is that of the King of Denmark.   Caspar Mayer vouches for his good
character.

10) Jacob Monheimer (D26), on December 2, 1818, filed his
Declaration of Intention, stating that he was born in the year 1786
in the County of Retzatkreis in the Kingdom of Bavaria, whence he
migrated in 1818.   He offers to renounce his allegiance to Joseph
Maxmilian, King of Bavaria.

11) Gideon Ibach (D35), on September 6, 1816, filed his Declaration of Intention, stating that he was born in the Dukedom of Berg
in the Circle of Westphalia, in the year 1785, whence he emigrated
in 1796 and made his home in Pennsylvania.   Offers to renounce the
sovereignty of the Emperor of Austria.   In September Term, 1823, he
filed his Petition for Naturalization (P34), at which time Gustavus
Ibach of the Borough of Northampton vouches for his good character,
having known him from infancy; Johannes Smith of the Borough of

Northampton likewise vouches for him.

12) Gustavus Ibach (D39), on September 7, 1816, filed his Declaration of Intention, stating that he was born in the Dukedom of Berg in the Circle of Westphalia, whence he emigrated in the year 1796. Offers to renounce the sovereignty of the Emperor of Austria. In September Term, 1823, he filed his Petition for Naturalization (P40), in which he gives the year of his birth as 1791. Gideon Ibach of South Whitehall Township vouches for his good character, as does Johannes J. Schmidt of the Borough of Northampton.

13) Henrich (Heyman) Woolf (D36), on August 31, 1818, filed his Declaration of Intention, stating that he was born April 15, 1787, in Oberdorf, in the Kingdom of Wirdenberg [Wuerttemberg], whence he migrated, May 8, 1817, to the United States. Offers to renounce the sovereignty of Frederich II, King of Wuerttemberg. Signs his name in German: Heyman Woolff. In his Report (DR36), filed at the same time, his name appears as "Hayman Woolff," and he states that, he landed at Philadelphia, December 20, 1817; has no parents, etc. In September Term, 1823, "Henry Wolf otherwise called Hayman Wolf," filed his Petition for Naturalization (P37), in which he signs himself in German: Henrich Woolf. Peter Gross vouches for his good character.

14) Daniel Albrecht (P54), on May 3, 1825, filed his Petition for Naturalization, which states that "Daniel Albright, a native of the Palatinate of Wurtemberg [sic] in Germany, now resident in the Township of Upper Milford in the said County" of Lehigh, was resident in the United States between June 18, 1796, and April 14, 1802, and has continued to reside there ever since, having also lived in Pennsylvania for more than one year last past. Signs his name: Daniel Albrecht. Renounces the sovereignty of the *Duke* of Wurttemberg [Evidently he did not know that little Wuerttemberg had become a Kingdom!]. His good character is vouched for by George Kemmerer.

15) John T. Hollmann (P85), on September 5, 1829, filed his Petition for Naturalization, stating that he is a native of Bremen, and was resident in the United States between April 14, 1802, and June 18, 1812, and has continued to reside here. Signs his name in English: John T. Hollmann. Renounces the sovereignty of the Government of Bremen and the Emperor of Austria. John F. Halbach and Henry Jarrett vouch for his good character.

16) Jacob Agster (P86), on September 8, 1829, filed his Petition for Naturalization, in which he states he is a native of Ilsfeld in the Kingdom of Wurtemberg, and was resident in the United States between April 14, 1802, and June 18, 1812, and has continued to reside here. Renounces the sovereignty of the King of Wuerttemberg. Signs his name in German: Jacob Agster. Henry Jarrett and Conrad Neymeyer vouch for his good character.

———

"List of German Passengers Arrived in the Port, Philadelphia, in the Ship Margaret, from Amsterdam, C. E. Gardner, Master, September 19th, 1804. As Taken from the Original Immigrant List on File in the Division of Public Records, Harrisburg, Pa.," *Journal of the Lycoming Historical Society*, 1 (1956), 9-12 [Lancour No. 191].

This list, containing 91 names with size of household and age, place of birth, county and country of origin, occupation, and physical characteristics of the head of household, has also been printed in Strassburger and Hinke [Lancour No. 146] and in Rupp [Lancour No. 145].

"Passenger List of the Ship 'Elizabeth,' Which Arrived at Philadelphia in 1819," *The Pennsylvania Magazine of History and Biography*, 25 (1901), 255-258 [Lancour No. 192].

This list, copied from the original in the Library of the Historical Society of Pennsylvania, contains 83 names and the contractual obligations of both the passengers and the captain, concluding "Amsterdam, 4 May, 1819."
In has been reprinted in *Emigrants to Pennsylvania, 1641-1819* (see Lancour No. 183, above).

G. B. Keen. "The Third Swedish Expedition to New Sweden," *The Pennsylvania Magazine of History and Biography*, 3 (1879), 462-464 [Lancour No. 193].

This article, compiled from copies in the Historical Society of Pennsylvania of original papers in the Royal Archives, Stockholm, names emigrants who embarked on the *Kalmar Nyckel* and *Charitas* for New Sweden [now Delaware] in 1641. It has been reprinted on pages 1-3 of *Emigrants to Pennsylvania, 1641-1819* (see Lancour No. 183, above). An article by C. T. Odhner, "The Founding of New Sweden, 1637-1642," in the same volume of *PMHB* (pages 269-284 and 395-411), has not been reprinted.

G. B. Keen. "The Eighth Swedish Expedition to New Sweden," *The Pennsylvania Magazine of History and Biography*, 8 (1884), 107-108 [Lancour No. 194].

This article, compiled from a copy in the Historical Society of Pennsylvania of the original in the Royal Archives at Stockholm,

lists both males and females who set out with Commandant Hans
Amundson for New Sweden on July 3, 1649. It has been reprinted on
pages 4 and 5 of *Emigrants to Pennsylvania, 1641-1819* (see Lancour
No. 183, above).

Louis P. de Boer. "Delaware Papers. Passenger List of Colonists
   to the South River (Delaware) Colony of New Netherland, 1661,"
   The New York Genealogical and Biographical Record, 60 (1929), 68-
   70 [Lancour No. 195].

It is well known that the settlements on the South River, the
Delaware, of New Netherland, often changed hands in the early days
of their existence.
   After the Dutch had colonies of small proportions and short dura-
tion there, the Swedes—chiefly through the guiding hand of Pierre
Minuit, at one time Director-General of New Netherland,—in 1638
formed a larger and more lasting settlement there, known in Ameri-
can colonial history by the name of New Sweden.
   During Pieter Stuyvesant's administration as Director-General of
New Netherland, New Sweden, in 1655, again became part of New
Netherland, the West India Company's colony on the North American
continent, under the sovereignty of The High Mighty Lords, the
States General of the United Netherlands.
   In 1661 the West India Company transferred the ownership of the
South River Colony to the City of Amsterdam, and in the records of
that city, the colony is often mentioned as the "Stadt's Colonie"
or the "City Colony."
   All documents relative to the history of this colony from 1661
till 1664, i.e., till the year of the English occupation of all of
New Netherland, are not found among the West India Company papers
in the General Archives of the Kingdom of the Netherlands, at the
Hague, but in the Old City Archives of Amsterdam.
   From the last named collection of documents, which in its entirety deserves to be copied and translated on behalf of early American
colonial history, the following data has been taken:
   "Lyste van de Coloniers en andere Vryeluyden soo hun reets hebben
aengegeven om na deses Stats Colonie in Nieu Nederlant te gaen.
   4.   Joris Florisse, tot Leyderdorp, met syn jongen en 2 knechts.
   3.   Cornelis Aertsen, tot Sevenhoven, met syn jongen en neeff.
   1.   Jan Leendertsen, in de Bent.
   3.   Jan Roemers, van Haserwoude, met syn huysvrou en dochter.
   2.   Gerrit de Grot, van Ryns(a)terwoude, en Jongen.
   1.   Pieter Adriaensen, tot Sevenhoven.
   1.   Een Jongman van Sardam.
   1.   Laurens de Geus, van Amsterdam.
   1.   Coort de metselaer, tot Amsterdam.
   3.   personen van Vreelandt.

10. Gerrit Sandersen, van Tuyl, met 10 personen.
 4. Joost Noorda, met syn vrou en 2 knechts.
 1. Anthony Willemsen, van Vreelandt, synde een metselaer.
 1. Arent Arentsen, van Oldenburg, boereknecht.
 1. Lourens Cornelissen, van der Wel.
 1. Jacob Pietersen, van Brugge, in de Angeliers Streat, boer-
       knecht."
Translation:—
"List of Colonists and other Freemen who have already applied for
going to the Colony of this City in New Netherland.
 4. Joris Florisse, at Leyderdorp, with his boy and 2 man-
       servants.
 3. Cornelis Aertsen, at Sevenhoven, with his Boy and nephew (or
       cousin).
 1. Jan Leendertsen, in the Bent.
 3. Jan Roemers, of Haserwoude, with his wife and daughter.
[On page 69 of the original the list is illustrated.]
 2. Gerrit de Grot, of Ryns(a)terwoude, and boy.
 1. Pieter Adriaensen, at Sevenhoven.
 1. A young man of Sardam (i.e., Saendam).
 1. Laurens de Geus, of Amsterdam.
 1. Coort, the mason, at Amsterdam.
 3. Persons of Vreelandt.
10. Gerrit Sandersen, of Tuyl, with 10 persons [This expression
       in old Dutch is often used to indicate 9 persons beside the
       one mentioned. This list therefore includes 38 persons, 14
       of whom are named.].
 4. Joost Noorda, with his wife and 2 man-servants.
 1. Anthony Willemsen, of Vreelandt, being a mason.
 1. Arent Arentsen, of Oldenburg, farmhand.
 1. Lourens Cornelissen, of Wel.
 1. Jacob Pietersen, of Bruges (living), in the Angeliers Street
       (at Amsterdam), farmhand."
No date is affixed to this document, which appears to be the preliminary list probably made for the use of some official. That it
antedates the following document, is shown from its place in the
collection, where it is under No. 65, whereas the following paper
falls under No. 88.
(See: S. II L., No. 12 [13], document No. 65, Old City Archives,
Amsterdam.)
The following document appears between the numbers 87 and 89, but
through some omission is not numbered No. 88 as it should be:
"Lyste van Passagiers die voor de Stadt Amsterdam derwaerts gaen,
naer de Colonie N. Amstel in de Suydt Revier.
 4. Sr. Gerrit van Schweringe, Schout, met syn vrouw, knecht en
       meydt.
 2. Claes Verbrack, met syn frauw.
 3. Mr. Jacob de Commer, met syn vrouw en twee kinderen.
 1. Neeltgen Willems.

1. Gerrit Otte, van Accoy.
8. 7. Kier Wolters, uyt Drendt, met syn vrou en 6 kinderen.
1. Gerrit Jansen van Beck.
1. Roelof Barentszen.
1. Ryck Gurtsen van As.
1. Jan Gerritsz.
2. Cornelis Aertsen en knecht.*
2. Willem Jansen en knecht.
1. Jan Evertsen van Gysel.
6. 4-1/2. Gerrit Sandersen, met syn huysfrau en 4 kinderen.*
1. Pieter Arise Thysvelt.
2. Joris Florissen en knecht.*
3. Jan Ramaere, huysvrou en dochter.*
1. Jan Hellegers.
1. Herman Otte, van Accoy.
1. Gerrit de Groott.*
1. Laurens de Geus.*
1. Willem Cornelissen Byckevryer.
45. 42-1/2 Zielen.

In kennisse van my ondergeschreve, syn dese bovenstaende personen gaende nae de colonie Nieuwr Amstel, gemonstert en syn als hier vooren opgereeq, to samen bestaende in twee ent veetich hoppen en een half, soo halven als heelen door een gerekent, de suygelingen vry.†

Actum int Texel, opt Schip "de Purmerender Kerck,"
    den 17 November, 1661.§   G. V. Sweringen."

Translation:—

"List of Passengers who go there for the City of Amsterdam; to the Colony of N. Amstel, on the South River.

4. Sr. Gerrit van Schweringe, Schout, with his wife, man-servant and maid.
2. Claes Verbrack, with his wife.
4. 3. Jacob de Commer, with his wife and two children.
1. Neeltgen Willems.
1. Gerrit Otte, of Accoy.
8. 7. Kier Wolters, from Drenthe, wife his wife and 6 children.
1. Gerrit Jansen van Beck.
1. Roelof Barentszen.
1. Ryck Gurtsen van As.
1. Jan Gerritsz.
2. Cornelis Aertsen and man-servant.*
1. Jan Evertsen van Gysel.
6. 4-1/2. Gerrit Sandersen, with his wife and 4 children.*
1. Pieter Arise Thysvelt.
2. Joris Florissen and man-servant.*
3. Jan Ramaere, wife and daughter.*
1. Jan Hellegers.
1. Herman Otte, of Accoy.
1. Gerrit de Groott.*

1.   Laurens de Geus.*
1.   Willem Cornelisse Byckevryer.
42-1/2
45 [in fact, 46] souls.

To the knowledge of me, the undersigned, these above listed persons have been examined, and they are as accounted for above,
existing altogether of forty two heads and a half, halves and
wholes all counted together; nursing children free.†

                    Done in the Texel Roadstead, on the Ship
                         The Purmerland Church,
                    the 17th of November, 1661.§

                                (w.s.:)   G. V. Sweringen."

---

* The names thus marked in the passenger-list also occur in the
preliminary list given above. The preliminary list in many
instances supplements this passenger-list, by giving the various
places of origin of the passengers.

Jan Ramaere is called Jan Roemers in the preliminary list.

There might have been a relationship between Gerrit Otte and Herman Otte, both names occuring in the passenger-list, and both persons from Accoy.

† The number of passengers was taken by "heads," who had to pay
full passage, "half-heads," for whom half-fare had to be paid
(these were presumably children under the age of five) and infants,
who had free passage.

Forty-two and a half heads would make forty-three persons. One
infant of Kier Wolters, and one of Gerrit Sandersen were exempt,
but they have been accounted for in the margin, this making Kier
Wolter's family amount to 8 instead of 7, and Gerrit Sandersen's
family to 6 instead of 5 (4-1/2), and making a total of forty-five
souls, as given in the margin.

The scribe, however, has omitted in the margin an infant of Mr.
Jacob de Commer, the surgeon of the expedition, whose family
although consisting of himself, his wife and two children, is
counted for only three.

Correcting this error we would reach a total of 46 passengers
sailing on 24 November, 1661, on "de Purmerlander Kerck," from
Texel Roadsteads for Newer Amstel, Delaware.

§ As a matter of record it must be stated here that the ship remained in Texel Roadsteads for a whole week, not sailing until the
24th of November, 1661, evidently waiting for further cargoes and
supplies.

An inventory of the medical outfit and surgical instruments taken
by Dr. Jacob de Kommer to the colony, on this ship, would be of
interest to students of medical history in America.

A. R. Dunlap. "Three Lists of Passengers to New Amstel," *Delaware History*, 8 (1959), 310-311 [Lancour No. 196].

The collections of the Historical Society of Delaware include a microfilm copy, from the Archives of the city of Amsterdam, of manuscript records (in Dutch) relating to the Delaware. These records accumulated in Amsterdam during the years 1656-1664, when that city was actively interested in the affairs of the New Amstel colony. Much of this material was translated and published in volumes I and II of *New York Colonial Documents*, but several items remain untranslated and unpublished, among them documents containing the following lists of passengers to New Amstel in the years 1661 and 1662. The names in these lists should be of great interest to students of Dutch influence on the history and culture of the Delaware River area.

The first list (item 87 of the numbered items in the microfilm), dated November 13, 1661, is of passengers who came out as servants of the city's colony of New Amstel; their ship was named the *Purmerlander Kerck* ("Church of Purmerland"). The second list (item 94 in the microfilm) gives the names of those who came to New Amstel on the *Gulden Arent* ("Golden Eagle") early in 1662. The third list (item 98 in the microfilm), part of a document dated November, 1662, is also of passengers aboard the *Purmerlander Kerck*.

I.

Sr. Gerrit van Schweringe, Schout, with wife, servant, and maid
Claes Shrack, with wife
Mr. Jacob de Commer, with wife and two children
Woltger Willems
Gerrit Otto van (?) Accoy
Kier Wolters from Drendt, with wife and six children
Gerrit Jansen van Beck
Roelofus Barentsen
Ryck Gurtsen van As
Jan Gerritsen
Cornelis Aertsen and servant
Willem Jansen and servant
Jan Guertsen van Gysel
Gerrit Sandersen, with wife and four children
Pieter Arise Thysvelt
Joris Florisen and servant
Jan Roemeren, wife and daughter
Jan Hellegers
Herman Otto van (?) Accoy
Gerritt de Groott
Laurens de Geus
Willem Cornelisen Ryckevryer

II.

In addition to Joost de la Grange, his wife, three children, six servants, and two maids there were aboard the *Gulden Arent*, on February 5, 1662, the following:

Peter Jansen van Ann...
Peter Jansen van Amsterdam
Theunis (?) Ducxszboer, with wife and three children
Guvert Pietersen van (?) Gieten

III.

Willem Rasenburg
Barent Stordeur
Marten van der N —— [sic]
Jan Barensen
Pieter Tergotski
Hans Rasmussen

Jan de Ruyter
Jacques du Payos
Hendrick Bilvelt
Hendrick Gerritsz van Ges[e]l
.(?) Eugenie van Diemen [perhaps
    wife of Willem van Diemen]

"Emigrants to the Colonie on the Delaware River." (in) Edmund
   Bailey O'Callaghan. *Documents Relative to the Colonial History
   of the State of New York.* Albany: Weed, Parsons & Co., 1858
   (Vol. 2, p. 183) [Lancour No. 197].

   List of the Colonists and other free people who have entered
            to go to this city's Colonie in New Netherland
Holland Documents,
XVI., 242.

Joris Herisse, of Leyderdorp, with his boy and 2 servants,	4
Cornelis Aertsen, of Zevenhoven, with his boy and nephew,	3
Jan Liendertsen, in the Bent,	1
Jan Roemer, of Hazerswoude, with his wife and daughter,	3
Gerrit de Grot, of Ryntsterwoude, and boy,	2
Pieter Adriaensen, of Sevenhoven,	1
One lad from Sardam,	1
Lourens de Geus, of Amsterdam,	1
Joost, the mason, of Amsterdam,	1
3 persons from Vreelandt,	3
Gerrit Sandersen, of Tuyl, with 10 persons,	10
Joost Noorda, wife and 2 servants,	4
Antony Willemsen, of Vreelandt, being a mason,	1
Arent Arentsen, of Oldenburg, farm servant,	1
Lourens Cornelissen van der Wel,	1
Jacob Pietersen van Brugge, in Angeliers Straat, farm servant,	1
	38

NOTES TO THE INDICES

The user of this volume should be particularly careful to check every page shown bearing the name in question. The "ship lists" to Pennsylvania and Delaware happen to offer a greater duplication of names than other lists, and in a number of instances the same person is found in two or more articles. Indeed, some names will be found on "ship lists" but another article will reveal that the person in question did not actually sail on that ship.

Ships will be found listed in the Index of Ship Names under both their original names and their names in English translation if both names are given in the text. Otherwise one should inspect the index under both languages, if that may be appropriate.

The Index of Place Names is, for the most part, an uncritical organization of the place names found in the text. The user should consider the fact that many such names were misspelled by officials and emigrants, and some were misunderstood. One should look under all possible variant spellings, and all possible geographic divisions.

While in this volume each local place name is given under the heading of a specific country, in the case of foreign listings, it should be pointed out that a number of German-sounding place names are listed under France, as these villages were located in the Alsace region, now in France. It is possible that some Dutch or Belgian places will be found listed under Germany.

The Index of Personal Names should be searched very carefully by those seeking the names of specific persons. Keep in mind that many officials were not good or consistent spellers, that many immigrants could not spell their own names, and foreign accents, in some cases, might have been misunderstood. In some cases names which are similar, but distinct, have been grouped together simply because the compiler could not be sure, for example, that a Stewart should not have been listed under Stuart, and felt it necessary to compel the user of this index to check all people with similar sounding names. Accent marks have been ignored in the alphabetical arrangement out of consideration for many readers not familiar with foreign systems of arranging the alphabet. First names, spelled inconsistently in the text, have been spelled with some degree of consistency in the Index of Personal Names, insofar as was reasonable.

INDEX OF SHIP NAMES

INDEX OF PLACE NAMES

America / United States of America

Foreign Nations

Germany (cont.)
  Zinnhain 32
  Zweibrücken 93 109 110 112
    122 123 125 136 147 148 152
    153 155-158 163 188 192 200
    202
  Zweikirchlein 138
  Zuzenhausen 101-104 185 202
Ireland 13 129
  Dublin 78 183
  Erthon 200
  Limerick County 128
Netherlands 25 26 116 128 129
  137 205
  Accoy 216-218
  Amsterdam 44 213-216 218 219
  Bent 214 215 219
  Drenthe 216 218
  Flanders 139
  den Haag 37 214
  Haserwoude 214 215 219
  Holland 20 23 26 42
  Leyderdorp 214 215 219
  Oldenburg 215 219
  Rotterdam 30 44 49-58 60 61
    63 73 75-82 84 85 126 142
    146
  Rynsaterwoude 214 215 219
  Saendam 214 215 219
  Sardam 214 215 219
  Sevenhoven 214 215 219
  Tuyl 215 219
  Vreelandt 214 215 219
  Wachbach 137
  Wel 215 219
Poland 18 168 172
  Dornfeld 171
  Galicia 168 171 189
  Reichenbach 171
Russia 37
Sweden
  Stockholm 213

Switzerland 9 121 127 130 133
  134 177
  Aesch 120
  Basle 15 200 202 210 211
  Bern 15 124 134 137 158 174
  Birken 202
  Birmensdorf 120
  Chateau d'Oex 130
  Diebeldorf 117
  Duebendorf 117
  Ebding 200
  Langenbruk 210
  Meinisberg 134
  Pieterlen 134
  Saletz 122
  Schaffhausen 166
  Tobelindorf 117
  Waadt 130
  Wallisellen 166
  Zell 119
  Zürich 15 117 120 122 166

United Kingdom

England 20 23
  Cheshire 10
  Cowes 33 52 56 60 61 64 67-70
    75 80-82 84
  Deal 50 53-55 58 66 72 73
  Dover 57 60 63 73 75 85 126
  Falmouth 49
  Lancashire 10
  Liverpool 10
  London 9 23 61 64 66 70 73 75
    76 79 81 82 116 128 152 167
    200
  Plymouth 51
  Portsmouth 54 163
  St. Catherines 129
Scotland
  Glasgow 57 125-127 129 131-133
  Sunderland 73

West Indies 92 158
  Cajenne 88

INDEX OF PERSONAL NAMES

The following index should be inspected very carefully by those seeking to find herein specific persons. Keep in mind that many officials were not good or consistent spellers, that many immigrants could not spell their own names, and foreign accents, in some cases, might have been misunderstood. In some cases names which are similar, but distinct, have been grouped together simply because the compiler could not be sure, for example, that a Schmitt should not have been a Schmidt or Smith, and felt it necessary to compel the user of this index to check all people with similar sounding names. Accent marks have been ignored in the alphabetical arrangement out of consideration for many readers not familiar with foreign systems of arranging the alphabet. First names, spelled inconsistently in the text, have been spelled more consistently here, insofar as was convenient.

Beidelman (cont.),
  Hans Marti/Marx 136
  Johan Dietrich 136
  Johan Jacob 136
  Johan Leonhard 136
  Maria Elis. 136
Beigel,
  Hans Jerig 54
  Jacob 54
Beil, Balthazar 122
Beisel, Peter 121
Beitighoffer,
  Philip 195
Belert/Boelert/
Böhlert/Belerth,
  Anna (Müller) 88
  Anna Margaretha 87
  Eva Margaretha 88
  Johan Adam 88
  Johan Christoph 88
  Johan Friedrich 88
  Johan Jacob 64
  Johan Michael 88
  Maria Barbara
    (Grehl) 88
  Philip Jacob 87 88
Belits, Laurence 54
Bell 141
Bellman,
  Hans Georg 70
Beltzner, Simon 71
Bender/Benner 24
  George 64
  Hans Adam 71
  Hans George 60
  Hans Jacob 50
  Henr. 22
  Henr. Peter 22
  Hermann 43
  Jacob 21 184
Bendler,
  Christian 64
  John 64
Bene, John
    Rinehard 124
Benengé, Gerrett 115
Bengal, Daniel 54
Beni, Abraham 49
Benker, Christoph. 53
Benler, Wilh. 44

Benlie, Hans 53
Benn., James 78
Benninger, Peter 103
Benter, Hisbert 56
Bentz, Georg 143
  Johan Chr. 46
Berbesdorf,
  Georg Fred. 54
Berends, Klaus 7
Berg, Anna Margaretha
    (Wagner) 148
  Gottlieb 43
  Jacob 148 149
  Marg. 43
Berger,
  Maria Agnes 193
Bergstroster,
  Johan Georg 61
Bergemer, Wilh. 65
Bergt[h]old,
  Isaac 142
  Jacob B. 142
  Susanna (Hirsch)
    142
Berkel, Hans Jacob 78
  Jacob 78
Berndheisel, Johan 65
  Wendel 65
Berne, Wilhelm 69
Beroth,
  Franz Ludwig 189
    190
  Susanna (--) 189
Berret, Henrich 65
  Johannes 49
Berry, Anna Eva 89
  Anna Elisabeth
    (Schwartz) 89
  Anna Marg. 89
  Eva Christina 89
  Isaak 89
  Johann Ludwig 89
  Maria Barbara 89
Bertolet, Mary 130
Bertsch, Georg 195
Besaker, Jacob 68
Besch, Wilhelm 184
Besinger, Andreas 76
Besser, Christoph. 72
Best, Joh. Georg 23

Better, Christoph. 57
Betz, Christoph 32
  Johan Chr. 42
  Johan Jost 42
Bevell, Simon 81
Bey 119
Beyer/Beier/Bayer/
Beir/Byer/Boyer,
  Adam 189
  Andreas 61 77 90
  Anna Apollonia (--)
    90
  Anna Barbara 89
  Anna Elis. (Ebert)
    169
  Anna Maria 169
  Catharina 189
  Christoph 89
  Christopher 61
  Clara Elis. 89
  Dewalt 83
  Eva Elis. 90
  Georg Jacob 89
  Hans Melchior 83
  Jacob 55
  Johan Adam 62 77
  Johan Andreas 90
    169
  Johan Christo. 67
  Johan Friedrich 169
  Johan Jacob 62
  Johan Kasimir 169
  Johan Martin 90
  Johan Matthias 155
  Johan Nickel/Niko-
    laus 89 112 155
    169
  Johan Philip 61 90
  Johan Wendel 89
  Johan Wilhelm 169
  Joseph 61
  Kunigunde (--) 89
  Maria Elis. (--) 89
  Maria Magdalena 89
  Marie (--) 189
  Martin 90
  Matthias 112 113
    155
  Thomas 90
  Valentine 66

Bonnett, Jacques 75
Bonun, Hans 63
Boog, Jerig 54
Books, Johan 84
Boors, Gisbertus 62
  Johannes 62
Boot, Joannes 53
Bootz,
  Johan Georg 66
Born, Anna Cath. 200
  Anna Maria 200
  Anna Marie (--) 200
  Christina Marg. 200
  Johan Daniel 200
  Johannes 200
  Ludwig 200
  Maria Barbara 200
  Samuel 200
Bornheker, John
  Gerlach 106
Bornhuetter, Johan
  Gerlach 106
Borst, Michael 118
Borstler, Hans
  George 70
Bort[e]ner,
  Baltzar 69 120
  Jacob 120
Bosch, Anna Maria 197
  Barbara (--) 197
  Jacob 197 199
  Johan Friedrich 197
  Johan Jacob 197
  Johannes 197
  Joseph 197
Boshart, Henrich 82
  Jacob 81
Boshung, Hans 62
Bossert, Johannes 154
  Margaretha 154
  Margaretha (--) 154
  Michael 187
Botikofer,
  Nicolas 82
Bott, Johan Balt. 67
Boucher,
  Hans Ulrich 68
Boudmond/Baudemont,
  Andreas 161
  Philipp 161

Bousser,
  Christian 78
  Matthias 78
Bowdoin, James 35
Bower,
  Hans Martin 70
  Johan Martin 67
Bowman, Albrecht 52
  Daniel 52
  Dorts 63
  Hans Jerig 49
  Jacob 52 56 80
  Johannes 67
  John George 117
Boyd 138
Brach, Nickel 147
Bradbury, Eliz. 10
  Ellenor 10
  Jacob 10
  Joseph 10
  Martha 10
  Roger 10
  Sarah 10
Braft,
  Johan Sebastian 59
Brandstetter/Brand-
stätter, Andreas 178
  Anna Barbara 178
  180
  Anna Barbara (Mag)
  177
  Anna Esther 177
  Anna Magd. 177
  Dorothea Barb. 177
  Johan Friedr. 177
  178
  Johan Michael 178
  Johannes 178
  Maria Catharina 177
  Maria Elisabetha
  178
  Marie Magdalene
  (Schaar) 178
  Matthias 178
  Michael 177 180
Brand, Elias 136
  Hans Wilhelm 67
  Johan Chr. 41
  Michael 68
  Samuel 64

Brandt, Albertus 14
Braun/Brown,
  Christoph 56 190
  191
  Fritz 86 113 125
  168 189
  Jacob 205
  Johan Jacob 43
  Johan Martin 79
  Joh. Peter 46
  Johannes 43
  Rudolph 69
Brechbil[1]/Brech-
biel/Brechbeil,
  Bendu 73
  Hans 73 142
  Hans Peter 73 142
  Jacob 73
  John 64
  Wendal 64
Brecher,
  Johan Nicol. 59
Brecht, Johan 100
  Stephan 100
Brechtlen,
  Barbara 198
  Elis. (--) 198
  Mattheus 198
Breckly,
  Christopher 64
  Hans Jacob 64
  Mathias 64
  Ulrick 64
Bregell,
  Friedrick 83
Breiner, George 120
Brendel/Springel,
  Anna Maria 201
  Elisabeth 201
  Eva Catharina 201
  Eva Cath. (--) 201
  George 201
  Heinrich 201
  Johan Georg 201
  Johan Marx 143
  Johannes 201
  Maria Barbara 201
Brengel,
  Anna Catharina 164
  Christian 164

Busshel, Anthony 10
Butler, Johannes 83
Butz, Peter 124

Cagnelin, Dietrich 84
  Jean 84
  Sebastien 84
Calb, Martin 54
Callar, Carles 59
Camerer/Cammerer,
  Joseph 195
  Ludwig 82
Camerloo, Anna (--)
  114
  John Frederick 114
Campbell, William J.
  12
Capp, George Fred. 66
Carl/Carle,
  Hans Michal 84
  Jacob 62
  Simon 84
Carlz, Simon 66
Carpenter, Emanuel 9
Carver, Nicolas 56
Casparing, Jasper 65
Cassel, Arnold 14
Cassels, Johannes 14
Casser, Alexander 76
Castle, Hillis 52
Caup, Michael 66
Cavel, Philip 65
Ceeker,
  Clemens Stout 83
Chambers,
  Theodore F. 17
Chriesmerg, Wilh. 66
Christ, Christian 143
Christaman, Jacob 85
Christian/Chrestien,
  Hendrick 65
  Jean Francois 85
  Johan Georg 169
  Johan Peter 169
  Johan Valentin 169
  Maria Elisabetha
    (Dorth) 169
  Philip Jacob 145
  169
  Rudolph 68

Christler,
  Johan Jacob 83
Christmann, Johan 31
Claas, Joh. Jost 32
Clap, Joseph 49
  Jurgh 49
  Lodowick 49
Class, Johan Nic. 22
Clauser,
  Hans Jerig 57
Clayton/Cleaton,
  James 10
  Jane 10
  John 10
  Lydia 10
  Mary 10
  Sarah 10
Cleiner, Henrick 59
  Johannes 59
Clementz, Anna Maria
  (Knoll) 154
  Cath. (Kuntz) 153
  Georg 153
  Johan Adam 154
  Johan Valentin 153
  Juliana 154
  Sebastian 153
Cless, Maria Dorothea
  170
  Philip Heinrich 170
Clever, Conrad 69
Cling, George 71
Clipton, Fredrick 86
Clymer, Christopher
  77
  William 58
Cobham, Elijah 10
Coch, Jurgh 49
Cogh, Hans Erick 57
Colehendurfer,
  Andreas 70
Coll, Dilman 55
Colmere, Daniel 68
Colon, Michael 10
Comer, Jean 84
Conderts, Tennis 14
Conrad/Conradt/Con-
raad/Conrath, Anna
  Maria (Wagner)
  169

Conrad (cont.),
  Christian 201
  Hans Leond. 66
  Jacob 201
  Johan Jacob 201
  Johannes 201
  Johann Henr. 23 24
  Johan Konrad 169
  Johan Nicolaus 169
  170
  Maria Cath. (--)
  201
  Mary Elizabeth 135
Contee, Hans 56
Cooble, Hans 51
Cook, Aaron 83
Cool, Johan Ulrich 75
Cooper, Daniel 209
Coopman, Joannes 53
Copenhaver, Michael
  66
  Wolf 66
Coplinger 119
Coppersmidt,
  Casper 83
Corber, Nicolas 64
Corbit, W. F. 15
Cornelissen,
  Lourens 215 219
Cornelius, Peter 74
Corr, Barbara (--)
  200
  Casper 200
  Christian 200
Cortes, Joannes 51
Couger, Johan
  Georg. 66
Coultas, James 55
  John 53
Cox, John 167
Crable,
  Hans Erick 51
  Michel 51
Craemen,
  Hans Jerig 49
Craigie, James 56
Cramer,
  Johan Matthias 63
Cranbach, Leonh. 83
Cranklook, Ulrick 66

Gerlinger (cont.),
    Andreas 42
    Maria Cath. 155
    Philip Jacob 155
Gerner, Johan Matthes
    185
Gerritsen/Gerritsz,
    Jan 216 218
Gerster,
    Hans Georg 84
Gertner, Jerg 54
Gery, Anna Maria Ger-
    draut (Griesemer)
    130
    Jacob 130
Gesel[1], Hans 68
    Wilhelm 82
Getz, Conrad 73
    Henrich 73
Geyer, Johannes 86
Geyser/Jayser,
    Anna Maria 198
    Barbara (--) 198
    Hans Jerg 198 199
    Johannes 198
Gibson, John 206
Giersbach, -- (--) 32
    Anna Christina 33
    Joh. Jost 32
Giesler/Gissler/Giez-
    ler/Gesler,
    Anna Catharina 90
    Hans Adam 90
    Johan Adam 90
    Johan Michel 90
    Maria Christina 90
    Maria Magd. (Roth-
    mayer) 90
Gift, Aaron K. 88 96
Gilbert, Anthorn 67
    Eva (Hautz) 135
    George 135
Gillingham,
    Harold E. 167
Ginsberg, Johan
    Jacob 41
Gis, Jacob 65
Gitting,
    Johannes 33
Giuseppi, M. 182

Glain,
    Johan Michel 60
Glantz, Hieronimus 69
Glaser, Philip 54
Glass, Fredrich 77
Glassbrenner/Glas-
    breuner, Conrad 72
    Johan George 64
Glat, Anna Maria 202
    Elisabeth 202
    Elisabeth (--) 202
    Georg 202
    Maria Cath. 202
    Nicholas 202
Glatz, Henrich 189
Gleich, Anna Catha-
    rina 150
    Henrich 150
Goadts, Felix 51
    Peter 51
Gobal, Hans Jurg 76
Goball, Henrick 70
Gochnaur/Gochnauer,
    Christian 65 119
    Jacob 65
Goebel[1] 24 34
    Joh. Georg 32
    Julius 17
    Maria Elis. 32 34
    40
Goedke, Hans George
    64
Goetschy, Anna 122
    John Henry 122
    Maurice 122
Gö[h]ringer,
    Johan Georg 204
Gölbert/Gelberth,
    Anna Rosina
    (Geiss) 98
    Henrich 98
    Maria Cath. 98
Gons, Jacob 49
Good, Samuel 51
Goodbroodt,
    Ludwig 60
Goodman, George 167
Gookar,
    Johan Bartel 61
Gordner, Johannes 77

Gordon, Patrick 49-52
    54-57 59-61 63 72
    81 82
Görg, Johan Jost 22
    Peter 23
Gothe, Eva Elis. 97
    Maria Elis. 97
    Velten 97
Gottschalk, Georg 7
Gotz, Frederich 77
Graeb[n]er, Emanuel
    195
Graff/Graf/Gravin/
Graaf/Grove/Gräff,
    Anna Katharina 170
    Barbara 187
    Christian 55
    Franz 108
    George 55
    Hans Geo. 66 85
    Jerich Palk 66
    Johan Wilhelm 80
    Johannes 33
    Michael 72
    Sebastian 85
Graffert, Anna Eva
    (Finkenauer) 145
    Christoph 145
    Johan Gerhard 145
    Philip Peter 145
Grairteus,
    Johannes 69
Gratz, Palatine 52
Gratzmann,
    Anna Margarethe 173
    Peter 173
Grau/Graw,
    Leonard 57 128
Grautter, Abraham 76
Gray/Grae/Graa,
    Conrad 31
    John 70
    Velde 53
Greb, Chr. Henr. 31
    Johan Deis 31
Greeseman, Dirick 56
    Johannes Dirick 56
Grehl, Maria Barb. 88
    Philip 88
Greiner/Creiner,

Heintz (cont.),
　Johanna (Ulm) 92
　Johannes 32
　Jost Henr. 43
　Maria Catharina
　　(Theiss) 94
　Susanna 156
　Wendell 92 93
Heinzelmännin,
　Anna Barbara 198
Heironimous, Peter 83
Heistand, Johan 62
Heit, Johannes 81
Held, Anna Maria 151
Helfeysen, Martin 33
Helfrich, John 119
Helfurt, John 65
Hellegers, Jan 216
　218
Heller/Heler,
　Christopher 123
　Roldolph 53
　Simon 123
Helli, Eva Cath. 176
　Matthäus 176
Helm, Johan Adam 41
　Johannes 42
Heltzel, Nicolaus 79
Hemburger/Humberger,
　Hans Bartel 59
　Henrich 76
Hemler, Andreas 67
Hemperl, Elis. 186
Heneberger, John 64
Henge, Catharina
　　(Mueller) 110 148
　Georg 110 148
　Philip 110 148
Hennel, Jacob 78
Henninger, Hans
　　Michael 62
Henrich/Hendrick[s]/
　Henerich/Heinrichs/
　Hendrick 34
　Christopr. 58 129
　Gerhard 7
　Jacob 73 75
　Jerig 61
　Johannes 22

Henrich (cont.),
　Turgen 60
　Valentine 80
Hensell, Bernard 53
Heppener, Johannes 42
Herbertz, Henric 62
Herburger,
　Johannes 72
Herdt/Hirt/Hert,
　Georg 179
　Jurgen 179
　Maria Magd.
　　(Dreher) 179
Hereylf, Hans J. 49
Herget/Hergedt,
　Johann Peter 190
　191
Herisse, Joris 219
Herlein, Michael 208
Herier, Johannes 59
Herman[n], Jacob 55
　78
　Johannes 64
　Marg. (Apfel) 151
　Michael 151
Hermans, Reinier 14
Hermel,
　Johan Henrick 60
Hermer, Johan Leonh.
　67
Herr, Johannes 86
Herre, Anna Maria
　　(Sassler) 105
　Hans Martin 105
　Simon 105
Herter, Andreas 105
Herttranft, Tobias 80
Herwig, Hans Jacob 33
Hertz 44
　Johan Henr. 43
　Johannes 43
Hertzel/Hurtzell/
Hertsell, Geo. 137
　Ludwig 137
　Paulus 68
Hess/Hes/Hees,
　Anna (--) 128
　Anna Margtta 114
　Augustinus 114

Hess (cont.),
　Balthasar 129
　Christian 129
　Elisabeth 129
　Hans Conrad 129
　Henr. 42 45 136
　Jeremias 57 128 129
　131
　Johannes 42 45 81
　131
　Maria (--) 114
　Maria (Heim) 129
　Thomas/Dommes 136
Hetrich, Corab 75
Hetser, Johan
　Philip 74
Hetterling,
　Wilhelm 83
Heun, Joh. Best 46
Heyd, Jacob 186
　Maria Apollonia 180
　Rudolph 180
Heyder, Hans Michael
　56
Heydering, Casper 53
Heydon, Melchior 63
Heydrich, Baltzar 80
　Caspar 80
　George 79
Heyl, Elis. Cath. 112
　153
　Jerig 64
　Johann Peter 153
　Susanna Catharina
　　(--) 153
Heylman[n], Anna
　　Maria/Regina 102
　Martin 69
Heymann, Johan Dan.
　43
Heynsman, Johannes 80
　Jorg. 80
Heyriger, Hans Erick
　51
Heyster,
　Johan Friedrich 70
Heystoe, Jacob 53
Hezel, Jacob 101
Hib, Catharina 151

Knoll (cont.),
  Johannes 75
Knop, Jacob 77
Knopp, Johan Henrick
  60
  Philip 60
Kobell, Jacob 62
Kober/Cover,
  Dietrich 58 137
Koberstein, Anna
  Cath. (--) 185
  Hans Georg 185
Koch, Georg
  Friedrich 157
  Jerg Adam 77
  Johan 22
  Johan Christian 146
  Michel 69
  Philip Carl 157
Kocher, Martin 123
Kochnour, Jacob 83
Koehler/Köhler/Koh-
ler, Andreas 159
  Anna Catherine
    (Zimmer) 159
  Anna Elisabetha 97
  Hans Jurg 76
  Jacob 194
  Johan Georg 194
  Johan Jacob 159
  Johannes 32
Koen, Abraham 74
  Fredrich 74
Koenig/König/Konigh,
  Abraham 93 158
  Anna Maria 92 93
  Balthasar 104 205
  Frantz 92 93 158
  Gabriel 66
  Johan Marcus 22
  Marcus 24
  Maria 158
  Maria Magdalena
    (Kauffmann) 93
  Rahel (--) 92 93
Koentz, Peter 74
Koepplinger/Köpplin-
ger/Kopplinger/Kep-
linger/Caplinger,

Koepplinger (cont.),
  Johannes 58 136
  Leonard 58 136
Koerner/Körner/
  Karner, Jacob 188 192
Koff, Laurence 58
Kolb, Conrats, 72
Kohl, George Dietric
  62
  Gertrud (Franck)
    159
  Hans George 71
  Henrich 159
  Jost Henr. 43
  Peter 85
Kolk, Dietrich 8
Koll, Leonart 59
Koller,
  Hans Conrad 81
Kollin,
  Johan Wilhelm 66
Kommer, Daniel 84
Koobler, Jacob 75
Koofman, Johan 74
Koog, Johan Jacob 68
Kooger, Jacob 73
  Nicolaus 73
Koogh, Conrad 61
Kooler, Frederich
  142
Kopp, Johan Georg 60
  Samuel Eberhard 124
Koppenhoffer,
  Thomas 55
Koppenstein,
  Johan Görg 22
Koppler,
  Hans Martin 72
Korber,
  Johan Casper 74
Korr, Michael 55
Koser, Jacob 80
Köster, Heinrich
  Bernhard 8
Kram, Hendrick 62
Kramer/Kraemer/Kremer
/Cramer/Cremer,
  Andreas 8 68
  Bartel 108

Kramer (cont.),
  Casper 70
  George 116
  Hans Adam 61
  Hans Andres 14
  Henrick 61
  Johan Friedrich
    145 146
  Johan Peter 145 146
  Matthias 68
Krafft, Gottfried 62
Kraler, Jacob 74
Krans, Wilhelm 76
Krantz, Joh. Henr. 24
Kratzmann, Johan
  Nikolaus 170
  Maria Christina 170
Kraus[s]/Grauss,
  George 188
  Hans Jacob 67
  Jacob 184
  Johannes 104
Krebs, Friedrich 16
  86 87 99 100 142
  143 160 166 167
  176 182 183 185
  187 189 191 192
  195 196 199 204
  205
Krehebuehl,
  Johan Adam 101
Kreider, Michael 64
Kresler,
  Hans Philip 72
Kretzer, Leonhardt 42
Kreuder/Kreuter 141
  Johan Conrad 22
  Karl 135
Kreyl, Thomas 67
Krichner, Johannes 75
Krieble, Caspar 79
  George 79
  Melchior 79
Krieg, Anna Barbara
  (--) 90
  Anna Maria 91
  Johan Philip 90
  Marg. Dorothea 90
Krieger/Griger,

Lutz/Luetz, Elisabetha Catharina (--) 112 157
Johan Philip 62
Johan Wilhelm 112 157
Margaretha 94 159
Matthes 112 157
Luycken, Jan 8
Lybert, Michael 50
Lydie, Jacob 51
Lyme, Palzer 51
Lyon, Jane 10
Lypersberger, Jacob 71

Maag/Maager, Johannes 22
Mack, Alexander 56
Felte 56
Jacob 194
Joannes 56
Mackinterfeer, Joannes 57
Madinger, George Sebald 60
Madter, Jacob 81
Mag, Anna Barb. 177
Peter 177
Mahn, Jurig Bernhardts 68
Mang, Gottfried 180 181
Maria Barbara (Jessrang) 181
Theobald 180 181
Manger, Johan Phil. 43
Mann, Chr. 32
Mans, Eva (--) 159
Matheis 159
Mansur, Matthais 142
Mantandon, David 56
Manton, Nath. 167
Mantz, Hans Michl. 71
Marker, Matthias 80
Marky, Hans David 85
Marcus 85
Marlborough 18

Marot, Peirre 77
Marquart, Michel 198
Marsh, Frederick 56
Marshall, James 82
Marsteller/Marstiller, Frederick Ludwig 118
Johan Peter 84
Philip 118
Mart, Derrick 83
Marta, Henrick 59
Marten, David 51
Jacob 51
Martin/Marthin 141
Caspar 74
Conrad 24
Georg/Joerg 104
Hans Georg 73
Hans Henrick 62
Johan/Hans Steffan 105
Martz, Ann (--) 114
Anna Marg. 114
Simon 114
Marx/Marck, John 210
Mastersundts, Rudolph 59
Matheis, Andres 205
Mather, Joseph 10
Matten, Christopher 57
Mattern/Matern, Peter 71 120
Thomas 66
Matthäi, Konrad 8
Matthes, Stephen 73
Matthis, Hans Jacob 74
Mattinger, Susanna 179
Matts, Stephen 142
Maul, Anna Elis. 23
Joh. Friedr. 24
Johann Friedr. 22
Johannes 22
Maurer/Mower/Maeurer, Anna Elis. (--) 173
Anna Eva 173
Catharine 138

Maurer (cont.), Jacob 81
Johan Jacob 151 173
Katharina Barb. 173
Paul 173
Philip Jacob 145
Mauritz, Nicolaus 78
Maus[s], Bernhard 77
Franz Carl 144
Friedrich 109 147 153
Georg Jacob 144
Margaretha 159
Maria Marg. 110
Samuel 109 147 153
Susannah (Mueller) 109 147 153
Mayes, Andrew 56
Maylaender, Anna Appolonia (Guenter) 165
Conrad 165
McCall, George 142
McCracken, George E. 11 12 125
Meck, Georg Michal 69
Meckel, Christian 109
Meckeling/Mechling/Meckli, Jacob 55 118
Johan Jacob 76
Theobald 55 117
Medart, Carl 153
Catharina 153
Johan Adam 153
Marg. (Kuntz) (Clementz) 153
Valentin 153
Mede, Jane 11
Marjory 11
Meder, Henry 74
Mehn, Johannes 75
Meidleman, Elias 58
Voldrick 58
Meikle, Henrich 79
Meinzer, Johannes 187
Martin 187
Meister, Anna Elisabetha 159
Anna Maria (Kesseler) 159

Mindhard/Minhart,
  Friedrick 83
  Hans Jorig 66
Minger, Jacob 81
Minicher,
  Johan Herb 64
Minier,
  Christian 71
Minuit, Peter 214
Mire, Hans Adam 54
  Philip 78
Miss, Anna Juliana
  (--) 200
  Catharina 200
  George 200
  Johan George 200
  Johan Gerhard 200
  Johan Heinrich 200
  Maria Christina 200
Mittelberger,
  Gottlieb 105
Moak, Johannes 72
Mock, Hans Peter 74
Moeser, Martin 55
Moesser, Hans Adam 55
Moessinger, John 119
Mohler/Moler/Mahler,
  Anna (--) 137
  Georg Adam 137
  Heinrich 137
  Jacob 137
  Lutwig 137
Moler, Lutwig 58
Molich, Johannes 81
Moll, Bartol 73
  Christofoll 61
  Johan Michael 61
  Peter 56
Momma, Leonhardt 67
Monheimer, Jacob 211
Moog, Hans Michl. 65
Moor, John Adam 55
Moore, Rudolph 56
Mooselback,
  Carol Arant 56
Moots, Jerig 54
Morgenstern/Morge-
stern, Joannes 54
  Johan Engelbert 148

Morgenstern (cont.),
  Johan Philip 148
  Maria Rosina (--)
  148
Morris, James 72
Morschheimer/
Moerschheimer/
Merschheimer,
  Henrich 205
Mortz, Bartholomius
  67
Moseke, Henry 81
Moseman, Andreas 77
  Christian 77
Moser, Andreas 71
  Elisabeth 110 163
  Jorig 69
  Leonhard 69
  Martin 118
  Michael 69
  Paulus 69
  Tobias 69 120
Mosiman, Hans 64
Moths, Michel 62
Moyer, Philip
  Melchior 73
Moyser, Christian 50
  Hans 50
  Jost 50
Mueckli, Jacob 121
Muehlschlagel,
  Johan Andreas 192
Mueller/Müller/Muller
/Miller/Millar/Mullar
/Moller/Möller,
  Abraham 76
  Andreas 65
  Anna Christina 42
  Anna Elis. (--) 202
  Anna Margaretha 135
  Anna Maria 135
  Anna Maria (--) 42
  Anna Maria (Jacob)
  24
  Anthony 58
  Anton 41
  Catharina 110 202
  Christian 49 59 62
  100

Mueller (cont.),
  Christopher 134 187
  Conrad 24 25 71
  Daniel 66
  David 104
  Dietrich 101
  Franziska Magdalena
  194
  Fredrick 67
  Friedrich 202
  Fulk 72
  Georg 8 70
  Gerard 56
  Hans 50 51 54 81
  Hans Adam 71
  Hans Georg 62
  Hans Henr. 25
  Hans Jacob 53 66
  Hans Jerig 52
  Hans Jörg 25
  Hans Lendert 53
  Hans Martin 53
  Hans Michael 68
  Henr. 33
  Herman 62
  Hieronimus 69
  Jacob 59 66 70 75
    84 100 101 202
  Jaebez 139
  James 51
  Jerem 52
  Joan Nicolas 65
  Johan Andreas 81
  Johan Conrad 22
  Johan Diess 22
  Johan Friedrich 185
  Johan Georg 66
  Johan George Antony
  81
  Johan Henr. 22
  Johan Jost 22
  Johan Michael 184
  Johan Nicolaus 71
  Johan Peter 138 139
  Johan Stoffel 22
  Johannes 22 24 25
    33 42 64 68 138
    194 202
  Johannes Kits 53

Pinklie (cont.),
    Peter 85
Pintnagle, Johannes
    70
Pixseler, Peter 52
Place, Lorentz 107
Platz/Plotz,
    Friedrich 108
Pleuler, Caspar 81
Plino, Hendrick 56
Plumm, Frans 59
Plumsted, Clement 50-
    52 54 61 63 82 85
    86
Plyger, Jacob 85
Podom, Jacob 72
Ponne, Andreas 56
Pontius, Andreas 144
    Anna Marie (--) 144
    Johan David 144
    Johan Philip 144
    John 123
Porter, Robert 209
Possart, Jacob 56 57
Post, Nicolas 84
Pott, Degenhart 80
    Wilhelm 80
Presel, Johan
    Valentine 77
Preston, Samuel 49 52
    86
Prill, Martin 49
Princeland,
    Christian 59
Pris, Johan Peter 85
Probst, Christoph 92
    Elis. Marg. 92
    Johs. Michael 74
    Michael 74
Prunder, Johannes 57
    Joseph 57
Pusey, Caleb 11
Putz, Michel 69

Qnukle, Johan Michal
    85
Quast, Johannes 164
Quattelban/Quattel
Ban, Peter 85

Quickell/Quickle,
    Hans Jerig 65
    Johan Georg 85
    Johan Phillippus 85

Raan, Hendrick 53
Rabe, Christopher 80
Radclif, Richard 10
Radler, Joannes 51
Rafer, Feltin 57
Ramb, Christian 108
Rambach, Asimus 78
Ramsaur, Henrick 64
Randecker, Johan Adam
    194
    Ursula 194
Ranhard, Michael 75
Rank, John Philip 55
    Michael 53
Ranseler/Randsailer,
    Hans Philip 69
    Jacob 69
Ransch, Johan Adam 85
Rape, Christian 70
Raper, Stephanus 57
Rapp, Apolonia 157
Rasenburg, Willem 219
Rasmussen, Hans 219
Rat, Hans 76
Ratgal, Hans Jacob 81
Ratsell, Frantz 75
Ratslue, Hans Jacob
    56
Rattenauer,
    Gottfried 194
Raub, Michael 70
    Philip 70
Rauch, Peter 70
Raudebush, Isaac 72
Rausch 119
Rausher, Jacob 74
Ray, George Michael
    70
Re, Johan Nicolas 61
Read, Charles 82
Rebell, Nicolas 83
Reblet, Christian 76
Rebsamen 181
Rech, A. M. (--) 112
    153

Rech (cont.), Johan
    Conrad 112 153
    Johan Michael 112
    153
Rechter, Johannes 80
Reckty, Christian 84
Reeche, Hans 63
Reehsh, Matthias 78
Reel, Simon 56
Reemer, Philip 52
Reep, Johannes 70
Regensberger, John
    Stephen 55
Rehberger, Anna
    Margaretha 134
Rehi, Johan Chr. 31
Rehrer, Johan Gott-
    fried 103
Reiber, Abraham 190
    Anna Margaretha
    (Reuther) 190
Reich, Mattheus 186
Reichenbach, Johs. 79
Reichert, Jacob 104
Reiffenberg, Johan
    Georg 22 24
Reimer/Reymer,
    Anna Barbara 131
    Balthasar 159
    Elisabetha 131
    Elis. (Weynacht)
    131
    Fredrick Reimer 57
    131
    Johan/John Peter
    131 132
    Johanna Maria 132
    Susanna Elisabetha
    131
Reiner, Anna Maria
    107
    Eberhardt Friedrich
    107
    Georg Philip 107
    Johan Christian 107
    Johan Dietrich 106
    107
    Johannes 107
    Maria Magdalena 107

Schapper[d]t/Schab-
  bert, Anna Barbara
    174
  Anna Barbara
    (Seiss) 174
  Anna Christina 175
  Anna Katharina
    (Grimm) 174
  Anna Katharina
    (Gutheil) 174
  Filb 174
  Johan Michael 174
  Johan Nikolaus 174
  Johannes 172 174
    175
  Maria Margarethe
    172
Schartz, Conrad 68
Schaub, Balthasar 162
  Heinrich 162
  Maria Dorothea 162
  Susanna Catharina
    162
Scheadecker, Felter
    73
Schedla/Schedler,
  Johan Christian 145
    146
  Johan Heinrich 146
Scheer/Schere,
  Johan Valentine 83
  Samuel 64
Scheertel,
  Bernhard 69
Scheid, Leonhardt 103
Scheive,
  Johan Jacob 60
Schelbert, Leo 15
Schell, A. Cath. 41
Schellig, Philip 72
Schelt, Joh. Conrad
    32
Schenefelt,
  Joannes 54
Schenemansgruber,
  George 78
Schenholl, Henry 52
Schenk, Andreas 70
  Anna Maria K. 90

Schenk (cont.),
  Johan Jacob 90
  Michel 50
Schen[c]kel[1],
  Heinrich 188
  Jacob 81 188
  Johan 61
  Johan Philip 188
  Philip Carl 188
Scheps, Friedrich 79
Scherges/Scherkes/
  David/Viet 8 14
Scherer/Scherrer/
Sherer/Sherar,
  Andreas 69
  Hans 78
  Jacob 68
  Johan Adam 69
  Johan Augustus 133
  Johan Justice 58
  Johannes 58 133
  Ulrich 132
Scheuchzer, Hendri 81
Schmeymer, Johan
    Conrad 67
Schiblen,
  Christian 85
Schickle, Georg 186
Schierwager,
  Gotfried 81
Schifferdecker,
  Jacob 104
Schindler, Heinrich
    194
Schlappig, Joh.
    Dan. 33
  Joh. Jost 33
Schleicher, Maria
    Margaretha 106
Schley, -- (Wintz)
    149
Schli[e]chter,
  Gallus 193
Schlickers, Ludwig
    187
Schlindwein,
  Anna Eva 87
Schloos, Kaplan 44
Schlosser, Leon. 72

Schlosser (cont.),
  Leonhard (cont.)
    120
  Peter 71
Schmätzlen,
  Agatha 197
  Barbara 197
  Eva (--) 197
  Jerg 197
  Simon 197
Schmeltzar,
  Johannes 70
Schmelzle,
  Rudolph 186
Schmidt/Schmitt/
Schmid/Schmit/Smit/
Smidt/Smith/Schmied/
Shmiet/Schmiedt/
Smiet/Smitt/Shmith/
Smitz/Shmitt,
  Abraham 111 150
  Andreas 95 161
  Anna Elisabetha 95
    161
  Anna Katharina 173
  Anna Magdalena
    (Rollauer) 169
  Anna Margaretha 95
  Anna Maria (--) 203
  Anna Maria (Heck-
    man) 99
  Balthasar 194 203
  Bernard 115
  Catharina 115
  Catharina (Jahraus)
    95 161
  Christian 61
  David 192
  Dirik 53
  Georg 111 150
  Georg Michl. 70
  Gilian 74
  Henr. 42 45 76 77
    203
  Jacob 33 81
  Jan 132
  Johan Andreas 23
  Johan Casper 57 86
    132

INDEX OF VARIANT SURNAME SPELLINGS

The following index is intended to assist the reader in locating variant spellings of surnames in the foregoing index of personal names. It is not a total index of the variant spellings in that those variations which would not be out of order, such as Schmitt with Schmidt, are not listed. In addition, it should be noted that while many names being checked against these indices will not be found under the same spelling, an imaginative use of this book with sounds, rather than spellings, in mind, should produce better results.

Almbach, Allenbach
Altspach, Alspach
Anderras, Andres
Angubrant, Ankenbrautt
Apfel, also Appel
Appel, also Apfel
Arets, Arens
Baach, Bach
Bach, also Back
Back, also Bach
Baire, Baer
Balsam, Balssel
Bartges, Baertges
Bartjes, Baertges
Basler, Baasler
Batter, Bader
Baub, Bub
Baudemont, Boudmond
Bauor, Bauer
Bayer, Beyer
Bear, Baer
Behr, Baer
Beier, Beyer
Bekker, Becker
Belritsch, Bayritsch
Benckle, Bingley
Benner, Bender
Ber, Baer
Bettle, Boettle
Beutelmann, Beidelman
Beydelmann, Beidelman
Bickle, Buckle
Bloom, Blum
Boelert, Belert
Böhlert, Belert
Böhm, Boehm
Bomgartner, Bumgartner

Bouquet, Bocke
Bowersox, Bauersachs
Boyer, Beyer
Brener, Brenner
Brown, Braun
Brückert, Brickert
Buckner, Buchner
Buettner, Bittner
Burckholter, Burkhalter
Burghalter, Burkhalter
Burghart, Burkhard
Büttner, Bittner
Byckevryer, Ryckevryer
Bydleman, Beidelman
Byer, Beyer
Byerle, Beyerle
Camerer, also Kemmerer
Cammerer, Camerer/Kemmerer
Caplinger, Koepplinger
Casner, Kastner
Cawbrisco, Zabriskie
Chrestien, Christian
Cleaton, Clayton
Copenhaver, also Koppenhoffer
Cover, Kober
Cramer, also Kramer
Crantz, also Krantz
Crown, Kron
Crum, Krum
Cuntz, also Kuntz
Cuntzer, Küntzer
Dauber, Dauwer
Deibellbissen, also Dreibelbis
Deiss, Theis
de Kommer, de Commer
Desch, Tesch
Deubendorffer, also Diebendörfer

Didrich, Dietrich
Diebendörfer, also Deubendorffer
Diedenhöffer, Düttenhöffer
Ditreich, Dietrich
Dittenhöffer, Düttenhöffer
Ditts, Dietz
Domie, Daum
Domm, Dom
Dorten, Doerter
Drautman, Trautmann
Dreibelbis, also Deibellbissen
Drexler, Trexler
Düdenhöffer, Düttenhöffer
du Payos, Payos
Duten, Doeden
Erhart, Ehrhard
Ernhardt, Ehrhard
Eshelman, Eschelman
Esleman, Eschelman
Faeber, Faber
Fath, Fauth
Favian, Fabian
Feezer, Fiser
Fegeley, Fegley
Felte, Fehlten
Fetherholf, Federolf
Fetterolf, Federolf
Fizer, Fiser
Foeser, Fiser
Foetsch, Fetsch
Fray, Frey
Fredrick, Freidrich
Freh, Frey
Friedrich, Freidrich
Fry, Frey
Fuisser, Fiser
Füsser, Fiser
Graa, Gray
Graaf, Graff
Grae, Gray
Graeff, Op den Graeff
Grauss, Krauss
Gravin, Graff
Gelberth, Gölbert
Gerhardt, Ehrhard
Gesler, Giesler
Gillich, Güelich
Gissler, Giesler
Graw, Grau

Griger, Krieger
Grisimer, Griesemer
Groscost, Grosscost
Grove, Graff
Hachman, Hackman
Hainz, Heintz
Halzapfel, Holzapeil
Hamman, also Hammann
Hammann, also Hamman
Hammon, Hamman
Hass, Haas
Hast, Haas
Hees, Hess
Heinrichs, Henrich
Heler, Heller
Hendricks, Henrich
Hershey, Hirsch
Hirt, Herdt
Hoffen, in den Hoffen
Hofman, Hoffman
Hoglander, Hochländer
Hooginunk, Hochgenug
Houfman, Hoffman
Hosuer, Houser
Huff, Hoff
Humberger, Hemberger
Hurtzell, Hertzel
Kargher, Kaercher
Karner, Koerner
Kastner, also Kistner
Keiser, Keyser
Kemmerer, also Camerer
Keplinger, Koepplinger
Kifer, Kieffer
Kinser, Küntzer
Kircher, Kercher
Kistner, also Kastner
Kleyn, Klein
Köhler, Koehler
Kolck, op de Kolck
König, Koenig
Konigh, Koenig
Koppenhoffer, also Copenhaver
Kopplinger, Koepplinger
Körner, Koerner
Kraemer, Kramer
Kramer, also Cramer
Krantz, also Crantz
Kremer, Kramer

Kroner, Groner
Kuehl, Kiel
Kuerlis, Kürlis
Kuntz, also Cuntz
Laam, Lahm
Lenkenberger, Lünberger
Lienenberger, Lünberger
Locke, Ludi
Loninacre, Longacre
Loudinback, Lautenbach
Lough, Ludi
Luchenbühl, Lukenbill
Luckenbill, Lukenbill
Luecker, Licker
Luetz, Lutz
Lugenbühl, Lukenbill
Maeurer, Mauer
Mahler, Mohler
Maier, Meyer
Marck, Marx
Marthin, Martin
Martin, also Mertin
Matern, Mattern
Mayer, Meyer
Mechling, Meckling
Meckeling, also Meikle
Meidelman, also Beidelman
Meikle, also Meckeling
Melchoir, Melchior
Merschheimer, Morschheimer
Mickle, Michael
Mier, Meyer
Miller, Mueller
Minch, Münch
Minech, Münch
Minigh, Münch
Minnich, Münch
Moerschheimer, Morschheimer
Moessinger, Messinger
Mohler, also Moler
Moler, also Mohler
Moller, Mueller
Morce, Mey
Mower, Mauer
Muehleysen, Mühleissen
Muench, Münch
Muenig, Münch
Müller, Mueller
Neuhard, also Newhard
Newhard, also Neuhard

Nick, Niecke
Noh, Noë
Oler, Ohler
Percy, Peircy
Petter, Peter
Pifer, Peifer
Plotz, Platz
Ramaere, Roemers
Randsailer, Ranseler
Rath, Roth
Rehsh, Reehsh
Reidebach, Reitenbach
Reitzel, Reutzel
Reser, also Rezer
Ressar, Reser/Rezer
Reutzel, Reitzel
Reymer, Reimer
Rezer, also Reser
Rheinhart, Reinhart
Rittinghuysen, also Rüttinghausen
Roller, Rollard
Rommigh, Roehmell
Rouyter, Reuther
Rumetsch, Rometsch
Rüpel, Reupel
Rüttinghausen, also Rittinghuysen
Saboroscus, Zabriskie
Schans, Shans
Schearman, Shearman
Scheitz, Shitz
Schelberger, Shelberger
Schever, Schaeffer
Schilling, Shilling
Schitz, Shitz
Schoeffer, Schaeffer
Scholtze, Schultz
Schuhl, Scholl
Schupp, Schoup
Segar, Sager
Seleberger, Shelberger
Seubert, Seibert
Seydler, Seidler
Seysen, Seiss
Seytz, Seiz
Shefer, Schaeffer
Sholts, Schultz
Sherer, Scherer
Shmith, Schmidt
Shoemaker, Schumacher
Shunk, Schunck